DATE DUE

MAR 2 4 1999	
FEB 2 8 2003	

BRODART   Cat. No. 23-221

The Paradise of Association

The Paradise of Association

Political Culture and Popular Organizations
in the Paris Commune of 1871

Martin Phillip Johnson

Ann Arbor

THE UNIVERSITY OF MICHIGAN PRESS

Copyright © by the University of Michigan 1996
All rights reserved
Published in the United States of America by
The University of Michigan Press
Manufactured in the United States of America
⊗ Printed on acid-free paper

1999   1998   1997   1996   4   3   2   1

A CIP catalog record for this book is available from the British Library

Library of Congress Cataloging-in-Publication Data

Johnson, Martin Phillip, 1959–
    The paradise of association : political culture and popular
organizations in the Paris Commune of 1871 / Martin Phillip Johnson.
        p.   cm.
    Includes bibliographical references and index.
    ISBN 0-472-10724-0 (cloth : acid-free paper)
    1. Political culture—France—Paris—History—19th century.
    2. Political clubs—France—Paris—History—19th century.   3. Paris
    (France)—History—Commune, 1871.   I. Title.
    JS5170.J64   1996
    306.2'0944—dc20   96-25345
                                                                  CIP

Paris is a true paradise. . . . all social groups have established themselves as federations and are masters of their own fate.

—Gustave Courbet, April 1871

Preface

Scholars often say they hope their work provides a foundation for future studies, and that hope has been fulfilled in this study of popular organizations. Indeed, this book may be considered the third volume of a collective trilogy on popular organizations from 1868 to 1871. The first volume is *Aux Origines de la Commune: Le Mouvement des réunions publiques à Paris 1868–1870,* by Alain Dalotel, Alain Faure, and Jean-Claude Freiermuth, which analyzes public meetings from June 1868 until they were outlawed in the spring of 1870. Although it ends a year before the insurrection of March 18, it concludes that the Commune was the result of revolutionary action. The second is R. D. Wolfe's similarly titled 1965 dissertation, "The Origins of the Commune: The Popular Organizations of 1868–71," which focuses on clubs and committees during the seige of Paris. The last pages of Wolfe's dissertation suggest that the Commune was born from a revolutionary socialist coalition, a supposition that has proven correct. These well-crafted works were necessary prerequisites for this study, and my readers and I owe their authors a debt of gratitude.

The aid and encouragement of many people and institutions made this study possible. Irwin Wall and David Gordon first introduced me to French history and the Commune; they and Kenneth Barkin at the University of California, Riverside, read some of the early papers and historiographical reviews that became the foundation for this study. In Paris, André Burguière and Pierre Nora provided assistance and orientation. At Brown University, Philip Benedict and R. Burr Litchfield gave generously of their time and expertise, and I am most grateful for the encouragement and incisive criticisms of my dissertation director, Joan Wallach Scott. Doug Cremer, Christopher Guthrie, Louise Tilly, and Irwin Wall read and commented on parts of the manuscript at various moments. My thanks and appreciation go especially to Nancy M. Wingfield, who gave the gift of her intelligence and love. Finally, I would like to acknowledge the financial assistance of the University of California, the Fulbright program, Brown University, and the National Endowment for the Humanities.

Contents

Introduction: Revolution and Political Culture

"So that's a club!" Gill says to me. "Its not very lively . . . And to think, historians will later make them out to be flamboyant spectacles . . . Ah! History . . ."

—Maxime Vuillaume

Early in April 1871, at the beginning of the civil war between the Paris Commune and the National Assembly at Versailles, the revolutionary municipal council of the 11th arrondissement publicly burned two guillotines that allegedly had been commissioned by the "odious" government. Amid shouts of "Down with the death penalty!" from the crowd, flames destroyed the "servile instruments of monarchist domination," sacrificed, in the words of the municipality, "for the purification of the arrondissement and the consecration of our new freedom."[1] Eight weeks later, as the French army reconquered the capital street by street, one of those who had destroyed the guillotines commanded defenders of the Commune. "Establish your line of defense between you and the Versaillais. Burn, incinerate everything that is against you," François David ordered. "No sorrow, nor discouragement," he urged; "the men of the 11th will hurl themselves to your rescue as soon as you are threatened. Courage, and if you act the Republic is saved this day."[2]

Epigraph from Maxime Vuillaume, *Mes Cahiers rouges au temps de la Commune* (Paris: Société d'Éditions Littéraires et Artistiques, 1909; reprint, Paris, Albin Michel, 1971), 277. Gill, a well-known satirist, and Vuillaume, a journalist, had just attended a club in the Saint Severin Church during the Commune.

1. *Le Journal Officiel de République Français*, April 10, 1871, translated in Steward Edwards, ed., *The Communards of Paris, 1871* (Ithaca: Cornell University Press, 1973), 150; Jean-Pierre Azéma and Michel Winock, *Les Communards* (Paris: Seuil, 1964), 124. Catulle Mendès described the burning of the guillotine in *Les 73 journées de la Commune (Du 18 mars au 29 mai 1871)* (Paris: Lachaud, 1871), 140.

2. Archives Historiques de la Ministère de la Guerre, Vincennes (AHG): Ly 22.

These scenes from a revolution highlight the relationship between symbolism and agency that lies at the heart of political action. François David had turned from the ceremonial gesture of burning guillotines to concrete measures against his enemies, yet comprehending this leap from ideational constructs to instrumental action raises difficulties for students of the human experience.[3] The analysis presented in this book contends that the linkages between discourses and deeds in history are best illuminated through the concept of political culture, which I define here as the confluence of symbols, practices, and contexts that constitutes making and implementing collective decisions. This definition owes much to Lynn Hunt and Keith M. Baker, who have helped transform the concept of political culture by infusing it with insights from critical theory and interpretive anthropology. But both scholars employ definitions of political culture that stress its representational aspects and neglect its instrumental elements.[4] Images and rituals reveal much, but incorporating practices and context into the concept of political culture allows exploration of the ways ideas translate into action. In this perspective, burning guillotines and incinerating enemy positions partake equally of political culture, as both practices arose within specific symbolic and social contexts, and as both express and implement political choices.

Specifically, I argue in this book that the Paris Commune resulted primarily from revolutionary action by popular organizations and was

---

3. In the face of this problem psychologists have emphasized innate drives, sociologists have investigated social structures, and political scientists have explored interest group dynamics. The anthropologist Clifford Geertz explored this issue in his celebrated essay differentiating between a wink and a twitch, "Thick Description: Toward an Interpretive Theory of Culture," in *The Interpretation of Cultures* (New York: Basic Books, 1973). See also Lynn Hunt, ed., *The New Cultural History* (Berkeley: University of California Press, 1989); Roy D'Andrade and Claudia Strauss, eds., *Human Motives and Cultural Models* (Cambridge: Cambridge University Press, 1992); Richard Munch and Neil J. Smelser, *Theory of Culture* (Berkeley: University of California Press, 1992).

4. Hunt's exploration of the French Revolution expands on her definition, for she investigates social structures while defining political culture as "symbolic practices, such as language, imagery, and gestures"; *Politics, Culture, and Class in the French Revolution* (Berkeley: University of California Press, 1984), 13. Baker has defined political culture as a "set of discourses or symbolic practices" in *Inventing the French Revolution: Essays on French Political Culture in the Eighteenth Century* (Cambridge: Cambridge University Press, 1990), 4; see also Baker's introduction to *The French Revolution and the Creation of Modern Political Culture*, vol. 1, *The Political Culture of the Old Regime*, ed. Keith M. Baker (New York: Pergamon, 1987), xiii. As Baker noted, an American political science school of political culture arose in the 1950s and has been recently revitalized; see Michael Brint, *A Genealogy of Political Culture* (Boulder: Westview, 1991); John Gaffney and Eva Kolinsky, eds. *Political Culture in France and Germany* (London: Routledge, 1991); Stephen Welch, *The Concept of Political Culture* (New York: St. Martin's, 1993).

shaped by the unique political culture fostered within them. When David ordered that fires be set to defend the Commune he did so in the name of the local vigilance committee; all across Paris members of similar clubs and committees administered arrondissements, secularized education and social services, and rallied the National Guard to fight for the cause. Against the backdrop of the *année terrible* of 1870–71, when France experienced a military and political crisis unequaled since 1793, members of the vigilance committee movement created the organizational and programmatic framework for the seizure and exercise of power. A string of defeats in the Franco-Prussian War had precipitated the fall of the Second Empire in September 1870, and while the capital was besieged by German forces a provisional government composed mainly of moderate republicans ruled France. After four months of hardship Paris capitulated, but the National Assembly that was elected in February to approve a humiliating peace was composed overwhelmingly of monarchists and conservatives. Under these conditions moderate and radical republicans feared a royalist restoration. Thus political divisions exacerbated a national military emergency, producing a period of enormous revolutionary potential and culminating in Paris with the largest urban uprising of the nineteenth century. The clubs and committees that sprang up in this atmosphere of crisis and fear were at the center of agitation. Yet the history of popular organizations has largely been neglected.[5] A coordinated movement composed of club and

---

5. One exception is R. D. Wolfe, "The Parisian *Club de la Révolution* of the 18th Arrondissement 1870–71," *Past and Present* 39 (April 1968): 81–119. Wolfe's dissertation covered only the siege of Paris; "The Origins of the Paris Commune: The Popular Organizations of 1868–71" (Ph.D. diss., Harvard University, 1965). For women's associations see Eugene Schulkind, "Socialist Women during the 1871 Paris Commune," *Past and Present* 106 (February 1985): 124–63; Schulkind also wrote a brief overview, "The Activity of Popular Organizations during the Paris Commune of 1871," *French Historical Studies* 1 (December 1960): 394–415. Jean Dautry and Lucien Scheler, *Le Comité Central Républicain des Vingt Arrondissements de Paris (september 1870–mai 1871)* (Paris: Éditions Sociales, 1960), described the most important group of the period, but it misconstrued the evolution of the Committee Central during the siege and is very incomplete for the Commune. Most general histories survey clubs but rely on published documents and secondary sources almost exclusively. Claude Perrot contributed a chapter on clubs to Jean Bruhat, Jean Dautry, and Emile Tersen, *La Commune de 1871,* 2d ed. (Paris: Éditions Sociales, 1971). See also Stewart Edwards, *The Paris Commune, 1871* (London: Eyre and Spottiswoode, 1971); Stéfane Rials, *Nouvelle histoire de Paris: De Trochu à Thiers (1870–1873)* (Paris: Hachette, 1985); William Serman, *La Commune de Paris (1871)* (Paris: Fayard, 1986). Jacques Rougerie consulted archival material extensively for his general studies *Procès des Communards* (Paris: Julliard, 1964) and *Paris Libre: 1871* (Paris: Seuil, 1971), which include much of interest on popular organizations, as did Maurice Choury in his study of the four central arrondissements of Paris, *La Commune au coeur de Paris* (Paris: Éditions Sociales, 1967).

committee militants organized three revolts in Paris against the provisional Government of National Defense during the winter of 1870–71. Then, in February 1871, club militants created a Revolutionary Socialist Party to bring about revolution and social equality: "No more bosses, no more proletariat, no more classes."[6] In February and March 1871 these revolutionary socialist militants consciously strove to fuse with and lead the Parisian National Guard. Eugène Varlin, one of the most important leaders of this movement, quite accurately predicted in mid-March, "one more week and we will be masters of seventeen of twenty arrondissements, then we will chase the prefecture of police from Paris, we will overthrow the government, and France will follow us."[7] The key leaders of the insurrection of March 18 that inaugurated the Commune were members of this revolutionary socialist movement who were acting as officers of guard units.

Not only did the Commune mainly originate in revolutionary action by club and committee militants, but popular organizations shaped the ideas and furnished the leadership of the new revolution. David was also the president of the Club des Prolétaires held in the Saint Ambroise Church, a club whose program called for direct democracy and economic reforms so that "the worker might fully profit from the fruit of his labor." While Communards differed in their ultimate aspirations for the revolution they were making, there was remarkable uniformity in the methods they proposed for reforming economic, political, and social life. The common vehicle for attaining these goals was association, or "political federation and social federation," according to the program of the Club des Prolétaires.[8] The Communard program of association was not new; its roots may be found in the popular assemblies of the Great Revolution, in the socialist manifestos of the 1840s, in mutual aid societies and artisanal *compagnongages,* in middle-class *cercles* and civic societies, and in the agitation surrounding the Luxembourg Commission in 1848.[9] Indeed, one reason that associationist principles pervaded so much Communard discourse and

---

6. From the revolutionary socialist Declaration of Principles, February 19, 1871; Archives Nationales (AN): BB24 498.

7. Letter to the Russian populist Pierre Lavrov, in which Varlin boasted that "a notable part" of the National Guard was already in socialist hands; cited in Michel Cordillot, *Eugène Varlin: Chronique d'un espoir assasiné* (Paris: Éditions Ouvrières, 1991), 207.

8. *Le Prolétaire* (the newspaper of the vigilance committee of the 11th arrondissement and of the Club des Prolétaires), May 10, 1871.

9. Rougerie has observed that the idea of the Commune as a federation was accepted by Communards of every political stripe; *Paris Libre,* 150. Choury, from the Marxist wing of the

action is that association and federation had correspondences with both the revolutionary tradition and liberal social theory and practices.[10] Communard associationism was not the preserve of one class or narrow political affiliation but a method of fraternal cooperation among republicans and revolutionaries of various hues and social positions. Communard association was a more radical set of practices and ideas than middle-class versions, however, since its fundamental principle was that of the sovereignty of citizens when assembled, an ideal derived from the revolutionary tradition. The popular organizations thus formed were not conceived as merely pressure groups or as part of a complex of institutions but rather as the embodiment of the people's will. As such, clubs and associations could legitimately disregard formal law or existing procedures and take whatever action was necessary to promote goals agreed on by their members.

Communard political culture was most forcibly expressed through associationism, which had economic, political, and social facets. Most socialists agreed that producer and consumer cooperatives should be the foundation of a socialist society, and during the Commune tailors, metalworkers, butchers, and laundresses organized to restructure their conditions of work. The Commune actively promoted worker associations and decreed that abandoned workshops were to be operated by producer associations. As a form of direct democracy, clubs and committees were also widely recognized to be the political foundation of the Commune. The newspaper of the Club Communal held in the Saint Nicolas des Champs Church urged, "People, govern yourselves by yourselves through your public meetings, through your press; pressure those who represent you,

---

social interpretation, described the Commune as a "new and original program" of federation—but also as "the democratic dictatorship of the proletariat"; *La Commune au coeur de Paris,* 315. On association see William H. Sewell, *Work and Revolution in France: The Language of Labor from the Old Regime to 1848* (New York: Cambridge University Press, 1980); Bernard H. Moss, *The Origins of the French Labor Movement (1830–1914): The Socialism of Skilled Workers* (Berkeley: University of California Press, 1976); Bernard Gibaud, *Au conflit de deux libertés: Révolution et droit d'association* (Paris: Mutualité Française, 1989); Philip G. Nord, *The Republican Moment: Struggles for Democracy in Nineteenth-Century France* (Cambridge: Harvard University Press, 1995); Maurice Agulhon, *Le Cercle dans la France Bourgeois* (Paris: Armand Colin, 1977).

10. Freemasonry united diverse generations and ideologies around a common "federalist, anticlerical, and ultrademocratic" program, according to Philip G. Nord, "Republicanism and Utopian Vision: French Freemasonry in the 1860s and 1870s," *Journal of Modern History* 63 (1991): 214. Middle-class salons remained a significant part of the republican movement into the Third Republic; S. Aprile, "La République au salon: Vie et mort d'une forme de sociabilité politique (1865–1885), *Revue d'Histoire Moderne et Contemporaine* 38 (1991): 473–87.

they will never go far enough along the path of revolution." The club then followed its own advice, holding an unauthorized election for a vacant seat on the Communal Council.[11] Through social association, popular organizations provided the framework through which teachers, parents, and students cooperated to improve education, shopkeepers and businesspeople elected magistrates, and artists governed the arts. Gustave Courbet, president of the Fédération des Artistes and member of the Communal Council, hailed the associationist movement when he wrote to his parents that "Paris is a true paradise. . . . all social groups have established themselves as federations and are masters of their own fate." The Club des Prolétaires summarized these practices when it proclaimed that "Communal power resides in each arrondissement wherever men are assembled who have a horror of the yoke and of servitude," echoing the description of the guillotines as servile instruments.[12]

Club rhetoric, action, and personnel offer a unique opportunity to assess the foundations of political action, because popular organizations provide the essential link between discourse and deeds in the Commune. At the three levels of power in the city—in the center at the Hôtel de ville; in the twenty arrondissement *mairies,* or district town halls; and in the streets, squares, and assembly halls where public opinion was formed and expressed—club members, or *clubistes,* were vital in creating and shaping the revolution. Two-thirds of the members of the Communal Council elected after the insurrection of March 18 were current or former militants of the revolutionary socialist vigilance committee movement. Eighteen of Paris's twenty arrondissements were administered or represented in majority by former or current members of vigilance committees. Through intimidation and revolutionary fervor Communards silenced opposition and subverted neutral organizations, effectively monopolizing public discussion and opening space for the elaboration of revolutionary projects. Analysis of 733 club participants reveals them to be socially diverse individuals very likely to have a history of revolutionary activity; nearly one-third also held positions of authority in the Commune. Clubistes constituted not a social class but rather a culturally and politically defined revolutionary community. By dominating the Commune at several levels

---

11. *Le Bulletin Communal: Organ des Clubs,* May 6, 1871. The club's choice, Bernard Landeck, does not appear to have tried to take a seat on the Communal Council; AHG: 17e conseil 742, dossier Landeck.

12. *Courbet raconté par lui-même et par ses amis* (Geneva: Pierre Cailler, 1950), 140; "To the members of the Club of Proletarians," *Le Prolétaire,* May 19, 1871.

of power, from meeting halls to the Hôtel de ville, militants of popular organizations imposed their visions and ideals on the nascent revolution.

This argument contradicts generally accepted interpretations of the Commune and calls into question a number of widely held conclusions about labor, socialist, and revolutionary movements at a critical moment in the history of France and Europe. The Commune forms a bridge between 1848 and 1917, both historically and theoretically. The Commune conditioned political and social developments, and interpretations of the Commune played a crucial role in forming political, especially revolutionary, ideologies across Europe.[13] This means that explaining the Commune has always been more than a historical exercise. From the earliest accounts to the most recent studies two broad interpretative schools have dominated the historiography of the Commune, although each encompasses considerable variation.[14] What may be called the *political interpretation* considers the revolt to have been primarily a response to specific circumstances. In explaining the origins of the Commune it emphasizes the hardships of the siege of Paris. Thus it depicts the Commune as a mainly patriotic and republican outburst of anger and frustration[15] or perhaps a decentralizing reaction to the Second Empire.[16] The second school may be

13. The literature on interpretations of the Commune by Marx, Bakunin, Lenin, and others is immense, but for a fine survey see the essays in James A. Leith, ed., *Images of the Commune* (Montreal: McGill-Queen's University Press, 1978).

14. Like all simplifications this typology based on mode of analysis is necessarily a distortion, but one that helps clarify the central issues in the Commune's historiography. In contrast, most discussions of the historiography of the Commune focus on a source's political stance or degree of sympathy with the Commune; see, for example, the bibiliographic essays in Henri Lefebvre, *La Proclamation de la Commune: 26 mars 1871* (Paris: Gallimard, 1965); Bruhat, Dautry, and Tersen, *La Commune de 1871;* Charles Rihs, *La Commune de Paris 1871: Sa Structure et ses doctrines* (1955; reprint, Paris: Seuil, 1973); Rials, *Nouvelle histoire de Paris.*

15. The major recent examples are Edwards, *The Paris Commune;* Robert Tombs, "Harbingers or Entrepreneurs? A Worker's Cooperative during the Paris Commune," *Historical Journal* 27 (1984): 969–77; William Serman, *La Commune de Paris.* This might also be called the orthodox view, as it is by far the most common in general histories. See, for example, Gordon Wright, *France in Modern Times: From the Enlightenment to the Present,* 5th ed. (New York: Norton, 1995); François Furet, *Revolutionary France, 1770–1880,* trans. Antonia Neville (Oxford: Blackwell, 1992). The triumph of this view has recently been so complete that Robert Tombs has suggested that the key questions of the Commune are no longer subject to partisanship; "L'année terrible, 1870–1871," *Historical Journal* 35 (1992): 713–24.

16. Louis M. Greenberg, *Sisters of Liberty: Marseilles, Lyon, Paris, and the Reaction to a Centralized State, 1868–1871* (Cambridge: Harvard University Press, 1971); for a vigorous restatement of this thesis see Roger V. Gould, *Insurgent Identities: Class, Community, and Protest in Paris from 1848 to the Commune* (Chicago: University of Chicago Press, 1995), 4, 135.

called the *social interpretation,* which considers the Commune to be the result of large-scale economic and social forces disrupting the traditional order. Many scholars in this second current of opinion are socialist historians who argue that the primary mechanism of the revolt was class struggle.[17] Yet the social interpretation is also composed of a curious alliance of socialists and conservatives, who agree that the Commune was a social war but support different sides.[18] Both opponents and supporters of the Commune have attempted to expropriate its legacy for their own purposes, whether that meant delegitimizing it as a criminal attack on civilization or exalting it as the fulfillment of a revolutionary destiny. A century and a quarter after the Commune its historians in large measure still tread the paths delineated by its contemporaries and participants. Reorienting this historiography requires considering two related questions.

First, the origins of the Commune have generally been debated around whether the Commune was inevitable or fortuitous. "What was the Commune?" Charles-Aimé Dauban asked in 1873. "a normal product of society, or an accidental event?" Dauban embraced a conservative social interpretation that was orthodoxy on the right: the Commune originated in the decline of respect and morality among the lower classes, leading them to accept criminal and socialist doctrines of envy and pillage.[19] Most Communards and sympathizers also suggested the Commune originated from long-term causes, but they emphasized its roots in social evolutions and

17. The finest socialist account is Bruhat, Dautry, and Tersen, *La Commune de 1871;* see also Choury, *La Commune au coeur de Paris;* Jacques Duclos, *La Commune de Paris à l'assaut du ciel* (Paris: Éditions Sociales, 1970); A. Molok, "Les Ouvriers de Paris pendant la Commune," *Cahiers du Communisme* 5–6 (May–June 1951): 608–22, 728–75.

18. The conservative literary critic Maxime Du Camp wrote that the Commune stood for "instant substitution of the proletariat for all other classes of society, in ownership, in administration, in the exercise of power"; quoted in Roger L. Williams, ed., *The Commune of Paris, 1871* (New York: John Wiley and Sons, 1969), 37. This analysis is remarkably similar to that of many socialists.

19. See the National Assembly's official inquiry, *L'Enquête Parlementaire sur l'Insurrection du Dix-Huit mars 1871* (Paris: A Wittersheim, 1873). Dauban crafted a sophisticated phenomenology, arguing that two parts are necessary to any history: the history of the "social foundation," what would later be called structures, and that of the events; *Le fond de la société sous la Commune* (1873; reprint, Geneva: Slatkine-Megariotis Reprints, 1977), 1. His argument suggests that the Commune arose from the social foundation and was not a mere event, placing him squarely in the social interpretation. The most recent history critical of the Commune uses the term *revolutionary vandalism* to describe the Communard destruction of symbols of the old order such as the Vendôme column and the house of Adolphe Thiers; Rials, *Nouvelle histoire de Paris,* 471.

the revolutionary tradition.[20] Just before the First World War Edmond Lepelletier described the Commune as "une grande évolution historique," and the finest account from the Marxist wing of the social interpretation agrees that the Commune expressed "a normal historical evolution, which consists of the decline of one class and the rise of a new class."[21] In contrast, scholars of the political interpretation sometimes reduce the causes of the Commune to the hardships of war and suggest, in the words of Stewart Edwards, that "it would be misleading to say that the Commune was an accident, but not wholly untrue."[22] Similarly, Jacques Rougerie has described the Commune as "the 'accident' of March 18. Meaning of course accident in the historical sense, as a brutally sudden event, and not for all that fortuitous, in no way foreseeable."[23] The political interpretation makes the Commune the product of a unique situation, which is why the word *accident* recurs in its analysis. The social interpretation sees general processes at work and so prefers terms like *inevitable* and *natural.*[24] Scholars of both standpoints reject the notion that the Commune arose primarily from revolutionary action.[25] While some have emphasized the importance of the revolutionary movement before the Commune, no

20. An article in the March 30, 1871 issue of *Le Vengeur,* the newspaper of the neo-Jacobin Felix Pyat, asserted that "the France of the people dates from March 18, an era that is new, like its flag. The France of the nobility died in '89, with the white flag! The France of the bourgeoisie died in '70, with the tricolor flag." The socialist Auguste Vermorel wrote that March 18 "consecrates the political arrival of the proletariat, like the revolution of 1789 consecrated the political arrival of the bourgeoisie"; *L'Ami du Peuple,* April 24, 1871.

21. Edmond Lepelletier, *Histoire de la Commune de 1871,* 3 vols. (Paris: Mercure de France, 1911–13), 1:13; Bruhat, Dautry and Tersen, *La Commune de 1871,* 88.

22. Stewart Edwards, *The Paris Commune,* 1; Rihs argued that the Commune "marks a kind of accident between the Second Empire and the Third Republic"; *La Commune de Paris,* 123. Tombs cites Serman approvingly, maintaining that "it was the war and its immediate consequences that transformed Paris into a political powder keg"; "L'année terrible," 720.

23. *Paris Libre,* 23. Rougerie is the most important of the Commune's recent historians, and his painstakingly nuanced description of the Commune as an accident is characteristic of his complex, even contradictory, interpretative framework. While he gives great attention to changes in the social geography of Paris, his analysis of the causes of the Commune places him in the political interpretation, as it centers on the circumstances of 1871: "the insurrection of 1871 was above all an awkward, late, exasperated nationalist reflex"; *Procès des Communards,* 241.

24. Hunt has made a similar analysis of the historiography of the French Revolution, pointing out that the characteristics of the revolution often appear either "predetermined or entirely accidental." Richard Cobb's assertion that the sansculotte "is not an economic being; he is a political accident" has clear interpretative affinities with the political interpretation of the Commune; cited in Hunt, *Politics, Culture, and Class,* 10.

25. V. I. Lenin asserted that "the Commune arose spontaneously, nobody deliberately and systematically planned it"; Lenin, *Lessons of the Commune: In Memory of the Commune.*

inquiry has demonstrated that the Commune was the result of an organized movement, because none has systematically investigated popular organizations before and during the insurrection.[26]

Second, the nature of the Commune has been debated around whether the Commune belongs to the past or the future.[27] Marx opened the debate in a letter written while the Commune still ruled Paris: "Whatever the immediate outcome may be, a new point of departure, of importance in world history, has been gained."[28] The opposing view, characteristic of the political interpretation, was put in poetic terms by the historian Jacques Chastenet: "Rather than a sunrise, the Paris Commune was a flamboyant sunset."[29] Was the Commune the last of the nineteenth-century revolutions or a brilliant harbinger of future world revolution? The political school argues that the Commune was mainly republican and patriotic, a reaction to the victories of Prussians in the war and of monarchists in the elections to the National Assembly; expression of socialist sentiment was the work of a few members of the Association International des Travailleurs and others who had a limited following among the mass of Communards. Although conservatives have argued that the Commune was a criminal enterprise, and though some Marxists have suggested it blazed the trail for Bolshevik successes, both wings of the social interpretation agree it expressed class or social divisions. Martial Delpit's contemporary condemnation of Communards as new barbarians bent on demolishing

(Moscow: Foreign Languages Press, n.d.), 12. Bruhat, Dautry, and Tersen echo his conclusion: "the Commune was born spontaneously. Nobody consciously prepared it"; *La Commune de 1871,* 22. Roger Magraw has argued that members of the Association International des Travailleurs and other revolutionaries were "overtaken by the events of March," and that "spontaneous popular mobilization appeared to be overwhelming the International's cadres"; *A History of the French Working Class,* 2 vols. (Cambridge, Mass.: Blackwell, 1992), 1:264.

26. However, both monographs on popular organizations before the Commune suggest it arose from revolutionary action, although both end their analyses well before the Commune began: Wolfe, "The Origins of the Paris Commune"; Alain Dalotel, Alain Faure, and Jean-Claude Freiermuth, *Aux Origines de la Commune: Le Mouvement de réunions publiques à Paris 1868–1870* (Paris: Maspero, 1980).

27. Or as Rials phrases this "classic question": "Insurrection du passé? Insurrection porteuse d'avenir?"; *Nouvelle histoire de Paris,* 514.

28. Letter to Ludwig Kugelmann dated April 17, 1871, quoted in Eugene Schulkind, ed., *The Paris Commune of 1871: The View From the Left* (New York: Grove, 1972), 199.

29. Jacques Chastenet, "La Commune, aube des révolutions modernes ou flamboyant crépuscule?" preface to *La Commune de Paris,* by Pierre Dominique (1948; reprint, Paris: Hachette, 1962). In contrast, Bruhat, Dautry, and Tersen make the history of the Commune into a weapon of political struggle, when they hint darkly that "the bourgeoisie has not heard the last of the Commune of Paris"; *La Commune de 1871,* 8.

religion, the family, and society is as much a class interpretation as is the assertion by Jacques Duclos, a major figure in the French Communist Party, that the Commune was the first proletarian revolution.[30]

The debate between the political and social interpretations is often fruitful, but the nature of the questions raised admits only a limited range of responses. An approach founded on analysis of political culture rearranges the terms of discussion. Rather than debating binary oppositions, such as circumstances versus inevitability or legacy of the past versus harbinger of the future, the concept of political culture as defined here encompasses the symbols, practices, and contexts that constituted the Communard revolution. Communards defined their revolution through objects, words, and gestures laden with symbolic significance, such as wearing and waving red emblems, denying the title *citoyen* or *citoyenne* to those who did not support the cause, or singing the Marseillaise from the pulpit of a church hosting a revolutionary assembly rather than a religious congregation. Club language and ceremony described the "new world" that Communards sought to create. Unlike the political interpretation, this view recognizes the Commune's transformative content; it was not a criminal or narrowly political event. The "new world" that many Communards believed had dawned on March 18 was not the same as that described by scholars of the social interpretation, however, for it was defined primarily by culture, not determined by historical materialism. Without regard to class, women in the Union des Femmes and other organizations, for example, elaborated a vision of citizenship for women based on equality of sacrifice, devotion to the cause, and traditions of women's revolutionary action. Fulfilling aspirations voiced in 1792 and 1848 that women should enjoy the full rights and duties of citizenship, including military service, Communard women in the Légion des Fédérées and other armed women's groups arrested opponents and fought in organized units on the barricades of Bloody Week. Although women's rights in the Communal hierarchy were generally deemed inferior to those of Communard men, women in popular organizations exercised a large degree of functional equality with men, and the status of women in these organizations was one of the Commune's most revolutionary challenges to the social order.

---

30. Martial Delpit supervised the National Assembly's official report on the Commune, *Le Dix-Huit mars: Récit des faits et recherche des causes de l'insurrection. Rapport fait à l'Assemblée Nationale au nom de la Commission d'Enquête sur le 18 mars 1871* (Paris: L. Techener, 1872); Duclos, *La Commune de Paris à l'assaut du ciel.*

Clubiste practices and action were rooted in and coincided with the language and symbolics of club discourse. A prominent feature of popular organizations was the cult of revolutionary violence, which was based in large part on the historical memory of the Great Revolution.[31] Armed with weapons that served as both icons and tools of revolutionary power, and arrayed and surrounded by symbols that legitimated contentious action, clubistes explicitly defended their right to threaten and inflict violence on opponents. Threats and acts of violence were more than criminality or theatrics. By arresting clerics and former police officials, evicting nuns from charity and educational institutions, and intimidating landlords and draft evaders, clubistes and other Communards carried out the programs announced in popular organizations. Since most Communards were from the working classes, such actions constituted a revolutionary inversion of social and power relations that was analogous to the partial inversion of gender relations carried out explicitly and implicitly in the words and actions of armed women's units such as the Légion des Fédérées. But Communards did not implement the dictatorship of the proletariat. Rather, clubistes and Communards generally spoke and acted in the name of the people, a category constructed from a variety of oppositions, not just in relationship to the means of production. Here again, the characteristics of association framed the nature of Communard political culture, as organizations composed of diverse social categories and classes stressed conceptions of identity that bound together, rather than divided, the Communard community. Communards drew much more readily on the collective memory of the revolutionary tradition for inspiration and guidance than on more limited doctrines of purely economic exploitation, although some did emphasize class in their analyses and goals. This use of the past does not, however, mean that Communards on the whole were backward-looking. While Communards and clubistes differed in the degree of inspiration they sought from the revolutionary past, nearly all believed they were taking part in a new stage of an old struggle. Specific formulations of this idea varied, but most supporters agreed or hoped that the Commune represented a "new world," a new era of social progress and political freedom.

Symbols and practices were bound together in institutional and social contexts provided by clubs and committees. Contemporaries considered any series of public meetings a club, no matter how informally organized

---

31. Collective memory was an important aspect of clubiste political culture, but Robert Gildea goes too far in reducing French political culture to "the collective construction of the past"; *The Past in French History* (New Haven: Yale University Press, 1994), 10.

the meetings were. Committees, however, were special purpose membership organizations that often sponsored public assemblies to enlarge their
field of action. These popular organizations were at the same time physical, social, and discursive spaces, with institutional characteristics and histories that conditioned club culture.[32] From the streets, to the arrondissement mairies, to the Hôtel de ville, clubiste political culture then stamped
the Commune with its particular mixture of contentious democracy, bois-
terous fraternalism, and rhetorical violence. The social identity of club
participants affected the problems raised and solutions proposed in club
assemblies, although not in a linear or unmediated manner. In the last two
decades the explanatory role of class and other forms of social identity has
been undermined by critical theory, or discourse analysis, in what some
scholars have called the "linguistic turn" in the social sciences.[33] Such
analyses are often useful as correctives to overly schematic conceptions of
how class and politics interact, but when they deny the validity of class or
social position entirely they remove a powerful analytical tool from the
repertoire of social theory. For example, in defining political culture as
exclusively symbolic and representational, Baker has denied that there are

---

32. Leading what may be called the "new institutional history," Theda Skocpol has
underscored the importance of state structures in conditioning politics; "Bringing the State
Back In," in *Bringing the State Back In,* ed. Peter B. Evans, Dietrich Rueschemeyer, and
Theda Skocpol (New York: Cambridge University Press, 1990): 3–43. Institutional determinants of political and class developments have also been recently underscored by French historians. Mark Traugott has argued that the difference between insurgents and government
forces in 1848 was institutional; *Armies of the Poor: Determinants of Working-Class Participation in the Parisian Insurrection of June 1848* (Princeton: Princeton University Press, 1985).
Tony Judt has emphasized the role of the legal framework of the Second Empire in forming
socialism after 1848; *Marxism and the French Left: Studies in Labour and Politics in France,
1830–1981* (New York: Oxford University Press, 1986), 84. Gould notes that "formal institutions" are pivotal in forming social identity; *Insurgent Identities,* 18. See also Ira Katznelson and Aristide R. Zolberg, *Working-Class Formation: Nineteenth-Century Patterns in
Western Europe and the United States* (Princeton: Princeton University Press, 1986).

33. Gareth Stedman Jones has redefined class as "a discursive rather than an ontological
phenomenon"; *Languages of Class: Studies in English Working Class History, 1832–1982,*
(New York: Cambridge University Press, 1983), 8. William Reddy has suggested jettisoning
the category of class "and all it entails"; *Money and Liberty in Europe: A Critique of Historical Understanding* (New York: Cambridge University Press, 1987), xi. Patrick Joyce
described class as "less an objective reality than a social construct"; *Visions of the People:
Industrial England and the Question of Class, 1848–1914,* (Cambridge: Cambridge University
Press, 1991), 9. Joan Wallach Scott has explored the ways gender and class intersect in *Gender and the Politics of History* (New York: Columbia University Press, 1988). For a critique
of critical theory and a defense of historical materialism see Bryan D. Palmer, *Descent into
Discourse: The Reification of Language and the Writing of Social History* (Philadelphia: Tem-
ple University Press, 1990); see also Leonard R. Berlanstein, ed., *Rethinking Labor History:
Essays on Discourse and Class Analysis* (Urbana: University of Illinois Press, 1993).

"social realities independent of symbolic meaning" and argued against distinguishing between discursive and nondiscursive phenomena.[34] In this argument, Baker was expressing a larger project of the "new cultural history," which according to Hunt is characterized by concern with the relationship between "culture and the social world."[35] More broadly, a central project of the new cultural studies in history, political science, sociology, anthropology, and literary studies during the 1980s and 1990s has been to reject even the modifications of the base-superstructure model that implicitly informed much social theory in the twentieth century.

If indeed all experience is construed experience, that is, a cultural construction, it is still necessary to explore the factors affecting the architecture of the construction, including contexts of time, place, and social position. The social and institutional contexts within which groups and societies form a political culture are important elements in shaping how that experience is construed. In particular, one must pay special attention to the historical context, since Parisians reacted to and molded events that unfolded with breathtaking rapidity during the *année terrible* of 1870–71. François David, a common mason, and his fellow members of the Club des Prolétaires, many of whom administered the 11th arrondissement, had a long history of revolutionary action behind them by the spring of 1871. They cast their struggle as one between servitude and freedom, between despotism and the Republic. They burned symbols of "monarchist domination" to consecrate their "new freedom." Club rhetoric and practices were imbued with the conviction that the Commune inaugurated a new era of democracy and social equality. The first three chapters of this study address the institutional and political origins of the Commune in the club movement. The remaining chapters explore the nature of the revolution. Symbols, practices, and context can be separated for analysis, but popular organizations united them in a revolutionary political culture that created and shaped the Commune.

---

34. Baker, *Inventing the French Revolution*, 5.

35. Hunt, *The New Cultural History*, 10. On the relationship between the cultural and the social, a particular concern of the Center for Contemporary Cultural Studies at the University of Birmingham (United Kingdom), see also Nicolas B. Dirks, Geoff Eley, and Sherry B. Ortner, eds., *Culture/Power/History: A Reader in Contemporary Social Theory* (Princeton: Princeton University Press, 1994); Jeffrey C. Alexander and Steven Seidman, eds., *Culture and Society: Contemporary Debates* (New York: Cambridge University Press, 1990); Tony Bennett, et al., eds., *Culture, Ideology, and Social Process: A Reader* (London: Open University Press, 1981.

Part 1
The Origins of the Commune

CHAPTER 1

Club Politics during the Siege of Paris

Today everyone should be on the ramparts or at the public meetings.
—A. de Fonvielle

On July 15, 1870, Napoleon III declared war on Prussia and sealed his fate. His rule was in its nineteenth year, and France was increasingly impatient with the authoritarianism that had been welcomed by many after the disorder and conflict of the Second Republic. Only five republican candidates had been elected to the Second Empire's Corps Législative in 1857, but moderate republicans won the majority of seats for the large cities in 1863, and in 1869 republicans swept the urban centers, with opposition candidates gaining nearly 43 percent of the total vote.[1] Furthermore, in the late 1860s a militant labor movement reappeared for the first time since the Second Republic.[2] Critics of the regime grew more daring, emboldened by the immense success of journalist Henri Rochefort's satirical newspaper *La Lantern*.[3] Still, Napoleon III had won an enormous majority in a plebescite of May 1870 ratifying limited liberal alterations in his regime, and many foreign and domestic observers believed that the near-certain victory over Prussia would further consolidate his rule. Instead, on September 3 news reached Paris that the emperor, at the head of an army that

---

Epigraph from A. de Fonvielle in *La Patrie en Danger*, September 22, 1870, describing the dual struggle facing those on the left during the siege: the military contest against the Prussians on the battlefield, and the political fight through popular organizations for the Republic.

1. Alain Plessis, *The Rise and Fall of the Second Empire, 1852–1871*, trans. Jonathan Mandelbaum (New York: Cambridge University Press, 1985; French ed., 1979); see also Louis Girard, *Napoleon III* (Paris: Hachette-Pluriel, 1993); Pierre Miquel, *Le Second Empire* (Paris: Plon, 1992).

2. Worker "coalitions" were granted limited legal rights in 1864. The strikes of the late Empire had an 80 percent success rate due to the strong economic expansion; Michele Perrot, *Les Ouvriers en grève, France 1871–1890*, 2 vols. (Paris: Mouton, 1974), 1:80.

3. Rochefort's most famous quip was that France had "thirty-six million subjects, not counting subjects of discontent"; quoted in Edwards, *The Paris Commune*, 30.

was confidently expected to occupy Berlin, had been trapped and defeated at the border fortress of Sedan.

The next day, September 4, 1870, crowds in the grip of that singular combination of revelry and outrage that characterizes revolution filled the streets of the capital; some burst into the Palais Bourbon and forced the Corps Législative to disband, others pushed into the Imperial Suite at the Tuileries as the Empress Eugénie fled from a side door to find refuge with her dentist. Meanwhile a crowd in front of the Hôtel de ville variously acclaimed or rejected candidates for a "Government of National Defense" whose names were communicated to the public by slips of paper thrown out the windows of the building to the square below.[4] Rochefort and the radical republican tribune Léon Gambetta were among those accepted, but the government was composed mainly of moderate republicans who would not unduly frighten conservatives, a concern that prompted the government to declare "we are not in power but in combat."[5] Paris had made another revolution, but with triumphant Prussian armies marching on the city the fate of the new regime was very much in doubt.

Every major political faction both within Paris and without rallied to the Government of National Defense in the early days of the ensuing siege, which was endured by some two million inhabitants for four months from September to January, a record surpassed in modern times only by the siege of Leningrad during the Second World War. Beginning in early October, however, several demonstrations of military ineptness and news of attempts to negotiate with Bismarck quickly turned many factions, especially those on the left, against the government. Opponents of the government accused it first of incompetence, then of treason. They formed two successive coalitions based in popular organizations that sought victory through revolution. The first coalition, which was relatively moderate and unstructured, attempted to replace the government with an elected city council, or Commune, in October 1870. The failure of this insurrection provoked a more radical and better-organized "revolutionary socialist" movement in the popular organizations of the capital. This second coalition created a "revolutionary Commune" drawn from clubs and popular committees without recourse to general elections, and in January 1871

---

4. Alistair Horne, *The Fall of Paris: The Siege and the Commune, 1870–71* (New York: Penguin, 1965; reprint, 1981), 84; Edmond Goncourt, *Paris under Siege, 1870–1871: From the Goncourt "Journal,"* ed. and trans. George J. Becker (Ithaca: Cornell University Press, 1969), 51.

5. Michael Howard, *The Franco-Prussian War* (New York: Methuen, 1961), 226.

it attempted two unsuccessful uprisings to install it at the Hôtel de ville. Although the revolutionaries could not prevent the surrender of the capital, the Paris Commune of 1871 resulted from the organizational framework they had created. The struggles of the siege, punctuated by three unsuccessful insurrections, crafted a unique political culture within the revolutionary clubs and committees of Paris. When revolutionary socialists seized power in March, this political culture in turn shaped the Commune.

In both incarnations of the revolutionary coalition, popular organizations such as clubs, public meetings, and committees were crucial for setting common goals and instigating coordinated action.[6] Napoleon III had legalized limited public meetings in June 1868 to win support for his regime, but they became instead workshops of revolt.[7] Opponents of the regime had originally met in cafés, as when "quelques vieux de '48" assembled at a café on the boulevard Montmartre or when Blanquists and other left-bank radicals made the Brasserie Rhénane a notorious foyer of revolution. More famous and influential opponents of the regime, such as Rochefort and Gambetta, could be found in the sumptuous cafés of the Grands Boulevards.[8] Yet because of their public nature cafés were obviously unsuited for serious revolutionary organization. After the legalization of public meetings cafés were no longer central to the revolutionary movement, though they remained informal meeting places where opponents of the Empire socialized and learned to trust or detest one another.[9]

For many revolutionaries, popularity in the public meetings of the

---

6. The head of the Ministry of Interior's security division later testified that "The clubs and associations did all the harm. . . . I attribute all the events that just occurred to the clubs and associations"; *L'Enquête Parlementaire sur l'Insurrection du Dix-Huit mars,* 343.

7. Dalotel, Faure, and Freiermuth coined the phrase "workshops of revolt"; *Aux Origines,* 323.

8. The prominent socialist Gustave Lefrançais described this revolutionary nightlife and its regulars in *Souvenirs d'un révolutionnaire* (Brussels: Bibliothique des Temps Nouveaux, 1902), 287. Raoul Rigault was one of those who frequented the Brasserie Rhénane, also known as the Café Glaser, on the rue Saint Séverine; he and Maxime Vuillaume broke into it to have a drink just moments before Rigault was seized and shot during the *semaine sanglante;* Vuillaume, *Mes Cahiers rouges,* 215; Henri Bauer, *Mémoires d'un jeune homme* (Paris: Charpentier, 1895), 82. See also Robert Courtine, *La Vie Parisienne: Cafés et restaurants des boulevards, 1814–1914* (Paris: Perrin, 1984), 93; W. Scott Haine, "'Café-Friend': Friendship and Fraternity in Parisian Working-Class Cafés, 1850–1914," *Journal of Contemporary History* 27 (October 1992): 607–27.

9. Lefrançais noted that cafés fragmented opposition and that they were too public. Police easily penetrated such meetings, as in the "affaire" of the Café La Renaissance, when a group of Blanquist conspirators were arrested during a meeting in 1864; Lefrançais, *Souvenirs d'un révolutionnaire,* 282.

Empire was the first step on the road to the Commune.[10] The most radical orators were the Blanquists, an assortment of students, workers, and old revolutionaries that placed themselves under the guidance of "le vieux," Auguste Blanqui. By the late 1860s Blanqui had forty years of revolutionary action behind him and had spent nearly half his life in the prisons of every French government since the Restoration. He and his followers were, and are, sometimes portrayed as only political revolutionaries, but Blanqui had a well-developed vision of a socialist future.[11] Unlike most other socialists of the Second Empire, Blanquists argued that political revolution must precede any attempt at social and economic change; there was no place in the Blanquist program for compromises with the established order or for gradual evolution.[12] Armed with their revolutionary convictions and a secret, paramilitary organization, Blanquists made the rounds of the public meetings, gaining notoriety for their willingness to face prison and fines.

By the spring of 1870 the Blanquists had formed personal and political connections with some of the leaders of the Association International des Travailleurs.[13] A small group of workers had founded the AIT in 1864 on the Proudhonian assumption that social and economic reform within existing political conditions was possible through the association of pro-

10. Henri Bauer, a student opposed to the Empire, admitted being put off at first by the "somewhat rude and gross, strongly smelling, plebeian public," but he found that "after the stammering of the first evening and the agitation of an apprentice orator, I was soon master of the lexicon, an expert at attracting the warning of the police agent by lancing a few injurious attacks at the December Dynasty"; *Mémoires,* 108–9.

11. According to Blanqui one of the first steps of a revolutionary government would be to "lay the foundations of worker associations"; *Textes choisis,* ed. V. P. Volguine (Paris: Éditions Sociales, 1971), 165. Blanqui argued as well that a revolutionary dictatorship may be necessary for some time after seizing power, in order to adequately prepare the mass of rural French peasants for elections. See also Maurice Dommanget, *Blanqui, la guerre de 1870–71 et la Commune* (Paris: Domat, 1947) and *Les Idées politiques et sociales d'Auguste Blanqui* (Paris: Marcel Rivière, 1957).

12. In the mid-1860s Blanqui was imprisoned in the Ste-Pèlagie Prison in Paris, where students from the left bank and young workers visited him to discuss politics and past revolutions. Patrick Hutton, however, distorts Blanquism when he suggests it was backward-looking; *The Cult of the Revolutionary Tradition: The Blanquists in French Politics, 1864–93* (Berkeley: University of California Press, 1981). The struggle against clericalism, for example, which he qualifies as anachronistic, reflected the realities of contemporary politics. Dalotel, Faure, and Freiermuth have argued that the Blanquists were the most active element of the socialist movement at the end of the Empire; *Aux Origines,* 107.

13. Both Wolfe, in "The Origins of the Paris Commune," 41, and Dalotel, Faure, and Freiermuth, in *Aux Origines,* 355, see the same evolution toward cooperation.

duction, which would gradually create the basis for new political relations as well. Partly as a result of their association with Blanquists in public meetings, some leaders of the International came to accept the need for direct political action. "For us," wrote Eugène Varlin, one of the most important leaders of the AIT in the later Empire, "political revolution and social reforms are linked, and cannot go one without the other."[14] But the International was in no sense ideologically unified.[15] Other elements of opposition to the Empire were even less structured. Personal disputes and past grievances split the neo-Jacobins into several factions. Radical republicanism represented more a state of mind than an organized group.

Public assemblies provided effective platforms for these opponents of Napoleon III. The revolutionary *journées* of the late Empire, including the agitation surrounding the elections of 1869, the plebiscite of 1870, and the funeral of the journalist Victor Noir, can in whole or in large part be traced to the public meetings.[16] Yet the violent language of socialists and radicals in the capital often went far beyond what most French were willing to contemplate, and in the wake of the plebiscite riots of May 1870 the government closed the public meetings.[17] By July Paris was caught up in war fever over the crisis with Prussia, and attention shifted momentarily from politics to patriotism. When the Empire was toppled after the defeat at Sedan, however, public meetings immediately sprang up again. Blanqui

---

14. Varlin was roundly criticized within the AIT for advocating political action. Rougerie dates the AIT's turn toward politics to around 1867, when Varlin and Benôit Malon became ascendant; Rougerie, "Les Sections françaises de l'Association Internationale des Travailleurs," in *La Première Internationale: L'Institution, l'implantation, le rayonnement*, ed. Jacques Rougerie (Paris: Centre National des Recherches Scientifiques, 1968), 104. Moss ascribes this development to Bakunin's influence; *The Origins of the French Labor Movement*, 75.

15. Serman has described the International as "a kind of crossroads" and "a kind of thinking society," underscoring the confusion about the International's ideological character; *La Commune de Paris*, 62. Bruhat, Dautry, and Tersen agree that the International was divided within itself, mainly between Proudhonians and Blanquists. They maintain that it "in no way formed a homogeneous ideological bloc"; *La Commune de 1871*, 151.

16. Dalotel, Faure, and Freiermuth, *Aux Origines*, 355. Wolfe has credited these meetings with the election of Rochefort and stresses the role they played in creating an organized revolutionary opposition; "The Origins of the Commune," 41, 44, 68. A cousin of Napoleon III killed the journalist Victor Noir, probably in the belief that he was Rochefort; Noir's funeral in January 1870 attracted a huge crowd and nearly became an insurrection.

17. In prohibiting meetings the government of Emile Ollivier sought to appear "strong, as well as liberal"; Theodore Zeldin, *Emile Ollivier and the Liberal Empire of Napoleon III* (Oxford: Clarendon, 1963), 159.

led the first, which was especially fitting as he had organized the first club in 1848 as well.[18] His club, La Patrie en Danger, differed from the public meetings in that its organizers retained the right to limit discussion and select its members.

In addition to the individual clubs, committees, and public meetings that arose after the revolution of September 4, leaders of popular organizations coordinated their forces through the Comité Central Républicain de Défense National des Vingt Arrondissements de Paris (Republican Central Committee of National Defense of the Twenty Arrondissements), the group which was the most responsible for nurturing the Communal movement. While militants of the International were the principal instigators of the Republican Central Committee, it was formed by delegates sent from diverse clubs, assemblies, and vigilance committees and should not be considered merely a front for the AIT.[19] The Republican Central Committee became the crucial center of revolutionary activity in part because the AIT was divided about the role the working-class movement should play in political events during this uncertain period. Gustave Lefrançais, a prominent socialist, proposed that the AIT openly direct the vigilance committee movement, but the majority of Internationals feared that the existence of the AIT could be compromised if events turned against the committees. Even Varlin, generally a voice in favor of political action by the AIT, applauded the decision to insulate the AIT from a possible backlash.[20] The usefulness of such sleight of hand can be seen in the line taken

18. As early as 1832, when speaking before his judges at the "procès des quinze," Blanqui had argued for more democratic access to forums of discussion: "all the voices that echo in the public sphere, the voices of the salons, those of the shops, of the cafés—that is to say all the places where what one might call 'public opinion' is formed—these voices are those of the privileged. Not one belongs to the people"; *Textes choisis*, 76.

19. Dautry and Scheler suggest it was simply a manifestation of the International in another form; *Le Comité Central.* Rougerie and Wolfe show that members of the International were influential in some of the Republican Central Committee's arrondissement groups, though not in the majority of them; Rougerie, "Quelques documents nouveaux pour l'histoire du Comité Central Républicain des Vingt Arrondissements," *Le Mouvement Social* 37 (October–December, 1961): 3–29; Wolfe, "The Origins of the Paris Commune," 45. Louise Michel, later known as the "Red Virgin," described the creation of the committee: "The Federal Council of the International met on Corderie du Temple street; there too the delegates of the clubs met; thus was formed the Republican Central Committee of the Twenty Arrondissements, which in turn created vigilance committees in each arrondissement, formed by ardent revolutionaries"; *La Commune* (Paris: Stock, 1898), 93.

20. Gustave Lefrançais, *Étude sur la mouvement Communaliste à Paris en 1871* (Neuchâtel: Guillaume, 1871), 90–91. In January 1871 Varlin noted that "the International did not wish to pursue its policies itself; it left that to the public meetings. For my part, I do not regret it"; *L'Enquête Parlementaire sur l'insurrection du Dix-Huitmars 1871,* 526.

by many members of the International when they were arrested after the Commune. Eugène Bestetti, for example, claimed that "in our meetings we spoke only of workers' issues, the ways to ameliorate workers' conditions, and we never dealt with political issues," but he was careful not to mention his role in the vigilance committee of the 5th arrondissement, by virtue of which he held important administrative positions during the Commune.[21]

The early members of the Republican Central Committee were drawn mainly from the leadership of the public meetings of the late Empire. According to Benôit Malon, an important figure in the AIT, "the club delegates came to these meetings and brought there the violent language of the popular assemblies," underscoring the new dimension added to the Republican Central Committee by these militants. The admixture of these disparate groups in the local vigilance committees and in the Republican Central Committee that coordinated their activities goes far in explaining the way the revolutionary coalitions of 1870–71 were formed. The Republican Central Committee was the single most important organization in the revolutionary movement that preceded the Commune. According to Jules Vallès, a participant and later a member of the Commune, "from there came the Eighteenth of March."[22]

Due to its origins in various clubs, public meetings, and the AIT, the Republican Central Committee in its early days was divided not only in its members but also in its objectives. This was especially apparent in early October, as agitation for a Commune began to build. On October 5 the revolutionary adventurer Gustave Flourens led the first demonstration by armed National Guard battalions at the Hôtel de ville, demanding elections and a mass sortie against the Germans. Two days later a Blanquist, Théodore Sapia, attempted another armed demonstration but was arrested by his own men. Finally, Lefrançais and the leftists in the Republican Central Committee tried to initiate coordinated action, calling a public demonstration on October 8 to protest the cancellation of municipal elections. Perhaps as many as seven thousand guardsmen responded, but the government was well prepared, having stationed loyal National Guardsmen in front of the Hôtel de ville. The leaders of the demonstration were not allowed to present their petition to the government, and the crowd simply dispersed. The main effect of the demonstration of October 8 was to split the Republican Central Committee. Both moderates and

---

21. AHG: 25e conseil 203, dossier Bestetti.

22. Benôit Malon, *La Troisième défaite du prolétariate français* (Neuchâtel: G. Guillaume fils, 1871), 41; *Le Cri du Peuple,* January 7, 1884.

radicals dropped out of the committee in disgust with its incompetence, leaving only the central arrondissements fully represented.[23]

While the agitation for a Commune to organize decisive action against the Germans continued in popular organizations, the Republican Central Committee was momentarily weakened. Most Parisians distrusted the motives of the revolutionaries after the October 8 demonstration, and throughout October the press was filled with denunciations of radicals who betrayed the nation for their own political ambitions. Circumstances were changing, however, in favor of those who sought forceful action against the government. French armies continued their dismal performance against the Germans, and Orleans fell at midmonth. The siege of Paris was beginning to bite, with necessities such as bread and firewood expensive and scarce. These factors, and the continuing patriotic fury of the capital, help explain why a veritable flood of new clubs and committees formed in October. By the end of the month dozens of clubs were functioning, each with their particular clientele and atmosphere. Most arrondissement vigilance committees founded clubs to mobilize support for their goals and thus contributed to the flourishing of club life.[24] In addition, vigilance committees in some arrondissements were able to insinuate themselves into the local town halls, performing such functions as supervising rationing or outfitting guard units.

Sparked mainly by outraged patriotism and deteriorating conditions in the city, club oratory grew more critical of the government during October. This evolution was transformed into a revolutionary movement by three events on October 30 that unleashed an intense, though ultimately unsuccessful, insurrection. First, the government announced the surrender of the citadel of Metz by its commander, Marshall Bazaine; along with the fortress fell the last well-trained French army.[25] The government also announced that Adolphe Thiers and Otto von Bismarck were negotiating

<hr>

23. Flourens, a former professor of history, was one of the most charismatic figures of the period; see Richard-Pierre Guiraudon and Michel Rebondy, *Gustave Flourens: Le Chevalier rouge* (Paris: Pré au Clercs, 1987). Lefrançais, who had hoped for an armed uprising, blamed the failure of the October 8 demonstration on the commanders of the National Guard battalions who had not supported the Republican Central Committee in sufficient numbers; Dautry and Scheler, *Le Comité Central,* 95; Wolfe, "The Origins of the Paris Commune," 319.

24. For example, Raoul Urbain, later a member of the Commune, started the Club du Pré-aux-Clercs, whose formal title was *Republican Socialist Club of the Seventh Arrondissement,* as an adjunct to the vigilance committee; AHG: 3e conseil 29/15, dossier Urbain.

25. Bazaine's "treason" added to the impression that the government was only playing at resistance. Indeed, the government was dominated by politicians who believed from the first

an armistice that would allow the reprovisioning of Paris. Perhaps the government hoped this news would assuage the anger of Parisians who had become resentful of lines and high prices, but if so it misjudged the mood of the capital. An armistice with reprovisioning could only be a veiled surrender, and most Parisians still believed victory was possible. Finally, on October 30 several battalions of the National Guard were forced to retreat from a position after General Trochu, the commander of Paris, had refused to send reinforcements.[26] The triple blow delivered on October 30 shocked Paris; a storm of anger quickly gathered force, and it broke on the government on the afternoon of the next day.

While spontaneous Parisian anger was the foundation for the insurrection of October 31, popular organizations—especially the Republican Central Committee—provided the leadership and organizational framework for the revolt. Although its prestige and influence had been weakened by the failure of October 8, the Republican Central Committee and its local vigilance committees were able to react to the new situation with some effectiveness. Such a movement had long been anticipated, and the revolutionary clubs and committees were prepared to act when the favorable moment arrived.[27] Vigilance committees convoked special meetings, and the assembly at the salle Favié, for example, voted unanimously to march on the Hôtel de ville. The AIT, however, refused to endorse the movement, not wishing to become involved in purely political matters.[28]

The insurrection of October 31 took place at two levels, at the Hôtel de ville and at the mairies, or town halls, of the twenty arrondissements. That morning a large crowd gathered in front of the Hôtel de ville to protest armistice negotiations, shouting, "Vive la Commune," and calling for elec-

---

that victory was impossible; Gambetta was the main exception. Jules Simon was quite explicit about the government's lack of illusions; *The Government of M. Thiers, from 8th February 1871 to 24th May 1873,* 2 vols. (New York: Scribner's, 1879), 1:118.

26. The guardsmen had taken the position without orders, and Trochu was convinced it had no military importance, but the retreat had become a rout and resulted in twelve hundred French casualties. "In every public meeting, in every café, on every boulevard, and in every street a unanimous shout of curses arose against Trochu, whose incompetence had become obvious," Lefrançais recalled, reflecting the anger of the capital and illustrating some of the ways Parisians gathered and passed along news; *Étude,* 86

27. Both Rougerie, in *Procès des Communards,* 39, and Wolfe, in "The Origins of the Paris Commune," 229, reject the notion that the insurrection was prepared in the clubs.

28. Jacques Rougerie, "L'AIT et le mouvement ouvrier à Paris pendant les événements de 1870–1871," *International Review of Social History* 27 (1972): 25; Gustave de Molinari, *Les Clubs rouges pendant la siège de Paris* (Paris: Garnier. 1871), 213; Lefrançais, *Étude,* 92. Some newspapers reported the fall of Metz in the evening editions of the 29th.

tions. At the place de la Corderie, the headquarters of the Republican Central Committee, the International, and the Federation of Worker's Councils, a meeting was held to assess possible action. The diverse group also included Felix Pyat, an influential Jacobin not usually associated with the International or the Republican Central Committee. According to Lefrançais, "the delegates of the twenty arrondissements, united to the vigilance committees," decided to tell the government to hold elections or be removed. At two o'clock "the united committees" arrived on the place de l'Hôtel de ville, and delegates went in to confront the government.[29] Inside they found the members of the government trying to salvage the situation, promising resistance to the Germans and elections for a municipal council. Lefrançais would have none of it and began to read out a list of names of persons to be appointed to a Commune that would oversee elections. This list had evidently been decided on at the earlier meeting of the Republican Central Committee. At some point in the afternoon Etienne Arago, the mayor of Paris, who had been appointed by the government, gave permission for elections to be held, and orders went out to print posters announcing that fact. At four o'clock the unpredictable Flourens arrived, jumped on the table in the now crowded room, and read out his own list for a Committee of Public Safety. All semblance of order vanished when the table broke under this assault, and in the confusion some members of the government escaped from the building, only to immediately begin planning a counterattack. With the arrival of Blanqui in the evening the entire revolutionary spectrum was present, and despite confusion over who was in charge it appeared that the day had been won. Lefrançais and many others went to a meeting of the Republican Central Committee to decide on a combined list of nominees for the elected Commune, while Blanqui and Flourens, as members of a Committee of Public Safety, set about organizing the seizure of the Prefecture of Police, the mairies, and other key points in the city.[30]

In the arrondissements the local clubs and vigilance committees had

---

29. Archives de la Préfecture de Police (APP): Ba 362–6; Pyat described his actions in *Le Gaulois,* November 8; Lefrançais, *Étude,* 94. At his trial four months after the insurrection Lefrançais said that he, along with about thirty other people, entered the Hôtel de ville "as a delegate from a central club." The Republican Central Committee was never referred to as a central club, and no other group was known by that appellation except a group (described later in this chapter) that had just been formed. This helps demonstrate that the events of October 31 involved the coordination of several parts of the revolutionary movement, including local clubs, the Republican Central Committee, and the Club Central; *Gazette des Tribunaux,* February 24, 1871.

30. Lefrançais, *Étude,* 91; Flourens gave his version of events in *La Patrie en Danger,* November 4, 1870, and in *Paris Livré* (Paris: Librairie Internationale, 1871); the Republican

been equally busy. The salle de la Vieux-Chêne, which was associated with the vigilance committee in the 5th arrondissement, sent one hundred twenty men to swell the crowd in front of the Hôtel de ville. Similarly, vigilance committees in the 19th and 20th arrondissements assembled guard battalions to march in support of the revolt.[31] It is likely that a large number of the demonstrators who gathered in front of the city hall had been assembled at the behest of local clubs and committees, though only fragmentary evidence of this involvement survives. At the same time, many clubs and committees actually seized control of their local mairies, just as the revolutionaries were doing at the city level. Historians have long been aware of the insurrections in the arrondissements, but none of them has recognized the pattern of organized action that emerges when the insurrections are studied in light of the club and committee movement. Ultimately ten mairies were assaulted, which, when combined with the connections among the militants concerned, leaves little doubt that popular organizations were acting in a coordinated manner.

In the 19th arrondissement Jules Vallès and about three hundred guardsmen invaded the mairie at about five o'clock, taking possession in the name of the vigilance committee of the 19th arrondissement.[32] Meanwhile, Pierre Vésinier and perhaps thirty delegates of the Club Favié occupied the mairie of the 20th arrondissement, again supported by a crowd of guardsmen who had probably come from the club.[33] In the 13th arrondissement the Club Révolutionnaire de 190 avenue de Choisy, led by Leo Meilliet and Marie Sérizier, both of whom would later be influential Communards, invaded the mairie and raised the red flag above it.[34] In the 5th arrondissement the Club de la rue d'Arras forced out the mayor and,

---

Central Committee list is in AHG: Ly 12. Wolfe argued that the Republican Central Committee played no role in these events; "The Origins of the Paris Commune," 242.

31. Rougerie, *Procès des Communards,* 165; AHG: 4e conseil 1432.

32. At his trial for his role in this revolt Vallès understandably stressed the spontaneous nature of his actions, but the orders signed by him and the rest of the vigilance committee show their actions to be concerted and organized. Vallès was also charged with pillaging the mairie because he had distributed wine and herring to the guardsmen; AHG: Ly 26, dossier 19e arrondissement; *Gazette des Tribunaux,* March 10, 1871.

33. "I was named," Vésinier later explained, "like the other members of the commission, by the public meeting of Belleville." He added that "we only took possession of the mairie temporarily in order to watch over the elections for the Commune, which were supposed to take place the next day." As in the 19th arrondissement, Vésinier and the commission in the 20th had the drums beaten, summoning the National Guard to protect the insurrection at the Hôtel de ville. They also requisitioned ten thousand cartridges, as guardsmen were usually only issued ammunition at the front; AHG: Ly 12; *Gazette des Tribunaux,* February 24, 1871.

34. Gérard Conte, *Éléments pour une histoire de la Commune dans le XIIIe arrondissement, 5 mars–25 mai 1871* (Paris: Éditions de la Butte aux Cailles, 1981), 27–28.

having first contacted the Republican Central Committee, established a provisional municipal council.[35] A crowd from the Club de la rue Levis also expelled the mayor from the mairie of the 17th arrondissement.[36]

Things did not go so well for revolutionaries in the 14th arrondissement, where "the entire popular assembly of the Montparnass Theater" tried to take control of the mairie.[37] The guards refused to let them enter, and the crowd, said to be composed mostly of women, dispersed without attaining its objective.[38] The vigilance committee of the 12th arrondissement was also refused entry to the mairie and wrote to the Hôtel de ville asking for instructions. Over the seal of the Government of National Defense, Blanqui wrote an order giving the committee authority to occupy the mairie, and led by Jules Montels it did so.[39] In the 11th arrondissement a similar note from Blanqui authorized Jules Mottu and about fifty other militants to take possession of the mairie from its mayor, who had previously refused to give up his office.[40] The same pattern of events occurred at the mairie of the 1st arrondissement, where a crowd invaded the building but the mayor declined to leave. Jean-Jacques Pillot, who presided over the public meeting of the rue Jean Lantier, the club of the vigilance committee, intervened with an order Blanqui had written over the seal of the government, to which the mayor submitted.[41] In the 6th arrondissement Edmond Goupil, a member of the local vigilance committee, seized the mairie after having participated in the earlier invasion of the Hôtel de

35. It included four battalion chiefs, five members of the vigilance committee, and five members of the arrondissement's commission on armaments; AHG: Ly 12; *Le Combat,* November 2, 1870.

36. The mayor, François Favre, later testified that the group that invaded his mairie was the same one that did so on January 22, a group from the Club Levis; *L'Enquête Parlementaire sur l'Insurrection du Dix-Huit,* 344.

37. Ducoudray led the crowd; after September 4 he had installed himself as mayor, but he had recently resigned due to opposition from the government; *La Patrie en Danger,* November 5, 1870.

38. Even here, however, there had been preparations for an eventual seizure of the mairie. An accountant, Michael Astaix, testified that some days before the revolt he had been approached by leaders of the Club Gaieté (Théâtre Montparnasse) about being on a municipal council; AHG: Ly 12.

39. AHG: Ly 12; Jean Maitron, ed., *Dictionnaire biographique du mouvement ouvrier français, deuxième partie, 1864–71,* 6 vols. (Paris: Éditions Ouvrières, 1967–71), 7:394, referred to hereafter as *DBMOF.*

40. *Le Gaulois,* November 3, 1870.

41. Pillot then informed the Hôtel de ville that the "Republican Committee" of the arrondissement had successfully taken control of the mairie; AHG: Ly 12; *Gazette des Tribunaux,* February 24, 1871.

ville; it is likely that he too had some official instruction from the revolutionary government.[42]

Thus at both the Hôtel de ville and the arrondissement mairies, militants from popular organizations initiated and led the insurrection of October 31. Since their inception in early September the local vigilance committees had, like the Republican Central Committee at the citywide level, the dual role of watching over the local municipal authorities and of replacing them if possible. This is not to say that the hour or day of the insurrection was decreed long in advance or that the revolutionaries acted in complete unity. The intervention of Flourens at the Hôtel de ville proves otherwise. Lefrançais himself later concluded that the diversity of lists circulated for a Commune or a Committee of Public Safety revealed a lack of sufficient prior entente. Yet it is not fully accurate to suggest, as he does, that "this proves events alone produced the explosion."[43] The "explosion" was not produced by any individual or group; it was guided by the diverse elements of a fragile revolutionary coalition. Spontaneity alone would not have created the script that was played out at the Hôtel de ville and the mairies. Discussions in the Republican Central Committee, in the arrondissement committees, and in the other popular organizations had convinced radicals of the necessity of seizing power and had provided a means to organize the attempt when conditions were favorable.

In the early morning hours of November 1 the government was finally able to rally some guard battalions to its defense. Troops of the line were also brought into action. Remarkably, there was no blood shed as government forces entered the Hôtel de ville through an underground passage; believing victory assured, most of the revolutionaries had simply gone home. Blanqui and the others remaining inside agreed to leave peacefully when they were told elections would be held, and after this compromise the commander of the Parisian National Guard himself escorted Blanqui and the other insurgents out of the Hôtel de ville to safety. Once in control again, however, the government announced that instead of the citywide council that had been promised, elections would be held for arrondissement officials only. Having declared that it was committed to fighting the Germans to the finish, the government received a huge majority in a plebiscite held on November 3, and outside of the radical arrondissements in the northeastern working-class sections of Paris, the government could

---

42. Maitron, *DBMOF,* 6:222.
43. Lefrançais, *Étude,* 96.

even be satisfied with the mayoral elections, in which solid liberals and republicans won the day. Breaking a formal promise, the government then arrested all the insurrection participants that could be found, depriving the revolutionary movement of some of its key leaders for the duration of the siege.[44] For the government the main result of October 31 was that Paris had demonstrated it would not tolerate surrender. Three more months of siege were required before the capital would accept capitulation.

For those who had prepared and carried it out the effects of the failed insurrection were far more momentous. Even aside from the arrest or marginalization of key militants, the revolutionary movement received a demoralizing setback in the November plebiscite, when 322,000 Parisians supported the government while only 54,000 voted against it. In response to this spectacular repudiation and the failure of the revolt, many leaders of popular organizations reconsidered the program and tactics of the revolutionary movement. The events of October 31, an insurrection launched with at most thirty-six hours preparation, demonstrated both the strengths and weaknesses of clubs as revolutionary organizations. Clubs could directly reflect the sentiments of their members, allowing rapid execution of strongly felt dispositions. Groups such as the Republican Central Committee coordinated local club initiatives, multiplying their effectiveness. Yet clubs had several weaknesses as organizing structures, especially lack of unity, discipline, and secrecy. Popular organizations remained independent even while participating in the Republican Central Committee; their members, most of whom were only casual participants, regularly changed; and the government was well informed about any decisions that were taken. Many revolutionaries were aware of these deficiencies and took specific measures to correct them. During the latter half of the siege, club and committee militants learned lessons from their failures and forged a new coalition to safeguard the nation and their vision of the Republic.

This new revolutionary coalition arose from the ashes of the Republican Central Committee. The demoralization and arrests that followed the October 31 insurrection shattered the committee, which had only just recovered its strength after the demonstration of October 8. Most vigilance committees and clubs stopped sending delegates to the committee,

44. They were held without trial until February 1871, when all were acquitted except Vallès, who managed to escape. Others, such as Flourens and Blanqui, were forced into hiding, though Flourens was sometimes observed in the working-class districts, reportedly surrounded by a bodyguard of one hundred trusted men. In March both Blanqui and Flourens were sentenced to death *in absentia* for their role in the insurrection; AHG: Ly 12.

and by mid-November only five arrondissements were regularly represented.[45] With the momentary eclipse of the Republican Central Committee the revolutionary club and committee movement lacked an organized
center, giving it an especially chaotic aspect. To overcome this lack of
coordination, many clubs and meetings sponsored projects to combine
their forces on both an *ad hoc* and a more permanent basis.[46] Indeed, a
number of popular initiatives were launched or given renewed life in
November, and altogether they reveal a clear radicalization in club and
committee rhetoric and action. The new and renewed organizations
brought new participants into the revolutionary movement and set out
new goals and strategies.

The most important of the new organizations were the Légion Garibaldienne, the Club Central, and the Ligue Républicaine de Défense à Outrance. The Légion Garibaldienne had been formed in October as a semisecret federation of revolutionaries. It extended its activities to new clubs
and meetings in the later siege, eventually receiving the support of nine
clubs in eight arrondissements. The Légion was formed by militants with
close ties to the International, and the influence of that organization can
be seen in its membership card, which reads in part, "Universal Democratic and Social Republic. War to despots—peace to proletarians." It also
asserted that "the legionnaires, all workers, not recognizing any other government than that of the people by themselves and their servants," agreed
to never accept any "theocratic, monarchic, oligarchic, or dictatorial"
government and to bear arms only against the enemies of the Social
Republic.[47] The Club Central had originally been formed in mid-October
by delegates from several popular organizations, to collect and dissemi-
nate the propositions of every public meeting.[48] It appears to have ceased

45. They were the 1st, 3d, 4th, 5th, and 6th, again showing that the city's old core was the
Republican Central Committee's main base of support at this time; Wolfe, "The Origins of
the Paris Commune," 324.

46. See, for example, *Le Combat,* November 14 and 25, 1870.

47. AHG: 3e conseil 1112. Wolfe has given considerable attention to the Légion; "The
Origins of the Paris Commune," 330–36.

48. Pierre Vésinier first suggested a central club at the salle Favié on October 10, 1870,
and a committee was elected to organize one. Vésinier later made the same proposal to the
Pantheon section of the International, and an organizational meeting for the "central committee of public meetings" was held on October 15 at the salle d'Arras in the 5th arrondissement. Some days later another notice asked republican and socialist clubs to send three delegates to a meeting at the salle Ba-ta-clan on October 28 to organize a "league of clubs, or
central club," composed of delegates from all the republican clubs of Paris; *La Patrie en Danger,* October 14 and 28, 1870; *Le Combat,* October 16, 1870.

to function after the insurrection of October 31, but the idea of a central club resurfaced in late November, this time under the direct tutelage of the Republican Central Committee.[49] In its new incarnation the Club Central had its first public meeting on December 7 at the salle de la Redoute (1st arrondissement), and it continued holding meetings up to the end of the siege.[50]

The Ligue Républicaine de Défense à Outrance played the greatest role of the three in crystallizing the new revolutionary coalition of the later siege. Initiated by Blanquists and led by Eugène Chatelain and other members of the Republican Central Committee, it was a semisecret organization similar in structure to the Légion Garibaldienne. Its most vital contribution to the revolutionary movement lay in uniting several sections of the republican and revolutionary spectrum, including radicals such as Rochefort, moderate socialists such as Charles Beslay, and Blanquists, especially those from the 13th and 14th arrondissements who had not previously been well integrated into the larger Parisian movement. To promote greater coordination among popular organizations, the Ligue Républicaine supported two newspapers[51] and sponsored a Club de la Solidarité, which sought affiliations from other clubs and meetings. Taken together, these three groups show the club and committee movement to be rapidly evolving in November and December. Those moderates who had remained in the movement after the October 8 demonstration—including

---

49. The minutes of several meetings have been published in Rougerie, "Quelques documents nouveaux," 181. The unpublished minutes of one meeting, probably held at the Ba-taclan on October 28, 1870, reflect dissatisfaction with the Republican Central Committee; APP: Ba 363-5.

50. Napoleon Gaillard, who had been part of the delegation created by the Club Favié on 10 October to organize the first Club Central, presented a draft set of statutes at a Republican Central Committee meeting of November 23 for the Club Central du Comité Républicain Socialiste des Vingt Arrondissements de Paris. The statutes were published in *La Patrie en Danger,* November 28, 1870, and reprinted in Dautry and Scheler, *Le Comité Central,* 137, in the latter of which the authors make no mention of the Club Central of October. A complex process for admitting members and regulating discussion was prescribed, limiting the Club Central to those who agreed with "the fundamental and immutable principles of the Democratic and Social Republic"; *Le Combat,* December 8, 1870, and January 16, 1871; Rougerie, "Quelques documents nouveaux," 15.

51. One was *L'Oeil de Marat, Moniteur des XIXe et XXe Arrondissements adherent à la Ligue Républicaine,* published with the collaboration of Republican Central Committee leaders such as Gaillard, Chatelain, Vaillant, and Charles Dumont. The other was *La Résistance, organ démocratique et sociale, journal de la Ligue Républicaine,* which was also the newspaper of the Club Maison-Dieu (in the 14th arrondissement). See also Wolfe, "The Origins of the Paris Commune," 352.

many members of the International—appear to have definitively fallen away after October 31, their place in the clubs and committees being taken by increasing numbers of Blanquists.[52]

There was also a marked evolution in the tactics of the movement in the later siege. After defeat in the November plebiscite, revolutionaries came to rely less on public meetings and clubs for action than on new semisecret organizations such as the Légion Garibaldienne and the Ligue Républicaine, as well as on other secret meetings of club leaders and members. This change in tactics was a conscious choice. Already on October 28 Jules Andrieux, later a member of the Communal Council, had asserted that given the intensity of police surveillance "the door must be open and closed. Open for political discussion; closed for decisions to be taken."[53] In December Baillet declared that the clubs should disband because the police know everything that is said in them. Instead, he counseled citizens to join the Ligue Républicaine de Défense à Outrance, where "truly revolutionary decisions are taken, without fear of the police; one can speak freely." Baillet added that "in case the Ligue must act, orders would be carried to the twenty arrondissements; in a few hours everyone will be in arms." Other clubs also held private membership meetings in addition to public sessions. The effectiveness of this tactic is shown in the police reports of the period, in which frequent mention is made of private meetings that the police agent was unable to enter.[54]

The final and most significant transformation in the revolutionary coalition was a change in the goal of the movement. The Commune was still the touchstone of all revolutionary activity, but a new conception of the Commune gradually took shape and grew to dominance, that of the "revolutionary Commune." The distinction between the Commune of the early siege and the revolutionary Commune lies in the method of its formation, for both were intended to lead France to victory and the Republic. The Commune was originally conceived as an elected body, even if

---

52. Both Rougerie, in "Quelques documents nouveaux," and Wolfe, in "The Origins of the Paris Commune," 275, have drawn attention to this change in personnel.

53. Andrieux spoke at the Club Central; APP: Ba 363-5.

54. Baillet, speaking at the Club Maison-Dieu on December 5, also evoked the same dual struggle mentioned by Fonvielle in the epigraph to this chapter: "we must fight the Prussians and enemies of the Republic"; Bibliothèque Historique de la Ville de Paris (BHVP): Ms. 1083. The danger of police spies is ironically confirmed by the fact that the agent that left this report was present at the meeting. On secret meetings, see BHVP: Ms. 1083, December 24, 1870, and January 2, 1871. Molinari also laments his inability to enter many clubs at this time; Les Clubs rouges, 175.

government opposition meant that the elections would have to be held
after an insurrection. This concept had motivated the events of October 8
and October 31. Yet the failure of those revolutionary *journées,* especially
the results of the November plebiscite, indicated that revolutionaries could
never hope to rally a majority behind them; elections in those circumstances would likely result in victory for moderate republicans. The solution was a revolutionary Commune, drawn directly from the clubs and
committees of Paris, without recourse to general elections. While the idea
of a revolutionary Commune gained strength at the same time that
increasing numbers of Blanquists entered the vigilance committee movement, the change in strategy is not attributable simply to growing Blanquist influence. In the early siege the Blanquists had confined their aspirations to creating an elected Commune, as their actions on October 31
demonstrated. Each segment of the revolutionary coalition evolved
toward the revolutionary Commune, though at different rates and with
varying degrees of eagerness.[55]

The revolutionary Commune conceived in the later siege was recognized to be the government of a revolutionary minority. At the salle Favié
on December 18 a speaker explained that the November plebiscite had
shown that elections would be a gamble. The unnamed orator advocated
instead "election by the revolutionary path. We must ourselves choose
eighty pure republicans who will form the Commune and will save the
Republic like they saved it in 93! *(Yes, yes, that's it! the revolutionary Commune!)*"[56] At the Club Central on December 28 an important debate took
place around the idea of the revolutionary Commune. Jules Babick, a
future member of the Commune, declared, "the revolutionary method is
the only one which could today be put at the disposition of the people.
Governed for a long time by conspiratorial monarchic minorities, we must
today be guided by a minority devoted to the interests of the people."[57] In

---

55. In part, Blanquists became influential because, being predisposed toward direct
action, they were among the first to undergo this evolution and the most fervently devoted to
it. Gustave Tridon, a Blanquist, wrote that the Commune should be like that of 1792: revolutionary, illegal, and violent; *La Patrie en Danger,* October 8, 1870.

56. Quoted in Molinari, *Les Clubs rouges,* 160.

57. Babick then called for popular organizations to present their nominations to the
Republican Central Committee in order to organize the revolutionary Commune. Two other
speakers echoed Babick's remarks. Pessant demanded "the revolutionary Commune, whose
members should be chosen like the generals chosen by Gambetta, from among the young
who will be found there, ready to carry the weight of the situation"; and Siaux-Lavigne also
demanded "the revolutionary Commune, which, for him as well, is the only means of salvation." The full transcript is in Rougerie, "Quelques documents nouveaux," 20.

January an orator repudiated elections, proclaiming, "universal suffrage will be fine when France has stopped being raised by the *petits frères,* when everyone will have received free and obligatory education; but right now, what we need to save us is the revolutionary Commune! *(Acclamations: That's right!)*"[58] Militants in popular organizations not only conceived of a revolutionary seizure of power but took purposeful, and eventually successful, steps to bring it about. From the later siege to the Commune of March 18 runs a long-obscured, but unmistakable, thread of continuity in personnel, ideas, and organization.

The agitation to create a revolutionary Commune began as just a few comments in scattered clubs and meetings after the November plebescite. At the Club de la Vengeance on November 12 Eugene Dupas proposed the creation of "councils of the arrondissements, whose general meeting would form the Commune."[59] Militants of the Republican Central Committee then led a coordinated effort to form the revolutionary Commune, which was often mentioned in connection with the Ligue Républicaine de Défense à Outrance. Two weeks after Dupas's proposal, Gérardin outlined what very nearly was the exact trajectory of the revolutionary club and committee movement up to the insurrection of March 18. He told fifteen hundred persons at the Société Républicaine Socialiste du 17e Arrondissement that "the issue is to form a Central Revolutionary Committee, which, in accord with the other committees of the arrondissements, will form a federation with the International Association and the 'Comité de la Défense à Outrance.' " The new group would then send to the rest of France delegates appealing for the overthrow of the "government of shame and contempt" and for the establishment of the Social Republic, "the only government where the people are sovereign."[60] Gérardin thus revealed a mature plan to create a new version of the Republican Central Committee, under the name Comité Central Révolutionnaire, which would undertake united action with the AIT.[61] The Republican Central

58. An anonymous speaker at the Club Reine-Blanche, January 10; quoted in Molinari, *Les Clubs rouges,* 222.

59. Dupas, a socialist, veteran of the 1848 Luxembourg Commission, and founder of the Republican Central Committee, was very active in the clubs of the 18th arrondissement. Maitron, *DBMOF,* 5:416; Molinari, *Les Clubs rouges,* 88.

60. BHVP: Ms. 1083; the report does not give Gérardin's first name, but it was no doubt Charles, a future member of the Commune for the 17th arrondissement.

61. Gérardin may have only had the agreement of a local section or a dissident group of sections. Rougerie has clearly shown the divisions in the International in "L'AIT et le mouvement ouvrier." Sections in Gérardin's arrondissement, the 17th, were particularly independent.

Committee did change its name when it transformed itself into the revolutionary Commune on January 1, calling itself the Delegation of the Twenty Arrondissements. As Gérardin also suggested, the new organization sent to the provinces in February and March delegates who were instrumental in fomenting short-lived Communes. Meanwhile, something like Gérardin's plan was being implemented in the 18th arrondissement. Under the name Club de la Révolution several clubs organized a federation whose central purpose was to form a revolutionary Commune. As part of this initiative, the Club Reine-Blanche elected ten men on December 6 who were "to arrive, by means of the Commune, at a prompt and decisive action concerning the defense of Paris, and also to bring about social and economic reforms leading to the emancipation of the proletariat."[62]

The prominence of the Ligue Républicaine de Défense à Outrance in Gérardin's statement is likewise notable, as it had only recently been created, under the auspices of the Republican Central Committee. Given the role assigned to it by Gérardin, the Ligue Républicaine may well have been formed specifically to facilitate the creation of the revolutionary Commune.[63] Indeed, on December 18 Gabriel Ranvier, an important revolutionary militant and future member of the Communal Council, announced at the Club Favié that a new government was being formed by the "Ligue Républicaine de la Défense à Outrance and the Ligue Républicaine."[64] On the next day, police reported that the vigilance committee associated with the Club Favié had issued a poster calling for an insurrection at a specific date and hour.[65] At the same time, Albert Goullé proposed that the Club Central "put the government on notice to attack vig-

---

62. *Le Combat,* December 12. The police believed this meeting was called by Felix Pyat as part of his Ligue Anti-Monarchique; BHVP: Ms. 1083, December 6, 1870. Wolfe, unaware of the police reports in BHVP: Ms. 1083, overemphasized the role that the clubs in the 18th arrondissement had in forming the revolutionary Commune; "The Parisian *Club de la Révolution.*"

63. Wolfe, in "The Origins of the Commune," 336, argued that the Ligue was ineffectual; Serman makes the same claim in *La Commune de Paris,* 157.

64. It is unclear what was meant by the second "Ligue Républicaine," but it may be a garbled reference to the Comité Républicain, a common designation for the Republican Central Committee. Ranvier is quoted by Prefect of Police E. Cresson, in *Cent jours du siège à la Préfecture de Police, 2 novembre 1870–11 fevrier 1871* (Paris: Plon, 1901), 127.

65. The committee had the posters pulled down because military operations then underway had taken guardsmen away to the front. The report on this incident described alleged divisions in the revolutionary movement: the Ligue Républicaine could not get its members to join the revolt, and the faubourg Saint Antoine would not follow the lead of the 20th arrondissement; BHVP: Ms. 1083.

orously the Prussian lines within three days." Two days later members of
the Club Reine-Blanche discussed an ultimatum to the government to
break the siege within forty-eight hours or face a mass march on the Hôtel
de ville.[66] These reports were only the first of several alarms that sounded
around the end of the year and warned of an impending insurrection. The
nascent revolutionary Commune made its influence felt.

By the end of December the revolutionary club movement had fully
recovered from the debacle of October 31 and was ready to go on the
offensive. On December 23 the Republican Central Committee named a
delegate for each arrondissement to coordinate the local clubs and prepare
them for action. Additional clubs and committees elected their delegates
to the revolutionary Commune.[67] The Club de la Révolution at the Elysée-
Montmartre, for example, delegated four members to the Republican
Central Committee, "which," in the words of one orator, "will be called on
to play a decisive role when the moment comes—and it will hardly wait—
to march on the Hôtel de ville."[68] The Republican Central Committee
meeting of December 28 reflected the renewed belligerence of the revolutionary club and committee movement. Constant Martin requested that
vigilance committees tell the committee "as soon as possible the state of
the forces that each arrondissement could dispose of at an opportune
moment for installing the revolutionary commune." Montels then put a
key question to the assembly, asking "whether the committee should wait
to provoke the installation of the commune until events naturally occur, or
whether we should act through specific measures." The issue was not
resolved, though Gervais of the 18th arrondissement said he thought "an
event is close which will naturally lead democrats to act," a possible refer-

---

66. Goullé's proposal is reprinted in Rougerie, "Quelques documents nouveaux," 20; on
the subsequent ultimatum see Molinari, *Les Clubs rouges,* 166.

67. Rougerie, "Quelques documents nouveaux," 23; Wolfe, "The Parisian *Club de la
Révolution,*" 101. That evening, December 23, the Club de l'École de Médecine "organized a
new government" by dividing Paris into districts, each of which would name delegates to the
Commune; Cresson, *Cent jours,* 128.

68. Molinari, *Les Clubs rouges,* 172. On December 25 the Club des Révolutionnaires du
XIe Arrondissement held a meeting to decide on its list of names of those "delegated to take
measures for the public safety," inviting all club presidents from Paris to bring their lists. This
group had recently helped organize local sections of the Ligue Républicaine de Défense à
Outrance and the Légion Garibaldienne, which were no doubt part of this effort; *Le Combat,*
December 21 and 25, 1870. By December 25 popular organizations in seven arrondissements
(the 5th, 6th, 8th, 11th, 14th, 17th, and 18th) are known to have chosen members of the revolutionary Commune; given the events that followed, five other organizations (in the 1st, 4th,
13th, 19th, and 20th arrondissements) had also most likely elected their members.

ence to the retreat of Parisian forces from the strategic Avron plateau, ordered that night by General Trochu. The agenda for the next meeting was then determined: "On the Revolutionary Commune and the practical means of its revolutionary installation." That evening, at the Club Pré-aux-Clercs, the Blanquist Théodore Sapia, one of the initiators of the Ligue Républicaine de Défense à Outrance, announced that the 8th and 18th arrondissements had organized the Commune, and he reportedly urged that guillotines be placed at every intersection until victory was achieved.[69]

Preparations for the revolutionary Commune fully matured in the last two days of December. On the 30th the Republican Central Committee decided to call a general assembly of vigilance committees on the morning of New Year's Day, to present and discuss lists for the members of the Commune. "Never has the moment been better for us," Israel Schneider proclaimed that evening at the Elysée-Montmartre. "Be ready to march at every instant," he urged, "and above all don't forget your rifle."[70] The vigilance committees in the 19th and 20th arrondissements went into permanent session, a denotation of preparations for some important event. These committees told the members of the salle Favié that "they may ask their assistance for an action against what they called the Prussians of the interior." The next day, December 31, police reported that the Légion Garibaldienne and the Ligue Républicaine de Défense à Outrance were trying to coordinate with other groups and that their section chiefs appeared to have decided on a "projet d'un movement." A meeting to be held that night at the salle de la Redoute, the home of the Republican Central Committee's Club Central, was supposed to confirm this project. The usually sanguinary police report ended with a warning that things seemed to be getting more dangerous.[71]

This alarm was well founded. On January 1, 1871, a general assembly of vigilance committees inaugurated the revolutionary Commune, under the title Delegation of the Twenty Arrondissements. This entailed more than simply changing the name of the Republican Central Committee, for the new organization was intended to be the government of Paris. "The Cen-

---

69. The transcript from the Republican Central Committee meeting of December 28 is reprinted in Rougerie, "Quelques documents nouveaux," 24. BHVP: Ms. 1083.

70. The police report does not give Schneider's first name, but it was no doubt Israel, a militant of the committee of vigilance in the 18th arrondissement, and a member of the revolutionary Commune chosen by the Club de la Révolution on December 6, 1870; BHVP: Ms. 1083; Rougerie, "Quelques documents nouveaux," 24.

71. BHVP: Ms. 1083, report of December 31.

tral Committee is dissolved," Armand Levy explained at a club that night, "and delegates have been named by the twenty arrondissements for establishing the Paris Commune."[72] The Delegation embodied a new coalition of the left, formed after the catastrophe of October 31, around the idea of a revolutionary Commune. Fully 70 percent of known participants in the key meetings of December 23, December 28, and January 6 (thirty-six of fifty-one) had first been noted at Republican Central Committee meetings in November or December; almost all the new participants were members of the Légion Garibaldienne or the Ligue Républicain de Défense à Outrance. Nearly all the 140 members of the Delegation itself were working-class militants who had merged into the revolutionary movement through arrondissement vigilance committees and clubs.[73] While many were Blanquists or members of the International, the new coalition crystallized in the Delegation because it alone could unite the energy of the myriad popular organizations of Paris.[74] The Delegation of the Twenty Arrondissements formed on January 1 united the revolutionary elite of the capital, and in three months they would rule Paris.

On January 2 the Delegation set about organizing an insurrection to install the revolutionary Commune in the Hôtel de ville. According to the papers of Charles Chassin, the meeting opened with a roll call of "the representatives of the twenty arrondissements," that is, the members of the revolutionary Commune.[75] Théophile Ferré, a Blanquist who presided

---

72. Rougerie, in "Quelques documents nouveaux," 25, was the first to realize that the Delegation was in fact the revolutionary Commune, "a point," as Wolfe notes, "which Dautry and Scheler had completely missed"; "The Parisian *Club de la Révolution*," 102. Levy spoke at the salle d'Arras, where the general meeting of vigilance committees that formed the Delegation had met earlier that day; *La Lutte à Outrance,* 19 Nivôse 79 [January 9, 1871?].

73. Rougerie has emphasized the participation of members of the AIT from the left bank, grouped in the Democratic and Socialist Club of the 13th arrondissement, while Wolfe has stressed the Blanquist influence. Both are correct, as many members of the AIT were also Blanquists and vice versa; assigning single labels to militants in this period sometimes creates a false sense of precision. Rougerie, "L'AIT et le mouvement ouvrier," 38; Wolfe, "The Origins of the Paris Commune," 377.

74. The night of January 1 the salle Favié heard an announcement that "their committees [of the 19th and 20th arrondissements] were united and *en permanence,* and had organized a government in which figured Blanqui, Pyat, Ranvier, Chatelain, Lefrançais, Millière, Flourens." Citizens who wished to replace the government were invited to sign up with the committee; BHVP: Ms. 1083, January 2. Wolfe has argued that the Club de la Révolution of the 18th was alone in seeking revolutionary action; "The Parisian *Club de la Révolution*," 102.

75. Chassin had dropped out of the Republican Central Committee in protest over the demonstration of October 8, and he wanted nothing to do with the revolutionary Commune; his papers are reprinted in Rougerie, "Quelques documents nouveaux," 25.

over the meeting, then rose. "There is no need to discuss what was done yesterday. The Commune has been constituted," he said. "It remains only to agree on the measures to be taken," he continued, "so that it might exercise in a revolutionary manner the mission with which it has been entrusted." To that end he proposed creating a "*comité d'éxécution* composed of a small number of resolute members." Several speakers called for immediate revolution, saying, according to Chassin, "the hour has come to act and we must not lose a minute." "Their men, they claimed, were *en permanence*, with arms and munitions," writes Chassin, "the clubs as well." The majority of the Delegation, however, decided to prepare the ground by issuing what would later be called the Red Poster, "announcing to the people," in the words of Tridon as recorded by Chassin, "what we wish to do in their name, and indicating their duty."[76]

The *comité d'éxécution* called for by Ferré and the other delegates at the January 2 meeting was clearly intended to prepare and carry out an insurrection. The minutes of a Delegation meeting on January 6 list a nine-member *comité d'initiative* that is probably the same committee.[77] Edouard Vaillant, a member of this committee, later recalled:

> In the first days of January a commission of twenty-two members was formed at the Corderie in view of a movement that would be our revenge for October 31. This commission named a secret subcommission of five members, charged with preparing the insurrection. The five members delegated were: Ferré, Leverdays, Tridon, Sapia, and me.
>
> We met *en permanence,* Tridon, Sapia, and me. . . . We set about rallying, through the help of our most trusted friends at the Corderie, the greatest possible force, in the popular arrondissements, for a date to be determined.[78]

---

76. The members of the commission to write the poster, according to Chassin, were Leverdays, Vaillant, and Tridon; reprinted in Rougerie, "Quelques documents nouveaux," 25.

77. The nine members were Blanquists or sympathizers: Tridon, Vaillant, Sapia, Duval, Ferré, Caria, Arnaud, Brideau, and Meilliet; Rougerie, "Quelques documents nouveau," 26. There are four committees mentioned in three sources, all of which are probably the same: Ferré's proposed *comité d'éxécution* of January 2, described by Chassin; the commission actually created on January 2 to write the Red Poster, also described by Chassin; Vaillant's secret subcommission; and the *comité d'initiative* listed in the minutes of the Delegation's January 6 meeting.

78. Just previous to this excerpt Vaillant stated that by the Corderie he meant the "Comité des Vingt Arrondissements"; quoted in Choury, *La Commune au coeur de Paris,*

The revolutionaries of popular organizations were now going beyond reacting to events, as they had done October 31, and were preparing the "specific measures" (for an insurrection) that Montels mentioned at the Republican Central Committee meeting of December 30.

The Red Poster as eventually written reiterated the demands that the radical clubs and committees of the city had been making since the beginning of the siege: requisition of foodstuffs and other necessities for free distribution to the needy, equality of hardship and of responsibilities, and a mass sortie to break the blockade. In addition, reflecting months of frustration and disappointment with the government, the Red Poster openly called for the government's overthrow: "The policy, strategy, and administration of the Government of September 4, continuations of those of the Empire, have been condemned. Make way for the People! Make way for the Commune!" Previously unknown sources reveal that the Red Poster was more than a cry of outrage against a government deemed incompetent and reactionary.[79] And it was not a provocation intended to unleash a spontaneous uprising.[80] The Red Poster announced an insurrection planned in advance and executed by revolutionary popular organizations. The proof is not only in Vaillant's recollection but in the words of club militants themselves, who on the nights of January 4 and 5 systematically prepared their assemblies for an insurrection. "Tomorrow evening, January 5, the poster of the manifesto of the Commune will be printed and posted in the night," Leulier told the Club de la Ligue Républicaine on January 4. "Soon," he continued, "arrangements shall be made to go at a fixed hour to the Hôtel de ville to install the Commune." He recommended arriving

---

120. Vaillant was incorrect about the number on the committee, but there was a separate executive commission of twenty (not twenty-two) members mentioned as well at the morning Delegation meeting of January 6, and Vaillant's statements on that day show that he was part of this commission, too; reprinted in Dautry and Scheler, *Le Comité Central,* 149.

79. The new evidence is the police reports in BHVP: Ms. 1083. Dautry and Scheler did not suggest the poster had any insurrectionary significance; *Le Comité Central,* 145. Rougerie has argued that there is no proof the Red Poster was intended to coincide with an insurrection; "Quelques documents nouveaux," 26. Gould calls it only "a fiery call for a full-scale attack on the Prussians"; *Insurgent Identities,* 154.

80. Wolfe has argued that the Delegation "decided to depend upon a mass uprising rather than an organized *coup* for the installation of the Commune," whereas the *comité d'éxécution* was feverishly organizing exactly such a coup. He recognized the Red Poster to be a general call to arms but did not show that it was part of an insurrectional strategy centered in the clubs and committees. The Delegation did not just post the *affiche rouge* and wait for a response, as he suggests; "The Parisian *Club de la Révolution,*" 103. The poster was a "spontaneous and abortive revolutionary proclamation," according to Cordillot; *Eugène Varlin,* 197.

armed.[81] At the salle d'Arras, Charles Ledroit, future member of the Commune and member of the local vigilance committee, outlined a detailed revolutionary scenario. "The moment is approaching when you will hear the tocsin call the people to arms. You will go to the Hôtel de ville, you will probably find Breton guardsmen [protecting it]," he said, "but before letting them range for battle you will hurl yourself on them, en masse, and you will enter. Each of you will grab a guardsman, you will be masters of the situation." He, too, recommended that all citizens come to the meeting the next day, "because there probably will be precise orders given."[82] At the salle Favié, Marcollier demanded that the assembly of four hundred march that minute on the Hôtel de ville, which made Lavalette sound almost moderate when he merely announced that "the Commune formed by 120 members is ready to function, that it sent to the government an invitation to give up its place Thursday at noon. He [Lavalette] asks that all citizens go to the Hôtel de ville, adding that those who do not are cowards."[83] Altogether ten orators in four meetings the night of January 4 spoke with relative uniformity about a planned insurrection. The Red Poster was indeed intended to coincide with an insurrectionary movement, one planned by the Delegation and orchestrated through the popular organizations of the city.[84]

The dawn of January 5 brought the first bombardment of the city by the German forces encircling it. During the next three weeks some 250 people were killed by the shelling, but far from bringing calls for surrender the explosions seemed only to stoke Parisian anger and defiance. Much greater sources of misery were famine and disease; by the beginning of January, more than a thousand people each week were dying from causes related to the siege. As the first shells fell the commission entrusted with

81. BHVP: Ms. 1083. Four other militants spoke in the same vein. One was Antoine Arnaud, an active member of the Republican Central Committee, founder of the Ligue Républicaine de Défense à Outrance, and future member of the Commune of 1871; the others were Ménager, Gerard, and Laurent. The police report did not give the location of the club, but it was probably the salle Molière, in the 3d arrondissement, where Arnaud and Laurent are known to been active.

82. BHVP: Ms. 1083; Ledroit's first name was not given. Citizen Tabard also repeated the call to come to the next meeting: "we will be *en permanence* to wait for news and orders that may be given."

83. BHVP: Ms. 1083. Just as Lavalette indicated, the Red Poster demanded that the government retire, but it gave no deadline.

84. After the Red Poster was issued and dozens of its signers arrested the Delegation protested that it was not a call to arms, but these words are belied by the Delegation's actions; *Le Combat,* January 10.

writing the Delegation's Red Poster finished its work, and the reports on the clubs that night show that preparations for the revolt continued.[85] At the salle passage du Genie, Sauvage told the crowd of about 250 "to be ready at the first signal to march on the Hôtel de ville to establish this Commune that will take us from this terrible situation." The anticipation was palpable at the salle d'Arras, where the thousand people assembled went into permanent session to await "important news that two citizens, devoted to the republican cause, have promised to bring. Perhaps," the president, Arthur Pieron, added, "the people will be asked to act even tonight." Inspired by the moment, Pieron gave a speech that seems to have been exceptional, even when transcribed in the police report:

> Last October 31 we committed a courageous act, we succeeded, but we let ourselves be fooled by MM. du gouvernement who promised us the establishment of the Commune.
> This time we will go to the Hôtel de ville and we will install the Commune. For that, we will not have recourse to universal suffrage. Even though democrats are in the minority, we must try to establish the Commune, because for too long we have let ourselves be disunited by the Bourgeoisie, which has taken, since 1789, the place of the nobility. But we will treat them as our fathers treated the nobility.
> Yes, MM. of the Bourgeoisie, we will take you and we will make you pay. For too long you have exploited us, you have stripped us.
> Patience, the hour approaches, let everyone march, let everyone act in concert, and let everyone do their duty!![86]

Waiting for word that the insurrection was to begin, Pieron brought together in this speech many elements of the revolutionary discourse in the clubs and committees of the siege: anger with a government thought guilty of treason and deception, a sense of continuity with the great revolutionary tradition, and popular struggle against an exploiting bourgeoisie. The

---

85. Vallès has left a vivid description of the drafting of the poster: working late in a small room on the rue Saint Jacques, he, Tridon, Vaillant, and Leverdays, exhausted, had fallen asleep. They were awakened by canon fire, and Leverdays then formulated the final phrase: "Place au Peuple! Place à la Commune!"; *Le Cri du Peuple,* January 7, 1884.

86. BHVP: Ms. 1083; the report gave the speaker's name as "Pirron," though it must have been Pieron, who was an active member of the vigilance committee of the 5th arrondissement, salle d'Arras.

solution was the revolutionary Commune, a minority government to pre-serve the Republic.

The expected messengers never arrived, however, and the meeting broke up near midnight without its attendees marching on the Hôtel de ville. When the Red Poster did appear on the walls of the capital in the early morning hours of January 6, the response disappointed the revolu-tionaries. Police reports describe groups milling about the place de l'Hôtel de ville and the Bastille all day on the sixth, but officials did not think they were particularly dangerous.[87] Five or six hundred demonstrators gath-ered at the Chateau d'Eau and then spread out by groups into other areas, although without effect. The government denounced the attempt to "use our suffering and our sacrifices against the defense." The poster "raised some emotions in the faubourgs," according to a police report of January 6, but in the center of Paris citizens tore it down.[88] By the evening of Jan-uary 6 so many posters had been destroyed that the six hundred people attending the Club Reine-Blanche unanimously approved another post-ing.[89]

Despite the tepid response to the Red Poster, there were still some hopes for an uprising at the salle Favié, where an unnamed orator declared, "everything is ready for action. The Commune is formed! It is a secret Commune, if you like, but we now know all its members." He added that "The 'Republican Central Committee' has modestly and patriotically ceded its place to the delegates; it only remains for us to install them." On January 9 the Club Révolutionnaire of the rue Levis (17th arrondisse-ment) voted an immediate descent on the Hôtel de ville. Led by signers of the "Red Poster," club members then marched out of the hall crying, "Long live the Commune! Down with Trochu! String up the curates and

---

87. BHVP: Ms. 1083, January 6, 1871.

88. Even in the faubourgs, it seems, many of the posters were torn down by common Parisians, though there was much talk in the clubs that paid government agents were respon-sible, as at the salle Favié on January 16; Molinari, *Les Clubs rouges,* 249; *Paris Journal,* Jan-uary 9, 1871; BHVP: Ms. 1083, January 6, 1871.

89. A revealing incident occurred on the boulevard Magenta, where Benjamin Le Moussu, a member of the vigilance committee in the 18th arrondissement, stationed himself in front of a Red Poster and exhorted passersby to overthrow the government. He was looked on with suspicion by the crowd that formed, and he was arrested by the police. The next morning more posters were put up in the 18th and 19th arrondissements, but they were again torn down. Le Moussu remained in jail until the Commune, when he arrested the policeman that had previously arrested him. AHG: 13e conseil 189; BHVP: Ms. 1083, January 6 and 7, 1871.

spies!"[90] Still, this period saw the first doubts expressed in revolutionary clubs that the Commune could be established in time to save France and the Republic. The calls for the Commune once again take on a hypothetical tone, and revolutionaries seem discouraged. This was due in part to the arrest of many signers of the Red Poster, but revolutionary leaders were forced to admit a lack of enthusiasm in their followers; in several clubs orators derided the assembly for lack of courage or initiative, as at the Reine-Blanche: "I would like to see you have this Red Poster in your hands, see you study it, and when you have well understood it, act and sanction what we have decreed for three months."[91]

By the middle of January, after four months of siege, entire districts of the city were denuded of trees, park benches, fences, and anything else that would burn.[92] Hungry crowds pillaged warehouses; breadlines grew unruly. The Government of National Defense, which had seen little hope of victory even at the beginning of the siege, set about preparing the population for an "armistice," a euphemism for the city's surrender. To avoid another October 31, the government initiated a last military gesture to convince Paris that further resistance was useless. General Trochu accordingly organized the first large sortie by National Guards, at Buzenval on January 19, "to appease public opinion."[93] After a series of tragicomic blunders, however, the sortie was called off with relatively light casualties. The greatest fatality of the day was the faith many Parisians still maintained in the government. Suddenly the conditions prior to the October 31 insurrection were re-created: an angry population, faced with surrender, seemed ready to listen to the revolutionaries once again.

---

90. On January 11 an orator correctly told the salle Bourdon that the Commune was already functioning semiofficially and was only awaiting the right moment to openly take up its duties; BHVP: Ms. 1083, January 9 and 11, 1871; Molinari, *Les Clubs rouges,* 208.

91. The Delegation's second meeting of January 6 was confused and panicky, as several members had by then been arrested. Still, Ferré's defiant character showed clearly in his motion that all members of the Delegation come to their meetings "armed and ready to resist"; reprinted in Rougerie, "Quelques documents nouveaux," 26. On the demoralization see BHVP: Ms. 1083; Molinari, *Les Clubs rouges,* 215.

92. An important theme of club oratory after January 6 was the cowardice and lack of energy of those who claimed to be ready to march for the Commune but did not match their words with deeds. At the salle Favié on January 18 an orator castigated the assembly, shouting that the situation was worse than ever now, ten days after the Red Poster, while the "captives" of October 31 and January 6 were still imprisoned; Molinari, *Les Clubs rouges,* 246.

93. Another member of the government was quoted by General Ducrot as saying, "there must be a big sortie by the National Guard because opinion will only be satisfied when there are 10,000 National Guards dead on the battlefield"; quoted in Edwards, *The Paris Commune,* 105. Even progovernment newspapers such as *Paris Journal* decried the lack of action.

While the Delegation was incapable of producing an insurrection on its own in early January, when defeat at Buzenval once again created a propitious climate for an uprising the clubs and committees were ready to organize and direct it. The opening act of the revolt was the funeral on January 20 of a popular colonel of the National Guard, Rochebrune, who had been killed on the field of battle. According to Amilcare Cipriani, a colonel in the Légion Garibaldienne, those attending Rochebrune's funeral wanted to march on the Hôtel de ville, but "there was not enough time to alert the members of the Légion Garibaldienne, the Ligue Républicaine, and the International, scattered in all the battalions of the National Guard." He added that "a handful of resolute men were at the rendezvous, but a handful all the more insufficient because those who had the confidence of the crowd were in prison."[94] Cipriani's account implies two necessary courses of action before a successful revolt could be mounted: prior coordination of all revolutionary elements, and the liberation of the prisoners of October 31 and the Red Poster. These events took place in the next two days, as militants in popular organizations organized another attempted seizure of power.

The Delegation was at the center of planning for the revolt. According to Vaillant, "January 22 was prepared at the Corderie, where the Committee of the Twenty Arrondissements met." His account indicates that the secret *comité d'éxécution* created in the first days of January to install the revolutionary Commune at the Hôtel de ville was still at work later in the month, rallying adherents to the proposed revolt. Although Blanquists played an important role in the *comité d'éxécution,* the revolt resulted from coordination among several revolutionary elements, including radical republican and Jacobin groups such as the Alliance Républicaine.[95] Its membership was small but influential, mainly men of 1848 such as Ledru-Rollin and Charles Delescluze. According to Arthur Arnould, a member of the Alliance Républicaine, on January 21 the group made contact with "a few delegates of the faubourgs and several sections of the International, who had promised the support of their battalions. The general rendezvous

---

94. Most sources date this funeral to January 21, following Molinari, *Les Clubs rouges,* 263, but Cipriani wrote that it was the 20th; his letter is reprinted in Louise Michel, *La Commune,* 115. Cipriani had once been a companion in arms of Garibaldi in Italy and Flourens in Greece. The account of Rochebrune's funeral, in *Paris Journal,* January 24, 1871, asserted that the army had forced the "zealots of the Commune" to disband.

95. Luc Willette argued that the revolt of January 22 was "100 percent Blanquist"; *Raoul Rigault, 25 ans, Communard, Chef de Police* (Paris: Syros, 1984), 71. Vaillant quoted in Choury, *La Commune au coeur de Paris,* 120.

was for two o'clock, on the place de l'Hôtel de ville." Another group that included some important moderate republicans, the Union Républicaine, was also involved. It too issued a manifesto the morning of January 22, calling for the election of a fifty-member "political assembly."[96]

The final element of the revolutionary coalition that created the revolt of January 22 was the arrondissement clubs and committees. The directing hand of the Delegation's *comité d'éxécution* can be discerned in the simultaneous announcement of insurrection in six clubs and committees (and no doubt others for which no record survives) on the night of January 21. The 13th and 14th arrondissements, for example, which were particularly well represented on the place de l'Hôtel de ville January 22, were the scene of secret meetings. At the salle Favié, the meeting place of the vigilance committee of the 20th arrondissement, the insurrection was planned with the aid of three of the members of the comité d'éxécution (Leverdays, Tridon, and Vaillant), along with members of the vigilance committees for the 6th (Varlin), 11th (Goullé), and 19th (Vallès) arrondissements. All except Varlin were also members of the Delegation. It was decided that the committee of the 20th would be "en permanence" until Paris had been "delivered."[97] At the Club de l'École de Médecine, the meeting place of the vigilance committee of the 6th arrondissement, Armand Levy, semipermanent president of the club and member of the Delegation, declared, "in the name of the democratic committees," a rendezvous of all patriots for noon the next day at the Hôtel de ville, to overthrow the government. He concluded, "let none of us return home tomorrow without having done his duty, that is, having contributed to the disappearance of a government

---

96. By "delegates of the faubourgs" Arnould most probably meant the Delegation, though he could be referring to individual vigilance committees. Sometime prior to January 22 the Alliance Républicaine had sent emissaries to several generals asking if they would replace the phlegmatic Trochu; when the generals declined the group decided a popular uprising was the only hope for France. It then prepared a proclamation to Paris that called for elections to establish a two-hundred-member "Sovereign Assembly" that would direct the defense. Arthur Arnould, *Histoire populaire et parlementaire de la Commune de Paris* 3 vols. (Brussels: Librairie Socialiste de Henri Kistemaeckers, 1878), 1:73; *La Patrie,* January 23, 1871.

97. Gaston Da Costa, *La Commune vécue,* 3 vols. (Paris: Ancienne Maison Quantin, 1903–5), 3:349; Statement of Albert Goullé to Maxime Vuillaume, quoted in Choury, *La Commune au coeur de Paris,* 121; the decision to remain "en permanence" was reported in *Le Combat,* January 23, 1871. Leverdays was also one of the founders of the Ligue Républicaine de Défense à Outrance, and Varlin was one of the most influential members of the Parisian AIT.

that dishonors us and delivers us to the enemy."[98] At the salle Bourdon, the meeting place of the club of the vigilance committee of the 4th arrondissement, Adolphe Clémence, Jules Montels, and Brandely led the assembly in deciding to march on the Hôtel de ville.[99] All three were members of the Delegation. In addition, Clémence was a member of the vigilance committee for the 4th arrondissement, while Montels and Brandely were on the committee of the 12th.

The most important preparatory meeting took place at the Club de la Révolution in the 18th arrondissement, where "a general agreement took place among the vigilance committees, the delegates of the clubs, and delegates of the National Guard," according to Louise Michel. An orator, who may well have been Cipriani, told the crowded hall of the failed attempt to march on the Hôtel de ville after Rochebrune's funeral. "The movement miscarried because it was not coordinated. Now the clubs and vigilance committees are agreed. The rendezvous is for tomorrow at noon, on the place de l'Hôtel de ville," he said to the applause of the assembly. "The National Guards are asked to come armed; the women will accompany them to protest against the rationing of bread and the other policies designed to starve the people *(Agreement by the feminine part of the audience)*." Delegates from both the Club Central Républicain, which was the club of the Republican Central Committee before January 1 and continued as the club of the Delegation, and from the École de Médecine arrived to confirm the rendezvous. Someone from the 17th arrondissement said the republicans of Batignolles, an allusion to the Société Républicain Socialiste, were going to demand that their mayor lead them to the Hôtel de ville wearing his banner of office. The assembly then sent delegates to their mairie to ask their municipality to do the same, and they later returned to report that the vice-mayor had accepted. They decided to meet at 10 o'clock at the mairie and then march on the Hôtel de ville, and the meeting broke up, cries of "Until Tomorrow!" ringing in the night.[100]

Some did not return home immediately, however, for the revolutionar-

---

98. He also remarked that the rendezvous was to help celebrate the anniversary of the execution of Louis XVI on January 21, 1793, which had ended the era of dynasties; *La Patrie,* January 23, 1871.

99. Choury, *La Commune au coeur de Paris,* 122.

100. Michel, *La Commune,* 117, 119; Molinari, *Les Clubs rouges,* 262. Cipriani's mention of women no doubt reflects the organizational work of the Comité de Vigilance des Citoyennes du 18e Arrondissement under the leadership of Louise Michel; see Edith Thomas, *The Women Incendiaries,* trans. James Atkinson and Starr Atkinson (New York: George Braziller, 1966).

ies arrested for October 31 and the Red Poster remained in prison. Among them were Flourens and Lefrançais, who had been alerted to their possible deliverance, their notification indicating once more the prior coordination involved in the revolt. A crowd of about six hundred, led by Blanquists from the 18th arrondissement, but also including large numbers from the salle Favié and the salle Bourdon, marched on Mazas Prison.[101] A prison official later testified that these delegates said they were from Belleville (20th arrondissement) and declared, "we represent the republican committees *en permanence* for the salvation of the country." *Le Combat,* Pyat's newspaper, which was generally well informed about the popular movement, noted that they were "delegates of the twenty republican committees," confirming the Delegation's role in liberating the prisoners and in the ensuing revolt.[102] The crowd eventually overpowered the prison officials, and several revolutionaries were released, including Flourens. The crowd then marched off toward Belleville, led by National Guard drummers. On arrival, Flourens, who had been elected vice-mayor in November, established himself at the mairie and beat the tocsin to summon the National Guard, later retreating to a safe house because the response to his call was insufficient. Thoroughly disgusted, Flourens sat out the next day's revolt.[103] The government was not ignorant of these events, and even before the night of January 21 it was aware that the defeat at Buzenval had created a dangerous situation. To assuage public opinion Trochu's colleagues in the government forced him to resign as governor of Paris. In view of the likelihood of resistance to surrender, General Vinoy, a veteran of Louis-Napoleon's coup of December 2, 1851, was placed in command of the army.[104] After the October 31 insurrection the govern-

101. Among the three delegates who met with prison officials and demanded the release of the prisoners was Marcollier, who on January 4 at the salle Favié had called for an immediate march on the Hôtel de ville. The other delegates were Pierre Leroux, nephew of the utopian socialist of the same name, and someone known only as Haran or Hasant. *Gazette des Tribunaux,* February 19 and 26, 1871; Michel, *La Commune,* 119.

102. *Gazette des Tribunaux,* February 19 and 26, 1871; *Le Soir,* January 24, reprinting an article from *Le Combat.* Historians have followed Dautry and Scheler, *Le Comité Central,* 154, and Rougerie, "Quelques documents nouveaux," 27, in denying the Delegation any role in the uprising. Wolfe has argued that the Club de la Révolution alone was responsible; "The Parisian *Club de la Révolution,*" 103–4.

103. The other six prisoners released were Humbert, Pillot, Meilliet, Bauer, A. Demay, and Dupas. Ranvier, Lefrançais, and several others were held at Vincennes. *Le Soir,* January 24, 1871, reprinting an article from *Le Figaro;* Flourens, *Paris Livré,* 204–5.

104. Trochu had grandiloquently declared, "the governor of Paris will not capitulate," so that office was abolished when Trochu became president of the Council; Jules Favre, *Le Gouvernement de la Défense Nationale,* 2 vols. (Paris: Plon, 1871–72), 2:349. Vinoy's statement

ment had moved its offices to the Louvre, a more easily defended location. The city administration remained at the Hôtel de ville, however, which was filled with loyal National Guards and troops of the line. The government was resolved that there would be no repetition of October 31.

On the morning of January 22 Pyat's *Le Combat* printed the proclamations of both the Alliance Républicaine and the Union Républicaine Centrale calling for an elected council. Pyat also included his own denunciation of the government, concluding with an unambiguous call to arms: "Paris à l'Hôtel de ville!" By that afternoon the crowd in front of the city hall was reported at perhaps five thousand and was "churning like an open air club," according to Vallès. Many of the guardsmen assembled came from the 13th and 14th arrondissements, and battalions from the 5th, 18th, and 20th arrondissements had mustered at the Collège de France before marching on the Hôtel de ville. The leadership of the Alliance Républicaine was gathered at an apartment overlooking the square. Blanqui thought the revolt misguided because it was too late to save Paris from surrendering, but he was with the *comité d'éxécution* of the Delegation at a café on one side of the place de l'Hôtel de ville.[105] Several delegations were admitted to the Hôtel de ville, one from the Alliance Républicaine, one from the 18th arrondissement that included members of the Club de la Révolution and members of its municipal government, and another from the Delegation headed by Montels.[106] Gustave Chaudey, the only representative of the government present, refused the demand of the delegates for a Commune and stated that the government would resist any assault. Some time after this interview a battalion from Batignolles entered the square, with Mayor Benôit Malon leading the way wearing his sash of office, just as arranged the night before at the salle Levis. Shortly thereafter a shot was heard, and the defenders of the Hôtel de ville began firing into the square. The demonstrators returned fire from hastily built barricades, but the fighting ended after a short while. Some thirty people were

accepting his new post said nothing of the Prussians but denounced the "party of disorder"; *Paris Journal,* January 24, 1871.

105. Henri Labouchère, *Diary of the Besieged Resident in Paris* (London: Hurst and Blackett, 1871), 348; *Le Réveil,* March 13, 1882; Arnould, *Histoire populaire,* 75. Vaillant is the source for the *comité d'éxécution*'s observation point; quoted in Choury, *La Commune au coeur de Paris,* 119.

106. Serman, *La Commune de Paris,* 168. The delegates told Chaudey, "We are the delegates of the twenty arrondissements"; Etienne Arago, *L'Hôtel-de-ville de Paris au 4 septembre et pendant le siège* (Paris: Hetzel, n.d.), 335.

killed or wounded, marking the first bloodshed in all the disturbances of the siege.

The attempted revolt of January 22 was thus suppressed by force of arms, but the relatively small size of the insurrectionary force ultimately explains its failure. While the government could not count on the active support of the bourgeois battalions, which had not responded to the beating of the tocsin, the revolutionaries were also unable to rally their forces in sufficient number. Yet the failure of January 22 was not one of organization, as some historians and participants have suggested, for the clubs and committees of Paris were quite well organized.[107] The participation of a variety of groups, the liberation of the prisoners, and the preparations in many popular organizations are sufficient evidence for this conclusion. What was lacking was support—the physical presence of a large enough crowd to intimidate the government, as had been temporarily accomplished on October 31. Similarly, the reason the Red Poster of January 6 failed to incite an insurrection, despite its long preparation, was because the Delegation of the Twenty Arrondissements was fundamentally out of step with the vast majority of Parisians. Having constituted itself as the revolutionary Commune, prepared the clubs, and written a manifesto for revolt, the Delegation found that it lacked adequate support for its aspirations. Even a consciously minoritarian revolutionary movement needs a certain critical mass of partisans. The insurrection of October 31 had partially succeeded only because reports of an impending armistice momentarily linked national defense with the overthrow of the government. The government was able to reassert itself, however, and convinced most of the population that it would fight to the bitter end; revolt, then, constituted betrayal of the nation.

In contrast, rather than forswear revolt, club and committee militants had developed an even more revolutionary strategy. The November plebiscite had convinced revolutionaries that they were a minority in the city, and in response they crafted the revolutionary Commune and fomented two revolts in January intended to install it. Yet no amount of planning and dedication by militants in the clubs could overcome the fundamental aversion of most Parisians to overthrow a republican government during a national military crisis. The Delegation of the Twenty

---

107. No account has sufficiently revealed the role of the Delegation in the revolt. Wolfe wrote that it lacked "effective central direction"; "The Parisian *Club de la Révolution*," 82, 103. Da Costa blamed the timidity of the Alliance Républicaine and the lack of organization; *La Commune vecue*, 3:356–57.

Arrondissements and the popular organizations of the city had found a formula for seizing power but would only reap the benefit when the national emergency had passed and political issues had once again come to the fore. Although to members of the revolutionary Commune the national and revolutionary causes were indissoluble, moderates and conservatives depicted the agitation of January as criminal treason, noting that the Prussians must be overjoyed at the divisions in Paris.[108] Given the patriotic fervor that held Parisians in an iron grip in 1870–71, revolt was only possible when the national and revolutionary causes fused. That was the lesson of September 4, 1870; of October 31, 1870; and even of March 18, 1871. That lesson was again driven home on January 22, when a starving city, faced with surrender, witnessed a final attempt by militants of popular organizations to establish a revolutionary Commune.

As after October 31, so after January 22 the government went on the offensive against its enemies, with even greater severity. On January 23 it closed all clubs and meetings and suppressed the two major opposition newspapers, Pyat's *Le Combat* and Delescluze's *Le Réveil.* In the following days police arrested over eighty revolutionary leaders, virtually all of them signers of the Red Poster of January 6. As was feared, January 22 was indeed the last chance to avoid an armistice; the city surrendered at midnight on January 27. Despite the government's prior assurances to Gambetta, who was raising fresh armies in the provinces, the armistice encompassed not just Paris but all of France. For a few days Gambetta seemed determined to repudiate the agreement and continue the war, but instead he resigned and went into exile in Spain. Though technically only a pause in hostilities, the armistice was a *de facto* surrender. Bismarck granted the armistice so that France might hold elections for an assembly to sign a definitive peace; he did not believe an agreement with the provisional Government of National Defense would be sufficiently binding. Thiers, who was rapidly emerging as the voice of the war weary and of provincial France, knew very well that the armistice he had worked so long to achieve was the end of the war, and he immediately set about building a conservative coalition for the elections of February 8.

The closure of the clubs, the arrest of so many militants, and the conclusion of the armistice ended one chapter in the history of the club and committee movement. Popular organizations had failed repeatedly to

---

108. Trochu and the government echoed these sentiments, declaring that the agitators sought to undermine the defense; see *Paris Journal,* January 8 and 10, 1871.

establish a Commune in Paris, but the months of agitation and the experience of coordinating initiatives and combining efforts had forged a viable revolutionary coalition and a radical political culture. The Republican Central Committee and its successor, the Delegation of the Twenty Arrondissements, were at the center of this movement, as they united militants of the International, Blanquists, independent socialists, and Jacobins. Other groups associated with the Delegation, such as the Club Central and the Ligue Républicaine, cast an even wider net, including radical and even moderate republicans. None of these groups was a disciplined cohort ready to march at command into battle, but at moments of widespread discontent with the government's war effort they were able to multiply their impact through coordinated action. From the first hesitant demonstrations of September through the high hopes of October 31, the agitation of early January, and the bloody defeat of January 22, the personnel, tactics, and organization of the revolutionary movement evolved as conditions changed. Blanquists and others sympathetic to direct political action came to prominence, clubs and committees became centers of revolt instead of mere debate, and the revolutionary Commune was developed first as an idea, then as a reality. After the armistice the evolution of popular organizations continued at an even more rapid pace, and the most radical elements of the club movement were restructured into the Revolutionary Socialist Party. Unable to prevail when the Prussians were at the gates of Paris, militants from popular organizations finally attained the long awaited Commune when the Republic was threatened by a monarchist assembly.

CHAPTER 2

The Revolutionary Socialist Party

They were no longer just public meetings, they were truly centers of insurrection.

—Prefect of Police Choppin

Only eight weeks separated the armistice of January 27 and the insurrection of March 18 that inaugurated the Commune, but they were filled with political and revolutionary agitation. Monarchist candidates won a large majority in the February 8 elections by arguing that France needed peace to renew its spirit after a war that had brought only disasters. The overwhelming majority of Paris was incensed when the National Assembly voted to establish the government at Versailles and seemed intent on disbanding the Parisian National Guard, which was widely recognized as the guarantor of the Republic. On March 1 the Assembly ratified the Treaty of Frankfurt, prescribing large financial and territorial concessions to the new German Empire. Nationalist outrage in a city that believed itself betrayed into surrender and the political crisis over maintaining the Republic now reinforced each other, reversing the dynamic of the siege, when patriotic sentiment had inhibited civil strife in the face of the enemy. By mid-March a monarchist National Assembly faced a hostile republican capital, and a confrontation seemed inevitable.

In this overwrought atmosphere, which had the effect of continuing the tension brought by hardship and bombardment during the siege, revolutionaries in the club and committee movement strengthened their forces. The coalition embodied in the revolutionary Commune and tempered by the January revolts provided the framework for closer coordination. As the political crisis deepened, this coalition transformed itself into a "Revolutionary Socialist Party" dedicated to a "new world" of social and political equality. Meanwhile, in a related development, suspicious republi-

---

Epigraph from Prefect of Police Choppin, referring to popular organizations during the period of the armistice; *L'Enquête Parlementaire sur l'Insurrection du Dix-Huit mars,* 223.

cans—including many militants of the clubs and committees—formed the
Central Committee of the National Guard to protect the Republic, and
many leaders of the revolutionary socialist movement were elected to high
office in this Federation of the National Guard. This near fusion was a
conscious strategy adopted by key militants. The conjunction of these two
movements, one based on the National Guard, the other on clubs and
committees, made the insurrection of March 18 that created the Commune
appear spontaneous, when in fact it was prepared by a long period of revolutionary agitation. While the Central Committee of the National Guard
provided the structure through which the insurrection of March 18 was
carried out, most of the key leaders of the movement were militants of
popular organizations, veterans of the struggles waged through the vigilance committees and clubs of the siege. Furthermore, nine mairies were
assaulted or occupied on March 18, and in each instance club and committee militants had taken the initiative to seize power. The interpenetration of the two movements, club and guard, has not been recognized by
historians of the Commune, who have generally considered the National
Guard to be wholly distinct from previous revolutionary activity.[1] During
the Commune the revolutionary coalition formed in the popular organizations of Paris finally succeeded in establishing control of the city, and the
eight weeks of the armistice, when the Revolutionary Socialist Party crystallized, were crucial in this development.

Although the Government of National Defense prohibited clubs after
the revolt of January 22, within a week they reopened under the title of
electoral meetings, in preparation for the February 8 elections. In the context of a national electoral campaign the audience of these meetings was
much larger in size and broader in political sentiment than during the later
siege, in some cases diluting the revolutionary aspect these clubs and committees had previously exhibited. For example, at the salle de la Redoute,
which originally had been the Club Central of the Delegation of the
Twenty Arrondissements, an orator suggested that the assembly choose
candidates from among the "one hundred forty citizens who have been
designated to be part of the Commune," but his proposal met with
approval by only a portion of the assembly.[2] The Redoute was in the bourgeois 1st arrondissement, and the influx of new participants no doubt
reflected their predominantly moderate republican tendencies. In the

---

1. To cite only one example, Rougerie emphasizes the separation between the National
Guard and all other groups; *Paris Libre,* 81, 100.
2. Molinari, *Les Clubs Rouges,* 281.

mainly working-class districts, such as the 19th and 20th arrondissements, the same process did not appreciably alter the revolutionary nature of the clubs, as the new participants were evidently of similar social level and political persuasion as the participants during the siege. The Marseillaise and Favié were still in the forefront of the revolutionary movement during the armistice, as they had been during the later siege.

During the campaign, as in the later siege, the Delegation of the Twenty Arrondissements was the central pillar of the revolutionary movement. For a week after the January 22 revolt there is no record of activity by the Delegation, and with good reason: the clubs had been closed, over eighty of its members were either arrested or in hiding, and newspapers friendly to its cause had been suppressed. The minutes of several meetings during February have been preserved, however, and they show that in the days following the armistice the Delegation formed an electoral alliance with the two most important working-class organizations in the capital, the International and the Federal Chamber of Worker Societies. The Federal Chamber was composed of delegates from worker syndicates, unions, and mutual aid societies; in practice it was very close to the AIT, since the two shared many leaders. The novelty of the alliance of the Delegation, the AIT, and the Federal Chamber in February was that the AIT had always officially denied itself any purely political role. As one militant said at an AIT meeting of January 26, however, "the Republic is in danger; we must unite with republicans to defend it"; and this course was adopted.[3] From the end of the siege through the end of the Commune the International and the Delegation worked in close partnership, and their intersection in the electoral campaign of February was the cornerstone of the Revolutionary Socialist Party.

At the end of January the two groups and the Federal Chamber set about creating a combined list of candidates for the forty-three Parisian seats, and for this purpose they formed a "revolutionary socialist electoral committee" composed of delegates from each group.[4] The first indication that the electoral committee had agreed on candidates was on February 1 at the meeting at the Cour des Miracles, called by "delegates of the International." The vigilance committee of the 2d arrondissement was probably also behind this meeting, as it had sponsored public meetings at the Cour des Miracles during the siege and was dominated by members of the AIT. After the list of candidates was read, Auguste Serrailler, a member of

---

3. Hardy quoted in *L'Enquête Parlementaire sur l'Insurrection du Dix-Huit mars,* 526.
4. *Le Mot d'Ordre,* February 14, 1871.

both the AIT and the vigilance committee of the 2d arrondissement, explained the policies they represented: members of the government would be put on trial for treason, and the decision for war or peace would have to be made after finding out whether France was capable of continuing the struggle. Serrailler went on to argue that the war had been started to stifle the growth of the International, "but socialism is stronger than Bismarck, and if the candidates of the International are sent to the Assembly they will prepare the way for the advent of the Social Republic *(Applause)*."[5] Two days later, at a meeting sponsored by the vigilance committee of the 19th arrondissement, the unnamed president explained that the list of "revolutionary socialist" candidates had been agreed to by delegates from vigilance committees, the International, and worker federations. He explained that some had questioned the candidacy of workers—no doubt in favor of more widely known and electable names—but they had finally been accepted. "A choice had to be made between several hundred candidates," he announced. "Each of the members of the committee," he continued, "had to resign himself to sacrificing his own particular feelings to assure the success of the cause." The president then read from the manifesto that preceded the list of revolutionary socialist candidates, which later appeared on a poster printed by the Delegation, the AIT, and the Federal Chamber. "If there were only two republicans in France, then the Republic would still be our right," he said, echoing the rhetoric of the later siege, which had culminated in a consciously minoritarian revolutionary Commune. He emphasized that "it is not permitted to deny the Republic *(Energetic applause)*." He read other articles of the electoral manifesto proclaiming the political advent of the working class and the fall of industrial feudalism to an "explosion of bravos."[6]

---

5. Molinari, *Les Clubs rouges,* 282. The list read was not explicitly stated to be that of the combined groups, but all the names mentioned are on the list and Serrailler was an active participant in the combined meetings of the three groups in February.

6. Molinari, *Les Clubs rouges,* 297 and 311. Molinari's accuracy in reporting meetings is confirmed by the fact that some of these phrases he ascribed to the president at the Marseillaise repeat almost exactly, and in the same order, the phrases on the printed poster from which the president was reading. Besides the meetings at the Cour des Miracles and the Marseillaise the combined list of the three groups is known to have been proclaimed at two other meetings, both associated with vigilance committees: the old salle Favié (which at this time met in a dance hall called La Vielleuse) and the École de Médecine, associated with the committees of vigilance of the 20th and 6th arrondissements, respectively. When Henri Chouteau, a member of the AIT, suggested modifications to the list at the École de Médecine, Emile Lacord, a member of the vigilance committee, argued that it must be maintained intact; *Le Mot d'Ordre,* February 6.

Compiling this list of candidates was the first self-proclaimed act of an emerging revolutionary socialist movement, built on the foundation of the revolutionary Commune.[7] The phrase *revolutionary socialist* itself was not a new formulation, but its prominence in the combined electoral manifesto signaled a decisive shift to more radical positions by militants in popular organizations. In the public meetings of the late Empire and siege speakers occasionally designated themselves as revolutionary socialists, but during the siege the phrases *republican socialist* or *democratic socialist* were much more widely employed to designate socialist groups.[8] The term *revolutionary socialist* was used in isolated speeches and articles with somewhat greater frequency toward the end of the siege, precisely when the revolutionary coalition was restructuring itself into the revolutionary Commune of January 1. In December the newspaper of the Club Démocratique et Socialiste in the 14th arrondissement described itself as the journal of "the revolutionary socialist party," the first known usage of that phrase.[9] The Club Démocratique et Socialiste was one of the avenues by which Blanquists entered the vigilance committee movement, and the revolutionary Commune (that is, the Delegation of the Twenty Arrondissements), was the tangible expression of the importance of Blanquists in the second revolutionary coalition of the later siege. The revolutionary socialist electoral manifesto and list of February 1 was a key step in the transition of that coalition into a true party, formed for the most part from the intersection of Blanquists and members of the International in the Delegation, and based on a clearly defined set of ideas consciously described as revolutionary socialist.

---

7. Twenty of the forty-three candidates had signed the Red Poster of January 6. Only a few could be considered "grand names," including Garibaldi, Pyat, and Blanqui; the majority, perhaps twenty-four, were fairly obscure workers of the AIT and Federal Chamber who would be known only to those close to the socialist or club and committee movement, although Varlin, Malon, and Lefrançais were more widely known. Blanquists made up the next largest identifiable group of perhaps twelve, although given the fluidity of ideologies and overlapping allegiances it is sometimes hazardous to label militants too precisely. The rest were an assortment, including several "men of '48," such as Beslay and Gambon. The poster is reprinted in *Les Murailles Politiques françaises,* 3 vols. (Paris: Le Chevalier, 1873–74) 1:866.

8. The November statutes of the Club Central, for example, referred repeatedly to republican socialist organizations and militants; *La Patrie en Danger,* November 28, 1870. In October the Republican Central Committee had stated that its members must adhere to "revolutionary socialist principles," but it did not define them; reprinted in Dautry and Scheler, *Le Comité Central,* 107.

9. *La Resistance,* December 19, 1870. The word *parti* should be understood to mean section or element, rather than a fully defined political organization.

The meaning of the term *revolutionary socialist,* as distinct from *republican socialist,* is revealed in the problems encountered in devising the common revolutionary socialist list for the elections. The president at the salle Marseillaise meeting of February 3 explained that the electoral committee of the three revolutionary socialist groups—the AIT, the Delegation, and the Federal Chamber—had tried to negotiate a common list with "bourgeois republicans, who fired on the people in June 1848." At the last moment, however, the "bourgeois republicans" backed out of the agreement. What the president of the meeting did not explain was that a double schism had destroyed the tentative union between republicans, revolutionaries, and socialists. When the "bourgeois republicans" bolted they were joined by several moderate socialists and members of the International, and together the dissident groups issued their own list of candidates, known as the "list of the four committees."[10] Comparing their list with that of the three revolutionary socialist committees reveals the motive for the schism: while nearly a third of the revolutionary socialist list was composed of Blanquists, there were no Blanquists on the list of the four committees. As a radical revolutionary Blanqui was anathema to most republicans, but he and his followers could not have been left off the revolutionary socialist list without destroying the foundation of the coalition, which was the common action of Blanquists and Internationals. In view of the elections, the AIT, the Delegation, and the Federal Chamber had been willing to compromise with radical republicans to some degree, but to preserve their union intact they could not jettison the Blanquists. In the early months of the siege the republican socialist list of the four committees would very likely have been supported by the old Republican Central Committee of the Twenty Arrondissements. Two of the three radical republican groups on the schismatic list had in fact supported the revolt of January 22. Radical republicans and the revolutionary left had been able to work together at a moment of crisis during the siege, but in the more mundane electoral struggle of February this large coalition of the left was no longer possible. The schism went much deeper than mere electoral tactics, however, for it illuminates the evolution of the Republican Central

---

10. Molinari, *Les Clubs rouges,* 292. The list was issued in the name of the entire AIT, causing no little confusion. The "bourgeois republicans" were the Alliance Républicaine, Union Républicaine, and Défenseurs de la République. Without the revolutionary socialist context of this schism in the AIT several scholars have been unable to adequately explain it: Rougerie, "L'AIT et le mouvement ouvrier," 42; Serman, *La Commune de Paris,* 173; Stephen K. Vincent, *Between Marxism and Anarchism: Benôit Malon and French Reformist Socialism* (Berkeley: University of California Press, 1992).

Committee of the Twenty Arrondissements since the October 31 insurrection, a road not followed by the radical republican and moderate socialist left. One list was republican socialist; the other, revolutionary socialist.

The combined revolutionary socialist manifesto for the February 8 elections was a milestone on the road to the Commune.

> These revolutionary socialist candidates stand for:
> Prohibition of whomever it might be to question the Republic.
> The necessity of the political advent of workers.
> Destruction of the governing oligarchy and industrial feudalism.
> Organization of a republic that, in rendering to workers their instruments of work, as that of 1792 rendered land to the peasants, will realize political liberty through social equality.

More important than the specific provisions of this program, which were derived mainly from the International and from the radical clubs of the seige, the manifesto heralds a new phase in the organization of the revolutionary movement. Each time the phrase *revolutionary socialist* was used in the poster it referred to the candidates; *revolutionary socialist,* then, refers no longer to a tendency or set of sympathies but to a defined group in contention for political office, very nearly a party in fact, if not yet in name. The candidates were presented "in the name of a new world, by the party of the disinherited, an immense party" which has never been consulted by the classes that govern society. It reminded Parisians that during the siege this party had vainly denounced the "incapacity, even the perfidity" of the government—an implied criticism of the city for not listening to their recommendations earlier. "France is going to reconstitute itself anew," it continued, maintaining that "workers have the right to find and take their place in the order that is under preparation."[11] This explicit and forthright language is a further sign of evolution in the Delegation, which like the Republican Central Committee that preceded it had generally avoided clear statements of principle. Two considerations perhaps explain this new tone: the reemphasized cooperation between the Delegation and the AIT, and the shift in context from a national military struggle to a political contest. This new tone grew more emphatic in subsequent weeks.

Nonetheless, the socialist, revolutionary, and republican movements of

---

11. *Les Murailles Politiques,* 1:866.

the capital remained fragmented in the elections. Dozens of associations, clubs, meetings, and committees put forth candidates; umbrella groups, "fusions," and central committees of various sorts flourished. Unlike the revolutionary socialist list, which was presented as a fait accompli for acceptance by clubs and committees, almost all the lists presented by these groups originated in public assemblies as a result of the give and take of open debate. From this resulted both the almost indescribable confusion of the campaign and also its vitality. For example, at the salle d'Arras Arthur Pieron presided over a meeting bringing together delegates from the "démocratic socialiste" meetings of the 5th, 13th, and 14th arrondissements. During the siege the salle d'Arras had been one of the usual locales of the Comité Démocratique Socialiste of the 5th arrondissement, and there were other democratic socialist clubs linked to the vigilance committees in the 13th and 14th as well. The Red Poster of January 6 listing the members of the revolutionary Commune included many from these democratic socialist groups, but in this election they formed their own list of candidates under the heading "Fusion des Comités Républicains, Democrates, Socialiste."[12] Another list was presented by the Comité Central Révolutionnaire et Socialist des Clubs et Comités Électoraux des Vingt Arrondissements de Paris, chaired by Raoul Rigault, a young Blanquist militant and future member of the Commune. Despite the appellation *socialist,* though, the brief statement preceding the list was purely political.[13] Prefect of Police Choppin thought that Rigault's goal "was to bring about an agreement, in view of the elections, between the International and the Blanquists." This very likely was correct, as Rigault's list—though dominated by Blanquists and "great names" such as Louis Blanc—did include some workers of the International. Altogether, twenty-five of Rigault's forty-three candidates were also on the revolutionary socialist list. Indeed, the only time Rigault appeared at a joint Delegation and AIT meeting was on February 12, when he argued that "the diversity of lists did not hurt us [in the elections]," a sign of his cooperation with these groups.[14] In broad outlines the revolutionary socialist movement incar-

---

12. *Le Mot d'Order,* February 5 and 7. This list is not explicitly linked to the rue d'Arras meeting but is no doubt connected, as the "democratic socialist" label is very nearly the same, and as the list included Pieron as well as twenty of the forty-three names on the revolutionary socialist list; *Les Murailles Politiques,* 1:850.

13. *Les Murailles Politiques,* 1:868. This is probably the group referred to in newspaper notices as meeting on February 2, 5, and 6; *Le Mot d'Order,* February 7 and 8.

14. *L'Enquête Parlementaire sur l'Insurrection du Dix-Huit mars,* 221; Dautry and Scheler, *Le Comité Central,* 190.

nated the alliance of Blanquists and Internationalists described by Choppin.

The results of the February elections nationally were a stunning setback for republicans; the progressive urban centers seemed islands in an ocean of monarchist peasants. While the great majority of those elected in Paris were moderates and radicals such as Victor Hugo and Gambetta, a number of candidates of the far left were elected: Malon and Tolain of the AIT, the journalist Pyat, and representatives of 1848 who had evolved toward the left, such as Gambon and Delescluze. That only Jules Favre of the former Government of National Defense was (just barely) elected from Paris marked a contemptuous rejection by the city of those who had presided over the capitulation.[15] The only revolutionary socialist candidates elected were Malon, Tolain, and Gambon, and they were also candidates on many other lists. The list seems to have garnered from thirty thousand to fifty thousand votes, representing perhaps 15 percent of the votes cast. Due to duplications among lists further precision is impossible, but it is clear that the revolutionary socialists were still a minority, just as the revolutionary left had been in the plebiscite of November.

From the moment the results of the election were known many republicans, especially of the left, thought the Republic was in danger once again, as it had been during the war. The actions of the new National Assembly, which met on February 12 at Bordeaux, far from the front lines in what was still a nation officially at war, increased the anxiety of many Republicans and alienated nearly all of Paris. One of its first acts was to refuse to proclaim a republic, although Thiers was given the title chief of the executive power of the Republic. His cabinet was dominated by monarchists, and although it included three republicans, they were all from the former Government of National Defense, another slap at Parisian sensibilities. There was no doubt the Assembly would agree to a settlement with Germany, as conservatives believed continuing a war that was already lost would only play into the hands of extremists who still thought 1792 could be triumphantly reenacted. French finances were in shambles after the expenses of the Empire and the war, and many argued that only peace could revive prosperity. These considerations were behind the Assembly's decision on February 15 to stop paying Parisian National Guards who could not present evidence of poverty their daily compensation of one and

---

15. Henri Guillemin contends that even Favre only won election through massive fraud; *L'Avenement de M. Thiers et réflexions sur la Commune* (Paris: Gallimard, 1971), 40. See also Serman, *La Commune de Paris,* 175.

a half francs a day. Perhaps financially sound, this measure reduced a proud, armed citizenry to the status of humble beggars. Nearly all economic activity in the capital had ceased during the siege, and the guard pay, now threatened by monarchists, was the only sustenance for many. Personal and political motivations for opposing the Assembly began to merge, and not only among the revolutionary left and the poor.

Step-by-step the elements of a new revolutionary situation were rapidly coming together in Paris, but unlike during the siege, the balance of forces was tipped in favor of the revolutionaries. The government had very few reliable soldiers in Paris, the terms of the armistice having limited the army in the region to forty thousand, perhaps only fifteen thousand of whom were not demoralized by defeat and clamoring to be demobilized.[16] Yet the Parisian National Guard, 240,000 members strong, had been allowed to keep their weapons because the government knew very well that trying to disarm the guard with the Germans surrounding the city would have caused an instant revolt. Within the National Guard the balance was also turning, as perhaps one hundred thousand Parisians, most of them from the bourgeois districts, left the city in which they had been captive for five months, to find more plentiful provisions and a change of scenery in the provinces. On March 7 the commander of the Parisian guard convoked all the battalion commanders to test whether they would support the government if trouble arose. Only thirty or forty battalion chiefs responded, out of over two hundred battalions in Paris. Even they reported that their men would defend their arrondissements if attacked but would not go on the offensive against other elements of the guard.[17] On October 31 the "good" battalions had saved the government, but after the humiliation of the armistice and the insults of the Assembly they could no longer be counted on.

As the influence of the government waned, the revolutionary left was strengthening its organization in the capital. When viewed from the perspective of revolutionary popular organizations, the February elections had revealed two seemingly contradictory traits. First, the arrondissement clubs and committees that had been painstakingly coordinated into a fairly coherent movement over the course of the siege seem by and large to have gone their own way in naming candidates. Some of the public meetings associated with vigilance committees supported the revolutionary socialist list, even to the point of not allowing discussion of other candi-

16. Rials, *Nouvelle histoire de Paris*, 238.
17. Serman, *La Commune de Paris*, 196.

dates that might be in favor locally. But most public meetings reflected the divergent desires of the constituents who flocked to them in great numbers. In part, the formerly coordinated revolutionary elements were submerged, and in part some local militants sought to express their own views about appropriate candidates. Second, at the level of citywide politics, what might be termed the "center," the Delegation of the Twenty Arrondissements and the International were forming an increasingly close partnership born from electoral coordination: relative centralization at the city level, and relative fragmentation at the arrondissement level. The leaders of the revolutionary socialist movement in the Delegation of the Twenty Arrondissements well understood this divergent dynamic. Although they came from very disparate clubs, vigilance committees, and sections of the International, they had consciously sought to build a larger, more unified and integrated movement throughout the siege. For the most part they had behind them years of revolutionary experience in the battle against the Empire. They knew the advantages clubs and committees offered to the revolutionary struggle: immediate responsiveness to public demands, flexibility of tactics, and the potential to mobilize the population when conditions were favorable. Having experienced the fruitless quest to install the revolutionary Commune, they also knew the weaknesses of clubs and committees as weapons of combat: isolated action, difficulties of coordination, police scrutiny, and ideological division. In mid-February the revolutionary socialist leadership invented a strategy designed to reap the benefits of club and committee agitation and to counteract its deficiencies: the Revolutionary Socialist Party.

Several elements combined in mid-February to propel the revolutionary socialist movement toward greater integration. In the days after the February 8 elections the Delegation, the AIT, and the Federal Chamber met together to decide which candidates to support in the second round of elections. In the event, a second round was not needed, but their discussions revealed the need for more fundamental reshaping of the revolutionary socialist movement. In addition, the combined committees had gone into debt by nearly a thousand francs in the campaign and were without the means to pay, making an appeal to the local organizations necessary, and showing the desirability of more formal methods for assuring the financial health of the movement. Finally, some considered the moment ripe for revolutionary action, either in Paris or in the larger provincial cities, and sought to strengthen the organization of the revolutionary socialist movement as a first step.

The joint meetings of February 10 and 11 did little to resolve these pressing issues but do provide insight into the preoccupations of the left at this confused moment for Paris and France. On February 10 Vaillant, for example, proposed printing posters that called on Parisians to stay indoors and hang black flags during the anticipated symbolic occupation of the city by German forces. Leo Frankel suggested that in support of internationalism Parisians fly red flags bearing the words *Universal Republic* and the names of German democrats.[18] Pindy argued that the socialists elected to the Assembly should vote to put the government on trial for treason and then should retreat to Lyon, organize a revolutionary Commune, and continue the war to the finish. Parisel agreed and suggested as well that delegates from the committees should be sent "to the revolutionary communes that may be organized, as the Convention in times past sent delegates to the armies."[19] While no decisions were made, the joint meeting on the next day was more fruitful. The committees returned to Parisel's motion of the day before and decided to send delegates to the provinces, though Edmond Goupil warned against sending too many delegates, as committee members should stay in Paris to "regularize a movement that may sooner or later take place." Lacord supported sending delegates to Lyon especially, "where there is great interest in revolution," so that they might "organize, as soon as possible, on a solid basis, the revolutionary Commune." In February and March emissaries from the International and the Delegation traveled to the larger cities, and after March 18 they were partially responsible for sparking several insurrections, notably at Lyon and Le Creusot.[20]

The documents given to two such delegates, Albert Blanc and Parisel, described the Delegation as the Revolutionary Delegation of the Twenty Arrondissements. The addition of the word *revolutionary* indicates a renewed tendency toward extralegal action by the Delegation after the legalistic electoral politics of early February and demonstrates an aware-

---

18. Dautry and Scheler have published the minutes of the meeting (from which this and the subsequent quotes in this paragraph are drawn), in *Le Comité Central,* 180. Frankel, a Hungarian by birth, was one of the AIT's most fervent disciples of internationalism, at a time when even members of the International were sometimes carried away with patriotic fury.

19. After the isolation of the siege, Paris was only just learning of the revolutionary agitation that had developed in the major cities over the previous months. On March 29, the first day the Communal Council met, Parisel returned to his idea of calling on the departments; *Les Procès-Verbaux de la Commune de 1871,* ed. Georges Bourgin and Gabriel Henriot, 2 vols. (Paris: Ernest Leroux, 1924–45), 1:49.

20. *L'Enquête Parlementaire sur l'Insurrection du Dix-Huit mars,* 221; Jeanne Gaillard, *Communes de Province, Commune de Paris* (Paris: Flammarion, 1971).

ness that the moment presented revolutionary possibilities. The minutes of the February 11 combined meeting confirm this, stating, "Citizens Lacord and Viard insist on an attempt to bring together all the groups in view of a common action, which could not fail to give great force to the revolutionary idea."[21] From this proposal arose the Revolutionary Socialist Party, formalized on February 20 and 23 in general meetings of all revolutionary socialist clubs and committees. Ferré took up the motion, asking that "all of the new electoral committees of the twenty arrondissements, the International, and the Federal Chamber of Worker Societies" be convoked to a general assembly to decide on "the revolutionary socialist candidates" for the second round of the elections. By calling to the "new" electoral committees, Ferré must have been referring to the meetings during the electoral period that had been formed on the foundation of the Delegation's vigilance committees but had to some extent moved out of the control of the Delegation, that is, meetings that had modified the revolutionary socialist list. Ferré himself, one of the most active leaders of the Club de la Révolution in the 18th arrondissement, had most likely been involved in such meetings.[22] Ferré meant to include more than just revolutionary socialist committees, a point made by the meeting's vote on his proposition, which decided in contrast "that only the groups and committees in conformity with our program will be alone convoked," the phrasing underscoring a difference with Ferré's intent of including "all of the new" committees. Here again the tendency toward a more pure, exclusive organization is evident.

The meeting of February 12th is the last for which the minutes have survived before the formation of the Revolutionary Socialist Party, and those minutes offer a final opportunity to witness the processes by which the party was created. The meeting began with the question of the second round of elections. Rigault proposed a compromise with the influential journalist Rochefort. "Rochefort's men passed in the first round," he said, adding that "Rochefort can be used without danger. If he should betray us we can break him in several evenings in the public meetings."[23] That

21. Dautry and Scheler, *Le Comité Central,* 185.

22. Wolfe's study of the club states that it was the guiding force behind the list of the "republican electoral meetings of the 18th arrondissement," and Ferré could not fail to have been a part of any major club activity; "The Parisian *Club de la Révolution,*" 105–6.

23. Rigault's fine sense of the technology of power well suited one who later became the prosecutor of the Commune, reigning over its police and intelligence apparatus. The minutes (from which I draw this and subsequent quotes in this and the next paragraph) are published in Dautry and Scheler, *Le Comité Central,* 189.

Rigault, and earlier Ferré, sought an alliance with nonrevolutionaries is understandable in the Blanquist framework of seeking power first and social change after. Internationals tended to give greater weight to principles, a generalization confirmed in this meeting, when most agreed with Frankel that "compromises destroy all parties one after another." Vaillant agreed, adding that the list for the second round could be easily drawn up "since all our groups are in accord on principles, and do not impose any individuals [as candidates]." The discussion clearly reveals that the revolutionary socialist movement was considered to be more than the sum of the three committees. Goupil and Vaillant, for example, suggested that names from other revolutionary socialist lists be chosen if they had received a high vote. The meeting approved Goupil's resolution to that effect, then went on to discuss the related questions of finances and organization.

There seemed to be general agreement that the local committees needed restructuring. "Organization is lacking," said Lallement, who recommended, "let's begin by grouping our elements, each in our arrondissement." According to Perroche, "we must create an executive commission in each arrondissement." Treillard agreed, saying, "we have not studied the arrondissement committees enough. In the 5th there are many committees or groups. It would be necessary to know if each group of the arrondissement is represented and if the delegates who are here really represent the groups of the Central Committee." The lack of solid ties between the center and the arrondissements, and within the arrondissements themselves, aggravated the financial difficulties of the movement. Those most interested in initiating changes were arrondissement militants not usually seen at Delegation meetings. Six event-filled weeks had passed since the Delegation had been created as the revolutionary Commune of January 1, and conditions in the capital had greatly changed. While the center of the revolutionary movement was strong—no complaints were heard about the internal organization of the Delegation—the extremities, where the revolutionary socialist movement touched the mass of the population through clubs and committees, required attention. Members were assigned to ask committees for donations, and Varlin summed up a rather confused discussion by saying, "the cause is common, each arrondissement should give what it has without worrying about whether one arrondissement gives more than another." Certainly Vallès was right to complain about dissention in the meeting, and another "grand meeting" of all club and committee delegates was called for February 14.

Nothing is known of that meeting or of the those held on the 19th, 20th, or 23d, except that the revolutionary socialist movement emerged from them as the Revolutionary Socialist Party. The first step was taken on February 19, when a general assembly adopted a Declaration of Principles. This confirmed the emphasis on exclusivity evident since the later siege. Instead of enlarging its base as much as possible, the revolutionary socialist movement in February was most concerned with purity and fidelity to defined ideals. This exclusivity had already been expressed in the transformation of "republican socialists" into "revolutionary socialists" when the revolutionary Commune, in conscious disregard for electoral methods, was taking shape. The Declaration of Principles began:

> Every member of a vigilance committee declares allegiance to the Revolutionary Socialist Party. In consequence, he demands and seeks to obtain by all possible means the suppression of the privileges of the bourgeoisie, its downfall as the directing class, and the political advent of workers—in a word, social equality. No more bosses, no more proletariat, no more classes. He recognizes work as the only foundation of the social constitution, work of which the entire product should belong to the worker.[24]

Thus far the Declaration shows a very close relationship to the revolutionary socialist manifesto for the February 1 elections. There is a somewhat greater emphasis on socialism in the Declaration, which is defined in conformity with the innumerable declarations of the International that had appeared over the previous years. The formulation that "the entire product should belong to the worker," for example, referred to producer associations. The Declaration went on to state that the Republic represented a right above any discussion, reflecting a belief commonly expressed in the clubs and committees of the period. This was a direct response to the election results and the first decisions of the National Assembly.

The Declaration further asserted that members of the Revolutionary Socialist Party "will thus oppose, by force if necessary, the meeting of any Constituent or supposed National Assembly before the foundations of the current constitution of society have been changed by a revolutionary political and social liquidation." This frank statement of revolutionary intent,

---

24. The Declaration of the 19th and the Resolutions of the 20th and 23d (quoted in this and the following paragraph) are published in several places, notably in Dautry and Scheler, *Le Comité Central,* 196, and in Rougerie, *Paris Libre,* 78. The original manuscript does not appear to have survived, but an original printed version is in AN: BB24 498.

given the context of the meeting of the National Assembly, was in no way hypothetical. *Liquidation* should be taken in the sense of a final settlement or balancing of accounts and was a term borrowed from the world of finance and the stock market. The term was generally intended to denote the end of the bourgeois order, a clearing of accounts to allow the creation of new structures.[25] "While awaiting this definitive revolution," the Declaration of Principles continued, each member of the Revolutionary Socialist Party "recognizes no other government of the city than the revolutionary Commune originating from the delegation of revolutionary socialist groups of this same city." Furthermore, "he recognizes no other government of the country than the government of political liquidation arising from the delegation of revolutionary Communes of the country and the principle working-class centers." The principle of the Red Poster of January 6 was thus maintained, the Delegation being again formally recognized as the only legitimate government of Paris, an idea that had receded into the background during the electoral campaign. Now, however, this principle was extended to the nation, whose government was to be composed of delegates of the revolutionary Communes. The double revolution envisioned indicates the revolutionary left's long reflection on the failures of previous revolutions, especially that of 1848, which was often said to have failed because national elections were held before the peasantry had been freed from subservience to landlords and clergy. This double revolution also conjures up unfortunate comparisons with Marxist doctrine, a dictatorship of the proletariat presiding over the transition to communism.[26] Frankel and Serrailler were the only prominent members of the Delegation who may have been Marxists, and the intent of the Declaration was not dictatorship but equality. Work was recognized as the "only foundation of the social constitution," but nowhere does the Declaration hold that only workers should govern. Rather, only revolutionary socialists in popular organizations should govern, a key distinction: *workers* refers to class position, *revolutionary socialists* to an ideological position. The Dec-

---

25. The concept of a social and political liquidation had been developed by Proudhon, among others, and was widely discussed in the public meetings of the late Empire. A number of citations of this usage of the term *liquidation* may be found in Jean Dubois, *Le Vocabulaire politique et sociale en France de 1869 à 1872* (Paris: Librairie Larousse, 1962), 336.

26. Dautry and Scheler do not fail to make this connection; *Le Comité Central,* 199. Later Jean Dautry's position apparently evolved, as Bruhat, Dautry, and Tersen, in *La Commune de 1871,* 98, note Blanquist influence. One could easily hear echoes of Proudhon's federalism and of Bakunin, but the search for intellectual antecedents is less enlightening than the context of revolutionary experience gained over the previous months.

laration guaranteed workers the full value of their product, but not exclusive political domination.

The Revolutionary Socialist Declaration of Principles was nonetheless thoroughly revolutionary, a complete rejection of the current government in favor of one elected from revolutionary socialist clubs and committees. The Declaration ends by stating that each member of the Revolutionary Socialist Party will "struggle for these ideas and to propagate them by forming revolutionary socialist groups wherever they do not exist. He will federate these groups with each other and place them in contact with the central Delegation. He must, finally, place all the means of which he disposes at the service of propaganda for the International Association of Workers." The Declaration, then, presents political, social, and organizational guidelines for members of vigilance committees. The attitude toward the AIT is important to note as well. It would have been very simple to state that members of revolutionary socialist vigilance committees also belonged thereby to the AIT, but instead the members are only to give the propagation of its ideals their full support. Again the distinction is important, especially for understanding the kind of association those who wrote and adopted the Declaration were constructing. The International was a specifically working-class organization. While it did include some bourgeois and petit bourgeois elements, such as professionals, intellectuals, journalists, and holders of small properties, it was dedicated to the advancement, through socialism, of the working classes. The Revolutionary Socialist Party had another, though related, aim. It was a political association designed to govern by revolutionary socialist principles until the definitive "liquidation." It was not to be a syndicate of workers fighting for better working conditions, which was the function of the Federal Chamber, nor was it intended to set a larger, socialist agenda and link workers around Europe in a common struggle, which was the role of the International. The Revolutionary Socialist Party was to be a vehicle for direct political action, based in popular organizations and directed against antirepublican forces.

Building on the Declaration of Principles of February 19, general assemblies of delegates from vigilance committees in the next four days adopted the Resolutions concerning Vigilance Committees. The Declaration presented the goals and ideals of the Revolutionary Socialist Party, while the Resolutions announced its structure. As their title indicates, the Resolutions concerned only the arrondissement committees; the structure of the Delegation of the Twenty Arrondissements was evidently considered satisfactory. The first task for vigilance committees was to "immediately proceed with their reconstruction, by leaving aside elements whose temperament is not sufficiently revolutionary socialist." In addition, every member had to approve and sign the Declaration of Principles of February 19. Again ideological purity and political exclusiveness were foremost, institutionalized by a purge and a positive act of adherence by the remaining members of the Revolutionary Socialist Party. The Resolutions were mainly administrative, but they demonstrate that the financial and organizational problems raised in the meetings of February 10, 11, and 12 prompted the restructuring of the vigilance committees. Committees were to have fixed offices, permanent officers, formal accounting procedures, and membership dues of .25 francs a week. Half of each committee's monthly surplus was to be given to the treasurer of the central Delegation. Other provisions clarified the organization of the vigilance committees. Each was to form in its arrondissement "groups of adherents in one form or another, which will fill its coffers by means of small weekly dues, in addition to the receipts produced by the public meetings." Committees would also "provoke the fusion within themselves, by means of delegates, of all the existing groups in their arrondissement whose character they recognize as revolutionary socialist." This structural plan envisioned three levels for the Revolutionary Socialist Party, a kind of federation of popular organizations. At the center would be the Delegation; then would come the arrondissement committees, whose members were also members of the Revolutionary Socialist Party, and finally, the adherent groups, whose members were not necessarily members of the party, but whose "character" must be revolutionary socialist. Just as the Delegation oversaw and coordinated the arrondissement committees, so within the arrondissements individual committees were to be centers of their own networks.

These Resolutions were designed to preserve the foundation of the revolutionary socialist movement, which was the arrondissement clubs and committees, while mitigating the deficiencies of popular organizations as weapons of combat. Popular organizations would knit together militants within arrondissements and keep the local clubs and committees in contact with the center. Resources of money and activists would be at the disposition of the central Delegation, which was the recognized revolutionary socialist government of the city. Above all, the new stress on ideological identity would allow united action of a cohort of loyal militants, unlike the heterogeneous clubs and committees of the siege, which could only be mobilized on occasions of unanimous outrage, and even then with great difficulty. The Declaration of February 19 and the Resolutions of February 20 and 23 point clearly in the direction of unified ideals, organization, and action. This analysis is confirmed by a brief passage in Jean Allemane's *Mémoires,* the only known description of the key February meetings. "On the left bank we had however made very laudable efforts to form an entente between all the arrondissements, and at various times we met as delegates," he recalled. "In the last meeting, held at the salle d'Arras," he continued, "we decided on the creation of committees of action and vigilance, forming a kind of federation of arrondissements, and maintaining constant contact." Allemane concluded, "the first measures of resistance to the coup of March 18 were due to these committees on the left bank."[27] A member of the vigilance committee of the 5th arrondissement on the left bank, Allemane perhaps naturally credited his area with initiating the reorganization. While the minutes of the meetings of February 10, 11, and 12 demonstrate that there was a general desire for restructuring, he may be accurate in suggesting that militants of the left bank were at the forefront of the Revolutionary Socialist Party. The Club Démocratique et Socialiste of the 13th arrondissement, which included militants from the entire left bank, had been an important element in the revolutionary Commune of January 1. In late February the club and the local sections of both the AIT and the Légion Garbaldienne fused with the AIT section of the Pantheon, in the 5th arrondissement, as the "sections réunis du Ve et XIIIe arrondissements." The Pantheon section and the vigilance committee of the 5th were nearly identical in leadership, and while Allemane apparently never joined the AIT, he noted that the committees of vigilance of the 5th and 13th closely coordinated their activities in March, all of which no doubt reflected the restructuring of local committees and clubs envisioned in the revolutionary socialist Resolutions of February 20 and 23.[28]

Six committees are known to have adhered to or restructured themselves in conformity to the Declaration of Principles of the Revolutionary Socialist Party, including the committees of the 5th and 13th arrondissements. In the 14th arrondissement Claude Sermet, president of the vigilance committee, signed the Declaration of Principles, and the vigilance committee was reorganized in the middle of March.[29] The committee of

---

27. Jean Allemane, *Mémoires d'un Communard: Des barricades au bagne* (Paris: Librairie Socialist, n.d.), 38.

28. Rougerie, "L'AIT et le mouvement ouvrier," 55; Allemane, *Mémoires d'un Communard,* 38.

29. AHG: 19e conseil 134, dossier Sermet.

the 15th arrondissement, which directed the salle Ragache, also signed the Declaration, as did the vigilance committee of the 19th.[30] The vigilance committee of the 4th arrondissement adopted a new set of statutes changing its name to Vigilance Committee of Revolutionary Socialists. The committee vowed to defend revolutionary socialist principles and propagate them "principally by means of public meetings." During the Commune this committee directed the Revolutionary Socialist Club of the 4th.[31]

The Revolutionary Socialist Party represented a radical break from the earlier conceptions of how to achieve a socialist society. From the moment when socialism first became a distinct system of ideas, socialists had thought of their systems as lying outside the realm of politics. Certainly the full realization of the projects of Leroux, Cabet, Fourier, and the other socialist pioneers were understood to have political consequences. Yet none, even Blanc, who envisioned government aid for his social workshops, considered direct political action a necessary first step. In the 1850s and 1860s Proudhon's influential conceptions specifically rejected political action. In the later Second Empire we can discern the beginnings of a revolutionary socialist mentality, in socialist's recognition of the need for political agitation to achieve socialism.[32] Yet it was the revolutionary experience of the siege and armistice that propelled militants down the path toward the Revolutionary Socialist Party. The political, economic and social prescriptions embodied in the revolutionary socialist movement of January and February were drafted within the organizational framework of the vigilance committee movement and could not have been created without the revolutionary experience of the previous months. The cumulative effect of October 31, the fruitless agitation to install the revolutionary Commune in early January, the failed insurrection of January 22, and the electoral campaign in February culminated in the discovery that a socialist society could be realized only after the seizure of power by a Revolutionary Socialist Party.

The restructuring of the revolutionary socialist movement occurred at a crucial moment in the developing crisis between the National Assembly

30. Georges Bourgin, *Histoire de la Commune* (Paris: Cornély, 1907), 59; AHG: 4e conseil 1432, dossier Pillioud.

31. AHG: Ly 27. The statutes are undated, but they have clear connections with the language of the Declaration of Principles and the Resolutions concerning Committees of Vigilance. The committee had twenty-six members and an executive commission of six.

32. Moss ascribes this change to the growing influence of Bakunin on some young militants of the AIT; *The Origins of the French Labor Movement*, 6.

and Paris. On February 21 negotiations with Bismarck were begun on the final Treaty of Frankfurt, which entailed ceding territory, a five-billion-franc indemnity, and a symbolic temporary occupation of Paris. The prospect of Germans triumphantly marching down the Champs-Élysées humiliated virtually all Parisians and brought to a head the simmering hostility toward the National Assembly. In this atmosphere of patriotic and political crisis an organization of National Guardsmen, begun as an electoral association in the early days of February, came into prominence as the voice of the armed Parisian citizenry. Every history of the Commune discusses the Fédération Républicaine de la Garde Nationale, or Federation of the National Guard, because it was guard units that seized strategic positions in the city on March 18, and because the Federation's central committee administered Paris until the Communal Council elected on March 26 took office.[33] Yet the connections between the Federation and the revolutionary movement arising from clubs and committees have not been sufficiently understood. The Federation was described by hostile contemporaries as a group of "unknowns," as "obscure men." When seen in the light of the revolutionary socialist movement, however, the Federation takes on a new aspect.

Even before the founding of the Federation, popular organizations and units of the National Guard had fused to some extent. Clubs and vigilance committees had mobilized battalions in all the *journées* of the siege, from October 8 to January 22. Even though the Federation was originally convoked by a conservative newspaper, some militants of the revolutionary left participated in its foundation. Edouard Vaillant was a member of the Federation's organizing commission of February 3, and Jules Minet, an active member of the International who had been on the revolutionary socialist list for the elections of February, took part in at least two early Federation meetings. He urged participants of the February 4 combined meeting of the Delegation, the AIT, and the Federal Chamber to take part in the Federation's elections for guard representatives.[34] After the meetings organizing the Revolutionary Socialist Party, the Delegation began seriously considering on February 27 how to use the current agitation to promote revolution. While some were suspicious of the reactionary origins

---

33. Oddly, there is only one monograph on the Federation, Dale Clifford's "Aux Armes, Citoyens! The National Guard in the Paris Commune of 1871" (Ph.D. diss., University of Tennessee, 1975).

34. Dale Clifford, "Aux Armes, Citoyens!" 77; Dautry and Scheler, *Le Comité Central,* 163. The Federation was formed by guard companies electing delegates to meetings, and the delegates then elected the Federation's Central Committee.

of the Federation, Debock argued that the guardsmen in Paris from the department of the Seine were willing to "second the revolutionary movement if it is judged opportune." Minet stated that the Federation of the National Guard, of which he was a member, was strong enough to arrest Vinoy should the general seek to hinder the Federation. Vallès revealed the clearest tactical vision, though, when he noted that "the revolution is on its way" and concluded that "since the committee of the National Guard is so patriotic in its sentiments, let us try a fusion."[35] Malon reports that at this time "proletarian socialists" in several clubs simultaneously developed the idea of federating the National Guard.[36] The idea of coordinating or even combining the guard and revolutionary socialist movements was also discussed at the meeting of the International on March 1. Varlin asked that four members of the AIT be delegated to the Federation to support it against the government, "if we remain isolated from such a force our influence will disappear, if we unite with this committee we take a giant step toward the socialist future." Both he and Clamouse stated that, in the words of the latter, "socialists are at the forefront of the affair." Varlin urged members of the International to have themselves elected to the Central Committee of the National Guard "and work to take over the spirit of that assembly."[37]

This is exactly what happened in the first two weeks of March, as members of vigilance committees gained elected positions in the Federation of the National Guard. On March 3 the Federation renewed its provisional Central Committee, and sixteen of the thirty-one members of the new committee were members of the International, including Varlin, Viard, Lacord, and Pindy, some of the key leaders of the International and the Delegation. The transformation of the Federation was so complete that the March 3 meeting was presided by Jules Bergeret, a member of the International, and of the seven other attendees noted in the minutes of the meeting, five were of the International (Gouhier, Goullé, Varlin, Lacord, Viard), and another, Verlet, was a Blanquist.[38] By March 15 the numerical dominance of militants of the revolutionary socialist movement was overwhelming. Two-thirds (twenty-eight of forty-two) of the members of the

---

35. The minutes are reprinted in Rougerie, "Quelques documents nouveaux," 27.
36. *La Troisième défaite,* 50.
37. *L'Enquête Parlementaire sur l'Insurrection du Dix-Huit mars,* 528.
38. *L'Enquête Parlementaire sur l'Insurrection du Dix-Huit mars,* 472. Clifford argues that the takeover by radicals "was more apparent than real," as it lasted only a brief time—but this was exactly the period of time when the Federation seized control of the city; "Aux Armes, Citoyens!" 106.

Central Committee or legion commanders named that day were either members of the International or Blanquists. Forty-three percent (eighteen of forty-two) are known to have been members of vigilance committees or the Delegation.[39] From the first days of March, then, the Central Committee should be considered as being dominated not by "unknowns" but by activists of the revolutionary socialist movement.

One way this dominance was achieved is illustrated in a remarkable episode in the 14th arrondissement. Henry, as legion chief, wrote and had adopted by the Legion Council a set of directives for candidates to National Guard positions, which informed the guardsmen who were voting that they had to follow an "imperative mandate" to "defend the Revolution." It furthermore stipulated death to any "pretender, protector, or propagator of monarchy" and stated that the "the right of association is guaranteed by the Revolution." So far the text is noteworthy only for the explicit devotion to revolution, which reflects the radicalization of the guard in early March. Henry's instructions to the guard rank and file concluded, however, that "candidates for no matter what rank must be democratic revolutionary socialists." The choice for guard officers was thus restricted to the revolutionary socialist element, the word *democratic* in this case being most likely an echo of the name of the Club Démocratique Socialiste in the 14th arrondissement, to which Henry and others on the Legion Council belonged. Henry and the Legion Council had the ability to restrict the choice of officers to those in keeping with their revolutionary tenets and did so: the two men elected under this rule were both active in the revolutionary socialist movement.[40] Through such tactics Vallès's notion of fusing the Delegation with the Federation of the National Guard and Varlin's proposal to "take over the spirit" of the Federation were becoming reality. In mid-March Varlin wrote to the Russian populist

---

39. Rougerie, *Paris Libre,* 96, provides a list of the members, which I cross-checked with a variety of sources, in particular Maitron, *DBMOF.* Oddly, Rougerie suggests the Federation was moving away from any relationship with revolutionary groups; *Paris Libre,* 100.

40. These instructions were read to a guard meeting on March 7 and were greeted with the "general approbation of the assembly," according to the minutes; AHG: Ly 27. The importance given the right of association is probably an answer to the government's attempts to prevent the Federation from meeting. Since the edict of January 23 prohibiting public meetings had never been rescinded, such meetings were officially illegal. Vinoy later boasted that he was able to prevent several from taking place; *L'Enquête Parlementaire sur l'Insurrection du Dix-Huit mars,* 213. The two elected in the 14th were Alfred Billioray and Maximilien Avoine. Billioray was a noted orator of the Club Maison-Dieu, who would later be elected to the Commune; Avoine was a member of the International, who served in the Central Committee during the Commune.

Pierre Lavrov that the system of electing guard commanders had already put "a notable part" of the National Guard in socialist hands. "One more week and we will be masters of seventeen of twenty arrondissements," he wrote—in part accurately predicting the events of March—"then we will chase the prefecture of police from Paris, we will overthrow the government, and France will follow us."[41]

The celebrations commemorating the beginning of the 1848 revolution on February 24 were the turning point in the Federation's development and should be considered the beginning of the revolutionary cycle that led to the Commune. Given the apparent threat to the Republic, and the fact that this was the first time since 1851 such celebrations were legal, the twenty-third anniversary of the Second Republic was greeted with fervor by Parisians. That day the fledgling Federation of the National Guard declared it would not recognize any officers except those elected by the ranks—a rejection of General d'Aurelle de Paladines, appointed commander of the guard by the government the day before. The Federation defiantly stated its opposition to the Prussian occupation of the city and said it would "resist by force" any attempt to disarm the guard. As part of a series of guard parades to honor the Republic, members of the Federation then marched to the July Column, place de la Bastille, where those who died in the fighting of February 1848 are buried. Speeches were given in praise of the Republic, and a red flag was placed in the hands of the Spirit of Liberty at the top of the column, a symbolic declaration of revolution that precisely translated the underlying insurrectionary reality. On the 26th, as the celebrations continued, a policeman was brutally murdered by a crowd that had caught him writing down the battalion numbers of units parading around the Bastille. Prefect of Police Choppin, who was on the scene, had to flee for his life. Over the next week General Vinoy, commander of the army in Paris, noted that ninety-seven battalions marched to the Bastille, a demonstration of the guard's intent to preserve the Republic.[42] According to Vinoy, when he called out the "good" National Guard battalions to restore order, almost no one responded to the muster. The army was the only remaining weapon for enforcing the government's authority, but its soldiers were increasingly unreliable, and

41. Cited in Cordillot, *Eugène Varlin*, 207.

42. No one group seems to have been responsible for these demonstrations; the International, with its usual prudence, decided on February 22 not to take part as an organization, leaving it up to individual members to decided for themselves; Rougerie, *Paris Libre*, 86–90; *L'Enquête Parlementaire sur l'Insurrection du Dix-Huit mars*, 527; Serman, *La Commune de Paris*, 180.

troops sent to suppress the demonstrations at the Bastille instead frater-
nized with the guard.[43] On February 27 Vinoy attempted to remove soldiers from the dangerous influence of the working-class population by
ordering the army to retreat from the disaffected eastern sections of the
city.

Popular organizations and militants associated with the Revolutionary
Socialist Party organized much of this agitation. On February 26 news of
the definitive peace terms reached Paris. The wording of the announcement seemed to indicate that the Prussians would enter the zone of occupation centering on the Champs-Élysées and place de la Concorde at midnight, though their entry was not actually scheduled until March 1. In
conformity with the Federation's decision, guardsmen mustered to repulse
the expected invaders and removed about four hundred cannons from
artillery parks near the zone of occupation to more distant areas of the
city—mainly Montmartre and Belleville—so they could not be seized by
the Prussians. The guards' seizure of the cannons greatly altered the balance of power between Paris and the government, for the cannons were
immediately understood to be a powerful potential weapon should the
Assembly attempt to restore monarchy; they were a physical guarantee of
the Republic. The salle Marseillaise was the center of resistance in the 19th
arrondissement, organizing the surveillance of the cannons under its control. The vigilance committee of the 5th arrondissement also controlled
some of the seized cannons. Members of the vigilance committee of the
18th arrondissement played a dominant role in the local National Guard
committee that had possession of the cannons of Montmartre. On the
night of February 26 members of the salle d'Arras, among them Pieron,
were instrumental in forcing the gates of the Sainte-Pélagie prison and
releasing several popular guard officers who had been arrested for resisting the armistice.[44] In early March the 18th and 19th arrondissements were
to a great extent controlled by their vigilance committees, the 20th by its
National Guard legion commander, Emile Eudes. In addition, Emile
Duval declared himself commander in chief of the 13th arrondissement
and, with fellow members of the Club Démocratique et Socialiste, ran the
arrondissement in open defiance of civil and military authorities. All were
participants in the revolutionary socialist movement, either in vigilance
committees or in the Delegation of the Twenty Arrondissements or both.

---

43. *L'Enquête Parlementaire sur l'Insurrection du Dix-Huit mars,* 212.
44. Simon, *The Government of M. Thiers,* 1:224; Rougerie, *Procès des Communards,* 165;
Wolfe, "The Parisian *Club de la Révolution,*" 107.

Eudes, for example, was a Blanquist who served as a liaison between the Delegation and Blanqui, and he had been a revolutionary socialist candidate in the February elections.

That certain arrondissements had escaped government control before March 18 has always been known, but because the context of the Revolutionary Socialist Party and the movement that gave rise to it have not been understood the connections between these events have not been recognized. Generally the militants are considered to be acting on their own initiative only or as part of the Federation of the National Guard. Certainly the local guard units were instruments through which some militants acted, but without the leadership's experience of revolutionary action and the organization provided by the revolutionary socialist movement, it is unlikely the guard organization on its own could or would have seized the opportunities presented by the situation. Indeed, at the level of the arrondissement there was often a near fusion of the guard and club movements: guard elections were held in the same places used for club and committee meetings, and the leaders elected were often club leaders as well.

The insurrectionary activity of militants of the revolutionary socialist movement was especially important in the 19th arrondissement, where the committee of the salle Marseillaise formed a Committee of Public Safety in the last days of February to oppose the entry of the Prussians. According to the president of the vigilance committee, Moise Pillioud, the Committee of Public Safety was established on the demand of Fortuné Henry, who was a member of the revolutionary Commune, having signed the Red Poster of January 6. Emile Oudet, a future member of the Paris Commune and another signer of the Red Poster of January 6, was also on the Committee. Pillioud admitted later at his trial that they gave orders to the National Guard to requisition arms and defend the ramparts, and the minutes of several meetings of the salle Marseillaise show that all this activity was coordinated through the club. Pillioud was named legion commander of the 19th arrondissement, though he tried to exculpate himself later at his trial by saying he was only following orders given by persons unknown to him. The astonished interrogator asked, "you found there was no [governmental] direction, and you, a small businessman, substituted yourself for the legal authorities in order to receive and expedite orders that came to you from an unknown authority?" Pillioud could only reply, "it's true."[45] A founding member of the vigilance committee of the 19th

---

45. Pillioud employed about thirty people in a tailor shop and is an example of why it is incorrect to apply the term *dictatorship of the proletariat* to the aspirations of the Revolutionary Socialist Party. He denied being a member of the International, although he said that

arrondissement and revolutionary of October 31, Pillioud was following the path envisioned by the revolutionary socialist Declaration of Principles, but he could hardly tell this to his interrogator.[46] At about this time two cannons stood before the entry of the Marseillaise, powerfully symbolizing the force of the club. And they were not only symbols: on March 18 the hall was protected from government attack by barricades and these same cannons. Similarly, in the 18th arrondissement the vigilance committee led by Ferré helped oversee the cannons of Montmartre. To protect these cannons from the government, fortifications and barricades were raised in the first week of March, clearly demonstrating the degree of power exercised in the arrondissement by the vigilance committee and the National Guard committee.[47]

Along with the 18th and 19th arrondissements, the 20th had by and large escaped government control before March 18. Legion Commander Eudes described in a letter of 1873 the way his actions were coordinated with other militants prior to March 18, and in particular with Legion Commander Duval in the 13th arrondissement.

> It was understood between he and me that our two legions, . . . to which would rally the 14th commanded by Henri, the 15th directed

Pindy had tried several times to get him to join, and that he had gone so far as to attend some AIT meetings at the Marseillaise. Jules Fleury, evidently another member of the Committee of Public Safety, was also on the Federation's provisional Central Committee of March 3, and he may have been the authority that gave the orders Pillioud referred to; Maitron, *DBMOF*, 6:52; AHG: 4e conseil 1432 and Ly 22.

46. Even after the agitation surrounding the Prussian occupation died down the assembly of the Marseillaise was a force in the arrondissement. Around March 12 guardsmen of the 147th battalion took several Prussians hostage, demanding the release of one of their officers imprisoned by the Prussians for causing a disturbance. The Prussian hostages were brought to the salle Marseillaise, where, despite the entreaties of several vigilance committee members and an entire battalion of police, the club members refused to free the Prussians. Only after several days of negotiations were the Prussians released—the fate of the officer of the 147th is not known. The police agent who reported these facts noted that the angry club assembly called the committee members "traitors and false friends" for helping the police; AHG: 13e conseil 185, dossier Etienne Canal.

47. AHG: 14e conseil 1432; *L'Enquête Parlementaire sur l'Insurrection du Dix-Huit mars,* 223; Michel, *La Commune,* especially 165; Wolfe, "The Parisian *Club de la Révolution,*" 107. Serman is incorrect to suggest that the National Guard arrondissement committee "acted without coordinating with the local vigilance committee," as its key members were all members of or the Club de la Révolution; *La Commune de Paris,* 163. Rougerie confirms that in the 18th arrondissement the real powers were the vigilance committee and the National Guard, not the government or the municipality; "Notes pour servir à l'histoire du 18 mars 1871," in *Melanges en Histoire Sociale offerts à Jean Maitron* (Paris: Éditions Ouvrières, 1976), 233; *Le Bien Public,* March 9. Unless indicated otherwise, all further newspaper references are to 1871.

by a committee of which Chauvière was the key man, the 18th in the
hands of the Committee of Vigilance of Montmartre of which Ferré
was president, and several battalions of the 11th arrondissement and
the 19th, would all be under our immediate direction without going
through the Central Committee [of the National Guard], which did
not offer the required trustworthiness.[48]

Eudes was to command the right bank, Duval the left, though he noted
that this "revolutionary army" was not able to be fully organized before
March 18. Chauvière and Duval were Blanquists who were also members
of the International, and with Ferré they had signed the Red Poster of January 6. Lucien Henry, called Henri by Eudes, was also a member of the
AIT and was elected legion commander of the 14th at a meeting of the
Club Maison-Dieu, where he was a constant orator; he was also a member
of the Ligue Républicaine de Defense à Outrance.[49] This "revolutionary
army" thus was linked by all its key leaders to the revolutionary socialist
club and committee movement, and on the day of March 18 these individuals seized large parts of the city at the head of their battalions and legions.

In Duval's 13th arrondissement the mayor resigned in late February,
leaving the arrondissement in the hands of its vice-mayors, one of whom
was Leo Meilliet. Meilliet had been a member of the revolutionary Commune of January 1 and, with Duval, was a leader of the Club Démocrate
Socialiste of the 13th. Duval, though a simple private in the National
Guard, ordered twenty-six cannons seized from the ramparts and placed
in defensive positions around the mairie on March 5. Vinoy sent a contingent to arrest him, but instead the contingent was arrested and its com-
manding officer very nearly shot. The vigilance committee established
itself in the mairie, and Duval issued a poster stating the National Guard
had the right to defend itself against those who would use the cannons
against the Republic.[50] Some of the arms and munitions seized in the 13th
were made available to the neighboring vigilance committee of the 5th
arrondissement, which held itself ready, according to committee member
Allemane, to resist any "coup" on the part of the government.[51] In four

48. Quoted in Maitron, *DBMOF,* 5:449.
49. Maitron, *DBMOF,* 6:313; a Henry also signed the Red Poster, and while there were
many Henrys in the city, Lucien's affiliation with the Ligue, a group closely associated with
the revolutionary Commune of January 1, makes it likely that he was the one who signed.
50. Conte, *Éleménts pour une histoire de la Commune dans le XIIIe arrondissement,* 37.
51. Allemane, *Mémoires d'un Communard,* 38.

arrondissements, then, militants of the revolutionary socialist movement moved into the vacuum created by the collapse of the government's authority in late February. The fusion of the revolutionary socialist movement and the Federation of the National Guard was the foundation of revolutionary action from late February up to and beyond March 18, a result of revolutionary socialist militants being elected, or just naming themselves, to positions of authority in the guard hierarchy.

Indeed, the influence of the Delegation and the AIT was instrumental in preventing a clash between the Federation and the Prussians when the latter finally did enter the city on March 1. On the night before, members of the Delegation and the AIT convinced the Federation that resistance would only compromise the Republic and serve the interests of reactionaries. Instead, the occupied sections of the city were cordoned off and Parisians in those areas remained indoors. Black flags of mourning were flown on many buildings. When the occupation ended on March 3 many Parisians felt they had denied the Prussians their triumph, and the Federation's ability to control the guard had been clearly demonstrated. Against this backdrop the government attempted several times to retake the cannons but was always turned back by guardsmen who suspected the government of royalist objectives. The National Assembly continued to exacerbate these suspicions, issuing on March 10 and 11 several decrees that alienated nearly the whole of Paris. It reconfirmed the decision to end payment to all but indigent National Guardsmen, suppressed five newspapers, and voted to close the clubs and public meetings. A military court sentenced Flourens and Blanqui to death *in absentia* for their role in the October 31 insurrection. The moratorium on payment of rent and bills of credit imposed during the siege was ended, payment now being due with interest; over the next week some 120,000 notices of inability to pay were recorded. Virtually the entire lower bourgeoisie was driven to the edge of bankruptcy, depriving the National Assembly of the support of those who generally have an interest in order and stability. Finally, on March 11 the Bordeaux Assembly adjourned until the 20th, but out of fear of the guard's cannons refused to reconvene in Paris, deciding instead on Versailles. This decapitalization convinced many Parisians that the Assembly was only waiting for the proper moment to install a monarch in the former abode of the Sun King.

The meeting of the Assembly at Versailles on March 20 became a *de facto* deadline for Thiers. Should large parts of Paris still be effectively out of government control on that date, should the cannons of the guard still loom over the city from the heights of Montmartre, then his leadership would come under serious scrutiny in the Assembly by those who already considered him too lenient on the "reds" in Paris. Thiers acknowledged that bankers and other businesspeople demanded that he "finish with" the agitators, resurrecting the ominous phrase of June 1848. In the early hours of March 18 Thiers sent the army back into the eastern district of the capital. Behind the columns of troops came police agents and gendarmes to arrest "all the chiefs of the insurrection," according to General Vinoy. Ex-Prefect of Police Choppin, who helped plan the attack, said members of the International were to be given particular attention.[52] Almost from the first the action went badly, as the bourgeois guard battalions refused to muster for the government. Although the troops managed to momentarily take possession of the cannons, they were surrounded by large crowds composed mainly of women, who urged them not to fire on the people. The troops began fraternizing, in some cases disobeying repeated commands to fire. General Lecomte, in charge of the units in Montmartre, was arrested by his men. Similar scenes were enacted in the other areas where government forces attempted to retake cannons. Despite the best efforts of vigilance committee members in the 18th, Lecomte and another general taken prisoner were shot later in the day by an angry crowd. By late morning not only were the cannons still held by the National Guard, but the army itself was disintegrating. To avoid losing the entire army, Thiers ordered the retreat of all government forces to Versailles in the midafternoon.

From midmorning onward some National Guard units went on the offensive, seizing important intersections and government buildings. Many of the leaders are familiar from the Red Poster of January 1 or the revolutionary socialist meetings of February. Pindy commanded a battalion that surrounded the mairie of the 3d arrondissement and later took control of the Imprimerie Nationale. Varlin momentarily occupied the mairie of the 17th and then commanded the guardsmen that seized the headquarters of the Parisian National Guard on the place Vendôme. Duval led the battalions of the 13th in taking the Pantheon and then the Prefecture of Police. Eudes commanded the first battalions to enter the

---

52. A statement was posted calling on the "good citizens" to aid the government against the Federation's Central Committee, which it said would "put Paris to pillage and France in the grave." On the day before, Blanqui was arrested in province, an indication of the completeness of the government's planning. Vinoy quoted in Choury, *La Commune au coeur de Paris*, 168; Choppin in *L'Enquête Parlementaire sur l'Insurrection du Dix-Huit mars*, 225.

Hôtel de ville. Arnaud coordinated the response from guard headquarters on the rue Basfroi. Other members of the Central Committee who had no known connection to the revolutionary socialist movement were also involved, such as Nestor Rousseau, but the predominant role of revolutionary socialist militants is clear. They were acting according to a generally understood idea of what would be necessary should the government attack—an expectation that had been building for several weeks, since the guard had seized the cannons at the end of February.

On March 18 and the days following revolutionaries also seized the twenty arrondissement mairies, and here too revolutionary socialist militants were notable for their energy. As on October 31, the vigilance committees rapidly transformed themselves from popular assemblies into governing bodies, a process envisioned by some of the revolutionary left at the very outset of the vigilance committee movement in September and codified in the February Declaration of Principles. On the day of March 18 revolutionaries led in every case by revolutionary socialist militants or popular organizations occupied nine mairies. Two were held only temporarily, those of the 6th and 7th arrondissements.[53] All seven mairies remaining in the hands of insurgents on the night of March 18 were controlled by revolutionary socialist militants, and all of them except that in the 5th arrondissement were in the extreme eastern and southern areas of the city, where the working classes predominated.[54] That the 5th was occupied by Communards so early was a result of the coordination of forces between Duval in the neighboring 13th and the local vigilance committee.[55] In the remaining mairies of Paris the mayors and vice-mayors elected

53. The mairie of the 6th was temporarily occupied by Tony Moilin, a member of the Association Républicaine du 6e Arrondissement, which functioned as the local vigilance committee. Moilin was a member of the Delegation, having signed the Red Poster of January 6. The mairie of the 7th arrondissement was invaded by Raoul Urbain and François Parisel, both members of the Club Républicaine Socialiste du 7e Arrondissement, popularly known as the Club Pré-aux-Clercs, which was run by the vigilance committee of the arrondissement. Goupil had also invaded the mairie on October 31. *Le Patriote,* March 21; Gustave Nast, "Les Mairies de Paris et le Comité Central," *Le Correspondant: Recueil Périodique* 84 (September 25, 1871): 1052; Maitron, *DBMOF,* 5:460, 7:377, 8:92, and 9:247; *L'Enquête Parlementaire sur l'insurrection du Dix-Huit mars,* 347.

54. These seven mairies were in the 5th, 13th, 14th, 15th, 18th, 19th, and 20th arrondissements. The 15th arrondissement was under the control of the local guard, led by Nicolas Faltot, a Blanquist who was part of the "revolutionary army" mentioned by Eudes; Dommanget, *Blanqui, la guerre de 1870–71 et la Commune,* 115.

55. Allemane, a member of this committee, wrote that he was awakened by other vigilance committee members early in the morning. They then set about organizing the defense of the arrondissement in conjunction with Duval's forces. Later in the day the mairie was

in November stayed on in an attempt to prevent civil war between the city and the Assembly. When conciliation failed, one by one the mairies were occupied by Communards. Vigilance committees eventually administered ten arrondissements during the Commune.[56] The rest were administered by guard delegations, by the members of the Communal Council elected on March 26, or by councils appointed by those members. In some arrondissements revolutionary socialist militants participated in the appointed councils, and in others the local vigilance committees helped these councils administer the arrondissements.[57]

The insurrection of March 18 culminated a long history of revolutionary action that began in the public meetings of the late Empire. From 1868 to 1871 there was fundamental continuity in the revolutionary movement's militants, leadership, goals, and structures. The Commune was not an insurrection born of circumstance, an accident. And given the history of revolutionary organization that created the Commune, it was more than a natural historical evolution. No revolutionary project would have succeeded without the revolutionary consciousness of club and committee militants and the organizational structures they created. A variety of fortuitous conjunctures were part of this process, such as the military factors that led to the isolation and bombardment of Paris, and an Assembly elected to bring peace but apparently determined as well to restore monarchy. Long-term evolutions in industrial capitalism and social structures certainly shaped the historical context of 1871. Yet the origins of the Commune as seen through the history of the clubs and committees demands that the revolutionary political culture of popular organizations be returned to the center of the equation.

Only in reconstructing the history of the popular organizations of Paris can we understand the exact mechanism for translating rhetoric and rituals into a revolutionary program during the Commune and illuminate the

---

seized, and Allemane—as "adjoint-delegate," or assistant to the mayor—issued an order to build barricades. Dominique Régère of the vigilance committee was appointed mayor. Allemane, *Memoires d'un Communard,* 39–40; Maitron, *DBMOF,* 4:103; *L'Enquête Parlementaire sur l'Insurrection du Dix-Huit mars,* 351; *La Verité,* March 29.

56. The 1st, 5th, 7th, 8th, 9th, 14th, 16th, 17th, 18th, and 19th.

57. This categorization of mairie administrations is based primarily on the dossiers on the municipalities in AHG: Ly 27, the testimony of the mayors and vice-mayors forced out by Communards in *L'Enquête Parlementaire sur l'Insurrection du Dix-Huit mars,* and Rougerie's "Notes pour servir à l'histoire du 18 mars 1871." There is no general history of the mairies of Paris during the Commune, and most histories ignore the topic. Clifford wrongly states that all mairies were administered by guard committees; "Aux Armes, Citoyens," 213.

continuity from siege to armistice to Commune. The insurrection of March 18 was not spontaneous; those who seized the centers of power on that day and the days following possessed a framework of organization, an expectation of the need to act, and a vision of desirable goals. Clubs and committees associated with the revolutionary socialist movement over the preceding seven months had attempted three insurrections, formed a revolutionary Commune drawn directly from popular organizations, and created the outlines of a Revolutionary Socialist Party that called for France to be governed by revolutionary socialist clubs and committees. During the Commune this program was in large part accomplished. To speak of spontaneity in this context falsifies the history of preparation behind most of those who created and led the Commune.

The Delegation of the Twenty Arrondissements did not plan the insurrection of March 18, but the revolutionary experience of its membership, the direction provided by its leadership, and its Parisian-wide structure were the foundations for the successful seizure of power. In early March the Delegation began calling itself the Delegation Communale des Vingt Arrondissements, the word *communale* being a prescient addition, underscoring that revolutionary socialist militants were as convinced as ever that their organization was the only legitimate government of the city.[58] This pretension was ambitious, but as the National Assembly progressively lost all authority in the capital the pretension moved ever closer to reality. In the vision of its founders, the Revolutionary Socialist Party was a far more ideologically and organizationally unified movement than the revolutionary clubs of the siege, being dedicated to precise goals: social equality; the destruction of bourgeois privileges and power; the political advent of workers; a Paris ruled by a revolutionary Commune formed from revolutionary socialist vigilance committees; and a France ruled by a federation of revolutionary Communes. And when the expected strike against the Republic occurred, it was revolutionary socialists who gained the victory and forged a revolution.

---

58. *Le Mot d'Ordre,* March 1 and 8.

CHAPTER 3

Shaping the Revolution

The initiative for revolutionary measures belongs to us. . . . Communal power resides in each arrondissement wherever men are assembled who have a horror of servitude and the yoke.

—*Le Prolétaire*

The Commune operated at three distinct levels, and at each level club and committee militants to a great extent both provided the leadership and shaped the program of the revolution. In the central civil and military administrations of the city, revolutionary socialist organizations and militants acted decisively to preserve and then to direct the insurrection. As a government the Communal Council at the Hôtel de ville was largely the work of revolutionary socialist militants. At the second level of power in Paris, that of the arrondissement mairies, or town halls, the club and committee movement was equally vital in shaping the revolution. Half of the twenty Parisian arrondissements were administered by municipal commissions created on the foundations of vigilance committees, while eight of the remaining districts were represented on the Communal Council by members of vigilance committees or the Delegation. At both the Hôtel de ville and the arrondissement mairies, militants moved directly from clubs and committees to revolutionary government, conforming in broad outlines to the Declaration of Principles of the Revolutionary Socialist Party. Militants of popular organizations were also crucial in consolidating the revolution at a third level, that of the squares, meeting halls, and streets where public opinion was formed and expressed. By intimidation and dedication Communards in clubs and committees, known as clubistes, monopolized the organized expression of opinion. The insurrection of March 18 became a revolution—one with a specific shape and content—because at these three levels of power and action revolutionary socialists

Epigraph from "To the members of the Club des Prolétaires," *Le Prolétaire*, May 19.

and clubistes elaborated and partially implemented their vision of a "new world."

At the center, the Delegation of the Twenty Arrondissements has been portrayed as initially hesitant to support the Commune, but in fact the Delegation was essential in preserving the new insurrection.[1] Late on March 19 the Central Committee of the National Guard reached a compromise with the elected mayors and deputies of Paris that called on the National Guard to relinquish the Hôtel de ville so that elections for a municipal council could be held. According to one participant the Delegation tipped the balance against this surrender, arguing that the agreement was a trap. One speaker carried the day with the argument "Citizens, don't listen to perfidious promises. You have retaken the cannons, keep them! You have the Hôtel de ville, keep it!"[2] The Delegation did not issue a public statement of support for the National Guard until March 21, but not because it was unsure about backing the insurrection. Until that day it was not clear that the National Guard needed a statement of support, since negotiations with the mayors were being carried out in an atmosphere of mutual respect for each side's authority.[3] That morning, however, twenty-eight Parisian newspapers issued a statement denying the right of the National Guard to call elections, and the mayors and deputies issued a poster seeming to challenge the National Guard's legitimacy. Positions were hardening, and only at this juncture did the leaders of the Delegation feel a public statement was required.

Furthermore, any doubts the Delegation had about the new insurrectionary government existed not because the Delegation's support was

---

1. Edwards, *The Paris Commune,* 174. Rougerie, *Paris Libre,* 126, suggests that the Delegation did not initially support the Central Committee of the National Guard.

2. Da Costa, *La Commune vécue,* 1:185. Da Costa, a Blanquist, emphasized the role of Blanquists in this decision. Prosper Oliver Lissagaray, a contemporary journalist, confirmed the intervention of the Delegation; *Histoire de la Commune* (1871; reprint, Paris: Éditions de Delphes, 1964), 93.

3. On March 21 Dumont suggested the Delegation "renew" its offer of support to the Central Committee of the National Guard, indicating that private assurances of support had already been given; Dautry and Scheler, *Le Comité Central,* 217. A poster of March 20 expressed the support of the "municipalities of the arrondissements," and it is difficult to see what groups this could mean except the arrondissement vigilance committees, as the elected municipalities were hostile to the insurrection. Citing a contemporary source, Rials, in *Nouvelle histoire de Paris,* 285, argued the poster was a fraud perpetrated by the Central Committee of the National Guard, but such a maneuver would be foreign to these men, who considered themselves honest and honorable. The International did not publicly declare its support for the Central Committee of the National Guard until March 22, fully three days after the Delegation had done so.

tepid but because many in the Delegation feared the National Guard was too moderate. An influential faction in the Delegation sought to push the National Guard to adopt more radical measures. Since its creation on January 1 the Delegation had argued that the only government of the city should be the revolutionary Commune arising from the clubs and committees of Paris, a decision reaffirmed in the revolutionary socialist Declaration of Principles of February 19. In the days just after March 18 some members of the Delegation hoped to implement that strategy. This would assure that the government of Paris would be revolutionary, while the results of an election could not be guaranteed. Speaking for one of the most important of the Delegation's committees, Claude Napias-Piquet forcefully argued the case against elections: "The 1st arrondissement wants revolutionary measures and not elections." He proposed transforming the Central Committee of the National Guard into a Committee of Public Safety, with the addition of members of the Delegation of the Twenty Arrondissements: "if we accept, the 1st arrondissement is with us; if not, no!"[4] Following the same argument Eugene Chatelain, also from the 1st arrondissement, refused to stand in the elections. Lefrançais hoped to preserve revolutionary government and avoid the "rut of parliamentarism" by having Paris administered by a committee formed from popular assemblies, just as the Delegation had been formed.[5] Vaillant also maintained faith in the revolutionary path of January, some years later lamenting the electoral strategy of March. "Instead of a revolutionary Commune, Paris had an elected Commune," he recalled. "It did its duty and did its best," he noted, "but because of its electoral origin it could not have the unity of action and the energy of a committee arising spontaneously, revolutionarily, from a people in revolt."[6]

This decision to support elections rather than a revolutionary line modified the Delegation's tactics of January and February, but most delegates in the meeting of March 21 implicitly agreed that circumstances required some changes in the revolutionary socialist program. It was not the Delegation that held power, but a committee had been initially suspect as reactionary, though many of its current members were revolutionary socialists. The existence of a government at Versailles meant that the rev-

4. The minutes are reprinted in Dautry and Scheler, *Le Comité Central,* 217.
5. After the bloodshed of the Friends of Order demonstration, however, Lefrançais supported elections as the best way to avoid civil war; Lefrançais, *Souvenirs d'un révolutionnaire,* 477.
6. *Ni Dieu, Ni Maître* (the Blanquist newspaper), March 20, 1881; quoted in Edwards, *The Paris Commune,* 294.

olution faced an external threat of the greatest magnitude. In the first days of the insurrection the memory of the June Days of 1848 was repeatedly invoked as an argument for elections, which seemed to present the best means of assuring harmony in Paris and a united front against the royalists at Versailles.[7] In choosing an electoral, rather than a revolutionary, strategy the Delegation gave precedence to republican unity rather than to its revolutionary socialist principles. This decision signaled a tactical reorientation that lasted throughout the Commune. After March 18 the tendency toward exclusiveness and ideological purity evident since the later siege gave way to an effort to unite as large a range of opinion as possible behind the insurrection. As early as the afternoon of March 21 the Delegation held a combined meeting with the Union Républicaine Centrale, a moderate group composed mainly of men of 1848, who previously would have been castigated as reactionaries by many Delegation members.[8] Once the issue was no longer seizing power but assuring the continuation of a revolutionary regime, however, the Delegation worked for greater coordination among all Communard groups, "from the most moderate to the most advanced."[9] During the Commune the Delegation in some ways returned to the tactics that the Republican Central Committee, which had been formed to aid the Government of National Defense in the fight against the national enemy, had used in the first half of the siege. Only when militants became convinced of the government's incompetence and defeatism did the Republican Central Committee, under the name Delegation of the Twenty Arrondissements, begin the evolution toward open opposition that resulted in the revolutionary Commune. After March 18 the Delegation reverted to the strategy of supporting a government with which it fundamentally agreed.

This change in the Delegation's approach was partially due to the fact that its personnel during the Commune was somewhat different from the group that had created the Revolutionary Socialist Party. Just over 40 per-

---

7. While negotiating with the Central Committee of the National Guard, Jean-Baptiste Millière, a deputy of Paris who later rallied to the Commune, warned of a repetition of the June Days; Serman, *La Commune de Paris,* 229. Armand Levy, an active participant in the revolutionary socialist movement, wrote an article calling for elections that demanded, "above all, no more June Days"; *Le Patriote,* March 20. He called somewhat contradictorily for "prudence, firmness, and conciliation." Rougerie has stressed the insurrection leaders' desire to preserve unanimity in the city; *Paris Libre,* 112.

8. *Le Cri du Peuple,* March 21 and 23; *Le Patriote,* March 23. The Delegation and the Union Républicaine had attempted to cooperate in the February elections, but the latter refused to endorse Blanquist candidates.

9. From a Delegation statement in *Le Cri du Peuple,* May 18.

cent[10] of the men known to attend Delegation meetings after March 18 had never been recorded as part of the Delegation or Central Committee during the siege or armistice. The new members of the Delegation were probably members of local vigilance committees during the siege and armistice, though the records of those committees are extremely fragmentary, so the transformation in personnel should not be overstated. Indeed, 38 percent had signed the Red Poster of January 6, an indication of continuity in the movement. Nonetheless, at the "center," that is, the Delegation, there was unarguably a renewal of personnel. Most of the former leadership of the Delegation was busy with responsibilities in the National Guard, the Communal Council (elected March 26), or the municipalities, leaving the field free for new leadership. For example, five of the most influential leaders in the Republican Central Committee and Delegation from September to March—Arnaud, Demay, Duval, Oudet, and Pindy— are not known to have participated in either group during the Commune. All except Demay held important posts after March 18, and all including Demay were elected to the Commune as candidates of the Delegation; they had made the long-projected transition from revolutionary opposition to governing. Of course a number of former leaders maintained their activity in the Delegation (especially in the first weeks of the Commune), including Beslay, Chatelain, Dumont, Levy, Martin, Napias-Piquet, Vaillant, and Vallès. Even with the addition of thirty-five new members, some of whom had a certain importance in the left, the Delegation lost many of its influential leaders as they took up administrative or military responsibilities. The Blanquists in particular, so important in the Delegation since the later part of the siege, turned their activity onto other paths during the Commune. Ferré and Vaillant are the only major Blanquists recorded as participating in the Delegation during the Commune, and their activity appears to have been infrequent.

Once the Delegation had agreed on an electoral strategy it became essential to mobilize the votes of moderate and radical republicans, the great majority of the Parisian electorate. The Delegation reverted to a minimum program, reversing the maximalism of the armistice. A large measure of the more moderate tone of the Delegation's pronouncements

---

10. That is, thirty-seven of ninety. These figures are based mainly on the index in Dautry and Scheler, *Le Comité Central,* which lists the dates the members were active, with the addition of some names they missed. After the first week there are very few sources for the names of Delegation members.

may be traced to the influence of Jules Vallès.[11] A romantic revolutionary, Vallès was concerned above all with avoiding civil war. Though he was an active member of the Republican Central Committee and later of the revolutionary Commune, he never ascribed to the International, preferring an independent socialist position. He and Pierre Denis, likewise a socialist of Proudhonian tendencies, appear to have been the predominant voices in the manifestos that the Delegation published before the elections of March 26, and the new strategy of inclusion was well suited to their sympathies. Vallès gave himself much of the credit for the conciliatory tone of a proposition voted in at the March 21 meeting with representatives of the Union Républicane Centrale. It confirmed the Delegation's support for the National Guard but requested that, "in the interest of political conciliation with all democratic forces," its arrondissement committees do all they can to encourage the mayors and deputies of Paris to agree to elections. In keeping with the moderate tone, the Delegation's statement said elections were for "the free municipality" and for "the communal administration," with no hint of the revolutionary Commune or of the Commune of 1792 that had been such a large part of revolutionary discourse during the siege.[12] This moderation reflected the wishes of the majority of the Delegation, for while the minutes of its meeting of March 23 reveal that the battle of tactics was still being waged by part of the membership, most preferred an electoral strategy. When Ambroise Lyaz, a member of the vigilance committee of the 12th arrondissement, announced that the committee had taken possession of the mairie, the debate about strategy reopened. "Elections are necessary. Don't change our path. The population would not follow us," Auguste Briosne said. He continued, "The reaction will probably abstain. It is thus necessary to try to get out the vote in order to augment our moral force."[13] Like that of the 21st, the statement issued by the meeting of the 23d very prudently defined exactly what the elections were about. It rallied support through a studied ambiguity, evoking "the movement begun on March 18" and "the work so courageously undertaken" by the National Guard.

This statement was presented as being by the Comité Central des Vingt Arrondissements, a return to a common name used for the Republican

---

11. See Roger Bellet, *Jules Vallès* (Paris: Fayard, 1995).

12. The meeting sent ten delegates to notify the Central Committee of the National Guard of its decisions, which were voted "unanimously, less two votes," probably two members who sought more radical measures; *Le Cri du Peuple,* March 23.

13. The minutes are in Dautry and Scheler, *Le Comité Central,* 226.

Central Committee until the formation of the Delegation of the Twenty
Arrondissements on January 1. Over the course of the Commune the two
names were used interchangeably. At times, notices for meetings read "the
Central Committee and the Delegation of the Twenty Arrondissements,"
as if the two names referred to different organizations.[14] Delegation is the
more common of the two names in the first half of the Commune, but in
late April the balance shifts in favor of the title Comité Central des Vingt
Arrondissements. The fluidity of name is another indication of evolution
within the movement. Since Paris was under a revolutionary government,
the Delegation no longer considered itself an alternative government
drawn from the clubs and committees of the city, which had been the original reason the Republican Central Committee changed its name to Delegation of the Twenty Arrondissements.[15] It is most likely that both the old
name and the new one were used during the Commune to encourage all
militants of the revolutionary club and committee movement of the siege
to attend the meetings, not just those that knew the organization as the
revolutionary Commune. The use of the two titles is another aspect of
increased moderation in the Delegation, as it opened up the organization
to militants who might have dropped out during the radicalization of the
later siege and armistice.[16]

There was an apparent contradiction in the Delegation's activity in late
March, highlighted by Lyaz's announcement on March 23 that the committee of the 12th arrondissement had seized the mairie. While the Delegation was calling for elections and using moderate language designed to
rally all of Paris to vote, some of the clubs and committees associated with
the revolutionary socialist movement continued to occupy mairies. These
two strategies were complementary, however, as it was necessary to have
control of the electoral lists in the mairies in order to hold elections. Revolutionary socialist militants or whole committees had assaulted nine

14. One also finds the more explicable designations "the Delegation of the Twenty
Arrondissements (former Central Committee)" and "the former Central Committee and the
Delegation of the Twenty Arrondissements"; *Le Cri du Peuple,* March 21; *La Sociale,* April
14 and 24; *Le National de 69,* May 7.

15. Recall that in late February the Delegation generally added the word *communale* to its
name, reaffirming its pretension to being a governing body. Napias-Piquet, who favored a
revolutionary strategy, used this title as late as the meeting of March 21; Dautry and Scheler,
Le Comité Central, 219.

16. Indeed, seven of the ninety men in the Delegation during the Commune are known to
have been active in the Committee Central des Vingt Arrondissements only in the period
before October, though it cannot be known whether they had left the movement because they
objected to its radicalization in the later siege.

mairies on the day of March 18,[17] and in the following week they occupied five more. Their efforts suggest a coordinated strategy. Each case is somewhat different, but they all demonstrate the strength of local popular organizations. The mairie of the 8th arrondissement, for example, was invaded by Jules Allix and other vigilance committee members on March 20. Some members of a local group called the Union Républicaine du 8e Arrondissement (which was not associated with the radical republican Union Républicaine Centrale) merged with the vigilance committee either shortly before or after the invasion of the mairie. The occupiers asked the mayor to help organize elections for the Communal Council and forced him to resign when he refused. From March 20th onward the vigilance committee helped administer the municipality.[18] In the 10th arrondissement several delegates from the Central Committee of the National Guard presented themselves at the mairie on March 20 to prepare the elections, but they were turned away. On the next day the mairie was invaded, and one of the four leaders involved was Frederic Force, a member of the vigilance committee; the identity of the others is not known. After the occupation of the mairie the mayor and one of the adjoints retired, but the second vice-mayor, André Murat, a member of the AIT, remained until April 1, when he resigned to take up a post at the Mint. Murat was also a member of the vigilance committee, formed in early September.[19]

The mairie of the 6th was temporarily occupied on both March 18 and 20 by Tony Moilin, a member of the Association Républicaine du 6e Arrondissement, which functioned as the local vigilance committee. It was also a local section of the International and directed the Club de l'École de Médecine. Moilin was forced to evacuate the mairie both times, under pressure from guardsmen loyal to the elected mayor, but by March 22 it

17. The arrondissements of the nine mairies were the 5th (Allemane, Régère, and the vigilance committee), 6th (Moilin), 7th (Urbain), 13th (Duval and the Club Démocratique Socialiste), 14th (Henri and the Club Maison-Dieu), 15th (Faltot), 18th (Ferré and the Club de la Révolution), 19th (the vigilance committee, salle Marseillaise), and 20th (Eudes).

18. Jean Trohel, a member of the vigilance committee, signed one of the Delegation's manifestos, indicating that this committee coordinated with the larger Parisian movement. According to Mayor Denormandie, the committee was supported by about four hundred guardsmen from outside the arrondissement; *L'Enquête Parlementaire sur l'Insurrection du Dix-Huit mars,* 337; AHG: 9e conseil 687, dossier Trohel; AHG: 3e conseil 901, dossier Piquet. Allix was mentally unstable, "believing himself to be a supernatural power," according to a report in his dossier; AHG: 3e conseil 548.

19. Force remained at the mairie until May 14, when he resigned after being accused of stealing public funds. *L'Enquête Parlementaire sur l'Insurrection du Dix-Huit mars,* 354; Maitron, *DBMOF,* 6:63, 8:22; Wolfe, "The Origins of the Paris Commune," 86.

was back in the hands of revolutionaries, this time with Edmond Goupil of the Association Républicaine as provisional mayor.[20] Goupil was elected to the Commune on March 26, and in early April Moilin was again called "provisional mayor" in a document from the mairie.[21] Like that of the 6th, the mairie of the 7th arrondissement was temporarily occupied on March 18, in this case by Raoul Urbain and François Parisel, both members of the Club Républicaine Socialiste du 7e Arrondissement, popularly known as the Club Pré-aux-Clercs, which was directed by the vigilance committee of the arrondissement. Evidently they had not retained possession of the mairie, as according to the vice-mayor on March 24 they and Jules Endrès, another member of the Club Pré-aux-Clercs, entered the mairie with authority from the Central Committee of the National Guard, to prepare for elections. The vice-mayor refused to cooperate and retired. Parisel and Urbain were elected to the Communal Council on March 26, and Urbain appointed a municipal commission drawn mainly from the vigilance committee of the arrondissement; five of its ten members are known to have been leaders and orators of the Club Pré-aux-Clercs.[22] Finally, the mairie in the 12th arrondissement was held after March 23 by a provisional municipality composed of Phillipe Fenouillas as mayor and Lyaz and Louis Magot as adjoints. Jules Audoyneau, known as "Little Robespierre," had also taken part in the occupation of the mairie. All four were members of either the Club des Terres Fortes, which was the public meeting associated with the local vigilance committee of the 12th, or the Club Eloi, which replaced the Club des Terres Fortes in May.[23]

No mairies were occupied after March 24, because the Central Committee of the National Guard and the mayors and deputies decided to cooperate in holding elections. The agreement called for the mayors who had been forced out to be "reintegrated" into their mairies, but the Central Committee of the National Guard simply published a revised version of the agreement that made no provision for allowing the mayors back into

20. Moilin also signed the Red Poster of January 6. Goupil had invaded the mairie on October 31. *Le Patriote,* March 21; Nast, "Les Mairies de Paris et le Comité Central," 1052; Maitron, *DBMOF,* 7:377.

21. *L'Enquête Parlementaire sur l'Insurrection du Dix-Huit mars,* 332; AHG: 5e conseil 590.

22. Urbain had founded the club, and both he and Parisel had signed the Red Poster of January 6. Maitron, *DBMOF,* 5:460, 8:92, 9:247; *L'Enquête Parlementaire sur l'Insurrection du Dix-Huit mars,* 347. AHG: Ly 27 lists the members of the municipal commission, while AHG: Ly 22 contains a list of speakers at a Club Pré-aux-Clercs meeting on February 4.

23. AHG: 4e conseil 100, dossier Magot; *Les Murailles Politiques,* 2:67; Maitron, *DBMOF,* 4:153.

the mairies from which they had been excluded. Thus the situation of the mairies when the elections were held on March 26 may be divided into three categories. In thirteen arrondissements the elections were supervised by arrondissement vigilance committees.[24] In five others the mayors elected in November maintained their place and cooperated with the Central Committee of the National Guard in holding elections.[25] Finally, two arrondissements (the 4th and 9th) were held by National Guard committees with little apparent association with other popular organizations. The role of the vigilance committees in occupying mairies and administering the vote has not been recognized by scholars, which has led to an underestimation of the place of the Delegation of the Twenty Arrondissements and its vigilance committees in the early days of the Commune. Jean Dautry and Lucien Scheler created the standard interpretation of the Delegation during the Commune when they argued that it was eclipsed by events, "passed up by larger history, but where that larger history was sketched out."[26] Years after the Commune, Vaillant suggested that the Delegation had been weakened by the confusing press of events in February and March.[27] To the contrary, it appears that Dautry and Scheler as well as Vaillant allowed the later relative diminution of the Delegation in April and May to color their assessments. In the first week of the insurrection, when at moments the continued control of the Central Committee of the National Guard over the Hôtel de ville was in doubt, and when the mayors of the city were determined to avoid elections, the Delegation and its arrondissement vigilance committees were vital in carrying out and strengthening the insurrection both in the mairies and at the Hôtel de ville.

The Delegation and the arrondissement vigilance committees, the only

---

24. The thirteen arrondissements were the 5th, 6th, 7th, 8th, 10th, 12th, 13th, 14th, 15th, 17th, 18th, 19th, and 20th.

25. Of these arrondissements the 1st, 2d, 3d, and 16th were predominantly bourgeois areas, where the moderate republican mayors had the support of most of the local guard units. Indeed, there had nearly been a bloody confrontation when the Central Committee of the National Guard had attempted to seize the mairie of the 2d. The 11th was administered by radical, and even socialist, officials who willingly cooperated with the Central Committee of the National Guard, even though there were some hesitations on this score immediately after March 18.

26. Dautry and Scheler, *Le Comité Central,* 258. "No more than a survival," according to Noel, "it no longer corresponded to the movement"; *Dictionnaire de la Commune* (Paris: Payot, 1971), 89.

27. *Enquête sur la Commune,* a special edition of *La Revue blanche* in 1900, quoted in Dautry and Scheler, *Le Comité Central,* 251. Lissagaray, *Histoire de la Commune,* 68, notes that the Delegation just before and during this time was "reduced to a dozen members," which is not true but does express the sense that the Delegation had dwindled.

organized citywide political movement, also played an absolutely dominant role in electing the Communal Council and thus in shaping the revolution. Due to the resistance of the mayors and deputies the date of the
elections was changed three times. Originally scheduled for March 22, the
final date of March 26 was chosen only two days earlier, when the mayors
and deputies agreed to cooperate. In this confused and brief electoral
period the experience and prior organization of the central Delegation and
the local vigilance committees was fundamental to the electoral victory of
revolutionaries. The revolutionary socialist left was the only element of the
political spectrum with an organized base of militants in virtually every
arrondissement. Although moderate and radical republicans won many
seats on the Communal Council, the Delegation, whose candidates polled
only about 15 percent of the electorate in February, fielded a list that
swept many arrondissements and elected candidates to the Communal
Council from sixteen of the twenty Parisian arrondissements. In addition
to the superior organization of the Delegation, whose vigilance committees served as ready-made electoral meetings, the radicalization of Paris
under the perceived provocations of the National Assembly helps explain
this result. A final factor of great importance was the electoral cooperation
of National Guard organizations and club and committee movement. At
the center, the Delegation and the Central Committee of the National
Guard worked in partnership, and at the arrondissement level the vigilance committees and local guard structures often fused their lists, with the
combined list in some arrondissements garnering 80 percent of the votes
cast. The electoral partnership between the club and guard movements at
these two levels, at the center and in the arrondissements, guaranteed the
victory of revolutionaries.[28]

The Central Committee of the National Guard relied on arrondissement vigilance committees to prepare and carry out the elections. A mes-
sage on Hôtel de ville letterhead from François Josselin, a member of the
Central Committee of the National Guard, to the Ministry of the Interior,
where Arnaud, a leader of the Delegation, was second in command, outlined the role projected for the vigilance committees. "Have each
arrondissement vigilance committee give Citizen Josselin the situation of
their mairie," Josselin wrote, "that is, if the municipality is hostile or
friendly, if the electoral lists are under their control, if they have urns, the

---

28. The International, however, was in disarray. It neither participated in the Delegation's campaign efforts nor presented its own list, leaving the Delegation as the dominant
voice of the revolutionary left. See Rougerie, "L'AIT et le mouvement ouvrier," 56.

number of their precincts."[29] Josselin, himself a member of the vigilance committee of the 18th arrondissement, added that the Hôtel de ville would provide two thousand francs to defray the costs incurred by the committees. In the 17th arrondissement, for example, the voting was organized by the Club de la rue Levis, which as the Republican Socialist Society had elected members to the revolutionary Commune of January 1. On the night of March 22 the club members invaded the mairie with the authorization of the Central Committee of the National Guard, to prepare the elections. Alerted by telegraph that the elections were postponed, the club evacuated the mairie, but two days later it received the two thousand francs promised by Josselin. When the elections were held on the 26th club members were presidents of all the precincts, even though the elected municipality was still technically in control of the mairie.[30]

Continuing the practical fusion of the club and guard movements evident in February, the Delegation, local vigilance committees, the International, and members of the Federation of the National Guard worked closely together on electoral strategy. On March 21 the Delegation and the Central Committee of the National Guard agreed to present a joint slate of candidates, although the Central Committee later decided not to present any recommendations.[31] On the evening of March 21 a general assembly of members of arrondissement vigilance committees was held in conjunction with the Delegation of the Twenty Arrondissements and was attended by several delegates of the guard Federation and the International. The participation of delegates from the Central Committee of the National Guard, many of whose members were associated with the revolutionary socialist movement, and of the International again reveals the role of the Delegation as a center for uniting the left. When combined with the note by Josselin about the preparations for elections being carried out

---

29. Archives du Département de la Seine (ADS): VD^{6}2347 5. Historians, including Rougerie in "Les Elections du 26 mars à la Commune de Paris" (Diplôme d'Études Supérieurs, n.d.), have not recognized the role of vigilance committees in the elections.

30. The mayor was Malon, who from fear of civil war had hesitated before endorsing the elections. ADS: VD^{6}2347 5 and VD^{6}2452 3; Maurice Foulon, *Eugène Varlin, relieur et membre de la Commune* (Clermont-Ferrand: Éditions Mont-Louis, 1934), 209.

31. In the same meeting Jean Bedouch presented the list of candidates adopted by the Legion Council of the 10th arrondissement, and all five names are found on a draft list of Delegation candidates drawn up by the meeting. The draft list also included five candidates that Laurent, an official at the Ministry of the Interior and active clubiste, asked Viard to support before the Delegation as well as before the Central Committee of the National Guard at the Hôtel de ville; Viard was a member of both groups. *Le Journal Officiel*, April 24; Dautry and Scheler, *Le Comité Central*, 218, 220, 240.

by vigilance committees, this suggests far greater coordination between the guard Federation and the Delegation than has previously been recognized. The Federation, the Delegation, and the arrondissement vigilance committees shared many members in common and were all working toward the same end: to complete the revolution begun on March 18, through elections facilitated by revolutionary seizures of the mairies.

The great majority of the candidates on the Delegation's list were long-time militants of the club and committee movement.[32] Unlike February, there were no "grand names." The only element that might be considered foreign to the revolutionary socialist movement was the inclusion of some members of the Central Committee of the National Guard, though some of these (Lacord, Maljournal, Arnaud, Moreau) were also active in vigilance committees or the Delegation. Although few known Blanquists were connected with the Delegation during the Commune, many Blanquists may be found on the list, including Blanqui himself, Ferré, Tridon, Brideau, and Rigault. Their presence on the list suggests that the basic elements of the revolutionary socialist coalition were still intact: militants of the International were in the forefront, Blanquists maintained an important secondary role, and independents such as Lefrançais and Vésinier held third position.

That the electoral list was presented by the "Committee of the Twenty Arrondissements" on the basis of lists "furnished by the various electoral committees" indicates coordination between the center and the arrondissements. When comparing this list with those presented by local clubs and committees, two patterns emerge: in some arrondissements the Delegation and local lists are essentially the same, but in others there are significant differences. In both cases, though, there is evidence that the local guard structures were working in conjunction with local clubs and committees, indicating that even while coordination between the Delegation and the arrondissement vigilance committees was not perfect, in many areas of the city the guard and club movements were well coordinated at the base—that is, the arrondissements. For example, in the 4th arrondissement delegates of eleven battalions presented a list of candidates: Amouroux, Arnould, Clemence, Gérardin, and Lefrançais. Only Gérardin was described as a member of the "Republican Committee of the Twenty Arrondissements," and the poster makes no mention of the arrondissement vigilance committee. Yet in fact all but Arnould (a radical republican journalist and vice-mayor at the mairie before the November elections) are known to have been members of the vigilance committee, and two of the twenty-seven people who signed the poster as battalion delegates were on the vigilance committee as well. Gérardin and Lefrançais participated in the Delegation in the first days of the insurrection, and this is the exact list presented by the Delegation on March 26. Guard, vigilance committee, and Delegation support combined in this case on a victorious slate, winning all five seats with about 60 percent of the votes cast. In the bourgeois 4th arrondissement this was a particularly impressive victory against a united moderate republican slate headed by Louis Blanc, who had been elected to the National Assembly in February at the top of the Parisian list. Here, as with most of the results of March 26, a radicalization of the electorate is evident.[33]

Another example of guard and committee cooperation occurred in the 8th arrondissement, where the Union Républicaine and the vigilance committee combined in running the mairie. On March 22 delegates of the National Guard and of the Union Républicaine met at the Triat Gymnasium to support the candidacies of Allix, Arnould, Vaillant, and Esquiros. Unlike the 4th arrondissement, however, the Delegation supported a different list, composed of Rigault, Bestetti, Denis, and Moreau; none of these candidates appears to have been connected with the arrondissement. In this instance the list of the Triat Gymnasium was victorious.[34] Similar instances of local guard and committee fusion may be found in the 10th, 11th, 12th, and 18th arrondissements and perhaps in others for which information is unavailable. In all these instances of guard and committee cooperation the combined list was overwhelmingly victorious, the candidate with the lowest vote gaining about 75 percent of the total vote in the 10th, 80 percent in the 11th, 78 percent in the 12th, and 76 percent in the 18th.

The cooperation between the local clubs and committees and the guard helps explain the victory of revolutionaries in the elections, but the relationship between the central Delegation and the arrondissement vigilance committees was more problematic. In a number of arrondissements the

---

33. *Les Murailles Politiques,* 3:105; AHG: Ly 27. Choury, who examines the elections in the first four arrondissements, does not mention the role of the vigilance committee; *La Commune au coeur de Paris,* 226.

34. AHG: 3e conseil 901, dossier Piquet. At a later Triat meeting Trohel, of the vigilance committee and the Delegation, nominated Raoul Rigault, who was elected in place of Esquiros; see Trohel's letter published in Paul Fontoulieu, *Les Églises de Paris sous la Commune* (Paris: Dentu, 1873), 284.

Delegation and its local committees differed on choices for candidates, although it is difficult to be precise given the incomplete evidence.[35] In the 6th arrondissement the Delegation list and that of the Club de l'École de Médecine agreed on only two of five candidacies. The Central Comité Électoral Républicain, Démocrate, Socialist du XIe Arrondissement, several of whose members participated in Delegation initiatives in the first weeks of the Commune, had four of six candidatures in common with the Delegation. None of the candidates of the Delegation for the 12th were on the list presented by the local National Guard and the vigilance committee. In the 18th the list of the vigilance committee and that of the Delegation agreed on all but one of the seven candidacies, where a last minute change was made by the local committee.[36] Compared with the elections of February, however, the center and periphery of the club and committee movement were far better coordinated in the Communal elections, indicating the success of the reorganization associated with the Revolutionary Socialist Party.

The list of arrondissement clubs and committees that were able to organize effective electoral meetings given the brevity and confusion of the campaign is testimony to the importance of a preexisting, structured, revolutionary movement. A rapid review of revolutionary socialist electoral activity is enlightening, for it demonstrates the strength of the movement in the first weeks of the Commune. In the 3d arrondissement the salle Molière, home of the vigilance committee of the 3d, held nightly public meetings beginning by at least March 23, under the agenda "Our municipal elections." As noted, the vigilance committee in the 4th arrondissement was evidently fundamental in the National Guard meetings in which the victorious slate was selected. The Comité Démocratique Socialiste du 5e coordinated public meetings in three locales, the salle d'Arras, the École de Droit, and the salle Vieux Chêne (rue Mouffetard).[37] The Club de l'École de Médecine in the 6th had stopped meeting due to General Vinoy's decree of March 11 prohibiting clubs, but beginning on March 21 it reopened for nightly meetings sponsored by the Association Républicaine du 6e. Electoral meetings were held throughout the week after March 18 by the Club Pré-aux-Clercs, which was associated with the vigi-

---

35. Evidence for the following candidate support ratios comes from the electoral posters in *Les Murailles Politiques*, vol. 3.

36. Wolfe, "The Parisian *Club de la Revolution*," 111. Dupas was dropped in favor of Grousset.

37. *La Commune*, March 24; *Les Murailles Politiques*, 3:105, 80.

lance committee of the 7th arrondissement. The Triat Gymnasium was the scene of meetings sponsored by the Comité Independente de l'Union Républicaine du 8e, which fused with the vigilance committee and sent delegates to the central Delegation. In the 10th the Club des Montagnards, Club Républicaine, and the Legion Council of the local National Guard formed a joint list that was adopted by the Delegation.[38] The vigilance committee of the 12th held meetings at the salle Terres-Fortes.[39] An "electoral committee" held public meetings in the 14th; it was probably the vigilance committee, because Claude Sermet, a member of the vigilance committee, signed a notice as a member of the bureau, and because the three persons elected from the 14th all had ties to the vigilance committee, even if only two are known to have been members. In the 17th arrondissement the salle Levis had several meetings with over three thousand participants each. The list adopted, which won all five seats, was composed exclusively of vigilance committee members who were also members of the AIT, but it was different from that of the Delegation.[40]

The success of the coordination among revolutionaries—between, on the one hand, the guard and the vigilance committees and, on the other, the vigilance committees and the central Delegation—may be measured by the success of Delegation candidates in the elections. About two-thirds of the candidates presented by the Delegation were elected.[41] Taking into account multiple elections, resignations, and the deaths of two members in battle, the definitive Communal Council after the April 16 supplementary elections counted seventy-eight members.[42] Of these, fifty are known to have been members of arrondissement vigilance committees, a proportion of 64 percent, the highest proportion of any identifiable social or political

38. *Le Mot d'Ordre,* March 21; *Le Patriote,* March 22; AHG: 3e conseil 901, dossier Piquet; Wolfe, "The Origins of the Paris Commune," 217.

39. The meetings were held under the name Club du faubourg Saint Antoine. Gilles Ragache, "Les clubs de la Commune," *Le Peuple Francais: Revue d'Histoire Populaire* 2 (April–June, 1971), 7.

40. AHG: Ly 22; Wolfe, "The Origins of the Paris Commune," 397; *Les Murailles Politiques,* 3:116; Paul Martine, *Souvenirs d'un insurgé, la Commune, 1871* (Paris: Perrin, 1971), 64.

41. Or fifty-four out of eighty-seven candidates; this includes candidates on the Delegation list that were successful in an arrondissement other than that for which they were presented. For a similar calculation see Dautry and Scheler, *Le Comité Central,* 242.

42. Rougerie, "L'AIT et le mouvement ouvrier," 59; Serman, *La Commune de Paris,* 276, counts 79, but included Blanchet, who was forced to resign because he had been a police informer under the Empire.

group in the Council.[43] Eighty-five percent (sixty-six of seventy-eight) of the people serving on the Communal Council were members of vigilance committees or had been supported by either a local vigilance committee or the central Delegation. Members of the Delegation and its vigilance committees were elected all across Paris, not just in certain revolutionary areas (see table 1 for a list of vigilance committee members who were members of the Commune, listed according to the arrondissement that elected them).

TABLE 1.   Vigilance Committee Members Elected to the Commune

Arrondissement	Proportion in Vigilance Committees	Vigilance Committee Members
1	2/3	Pillot, Vésinier
2	4/4	Pottier, Durand, Serrailler, Johannard
3	3/4	Demay, Arnaud, Pindy
4	4/5	Lefrançais, Clémence, Gérardin Amouroux
5	3/4	Régère, Tridon, Ledroit
6	2/3	Beslay, Varlin
7	3/4	Parisel, Urbain, Sicard
8	2/3	Allix, Vaillant
9	0/0	No representation in the Commune
10	4/6	Henry, Champy, Babick, Rastoul
11	2/7	Avrial, Verdure
12	0/3	No representation in the Commune
13	2/3	Meilliet, Chardon
14	2/3	Martelet, Billioray
15	3/3	Clément, Langevin, Vallès
16	1/1	Longuet
17	4/5	Clément, Gérardin, Malon, Chalain
18	4/8	Theisz, Dereure, Ferré, Clément
19	3/5	Oudet, Ostyn, Puget
20	2/4	Ranvier, Viard
Total 50/78, or 64%		

43. Wolfe identified most of these, but his numbers have been corrected to eliminate cases of multiple election, "The Origins of the Paris Commune," 397. Classifying the members of the Commune is a cottage industry among historians. Serman appears the best informed and most judicious; *La Commune de Paris,* 276. The AIT accounted for 43 percent of the Communal Council, and most members of the Council were also on vigilance committees.

Members of vigilance committees made up half or more of the Communal delegation in seventeen of the nineteen arrondissements represented in the Communal Council.[44]

There was fundamental continuity in the ideals and the personnel of the movement from the revolutionary Commune of January, through the Revolutionary Socialist Party, to the Communal Council. Just over one-third of the Communal Council had been members of the revolutionary Commune of January 1; two-thirds of the revolutionary socialist candidates in the February elections were elected to the Commune.[45] These figures underscore the role the central Delegation and the local vigilance committees played in creating the organizational framework for a successful insurrection, as well as their role as schools of revolutionary experience. The Communal Council was not delegated directly from the clubs and committees of the capital, as the revolutionary Commune of January 1 had been, but its members were in great majority militants of those clubs and committees. While the Communal Council was riven with personal and political divisions, its members also in large measure shared a common background of principles and experience, which helps account for the considerable legislation that resulted from a body that lasted fewer than sixty days. Certainly the diversity of opinions among Jacobins, Blanquists, socialists, and independents must not be underestimated; it led ultimately to a schism in the Communal Council. Yet the shared revolutionary vision of most members of the Communal Council is demonstrated by a host of decrees—many of which would not be passed for decades, if at all, under succeeding regimes—such as the separation of church and state; obligatory, secular education; eliminating the distinction between official and common-law marriages; and supporting worker associations of production. That the meetings during the Second Empire and those of the clubs of the seige and armistice shared the experience of radical opposition explains to a great extent the shape and nature of the government established after so much anticipation and preparation.

---

44. The two exceptions were the 11th and 12th. In the 11th the slate presented by the local National Guard won most of the seats, but most were also supported by the Delegation even though they were not members of the vigilance committee. In the 12th the vigilance committee slate won the elections of March 26, but most of those elected either resigned or opted to represent other districts that had also elected them. In the supplementary elections of April 16 the list presented by the local guard was victorious.

45. Two others elected to the Commune signed: Duval, who was killed in combat; and Fruneau, who resigned. Wolfe has made nearly the same calculation; "The Origins of the Paris Commune," 380.

The vigilance committee movement provided a large majority of the members of the Communal Council, and the same is true in the second level of administration, that of the arrondissement mairies. In administering portions of the city the vigilance committees fulfilled the political goals of the revolutionary Commune of January 1 and the Declaration of Principles of February 19. The mairies of Paris during the Commune have never been the subject of a general study, and this treatment cannot hope to meet that need. Yet any consideration of vigilance committees during the Commune leads inevitably to the mairies, where in many cases militants of vigilance committees, and often entire committees, were responsible for administering the revolution at the base. Consideration of the members of vigilance committees who served on the municipal commissions helps reveal another aspect of the way consolidation of the revolution depended on revolutionary socialist militants of clubs and committees, not only at the Hôtel de ville, but in the arrondissements. The Communal Council decided on March 30 that, with the aid of appointed municipal commissions, its members would administer the arrondissements that they represented.[46] When choosing a municipal commission it was only natural that many members of the Commune should rely on the vigilance committees, because at least two-thirds of the members had been part of those committees.

Vigilance committees administered seven arrondissements because the committee had directly seized power either before March 18, the day of the insurrection, or just afterward.[47] Two other arrondissements, the 1st and 16th, were run by municipal commissions appointed by the Commune because the moderate republicans that had been elected to the Commune on March 26 resigned. In both cases the Commune chose members of vigilance committees to be on the commissions. These commissions stayed at the mairies even after the supplementary elections of April 16. In addition, the mairie in the 9th arrondissement was run by the radical republican Jacques Bayeaux-Dumesnil until early May, when he was replaced by the local vigilance committee. In nearly all these cases people not associated with vigilance committees also served, but the local vigilance committee appears to have played the preponderant role. In ten mairies, then, mem-

---

46. The Council was motivated in part by a desire to avoid "dualism" of power, in which elected members of the Council could face competition or opposition from elected arrondissement officials; *Les Procès-Verbaux de la Commune,* 1:71–74.

47. These seven arrondissements were the 5th, 7th, 8th, 14th, 17th, 18th, and 19th.

bers of vigilance committees were the dominant force in the municipal commissions that administered the arrondissements during the Commune.[48] In all but two of the remaining arrondissements half or more of the elected members of the Communal Council were members of vigilance committees, meaning that eighteen of Paris's twenty arrondissements were administered or represented in majority by members of vigilance committees. The complexity of relations between guard organizations, vigilance committees, and sections of the International at the level of the arrondissement makes categorical classification of the municipal councils difficult, however, as individuals could be active members of two or all three. Rougerie has suggested, for example, that members of the International were the predominant force in eight mairies, three of which are described here as being primarily composed of vigilance committee members.[49] The two descriptions are compatible, however, as the AIT was of course the foundation of the vigilance committee movement and remained influential in a number of the local vigilance committees. The designation *vigilance committee* for these municipal commissions is based on contemporary usage, as no member of the municipal commissions was designated as a member of the International in the surviving records of the mairies or in other official contemporary sources, while there are numerous references to vigilance committees in those documents. The members of the International in these and other arrondissements were working through the vigilance committee structure—with its links to clubs and public meetings, and with its center in the Delegation—rather than through worker corporations, the local sections of the International, or the Federal Council. This was a result of the framework for revolutionary action through popular organizations that was created during the siege and armistice.

Vigilance committees functioned as reserves of revolutionary personnel for the administration of Paris's arrondissements. Members of the vigi-

---

48. These mairies were in the 1st, 5th, 7th, 8th, 9th, 14th, 16th, 17th, 18th, and 19th arrondissements. In the remaining mairies the municipal commissions appear to have been built around local guard units or sections of the International, although in most instances individual vigilance committee members also participated. In six other arrondissements (the 6th, 10th, 12th, 13th, 15th, and 20th) members of vigilance committees were instrumental in occupying the mairie but were not predominant in the municipal commissions that were subsequently formed. This categorization is based on evidence collected about the mairies by army prosecutors after the Commune (AHG: Ly 27) and individual *conseil de guerre* dossiers; Maitron's *DBMOF* was also indispensable for piecing together this fragmented history.

49. The eight mairies were in the 3d, 4th, 10th, 11th, 12th, 13th, 14th, and 17th arrondissements, while the three primarily composed of vigilance committee members were in the 4th, 14th, and 17th; Rougerie, "L'AIT et le mouvement ouvrier," 61.

lance committee of the 18th, which directed the Club de la Révolution, made up almost the entire municipal council in the district.[50] In the 7th, all four of the members of the Communal Council were members of the vigilance committee, and the municipal commission was drawn mainly from the Club Pré-aux-Clercs, which held the public meeting associated with the committee.[51] The Club Levis, the seat of the *committee révolutionnaire* in the 17th, after having invaded the mairie in order to hold elections on March 22, provided a majority of members of the municipal commission. Many of these were also members of the local section of the AIT, which was the core around which the vigilance committee had been formed during the siege.[52]

Reliance on vigilance committee personnel was especially apparent in four bourgeois arrondissements where vigilance committees administered despite the electoral weakness of the left in these areas. In the 8th arrondissement, complaints reached the Commune that Allix's unstable mental state was wreaking havoc in the administration. Vaillant and Rigault, who along with Allix were the local members of the Communal Council, seemingly did not spend much time at the mairie, being overburdened with duties elsewhere. Sometime in mid-April they appointed the vigilance committee to be their delegate at the mairie, but Allix refused to recognize the authority of the committee and had it thrown out of the mairie. A compromise was evidently reached, as the vigilance committee and Allix worked uneasily side by side until early May. It is unclear what broke this truce, but on May 9 the vigilance committee asked for and received permission from the Committee of Public Safety (created by the Commune in early May) to take over the administration of the arrondissement. Allix and several of his close associates were arrested on May 9 by members of the vigilance committee, but he was released the next day. He returned to the mairie, broke the seals that had been placed there by the vigilance committee, and tried to reestablish his control. Arrested again by the vigilance committee, he definitively retired from the mairie and the Communal Council.[53] The new administration quickly acted to make up for time lost under Allix's chaotic administration, prohibiting nuns from

50. Wolfe, "The Parisian *Club de la Révolution,*" 113.

51. AHG: Ly 27; C. Barral de Montaud, *Notes jounalières sur l'état de Paris durant la Commune* (Paris: Paul Dupont, 1871), 36.

52. AHG: Ly 27; Martine, *Souvenirs,* 52; V. D'Esboeufs, *Trahison et défection au sein de la Commune: Le Coin du voile* (Geneva: Blanchard, 1872), 21.

53. AHG: Ly 16; AHG: 3e conseil 548, dossier Allix; *Les Procès-Verbaux de la Commune,* 2:57, 344; Maitron, *DBMOF,* 4:109.

teaching in public schools, starting a census to expose men who refused to serve in the guard, and beginning the destruction of the Chapelle Expiatoire, which had been built in the memory of Louis XVI.[54]

Vigilance committees also functioned as reserves of revolutionary personnel in the 1st, 9th, and 16th arrondissements, where the moderate republicans elected to the Communal Council had resigned, leaving a power vacuum at the mairie.[55] In the 1st the Executive Commission of the Communal Council, most of whose members had participated in the vigilance committee movement or the Delegation, resorted to the simple expedient of asking the "committees of the arrondissement" to propose nominations for a municipal council until supplementary elections could be held. All seven of those chosen were members of the vigilance committee.[56] In the 16th arrondissement, P. E. Turpin, Napias-Piquet, and Charles Longuet, all members of vigilance committees in other parts of the city, had led the occupation of the mairie on April 2, although Turpin was the only one known to be connected to the local vigilance committee. At least four of the eight appointed to the municipal commission are known to have been part of the local vigilance committee or to have participated in other Delegation activities.[57]

The municipality of the 9th was appointed not by the Communal Council but by the radical republicans who had been elected to the Commune and then resigned. Their choice for acting mayor was Jacques Bayeux-Dumesnil, formerly a deputy under the Second Republic and more recently active in the Défenseurs de la République, a radical republican group. Bayeux-Dumesnil remained in charge of the mairie even after the supplementary elections of April 16, because the only candidate in the 9th

---

54. AHG: 3e conseil 901, dossier Piquet; AHG: Ly 27.

55. All the members for the 2d arrondissement also resigned, but Lioseau-Pinson, one of the adjoints elected in November, remained on until forced out after the April elections; AN: BB30 486.

56. *Le Vengeur,* April 4 and 5. Four of the seven had also signed the Red Poster of January 6. The two members of the Communal Council that signed the appointment of the seven were Lefrançais and Vaillant, both pillars of the vigilance committee movement.

57. The archives of the Prefecture of Police preserve some records of this mairie, which provide a window into the preoccupations of those in power at this little-known level of the Commune. One concern, for example, was to ensure that the municipal funerary administration gave "equality after death" to those killed in the service of the Commune. The four committee members were Turpin, J. H. Richard, Xavier Missol, and Napias-Piquet; APP: Ba 364-4; Maitron, *DBMOF,* 6:244, 9:244, 5:131. Longuet, who was on the vigilance committee of the 5th arrondissement and had the backing of the Delegation, was elected to represent the 16th in the April supplementary elections; the municipal commission remained unchanged.

who received enough votes to be seated on the Communal Council resigned. Alone of the twenty arrondissements, the 9th had no elected representatives during the Commune. As the struggle with Versailles continued and the revolution moved ineluctably onto more radical paths, however, the administration of Bayeux-Dumesnil no longer seemed sufficiently revolutionary. On April 29, at a time when many churches were being occupied by Communard clubs, he decreed that churches in the arrondissement should be evacuated by the National Guard and restored to religious services.[58] This decision was the final straw that prompted the vigilance committee of the arrondissement to replace him, although Bayeaux-Dumesnil and the committee had apparently never been on good terms. An employee at the mairie testified after the Commune that Bayeaux-Dumesnil was replaced because he hoped to reopen the churches, and that he "wanted to administer alone, and not permit the vigilance committee to involve itself in the affairs of the mairie."[59]

The story of how the vigilance committee was able to replace Bayeux-Dumesnil in the 9th arrondissement is an illuminating example of how such committees helped to carry out and consolidate the revolution in the arrondissements. This story also demonstrates that political struggles continued even within the Communal movement, as Communards of various hues vied to shape the revolution. The vigilance committee of the ninth was only loosely associated with the Delegation of the Twenty Arrondissements; it had stopped routinely sending delegates to the Republican Central Committee after the demonstration of October 8, which had split republican ranks over whether to support or replace the Government of National Defense.[60] The president of the committee was Jean-Baptiste Millière, a socialist and journalist whose credentials, like those of Bayeux-

---

58. Fontoulieu, *Les Églises,* 269. This highly biased source is crucial for the history of clubs in churches during the Commune, and I have verified its information whenever possible. In this case Bayeux-Dumesnil's May 4 order that this decision be executed is in AHG: 20e conseil 56, dossier Louis Guerin.

59. AHG: 20e conseil 643, dossier Bayeux-Dumesnil.

60. One of its members, Martial Portalier, did sign the Red Poster of January 6 and participated in Delegation meetings during the Commune. The committee also protested against the Delegation's choices of candidates in the April elections, a sign that it considered itself part of the Delegation, even if it disagreed with its decisions; Firmin Maillard, *Affiches, professions de foi, documents officiels, clubs et comités pendant la Commune* (Paris: Dentu, 1871), 204. For the February elections the committee sponsored its own list, which had few names in common with the revolutionary socialist list, being composed mainly of republican notables, although Blanqui and some workers of the AIT were included; *Les Murailles Politiques,* 1:878.

Dumesnil, dated to 1848. Millière had gained notoriety as editor of Rochefort's popular newspaper *La Marseillaise* during the late Empire, and after having played a prominent role in the October 31 insurrection he was elected vice-mayor of the 20th arrondissement. He was elected to the National Assembly in February, but after some hesitation, he resigned in order to serve the Commune. The vigilance committee that Millière presided over counted twenty members, but nothing is known of most. One member was Louis Brunereau, a member of the Luxembourg Commission in 1848 who was later closely associated with Felix Pyat. Another member of the vigilance committee, Brunereau's son-in-law Marc Gromier, was a journalist who had served under Garibaldi in Italy, and he later served as Pyat's secretary.[61] These connections with Pyat may be significant, because Pyat was on the Commune's Committee of Public Safety, which issued the decree revoking Bayeaux-Dumesnil as vice-mayor.

Two delegates replaced Bayeaux-Dumesnil: Louis Guerin, a lawyer, and Martial Portalier, a boot maker and active member of the International, both of whom were members of the vigilance committee.[62] Guerin and Portalier appear to have been merely front men, however, as the real authority in the arrondissement was the vigilance committee, which according to an employee at the mairie met every day after Bayeaux-Dumesnil was revoked. Guerin later told army prosecutors that Gromier and others had said the "vigilance committee, in agreement with the Commune, was going to take up the administration of the 9th arrondissement in replacement of Mr. Bayeaux-Dumesnil, found too reactionary." A statement by Guerin and Portalier announcing their installation in office

---

61. In 1869 Pyat circulated his famous "Toast to a Bullet," a thinly veiled call to assassinate Napoleon III, and went into hiding at Brunereau's house to avoid arrest. Gromier was sentenced to five years in prison for reading the toast in a public meeting. Millière, Brunereau, and Gromier were all battalion chiefs in the National Guard, a further indication of the interpenetration of the guard and committee movements; Maitron, *DBMOF*, 4:436, 7:247.

62. Guerin testified at his trial after the Commune that he had been asked by Gromier to join the committee on May 3, just three days before being made a delegate at the mairie. He excused his actions by saying that he hoped to increase his notoriety and thereby gain more clients. A friend of Guerin's said that Guerin told him he agreed to be a delegate because it paid five hundred francs a month, and Guerin's landlord said that Guerin had not paid his rent since before the siege. Yet while Guerin said all committee members were paid ten francs a day, another member testified that they did not receive a cent; AHG: 20e conseil 56, dossier Guerin. Portalier had been a member of the committee since September; Wolfe, "The Origins of the Paris Commune," 86.

pledged to work in conjunction with the vigilance committee instituted since September, asserting that the institution of a Committee of Public Safety by the Communal Council required "the most energetic measures" in the arrondissement to assure victory.[63] Their deliberate reference to the Committee of Public Safety underscores the point that the replacement of Bayeaux-Dumesnil was an episode in a larger struggle between the several factions of the revolutionary coalition for control of the revolution. The creation of the Committee of Public Safety, which badly split the Communal Council, represented the victory of those who considered that radical, and even violent, measures were needed to save the Commune. This explains Guerin and Portalier's statement about the need for "the most energetic measures," which was not mere rhetoric. One of the first steps of the arrondissement's new administration was to allow clubs to hold meetings in the churches of the district. More ominously there were mass arrests of men who refused to serve in the National Guard in the 9th, which previously had a reputation as a safe haven; Notre Dame de Lorette was used as a prison. Finally, the decree by the Communal Council demolishing the house of Adolphe Thiers was swiftly executed, which would have been highly unlikely had Bayeux-Dumesnil still been in charge. A Versailles police agent reported that several people opposed to the demolition were arrested. Leon Picard, a member of the vigilance committee who supervised the police of the arrondissement, later had the courage to admit to his prosecutors that "I did not think it my duty to refuse this post in the dangerous time we were going through. This *quartier* of reactionaries didn't leave me a free minute."[64] The installation of the vigilance committee in replacement of Bayeaux-Dumesnil signaled the victory of radical Communards in the 9th, just as the creation of the Committee of Public Safety indicated the victory of radical revolutionaries in the Communal Council.

Similar divisions among Communards may be found in several other arrondissements where vigilance committees held authority. In the 5th the mayor Dominique Régère was roundly condemned by Jean Allemane for his moderation and his attempts to protect the churches and clerics of the arrondissement, though both men were members of the vigilance committee.[65] Pillot, of the 1st arrondissement, later told prosecutors that his can-

63. AHG: 20e conseil 56 and 3e conseil 60; *Le Journal Officiel*, May 11.

64. APP: Ba 364–4; Fontoulieu, *Les Églises*, 270; Maitron, *DBMOF*, 8:165.

65. Allemane scornfully wrote of Régère's attempts to convince him that "one could be a practicing Catholic and a revolutionary socialist." Fontoulieu, *Les Églises*, 374, confirms

didature in the elections of April 16 was violently opposed by the Delegation, which accused him of "moderation" and "bourgeois honesty."[66] Divisions within vigilance committees were also evident in the 19th arrondissement, which appears to have broken apart in May. Both Moise Pillioud and Etienne Canal, active leaders of the committee, separately testified that they opposed the "majority" of the committee, and that it was dissolved because of internal dissention. Pillioud added that the committee was dissolved by the assembly of the salle Marseillaise on his recommendation, because "there were people [on the committee] who only sought to hoard positions." It is likely, though, that the committee split, rather than dissolved, because Pillioud twice stated that a "faction" of the committee left the Marseillaise and established itself in the Saint Christophe Church, known as the Church of La Villette. Pillioud said he was then charged with reconstituting the vigilance committee by the salle Marseillaise, but that he did not do so. A notice on the door of the salle Marseillaise moved its meetings to the Church of La Villette on April 27 because of overcrowding, but if Pillioud is correct some meetings were still held there.[67] Much remains obscure about this episode, but it is the only known example of a vigilance committee splitting apart during the Commune.

Some tensions may also be found within the vigilance committee in the 14th arrondissement. During the Commune this committee administered the mairie, and according to one of its members, Jules Delaruelle, it was somewhat disorganized after the elections of March 26.

> A vigilance committee had been created in the 14th arrondissement, as in all the arrondissements of Paris, after September 14, 1870. These committees were composed of members of the International. I wasn't a member. A few days before March 18, new vigilance committees were instituted, but on March 26 the old committee was

---

Régère's protection of Saint Etienne du Mont, where Régère had a son preparing his first communion. Witnesses later testified that several persons arrested by Allemane were freed by Régère; AHG: 5e conseil 338.

66. Pillot was on an early Delegation list, but his name is absent from the final one. His reason for deletion cannot be verified, but Pillot was a very active participant in the vigilance committee movement and systematically lied at his trial to save himself; Choury, *La Commune au coeur de Paris,* 274; AHG: 3e conseil 1519.

67. AHG: 4e conseil 1432, dossier Pillioud; AHG: 13e conseil 185, dossier Canal; Fontoulieu, *Les Églises,* 173.

joined to those recently named. As we did not know the members of the old committee there were skirmishes between us, and soon we stood apart from the other members.[68]

Delaruelle was apparently describing the restructuring of the old vigilance committee in accordance with the revolutionary socialist Resolutions concerning Committees of Vigilance adopted in February. When asked about the Declaration of Principles, he denied any knowledge of them, but Claude Sermet, president of the committee during the Commune, admitted signing them. The dissonance Delaruelle described between the two groups was phrased with some hesitation; he evidently did not wish to say that an actual break had occurred, only that there were differences between the two. This combined vigilance committee reorganized itself on April 9, dividing into commissions to better carry out its tasks, a reorganization rendered necessary by the Versaillais forces' capture of Lucien Henry, who had been the key leader of the revolutionary movement in the arrondissement. Six of those on the old vigilance committee were given positions on the new commissions, indicating cooperation between the two elements Delaruelle described.[69]

The administration of ten of Paris's twenty arrondissements by vigilance committees was the culmination of the movement as it was conceived by some revolutionaries as early as September. As a result of the radicalization of the movement following the failure of the October 31 insurrection the entire movement, both in the arrondissements and in the central Delegation of the Twenty Arrondissements, was dedicated to replacing the government with a revolutionary Commune drawn from the revolutionary socialist clubs and committees of the city. This program was embodied in the Red Poster of January 6 and reconfirmed in the revolutionary socialist Declaration of Principles of February 19. In March and April the militants of the local vigilance committees acted to make that program a reality, by seizing the mairies or stepping in to administer their

---

68. AHG: 4e conseil 1256, dossier Delaruelle. Most of the members of the vigilance committee of the 14th arrondissement during the siege were indeed members of the AIT; Wolfe, "The Origins of the Paris Commune," 86.

69. AHG: 19e conseil 134, dossier Sermet; AHG: 3e conseil, 1112, dossier Séné; AHG: Ly 27. This is one of the municipalities that Rougerie suggests was run by the AIT, but most of the members of the vigilance committee were not members of the International; Rougerie was evidently basing his assessment on the names printed on posters immediately after March 18, which reflects the old vigilance committee before it merged with the group of which Delaruelle was a member; Rougerie, "L'AIT et le mouvement ouvrier," 61.

arrondissements. Their action was essential for consolidating the revolution and extending it to the base, down into the individual arrondissements where the National Guard was organized and outfitted, where the schools were secularized, where the symbols and the realities of the old order were being destroyed, and where even a few workshops were converted to cooperative production—indeed, where the revolution had many of its most profound manifestations. Yet a third level, below the mairie—that of the public spaces and contested areas where opinion was formed and expressed—ultimately was the vital battleground in the defining of the Communal revolution. In this third level, beyond that of the Hôtel de ville and the arrondissement mairies, Communard militants in clubs and committees organized themselves through association to assure the success of the Commune over its many enemies. For despite the moderate pronouncements of the Central Committee of the National Guard and the Delegation, the insurrection did not have the support of the majority of Parisians. Communards had established themselves in the centers of power, but for the revolution to be victorious in the city they had to take effective control of the streets, squares, and assembly halls.

Three broad currents of organized opinion may be discerned during the Commune, each of which sometimes displayed great internal dissension, but which together nonetheless maintained an overall coherence: groups that supported the Commune, groups that supported the Assembly at Versailles, and groups that sought conciliation or a neutral third path between Versailles and Paris. Communards were by far the most active segment of opinion and are considered in depth in succeeding chapters. The other two segments of opinion require attention here because the repression of anti-Communard sentiment, and the transformation of most neutral groups into pro-Communard elements, forms the context in which Communard clubs and committees were able to dominate political discourse during the Commune and implement their vision of the new world they hoped to create. The story of these movements is thus a necessary part of the history of the shaping of the revolution, as it reflects the final stage of the seizure and consolidation of power by Communards. The repression of opposition helped create an atmosphere of fear for some Parisians, for whom the Commune was not a glorious harbinger of a new world but a reign of Terror.[70] In these conditions Communard popular organizations flourished unrestricted by opposition, unrestrained by contradiction.

---

70. Historians sympathetic to the Commune, which is to say almost all recent historians, tend to deny the element of terror during the Commune, probably because this might imply some interpretive link to the scurrilous anti-Communard works of the period just after 1871.

In the first weeks of the insurrection the streets of Paris were the scenes of contestation among the major currents of opinion. Congregating in the open air was a recognized Parisian tradition in times of crisis. When war fever swept Paris in August 1870, when the Empire was overthrown, when the surrender of the city was announced after the closing of the clubs in January, and again when the decree prohibiting clubs was reaffirmed on March 11, Parisians gathered in open air to discuss issues of moment. In the days after March 18, as on these other occasions, the numbers in any one of these groups ranged from several dozen to several hundred.[71] Some groups were merely knots of passersby who gathered momentarily around a poster or an overheard conversation, but others were continuations of organized clubs. When clubs were prohibited in late January, for example, semiorganized open-air meetings sprang up around the grands boulevards.[72] Similarly, the ethnologist Elie Reclus presided over an electoral open-air meeting on March 26; in forty-five minutes the participants drew up a list of candidates and adopted it with a unanimous vote, an indication that these informal groups could provide results as well as debate.

Reclus noted that this meeting gathered "citizens who, for the most part, had never spoken up until then."[73] Toward the end of the siege organized clubs had justifiably acquired a reputation for radicalism and had come to be considered somewhat plebeian by certain elements of opinion. The open-air meetings on the grands boulevards drew very different social and political groups than these clubs. Under an insurrectionary regime, going to a club was generally considered evidence of radicalism, so informal open-air clubs were favored by moderates and conservatives. In addition, moderates and conservatives might have been too intimidated to speak out in the organized clubs, dominated as they were by the revolutionary left, which was the only element of opinion to remain mobilized

Rials, *Nouvelle histoire de Paris,* is the most important recent history critical of the Commune and does give attention to this issue.

71. *Le Journal Officiel,* March 22, noted groups of "twenty-five, fifty, and even one hundred people." Philibert Audebrand estimated that there were 250 to 300 people; *Histoire intime de la Révolution du Dix-Huit mars* (Paris: Dentu, 1871), 29. Jean-Baptiste Larocque, who almost pathologically exaggerated his own importance in events, wrote that several thousand people listened to one of his speeches just before March 18; *1871: Souvenirs révolutionnaires* (Paris: Albert Savine, 1888), 260.

72. Larocque observed that an open-air meeting in Belleville had a bureau, and it appeared to be connected to the "committee d'arrondissement," probably the vigilance committee that normally held meetings at the salle Favié; *1871,* 260. See also Molinari, *Les Clubs rouges,* 273.

73. Quoted in Rougerie, "Les Elections du 26 mars," 19.

after the February elections. Moderate clubs, which had flourished during the national military crisis of the siege, had stopped meeting. Somewhat ironically, moderates and conservatives were left only the streets. This is only one of a series of reversals to be considered in which social, political, or power relations were inverted during the Commune: former prisoners arrested police officers, conservatives rallied in the streets, atheists spoke from pulpits, women marched to battle.

While some on the grands boulevards spoke in favor of the insurrection after March 18, the majority were opposed. The *Journal Officiel* complained of "reactionary" orators on the grands boulevards, while Vallès's *Le Cri du Peuple* ironically complained that the "so-called friends of order" were in fact disorderly because they hindered circulation. The orators in these groups reportedly argued that a municipal council was not necessary, that the Central Committee of the National Guard was in league with the Prussians, and that the National Assembly had shown goodwill and a conciliatory attitude. According to the *Journal Officiel* the dominant theme of these groups was that "what is needed now is work, and that the new government would be incapable of procuring it." The reference to "travail" is repeated by Charles Bergerand, who wrote that he saw a huge crowd near the mairie of the 9th arrondissement, which that day had been seized by guardsmen from "the heights," the working-class areas of Montmartre and Belleville. The crowd insulted a National Guard patrol that passed by, shouting, "Get to work! Long live order!" The generally bourgeois 9th arrondissement was thus expressing its disdain for workers who would rather rise up in revolt than go to work. Bergerand reports that two shots were fired, dispersing the crowd. Earlier that day Bergerand had seen a crowd of three thousand to four thousand "guards, workers, and bourgeois" marching behind a Tricolor flag bearing the words "Meeting of the Men of Order. Long Live France! Long Live the Republic!" Another demonstration, by two thousand to three thousand persons in the 6th arrondissement, marched behind a similar Tricolor to the Hôtel de ville, where it was turned back by a few shots. The next day several thousand Friends of Order marched on the headquarters of the National Guard on the place Vendôme, where they pressed forward on a cordon of guards, threatening to invade the square. Shots were exchanged, leaving on both sides perhaps a dozen killed and more wounded.[74]

---

74. Accounts of the events vary widely, but see *Le Journal Officiel,* March 22 and 25; Charles Bergerand, *Paris sous la Commune en 1871* (Paris: Lainé, 1871), 33–34; Serman, *La Commune de Paris,* 239; *Le Cri du Peuple,* March 23; APP: Ba 364-2; Rials, *Nouvelle histoire de Paris,* 287.

In these early days of the insurrection the streets of the bourgeois districts belonged to the anti-Communards, even if the National Guard had the weight of arms. Aminthe Dupont, the chief of municipal police, responded to the Friends of Order demonstrations with a project to "organize civil demonstrations in favor of the Commune. Let National Guardsmen, dressed in street clothes, circulate in groups of thirty or three hundred in the various *quartiers* of the center, crying Long Live the Republic and Long Live the Commune."[75] The street, then, was considered an important arena of struggle between partisans and opponents of the Commune. The Central Committee of the National Guard also decided to forcibly occupy the mairies of the 1st and 2d arrondissements, which had become the headquarters of resistance by the mayors and deputies as well as the Friends of Order. On March 24 there was very nearly a pitched battle in the streets between the two sides, but the mayors and deputies and the Central Committee of the National Guard finally agreed to elections.

While anti-Communard sentiment appeared to be in the majority on the grands boulevards of the bourgeois districts, neutral and pro-Communard elements were always present and predominated in other areas of the capital. The square in front of the Hôtel de ville was a particular gathering area for Communards, for example, due to the proximity to power and the intimidating presence of guard battalions protecting the revolutionary government. From there a group of guardsmen on March 19 delegated Pierre Vésinier, a socialist journalist and future member of the Commune, to petition the Central Committee of the National Guard to occupy the Bank of France and attack Versailles. A Versailles agent overheard groups on the square argue that the Central Committee of the National Guard should declare the separation of church and state. Conciliatory sentiments were also given voice on the streets of the city, though the Versailles agents only appear to have remarked on this fact when the speakers were workers or guardsmen.[76] Yet conflicts in the open-air groups were almost unknown. The possibilities for violence in a city in revolution, the killings of March 18, and the bloodshed on the place Vendôme no doubt discouraged confrontation in the open arena of the street, where social codes of

---

75. None of the many demonstrations in favor of the Commune can be directly linked to this project; AHG: 5e conseil 590, dossier Jean (Aminthe) Dupont. Versailles police reports of April 25 and May 16 noted, however, "agitators who ran through the groups" and, again, "those who went from group to group"; APP: Ba 364-5 and Ba 365-1.

76. Pierre Vésinier, *Comment a péri la Commune* (Paris: Albert Savine, 1892), 16; APP: Ba 364-3 and Ba 364-4.

behavior were less clearly defined and of more uncertain application than in indoor meetings. The one exception found in the Versailles police reports is the case of a guardsman who was forced out of a group of about twenty persons for speaking in favor of the Commune. The guard uniform and the context of power being in the hands of revolutionaries perhaps provided this individual with the courage necessary to contradict the views of the larger group.[77]

Those people hostile to the insurrection, notably students of the Latin Quarter, continued to meet after the affaire of the place Vendôme. Beginning on March 21, nightly meetings were held at the École de Médecine. On March 24 a statement was adopted rejecting the authority of the Central Committee of the National Guard, which was said to have no popular mandate to hold elections, and pledging aid to the mayors and deputies in their struggle. There were many students among the Friends of Order demonstrations, and students formed a large contingent of those under arms in the service of the mayors and deputies. At a March 27 meeting at the École Polytechnique there was some talk of attacking the mairie of the 5th arrondissement, which had been under the control of the vigilance committee since March 18.[78] By the end of the month, though, students supporting the Commune made inroads into this opposition. A speaker at one meeting decried the fusion of students and workers, most likely an indication that Communard elements were entering the meetings of students. In early April other meetings were called, obviously by Communards, to discuss "the role of students in revolution." Although these meetings had originally been called to oppose the Commune, they instead resulted in a Communard student organization, the Fédération des Écoles, or Federation of the Schools, which remained active until the end of the Commune. The withering of student opposition to the Commune may be related to the move of the École Polytechnique from Paris to Tours on March 29, but the organized anti-insurrectionary movement in general

---

77. APP: Ba 364-4, report dated April 2.

78. The statement also disclaimed any ties to reactionaries, saying that students would resist any attempted "coup d'état by the government," a reference to rumors of a royalist restoration; *Le Gazette des Tribuneaux,* March 25 and 26; Allemane, *Mémoires d'un Communard,* 73. Six thousand students were present according to Audebrand, *Histoire intime,* 98, but only three hundred according to Henri Dabot, *Griffonnages quotidiens d'un bourgeois du Quartier Latin du 14 mai 1869 au 2 décembre 1871* (Paris: Peronne, 1895), 180. Lepelletier, *Histoire de la Commune de 1871,* 2:270, explains that students were hostile to the insurrection because they were unfamiliar with its leaders, having just returned from the provinces where the Écoles had met during the siege.

lost momentum when the mayors and deputies agreed on March 24 to cooperate in holding elections.[79]

The reports of Versailles police agents contain many descriptions of open-air gatherings into the first days of April, but increasingly a note of fear and suspicion is heard in these groups. One report stated that "reactionaries" are as numerous as ever, "but they guard against openly stating their hostile dispositions." Another reported that "on the grands boulevards little is said; each appears suspicious of his neighbor." The military struggle between Paris and Versailles began on April 1 and ended tolerance for opposition. Three days later the Commune suppressed several conservative newspapers accused of reporting military secrets, and seven others voluntarily stopped publication to avoid punishment. At this same time police agents from Versailles began to complain of difficulty getting into and out of the city, because the Commune was more effectively policing its borders. They also mention increasing numbers of arrests.[80] The last public initiative by opponents of the Commune was to call public meetings at the Stock Exchange and the place de la Concorde for April 6 in order to propose conciliation between Paris and Versailles. The Executive Committee of the Commune banned the meetings, making the first official limitation on freedom of association after March 18. The Executive Committee's decree argued that conciliation was a mask for reaction and warned that any meeting that threatened public order would be "vigorously suppressed by force." Despite this decree a crowd of perhaps twelve hundred to fifteen hundred met at the Bourse and then marched about the boulevards.[81] Two days later Dupont urged guard patrols to "range over the larger streets, and put to silence alarmist and reactionary remarks." This action put an end to public opposition to the Commune. A Versailles agent on April 11 reported no more groups on the streets, as "any individual seeming to listen to conversations is considered as suspect, and immediately arrested and sent to the Prefecture." Prevented from organizing, those who opposed the Commune were generally silent and ineffectual.[82]

---

79. APP: Ba 364–3; *Le Mot d'Ordre,* April 1. Jacques Girault, "Les Étudiants et la Commune," in *Experiences et langage de la Commune de Paris* (Paris, 1970), 104, explains the students' conservatism by their elite backgrounds.

80. APP: 364–4, reports of April 1 and 2; Rials, *Nouvelle histoire de Paris,* 217. The use of the term *reactionaries* in a Versailles police report is an interesting comment on the way the two sides were perceived.

81. *Les Murailles Politiques,* 3:177, 197; *Le Gazette des Tribuneaux,* April 8; *La Verité,* April 8.

82. AHG: 5e conseil 590, dossier Dupont; APP: Ba 364–3. There are a few notices of groups of reactionaries after this, as in, for example, *La Sociale,* May 6.

The current of opinion consisting of neutral groups, the so-called third party between Paris and Versailles, continued to be tolerated even after the Friends of Order demonstrations. Yet this current underwent significant evolution, and by mid-May most neutral groups had declared their adhesion to the Commune.[83] Already by early April the semiorganized student movement opposed to the Commune had been subverted by Communards, and the same transformation was effected in other associations, such as the Masonic Lodges, the Défenseurs de la République, and the Union Républicaine Centrale, groups that had previously been suspicious of the insurrection. The Alliance Républicaine, another influential republican group, endorsed the revolt from the beginning. The common element in these transformations was the role of general assemblies, through which Communards were able to enter into these groups and vote propositions of support for the Commune. The method of association, then, was a powerful weapon Communards could use to redirect the original intent of the leadership of these groups. The most characteristic example is that of the Union Républicaine Centrale, which had met with the Delegation of the Twenty Arrondissements on March 21 to support elections. For the Union this support did not imply acceptance of the insurrection but rather was seen as the best way to avoid civil war. The leadership of the Union maintained a suspicious attitude, refusing in early April to declare themselves for the Commune. At a general assembly on April 14, however, the Union approved an address vilifying the Versailles government and declaring itself wholeheartedly in favor of the victory of Paris. This address pointed out at great length that royalists were waging a war against the Republic and employing Bonapartist generals for the extermination of Paris.[84] Similarly, the leadership of the Masonic Lodges of Paris attempted to keep its distance from the insurrection while trying to end the fighting. Yet general assemblies of Masons in late April declared their allegiance to the Commune, and in a grand celebration of April 29 thousands of Masons rallied in favor of the movement.[85]

---

83. Schulkind has argued to the contrary that moderate groups "were increasingly reserved in their support of the Commune as the civil war continued"; "The Activity of Popular Organizations," 407.

84. The key personage in the Union was Dupont de Bussac, a republican with impeccable credentials dating to before 1830; Lefrançais, *Souvenirs révolutionnaires,* 500; *Le Journal Officiel,* April 14; *Le Vengeur,* April 16.

85. Phillip G. Nord "The Party of Conciliation and the Paris Commune," *French Historical Studies* 15 (1987): 25. A Versaillais police agent noted with surprise that these meetings were calm and reasonable; APP: Ba 364-5.

The case of the Défenseurs de la République is somewhat more complex. The Défenseurs was a group of republican notables founded in November to unite all republicans in the struggle against monarchy. It had a central committee for coordination but seemingly had groups in only a few arrondissements. Its president was Bayeaux-Dumesnil, the radical republican who administered the 9th arrondissement until being replaced by the vigilance committee. The Défenseurs appear to have been deeply split over whether to support the Commune. On the one hand, the committees for the 2d and 3d arrondissements supported the mayors in the elections of March 26, and Lefrançais later wrote a scathing denunciation of the Défenseurs, who in his eyes were too cowardly to defend anything. On the other hand, the committee of the 17th arrondissement voted on March 19 for an immediate attack on Versailles.[86] By early May, however, several early leaders who supported conciliation left the organization. On May 7 a general assembly of all Défenseurs in Paris revoked their mandate of the Parisian deputies remaining at Versailles and declared their full adhesion to the "Revolution of March 18." The resolution noted that the bombardment of the city and the killing of guardsmen captured in battle demanded a clear statement of support for the Commune.[87]

In each of these cases the evolution toward supporting the Commune was initiated by general assemblies of the rank and file, which exerted its influence against even respected moderate republicans. While Communards were not a majority in Paris, pro-Communard militants were active and resolute devotees of their cause and thus were able in these instances and others to dominate clubs, committees, and public discourse in general. In addition, the dynamic of bombardment by Versailles, the stories of Versaillais soldiers killing captured guardsmen, and all the phenomena of ruthless civil war worked to heighten emotions in the capital. It was difficult to stand aside in such circumstances, especially as Communards constantly argued that attempts at conciliation demonstrated cowardice and insufficient republican zeal. It is noteworthy that no group evolved away from identification with the Commune.

Two organizations that began as neutral or conciliatory did resist these pressures, but their stories confirm the patterns found in the previous

---

86. Lefrançais, *Souvenirs révolutionnaires,* 470; AHG: Ly 22; *Les Murailles Politiques,* 3:107, 116; Choury, *La Commune au coeur de Paris,* 226–28. Paul Martine described the meeting in the 17th arrondissement in *Souvenirs,* 47–51.

87. *Le Journal Officiel,* May 9. Bayeux-Dumesnil presided over the meeting, which was held the day after he had been replaced at the mairie of the 9th arrondissement.

examples. The Ligue d'Union Républicaine des Droits de Paris, the most important and active of the conciliatory groups, and the Union Nationale de Commerce et de l'Industrie both saw attempts to force taking position for Paris. The case of the Ligue d'Union has been well studied, and it must only be pointed out here that while the leadership was able to maintain a neutral stance, in the public meetings held under the auspices of the Ligue d'Union at the salle Valentino pro-Communard sentiment grew to become a majority. The evolution in these meetings shows very clearly the process by which Communards were able to subvert the intent of the Ligue d'Union leadership. The first conciliatory meeting by the Ligue d'Union was held at the salle Valentino on April 6 and declared its support for the deputies and mayors of Paris against the Communal Council. Three days later Ostyn reported to the Commune that he had attended a conciliatory meeting of "bourgeois" at the salle Valentino. He said that the meeting had approved a motion blaming the deputies and mayors for not attending and had called on Parisians to vote in the supplementary elections to the Commune. Two days later a newspaper article stated that a meeting of "businessmen and bankers" voted that the "bourgeoisie would take up arms" if Versailles did not recognize Paris's rights. Finally, on April 20 *Le Cri du Peuple* reported that about one thousand people voted almost unanimously that "the League of Republican Unity for the Rights of Paris recognizes the principles proclaimed by the Commune to be just and legitimate."[88] In just under two weeks those favoring the Commune over Versailles were able to push their views into prominence in Ligue d'Union meetings, and the leadership had to work diligently to maintain a neutral stance.[89] Indeed, these pressures split the leadership of the Ligue d'Union, with some leaders forming the pro-Communard Équilibre Républicaine, an attempt to moderate the demands of revolutionaries by balancing them with radical republican views.[90] The story of the Union Nationale is much

88. *Les Murailles Politiques,* 3:161; *Les Procès-Verbaux de la Commune,* 1:153–54; *Paris Libre,* April 12; *Le Cri du Peuple,* April 21.

89. André Lefèvre, a founder of the Ligue d'Union, noted that "every day" partisans of the Commune tried to force an adhesion, and he wrote that the declaration of the salle Valentino was the work of a minority in the Ligue d'Union; *Histoire de la Ligue d'Union Républicaine des Droits de Paris* (Paris: Charpentier, 1881), 102. Jeanne Gaillard notes the pro-Communard element in the Ligue d'Union but does not attribute it to pressure from public meetings; "Les papiers de la Ligue d'Union Républicaine des Droits de Paris," *Le Mouvement Social* 56 (1966):" 65–87.

90. The remaining leaders of the Ligue d'Union met with Thiers a number of times, but neither Thiers nor the Commune would agree on the concessions necessary to end the civil

the same. Its leaders maintained a neutral stance and were able to prevent
its public manifestos from appearing overtly Communard, yet one of its
founders later wrote of his heroic efforts to stifle the Communard sentiment in its public meetings and noted that several members resigned
because they found the group too timid.[91] A participant in the public meetings of the Union Nationale reported that "after a few days of derisory discussions about conciliatory projects, they gave themselves over to echoing
the Hôtel de ville."[92] All of the evidence supports the conclusion that to the
extent that neutral or conciliatory groups were influenced by the desires
expressed in public meetings they were Communard. The leadership of
these groups sometimes split over whether to proclaim solidarity with the
Commune, and the neutralist stance was compromised by Communard
resolutions that welled up from the rank and file in public meetings.

With victory in the struggle for the streets, and with the subversion of
most conciliatory groups, Communards dominated public discourse in the
city. Communards not only controlled the city's administrative structures
but extended their power into the streets and meeting halls. From the first
days of the insurrection the club and committee movement, in particular
the Delegation of the Twenty Arrondissements, was vital for maintaining
and consolidating the revolution. This domination was in part the result of
oppression and intimidation and in part the effect of the devotion and
energy of clubistes, who immediately set about constructing the new world
envisioned in popular organizations.

war. Serman, *La Commune de Paris,* 439; Nord, "The Party of the Conciliation," 7; Gaillard,
"Les papiers de la Ligue," 9. Équilibre Républicaine issued several manifestos supporting the
Commune but does not appear to have sponsored any public meetings. When testifying
before the National Assembly, Corbon, a founder of the Ligue d'Union, tried to explain
away the Ligue d'Union's pronouncement that it would take up arms in defense of the rights
of Paris, by arguing that verbal "excesses" were required to placate extremists; *L'Enquête
Parlementaire sur l'Insurrection du Dix-Huit mars,* 450.

91. Jules Amigues, *Les Aveux d'un conspirateur Bonapartiste* (Paris: Lachaud et Burdin,
1874), 70. The Union Nationale also had interviews with Thiers, again to no avail; see *Le
Journal Officiel,* April 8; *Le Moniteur du Peuple,* April 7; *Le Bien Publique,* April 16.

92. Edmond de Pressensé, *Les Leçons du 18 mars* (Paris: Michel Lévy, 1871), 119.

Fig. 1. Paris during the Commune—Club in Saint Eustace Church. (From Antoine Darlet, *La Guerne et la Commune, 1870–1871: Deseins par les principaux artistes de la France et de l'étranger* [Paris: Levy, 1872], 97.)

Fig. 2. Club in Saint Eustace Church. (From Jules Clartie, *Histoire de la Révolution de 1870–1871* [Paris: L'Éclipse, 1872], 649.)

Part 2
The New World

CHAPTER 4

Association and the New World

> The reign of justice advances. The Federation of individual activities
> will soon make social equality inevitable.
>
> —Eugene Vermersch

It was by no means certain that the insurrection of March 18 would become a revolution. Just as revolutionary popular organizations help explain the origins of the insurrection, so too clubs and committees, and the larger movement of association of which they were a part, shaped the character of the revolution. For clubistes the theory and practice of how to attain a revolutionary transformation of society centered on association. Historians have long recognized that direct democracy through local assemblies was an essential feature of the Commune.[1] The Commune's reliance on worker associations has been the subject of much attention.[2] What is missing is an integral interpretation of these and other phenomena that can help in comprehending the nature of the Commune. The program of association implemented in popular organizations during the Commune—not wholly new, for it developed out of a long history of associationist projects in France—provides the key to understanding the apparent diffuseness of the Communal movement. In this regard the argument that Communards had only vague, contradictory, or confused notions of what they hoped to achieve—an argument found among adherents of both

---

Epigraph from Eugene Vermersch in *Le Cri du Peuple,* March 1, expressing a common understanding of the way association would transform society.

1. Dale Clifford, "Direct Democracy in the Paris Commune of 1871," *Proceedings of the Western Society for French History* 5 (1977); Bruhat, Dautry, and Tersen, *La Commune de 1871,* 162; Serman, *La Commune de Paris,* 348. Choury seeks to place direct democracy in a Marxist context, by calling it the "democratic dictatorship of the proletariat"; *La Commune au coeur de Paris,* 277.

2. Citations about this aspect of the Commune could be multiplied infinitely. Georges Bourgin observed the "syndicalist method" of relying on trade corporations; *Histoire de la Commune,* 110. Tombs, "Harbingers or Entrepreneurs?" argues that the Commune was not socialist but utilitarian.

schools of Communard historiography—must be rejected. The political interpretation suggests that clubistes lacked a clear idea of the path to the Social Republic and were without a unifying vision.[3] For the social interpretation, emphasizing the ideological confusion of Communards often serves a double purpose: it helps explain the failure of a theoretically inevitable social revolution, and in some cases it is used to validate Lenin's insights about the need for discipline and unity in a vanguard party.[4] Both interpretations have overlooked the underlying unity of the Commune.

A full understanding of association aids a reinterpretation of the Commune in several ways. Association brings together the action of Communards in diverse areas—in politics, the economy, and social institutions—demonstrating that there was indeed an underlying logic and common theme to the innumerable projects of renewal and transformation. Association provides a common ground among the several levels of action and power during the Commune, from the Communal Council and Central Committee of the National Guard, to the arrondissement mairie, to the streets and meeting halls. Revealing the associationist program inherent in the Commune also allows a reinterpretion of the Commune's social foundations. Participants in popular organizations came from a wide variety of social backgrounds and did not constitute a social class. Rather, they formed a politically and culturally defined revolutionary community. Finally, a fuller understanding of Communard associationism reveals that the "new world" was not some purely utopian vision, that Communards were day-by-day making the revolution that they discussed and planned.

The associationist foundations of the Commune reveal that the debate between the social interpretation of the Commune as a "flaming dawn" of world revolution and the political interpretation of it as a "spectacular sunset," the last of the nineteenth-century revolutions, may be circumvented as a false dichotomy. The origins of association misled students of

3. Schulkind, "The Activity of Popular Organizations," 414. Wolfe wrote that clubs and committees expressed "vague and contradictory aspirations; "The Parisian *Club de la Révolution,*" 119. André Decouflé suggested that clubistes sought to "march together toward one knows not what, toward those luminous and vague horizons" that inspire crowds; *La Commune de Paris (1871): Révolution populaire et pouvoir révolutionnaire* (Paris: Cujas, 1969), 95. This is doubly wrong, as the "crowd" was not led like a docile herd but rather was an active shaper of their revolution through clubs.

4. Bruhat, Dautry, and Tersen, echoing a dominant theme among Marxist adherents of the social interpretation, concluded that in large part the failure of the Commune was due to the lack of a worker's party; *La Commune de 1871,* 360. Choury, who belongs to the Marxist wing, argued that the Commune did indeed represent a "new and original program" of federation; *La Commune au coeur de Paris,* 315.

the Commune. Association had tripartite roots in the Great Revolution, in the labor and socialist movements of the previous fifty years, and in the experience of the revolutionary left in the late Empire and siege. When we look at the political current of association developed out of the revolutionary tradition it is possible to see a preponderance of seemingly backward-looking rhetoric, such as "our fathers of '92" and other almost ritualistic invocations; when we review the economic ideas and practices of Communards the balance might appear tipped toward the future socialist revolution. The actions and aspirations of Communards can be fully understood only if we recognize not only both the political and the economic meanings of association but the social meanings as well.

Association became an important force in France through the early socialist movement in the 1830s. The overarching goal of all the so-called Utopian socialists was the replacement of economic systems based on individualism and exploitation with a system that fostered harmony, cooperation, and community by the association of production. Economic association through worker cooperatives, mutual aid societies, or some other vehicle was only part of a larger program for most early socialists. Pierre Leroux wrote in 1841 that he saw a new era dawning in which "the general tendency of laws would have for goal not individualism but association," a conception that went beyond purely economic matters. Association would instead be the foundation of all social institutions. In that same year Charles Fourier similarly argued that "the goal of all social reform must be the absolute Realization of the Association of Individuals and Classes of Society."[5] While early socialist theorists were dedicated to more than just cooperative economic ventures, in practice the revolutionary and socialist movements focused almost exclusively on the economic aspects of association.[6] Workers formed producer cooperatives when the political and economic climate were favorable and established mutual aid and credit societies. In 1848 the Luxembourg Commission became the locus around which some in the labor movement sought to achieve a socialist reordering of society through the association of trades. While their projects were destroyed by the repression following the June Days, under the Second Empire producer cooperatives or associations in a variety of for-

---

5. Quoted in Dubois, *Le Vocabulaire politique*, 220. Moss has observed that association was common to all early socialists; *The Origins of the French Labor Movement*, 36.

6. Sewell credits Phillipe Buchez with the creation of the "practical and egalitarian" conception of association that became the foundation of worker action in the 1830s and 1840s; *Work and Revolution in France*, 203.

mulations continued to be the foundation of the labor and socialist movements.[7]

The restructuring of society envisioned by many Communards was founded on association not only in the economic sphere but in political and social matters as well. The historical memory of the sections and districts of the French Revolution was a vital element in constructing this integrated vision of association. Communal associationism also derived in part from the strong tradition of *cercles* and salons among the middling classes, who had long been accustomed to participation in civic, business, and religious voluntary organizations.[8] Indeed, political, economic, and social association was the central contemporary vision of how to achieve the revolutionary trinity of liberty, equality, and fraternity. While only a vocal minority in 1871 had an integrated conception of how these three faces of association related to each other, the pervasiveness of the basic tenets of associationism is such that nearly every major program or statement of principles created by Communards contained elements of the theory of association. Even more important than programs and statements are the examples of how Parisians acted to transform political, economic, and social relations. In a city under a second siege and renewed bombardment, club and committee militants not only described but also began to build the "new world" that was such a prominent theme of Communard discourse.

It is not surprising that Parisians joined together to effect change; what is significant is that association was not just a way of coordinating efforts to address particular issues but also the vehicle for transforming the world as well as the foundation of the new world to be created. In a liberal democracy membership organizations are conceived as pressure groups that compete for the allocation of resources; association as articulated and enacted by Communards made voluntary organizations the sovereign core of the political, economic, and social systems. The Delegation of the Twenty Arrondissements did not merely hope to influence the Government of National Defense; it sought to replace it. Worker associations did not seek only to negotiate with employers; they took steps to abolish "wage slavery" and make producer cooperatives the foundation of the

7. Jean Gaumont, *Histoire générale de la coopération en France,* 2 vols. (Paris: Fédération Nationale des Coopératives de Consommation, 1924); Sewell, *Work and Revolution in France,* 275.

8. See Agulhon, *Le Cercle dans la France Bourgeois;* Maurice Agulhon and Maryvonne Bodiguel, *Les Associations au Village* (Le Paradou: Actes Sud, 1981); Nord, *The Republican Moment.*

new economic order. When education, art, and theater were restructured the method was the same: assemblies of interested individuals formed associations to regulate their interests. The Communal Council as a political institution was the mechanism by which competing claims were reconciled, but within their domain of action these associations were theoretically sovereign.

One of the most striking aspects of association in 1871 was the extent to which it was a conscious and deliberate strategy. Official statements, newspaper articles, and club orators constantly urged Parisians to band together to strengthen the movement and inaugurate a new era. There was widespread agreement about the utility of association, not just in one area, such as producer cooperatives, but as a general principle for restructuring society. The Program of the Commune adopted by the Communal Council on April 19 called for "the permanent intervention of citizens in communal affairs by the free demonstration of their ideas and the free defense of their interests."[9] *Le Prolétaire,* the newspaper of the Club des Prolétaires in the 11th arrondissement, simply demanded "Political Federation and Social Federation" in its statement of principles of May 10. Jean-Baptiste Larocque, a member of the Central Committee of the National Guard, announced a whole program to a group on a boulevard in early March. "Expect nothing from the government; do it yourself. . . . Associate yourselves with your comrades in the workshop, with your neighbors in your *quartier.* Through association gain your subsistence at low price, gain guaranteed work. Raise your children at common expense."[10] Marc Gromier, a journalist and member of the vigilance committee of the 9th arrondissement, declared that "the integral organization of the Commune is in fact a social institution superior to Civilization, as the Democratic and Social Republic is a governmental form superior to monarchy. This Commune has popular sovereignty for its base, solidarity for means, and fraternity for goal."[11] This device of implicitly conflating association with the revolutionary motto "Liberty, Equality, Fraternity" is also found in the April 28 issue of *La Sociale,* which held that "the Commune is the antithesis of the old world; it personifies the just remuneration of producers: Solidarity, Equality, Unity." In both formulations solidarity through association was the means of assuring harmony and community, a func-

9. Reprinted in Rougerie, *Paris Libre,* 154.
10. Larocque, *1871,* 244.
11. Marc Gromier's newspaper articles were later reprinted in *Lettres d'un bon rouge à la Commune de Paris* (Paris: André Sagnier, 1873), 78.

tion revealing that the roots of Communard association lie in the doctrines of the early socialists.[12]

Some Communards enunciated even more elaborate theories of association, by which all aspects of society would be transformed. After being elected to the Communal Council, the realist painter Gustave Courbet, much influenced by Proudhon, issued a statement that presented a complete associationist program. "Let us establish a new order of things that belongs only to us, and derives only from us," he proclaimed. "Autonomous associations, constituted according to their own interests, will be our version of cantons," he continued, "and the more they govern themselves, the more they promote the task of the Commune. . . . In this way, the present Commune will become the federal council of associations."[13] Courbet implemented these ideas as president of the Fédération des Artistes, an association of painters, sculptors, and other artists, which administered museums and artistic education under the Commune. Writing to his parents at this time Courbet explained, "Paris is a true paradise. . . . all social groups [corps d'état] have established themselves as federations and are masters of their own fate."[14]

Gustave Lefrançais, the prominent socialist militant and orator, put forward perhaps the most far-reaching and coherent program of association. As one of the founders of the vigilance committee movement, he had long experience in the clubs and committees of the siege and knew firsthand the possibilities and deficiencies inherent in association. From November to late February he had been imprisoned for his actions on October 31, so he was not part of the revolutionary socialist movement of the armistice. But he was a vital presence in the Delegation in the crucial first week after the March 18 insurrection. Immediately on his election to the Communal Council he presented a "draft constitution" for the organization of the Commune along associationist lines.[15] The central idea of this project was the creation of public meetings in each of the eighty *quartiers* of the city. Not only would these "districts" keep the members of the Communal Council in contact with their electors, but they would also

---

12. Sanford Elwitt has shown that the concept of solidarity developed before the Commune reconciled divergent interests and classes; "Solidarity and Social Reaction: The Republic against the Commune," in *Images of the Commune*, ed. James A. Leith (Montreal: McGill-Queens University Press, 1978), 187.

13. Reprinted in Maillard, *Affiches*, 214.

14. Letter dated April 30, in *Courbet raconté par lui-même et par ses amis*, 140.

15. The draft constitution (quoted in this and the following paragraph) appears in *Les Procès-Verbaux de la Commune*, 1:49, 55.

elect judges, police officers, and other local public officials. Beyond the districts, Lefrançais envisioned diverse other associations, "which will arise naturally from some community of interests and sympathies," and which will "maintain and extend the rights that you [the citizens] have so painfully conquered."

In his draft constitution, Lefrançais provided two examples of how association could solve specific problems. In the first instance delegates from the worker syndicates, the chamber of commerce, the Bank of France, and the railroads would meet to regulate the economy and find the solution to "the social problem posed by our century." Similarly, delegates from associations of workers, merchants, and industrialists would resolve questions of credit and rents. "Therefore let public meetings be opened everywhere," he concluded, adding, "we are counting on your energetic support to pass through this supreme crisis, at the end of which we will irrevocably find freedom." Commenting on this project in a book written just after the Commune, Lefrançais argued that the goal of the Communal movement was "to give back to the citizens themselves, through their assemblies in the *quartiers*, the regulation of their collective and local interests." The Communal Council's role would merely be to execute and coordinate the decisions made in the assemblies.[16] Although the Communal Council found the statement "too long," many of the measures Lefrançais called for were followed in piecemeal fashion over the course of the Commune, both by the Communal Council and by various associations. The Communal Council decreed the election of public officials and made worker associations the core of its economic reorganization. The Communal Council asked worker syndicates, businesspeople, and industrialists to help solve the problems of debt and credit.[17] Members of the Commune also held public meetings for the express purpose of keeping Communards in touch with their elected representatives, exactly as Lefrançais had suggested. Lefrançais did not initiate these developments; he had simply formulated the practices that Communards followed daily.

The experience of meeting together and of shared action gained over the previous months, and reflection on that experience, was a key ingredient in the development of association in 1871. The two other sources, the historical memory of the French Revolution and the theory and practice of worker associations over the previous forty years, were especially

16. Lefrançais, *Étude,* 213.
17. See the announcement by the Delegation of Work and Exchange in *Le Vengeur,* April 2.

important in shaping the two dominant facets of associationism, those concerning politics and the economy. Though some Communards had an integrated conception of how association as an organizing principle would restructure society, in practice Communards tended to concern themselves with the solution of pressing economic and political problems through association.[18] The economic policies of the Communal Council and the economic aspirations of the Communal movement in general have been subjects of intense scrutiny and debate by historians. Indeed, this debate has become one of the defining issues in the historiography of the Commune. The political interpretation denies the Commune was at heart a socialist revolution—though all theorists grant that certain aspects or groups were socialist—and insists instead on its political dimensions and similarities to past revolutions. The social interpretation tends to depict the Commune as the origin of future socialist revolutions.

The Communal Council act most important for discerning the Council's socialist content was the decree of April 16 requisitioning abandoned factories and shops. These establishments were to be owned and operated "by the workers who were employed there," and the former owners would be indemnified on their return to Paris. The other major decision in this regard was that of May 12 giving preference to worker associations when awarding government contracts.[19] While these decrees have been subject to a variety of interpretations, there is abundant evidence that those Communards interested in economic reforms saw association as the means of abolishing the problems of the current economic system.[20] At the same time, association would also eliminate the political oppression of the laboring classes that prevented the realization of their visions for a new world. Even before the Commune, socialism through association was a favorite subject of the public meetings of the late Empire, and it continued

---

18. Serman has argued that club discourse was not about the "future world" but about immediate concerns, yet it was by addressing immediate concerns that Communards began to craft that future in the present; *La Commune de Paris,* 295.

19. *Les Procès-Verbaux de la Commune,* 1:243, 2:367.

20. Both Gaumont and Rougerie have suggested that the decree of April 16 was based on Louis Blanc's theories of cooperative workshops announced in 1839. Still, Rougerie argues against seeing the Commune as a step toward a socialist future, arguing that the Commune was dominated by past traditions: "this socialism of 1871 . . . did it not itself belong to the past?"; *Procès des Communards,* 241. Seven years later he reconfirmed this analysis after some hesitation; *Paris Libre,* 242. See Gaumont, *Histoire générale de la coopération,* 2:15.

to be a common theme in the clubs of the siege.[21] Eugène Varlin, for example, rejected statist or centralized socialism in favor of the path of association, when he wrote in 1870 that corporate and syndical societies were the "natural elements" for the rebuilding of society: "it is they that can easily be transformed into producer associations; it is they that can put into practice the retooling of society and the organization of production."[22] During the siege the public meeting of the rue Aumaire, sponsored by the local vigilance committee (composed of members of the International), adopted a resolution to expropriate all weapons factories, which would then be owned and run by the workers.[23] During the Commune Auguste Desmoulins, the son-in-law of the socialist pioneer Pierre Leroux, advocated the "universal establishment of association," which he described as a second economic and social revolution to complete the revolution of universal suffrage begun in 1848.[24]

Building on the foundation of ideas, debates, and practice of the previous years, Communards who took an interest in worker affairs knew fairly clearly what course to take on the seizure of power. The April 16 decree on abandoned workshops was passed with no discussion by the Communal Council; the only question in the debate over the decree of May 12 giving preference to worker associations when awarding contracts was whether they should be given exclusive rights.[25] With the April 16 decree as a stimulus and guide, dozens of worker syndicates and professions organized themselves through public meetings to create associations of production and mutual aid societies. "We want to overthrow the exploitation of workers by the right of labor [le droit au travail] and the association of workers in corporations," a group of metal workers proclaimed when they sought aid from the Communal Council in forming a producer association, "and the federation in a not too distant time of all these corporations, which would be a giant step for social democracy toward the final goal, which

---

21. Dalotel, Faure, and Freiermuth have suggested that Parisians had arrived at the concept of the "dictatorship of the proletariat"; *Aux Origines de la Commune,* 245. That phrase was never used in the meetings, and the citations these authors present refer instead to the seizure of power by common people, workers, and peasants.

22. *La Marseillaise,* March 11, 1870.

23. This was similar to the Commune's April 16 decree; *Le Combat,* October 17, 1870. The Club de l'École de Médecine passed a version of the same resolution; *Le Combat,* October 28, 1870.

24. Quoted in Schulkind, *The Paris Commune of 1871,* 99.

25. *Les Procès-Verbaux de la Commune,* 1:241, 2:349.

every social democrat must envision, that is, the federation of peoples and the downfall of kings."[26] Economic association was thus seen as part of a larger project with international political importance. Association would not only free France of monarchism but liberate Europe as well. While this passage echoes some of the rhetoric and ideals of 1848, it is difficult to read this as evidence of archaism when at that moment Communards were dying for those principles. Rather, the continued vitality of the associationist visions projected by even the earliest socialists must be recognized.

In putting these principles into action the Communal Council and Communards in general consciously carried out a program of association. "For us, workers, this is one of the great moments to definitively organize ourselves," wrote Victor Delahaye, an active member of the AIT, when he called on workers to carry out the decree of April 16, "and to finally put into practice our patient and laborious studies of recent years."[27] The tailors' syndicate put the movement for economic association into context, announcing, "never has a more favorable occasion been offered by a government to the class of workers—to abstain would be to betray the cause of the emancipation of labor."[28] In their notice for meetings to "suppress exploitation between the worker and the owner," slaughterhouse workers noted, "the movement that is underway in the bosom of the working classes forces us to speak and to act."[29] The press of the Commune contains dozens of such calls for organizational meetings to form worker associations and implement the April 16 decree. Although only one workshop was in fact expropriated, by the middle of May about forty-three cooperatives had been formed, thirty-four worker syndicates had been established, and a number of these syndicates had taken the first steps toward carrying out the decree.[30] Before the end of the Commune several general congresses of worker societies had been held under the auspices of the Communal Council's Delegation on Labor and Exchange, to form the federation of worker's associations envisioned even before 1848.[31]

In contrast to 1848, however, the revolutionaries of 1871 assigned a

26. Quoted in Dauban, *Le fond de la société*, 140; Rougerie reprints several such declarations, in *Paris Libre*, 238.
27. *La Verité*, April 30.
28. *La Sociale*, May 3.
29. *Le Cri du Peuple*, May 22.
30. For example, in accord with the April 16 decree, the shoemaker Theodore Piny, acting as agent for the syndicate, inventoried and placed seals on two shops; Maitron, *DBMOF*, 8:122; Edwards, *The Paris Commune*, 264.
31. Some of the best accounts of this activity are in Bruhat, Dautry, and Tersen, *La Commune de 1871*, 191; and Serman, *La Commune de Paris*, 368.

more limited role to worker associations. Some historians have argued that the Luxembourg Commission of 1848, formed by delegates from worker societies, was more than an economic initiative, and that it became a project for a kind of worker's government.[32] No such development occurred in 1871, when the movement for economic association remained strictly separate from the government of the city. The Communal Council was far more radical and revolutionary than the Provisional Government or Second Republic in 1848, but another element at work reveals a profound difference between the Revolution of 1848 and the Commune of 1871. While both 1848 and 1871 were preceded by years of labor and socialist agitation, in 1871 the additional factor of the Franco-Prussian War provided a decisive difference. In 1848 the absence of a national military crisis meant that many Parisian men, building on the labor agitation of the previous years, defined themselves—and acted—as workers. The June Days, initiated in response to threats against the Luxembourg Commission and the National Workshops, testified to that identification. In 1871 Parisians had come to think of their city as an armed camp, and service in the national struggle had become a defining element of what it meant to be a citizen. Hence the Federation of the National Guard exhibited irresistible power when the National Assembly appeared intent on disarming the capital, and hence Parisian interests were divided in 1871 between economic projects to bring about the association of production, on the one hand, and political governance of the city, on the other.

Communard men defined themselves above all as citizens, who had fought for the nation and would fight for the Commune; they identified themselves as workers only in specific circumstances and with limited intent. Communards often used words like *workers* and *proletariat* in a general way to mean what in 1848 would have been called "the people." Society was thought of as comprising two groups, variously defined either as privileged and exploited or as propertied and proletarian; this was certainly a class-based analysis, but not one that suggested only one segment of the people should form a dictatorship over the other elements.[33] *Proletariat,* in particular, cast a wide net, as when an electoral meeting in the 5th

---

32. Sewell, *Work and Revolution in France,* 253; Rémi Gossez, *Les Ouvriers de Paris* (La Roche-sur-Yon: Bibliothèque de la Révolution, 1967), 233.

33. Jean Dubois has assembled many citations of the word *proletariat* in *Le Vocabulaire politique* (386) and concludes that "above all" it referred to the poor, the disinherited, and those living in poverty (43). Gould explores differences in class identity between 1848 and 1871, finding that Communards formed an "urban community," while the analysis here emphasizes a new conception of citizenship; *Insurgent Identities,* 27, 150.

arrondissement counseled, "open the door to the intelligent proletariat, to the true people. . . ."[34] The lead article of the first issue of *Le Prolétaire,* which is particularly germane because it was the newspaper of the Club des Prolétaires, dealt directly with the question of identity and class consciousness. "We are the proletariat, that is to say that manly people [homme-peuple] who searches only for light, honesty, the just, and the true, abhorring the lie, the base, and betrayal," the article began, "eternal Sisyphuses who have never ceased to push upward the infernal rock, which falls eternally on our shoulders, never leaving us in peace."[35] Endless labor is thus a defining feature of the proletarian, and a moral and political dimension is also evident, clearly expressed when the proletariat, "that is, the people," as it is also characterized, was contrasted with Legitimists, Orleanists, Bonapartists, and republicans such as Favre and Ferry of the old Government of National Defense. In a passage informed with the concept of new world the proletarian was said to reject "all your old prejudices, all your old dogmas, all your superannuated and enslaving doctrines of monarchism" from Louis XIV to Napoleon I, from Pius VII to Pius IX. The proletariat was thus defined as the working people, the oppressed majority, who have specific values and political ideals. This conception of the working classes or proletariat undermines the contention of some scholars who use the social interpretation and argue that the Commune was the "dictatorship of the proletariat." In 1871 the key mechanisms of revolt—the Federation of the National Guard and the clubs and committees that organized and prepared for the Commune—were organizations of citizens. Both were based on the *quartier,* not the workshop, and both were linked primarily to conceptions of citizenship, not class or occupation. The Luxembourg Commission was founded on worker corporations and societies; the Communal Council was the expression of sovereign electors. I am not suggesting that the Commune was not socialist or was not supported by workers. Rather, the Commune was more than a worker's movement or an attempt to initiate socialism. *Citizen* is a larger concept than *worker,* and for Communards it meant that all relations—political, economic, and social—would be founded on equality. Thus economic association was only one of the three faces of association, for the Commune was a global revolution encompassing in addition social and political transformations—not as dependencies or consequences of socialism, but as occurrences concurrent with economic restructuring.

34. *Les Murailles Politiques,* 3:128,
35. *Le Prolétaire,* May 10.

The Commune's program of economic association did not derive from any one version of socialism; there is only one example known in which Communards cited a socialist as the origin of their projects.[36] Just as in the process culminating in the formation of the Revolutionary Socialist Party, where various influences might be descried, here too Communard practice was eclectic, founded more on practical experience during the Second Empire than on books or the guidance of theorists. That is why the Revolutionary Socialist Party conformed to no single vision of revolutionary theory, and why the economic associationism of the Commune was not linked by Communards to one source. This point emerges clearly when considering some of those Communards who were at the forefront of the worker movement. Whether in the Communal Council, the AIT, or the various syndicates, collectively they could marshall many years of experience in the cooperative, worker, and political movements. Jean Gaumont identified ten members of the Communal Council, for example, who were among the most important leaders of the cooperative movement in the 1860s, having founded cooperative banks, producer associations, socialist newspapers, and worker syndicates. At a less exalted level, many of the foot soldiers in the efforts to associate production in syndicates and corporations during the Commune had their own histories of militancy.[37] In many cases they began their activity as early as 1848.

Producer cooperatives were part of a larger project for the regeneration of society. It is impossible to read the posters, official proclamations, newspaper articles, or club speeches of the Commune without quickly encountering the pervasive concept that the Commune inaugurated a new era of social equality and justice. For Auguste Vermorel, an active socialist, March 18 "consecrates the political ascension of the proletariat, as the revolution of 1789 consecrated the political ascension of the bourgeoisie." For the editors of *Le Fédéraliste* Paris is the pioneer of a new civilization that will be based on Federation—that is, association, "thus March 18 will be in the future, I do not hesitate to affirm, a date even more memorable than July 14, 1789, and August 10, 1792."[38] When clubistes and Communards wore red symbols such as belts, sashes, and shirts they affirmed that the Commune represented a new stage in history. A Versailles report on

---

36. An orator at the Club des Prolétiares on May 9 outlined the theories of Paul Courier; AHG: Ly 22.

37. Gaumont, *Histoire générale de la coopération,* 2:10; see the notices in Maitron, *DBMOF,* for Bibé, Alexander Rigault, and Jules Minet, to cite only three such militants among legions.

38. Vermorel in *L'Ami du Peuple,* April 24; *Le Fédéraliste,* May 21.

women during the Commune concluded, "many of them, seduced by the socialist theories developed in the clubs, believed that a new era was beginning."[39] "The political unity that Paris seeks is the voluntary association of all local initiatives," proclaimed the Program of the Commune, which stated that "the Communal revolution, begun by popular initiative on March 18, inaugurates a new era of experimental, positivist, scientific politics."[40] In a period in which the *Origin of Species* was still controversial and the *Syllabus of Errors* elaborated a conservative indictment of contemporary thought and society, connecting the Commune to science and positivism reinforced the modernism inherent in the Program of the Commune. Similarly, the association of workers in producer cooperatives was to be the economic foundation of the new world, an ideal stated forcefully in a meeting of women at the Trinity Church on May 12. "The day of revindication and justice approaches with giant strides," said one woman, who proclaimed, "the workshops in which you are packed will belong to you; the tools that are put into your hands will be yours; the gain resulting from your efforts, from your troubles, and from the loss of your health will be shared among you. Proletarians, you will be reborn."[41] Beyond political and economic association, what gave Communard attempts to create a "new world" the character of an integral revolution was the element of social association, the restructuring of collective activities using voluntary, sovereign organizations to express and implement the people's interests. Doctors, parents and teachers, artists, deaf-mutes, actors and actresses, musicians, veterans of the Second Republic, students—all held public meetings or formed associations during the Commune that were designed in part to safeguard their interests. They acted as independent assemblies of citizens, sovereign in their own domain. Courbet's aspiration for the Communal Council to be a federal council of associations and Lefrançais' hope to give back to the citizens themselves "the regulation of their collective and local interests" were in part realized by these groups.

The Doyens d'Age, or Elders, for example—a group of republicans

---

39. But greed was alleged to be the greatest cause of Communard sympathy; *L'Enquête Parlementaire sur l'Insurrection du Dix-Huit mars,* 345.

40. The Program of the Commune described the features of the "governmental and clerical old world," including militarism, bureaucracy, exploitation, stockjobbing, monopolies, and privileges, "to which the proletariat owes it serviage, and the Nation its troubles and disasters"; reprinted in Rougerie, *Paris Libre,* 155.

41. Reported by a conservative eyewitness; Audebrand, *Histoire intime,* 211. This was a meeting of the Women's Union for the Defense of Paris and Care for the Wounded, an organization closely linked to the International.

over fifty years of age—held a "splendid and magnificent" demonstration
at the place de la Bastille on May 7. They issued a declaration arguing that
Versailles and the men of the old Government of National Defense represented the past, whose features were monarchy and divisiveness. In contrast, the members of the Communal Council were "preparing the future"
of peace, work, and communal liberty.[42] They asked that the Communal
Council confer on them the guard of the city as a "Communal Militia"
while the younger guardsmen were at the ramparts fighting, an honor that
would mean that "under your auspices, the people will have themselves
founded their first institution for those who may no longer work." The
success of the revolution and the creation of the new future world was
thereby connected to the group's efforts to promote republican institutions. Another group of veteran republicans, the Society of Former Political Criminals and Exiles, organized a battalion to fight for the Commune.[43]

Social association involved areas where the public interest intersected
with the particular interests of specific groups. Medical education, theaters, art, and public education were the scenes of the best articulated
attempts to make association the basis of the new society. The École de
Médecine was reorganized on the initiative of the Communal Council's
Education Delegation. Doctors met in each of the twenty arrondissements
to name delegates, students met at the École de Médecine to elect ten delegates, and independent medical professors elected three delegates. All
interested groups were thereby brought into the project of reorganization
through the method of public meeting and delegation. The delegates then
began a series of meetings twice weekly to draft new guidelines for medical
training. Once this work was completed, the Communal Council was to
have the final decision on implementing the findings.[44] The several meetings that medical students held to fulfill this project appear to have been
the origin of the Fédération des Écoles, a student group that placed itself
at the service of the Commune.[45] The draft statutes for the Fédération des
Écoles, at the time known as the Association Républicaine des Écoles, out-

42. *La Sociale*, May 13.
43. *Le Vengeur*, April 3, 5, and 7.
44. *Le Mot d'Ordre*, April 20 and 26; *Le Journal Officiel*, April 27; *Le Bien Publique*, April 27.
45. Some hesitation to support the Commune was still expressed in the medical student meetings of late April, when some attendees would only shout, "Long live the Republic!" rather than shouting, "Long live the Commune!" Dabot, *Griffonnages quotidiens*, 202; *Le Bien Publique*, April 27.

lined the goals of the group, which also reveal the several aspects of social association.[46] The "political goal" of the Fédération des Écoles was to assure the triumph of the "universal republic" through the principles of liberty and justice. The "scientific goal" was to "struggle against all opinions founded on faith and tradition, through the propagation of science and history," and to "concern ourselves with all issues relative to instruction at the various Schools." The "material goal," founded on fraternity and solidarity, was to create the means for mutual security and protection against economic difficulties. The Fédération des Écoles placed the activity of students in the context of the political struggle between Paris and Versailles, sought to promote the interests of students in educational institutions, and hoped to assure the material life of its members.

There was some dispute within the Fédération des Écoles about the methods to be employed in aiding the Commune. The Fédération sent several delegates to the Ligue d'Union Républicaine des Droits de Paris, the conciliatory group of moderate republicans. "Two currents are found in our federation," a delegate told the Ligue. "One," he continued, "tends toward a pure and simple adhesion to the program of Ligue; the other, which I represent, calls for immediately taking up arms for municipal rights against monarchism."[47] Indeed, in early May a group broke away from the Fédération and founded the Club of Atheist Republican Students, motivated by the Fédération's perceived moderation in combating clericalism and monarchism. The occasion for this schism was most likely the drafting of a long declaration "to the Schools of France," intended to gain the support of provincial students for the Commune.[48] The tone of the declaration was temperate and reasonable, stressing the need for moral force and for enlightening France about the real nature of the conflict between Paris and Versailles, described as the struggle for communal liberty versus monarchy. Only in the last paragraph did the Fédération des Écoles counsel armed resistance. The moderate tone, which most likely precipitated the schism with the more radical elements, was clearly a tactic to gain a larger audience; five of the six people who signed the declaration served the Commune as medical personnel or in the Ministry of War.

---

46. The statutes are reprinted in Girault, "Les Étudiants et la Commune," 101. Girault suggests that this was "perhaps the first student formation of the syndicalist type."

47. As described by Lefèvre, a Ligue official; *Histoire de la Ligue d'Union,* 180.

48. The club statutes are reprinted in Girault, "Les Étudiants et la Commune," 102; *Le Cri du Peuple,* May 14. This was only one of many appeals to France drawn up in late April and May, when it was evident that Paris could not defeat Versailles on its own. The declaration is dated May 8 and was written at least in part in a meeting of May 4; APP: 364-6.

The most important association involved in education under the Commune was Education Nouvelle, or New Education. This group had its origins in the siege, when a group of teachers and parents began meeting at the École Turgot to discuss reforms in education.[49] Education Nouvelle was thus able to present its program for educational reforms to the Commune as early as April 1. It outlined a republican project for free, obligatory, and secular education based exclusively on "the experimental or scientific method" rather than on religious principles. The Falloux Law of 1850 had placed primary education under the auspices of the Catholic Church, although in Paris almost as many students attended secular municipal schools as religious ones.[50] Many republicans identified the church with monarchism and obscurantism, and the struggle against religious education was an important theme in republican ideology in the late Second Empire. The members of the Commune told the delegates from Education Nouvelle that they fully agreed with the program and were strengthened in their resolve to implement its reforms. This began a fruitful collaboration between the Commune and Education Nouvelle to secularize education, modernize the curriculum, and foster vocational education.[51] It was Joanny Rama, a member of Education Nouvelle, who suggested that the Communal Council's Delegation of Education name a committee composed only of persons "devoted to the cause of rational education," to reorganize education.[52] Several members of Education Nouvelle were appointed to the commission, and in late April the group was holding meetings to discuss a new law on public education. As Delegate for Instruction in the 17th arrondissement Rama secularized municipal schools and introduced "the experimental or scientific method," the exact formulation found in Education Nouvelle's statement of April 1.

---

49. For example, one orator insisted that "only secular education can produce honest and good citizens." One member of this group was Rheims, who continued to be active in Education Nouvelle. Another member was Elie Ducoudray, who was for a time mayor of the 14th arrondissement, and who on October 31 attempted to invade the mairie at the head of the Club Maison-Dieu; *Le Combat,* November 28, 1870; *La Cloche,* November 14, 1870; *Le Gaulois,* November 27, 1870.

50. *Le Journal Officiel,* April 2. About one-third of Parisian students did not attend any schools at all; Edwards, *The Paris Commune,* 267. See also Maurice Dommanget, *L'Enseignement, l'enfance, et la culture sous la Commune* (Paris: Éditions Sociales, 1964).

51. *Le Mot d'Ordre,* April 4; *La Sociale,* April 28. Education Nouvelle also met with Jules Allix's mutual aid society La Commune Sociale, to coordinate their initiatives for education and social welfare; *Le Cri du Peuple,* April 22.

52. The initiative for creating this committee has always been ascribed to Vaillant, the head of the Delegation of Education, but Rama's proposal to Vaillant is in APP: Ba 364-6.

Other arrondissement administrators followed a similar pattern of organizing secular public education through public assemblies.[53]

Secular education was part of a larger program of social renovation for the reformers of Education Nouvelle, which considered education to be "the key question that embraces and dominates all political and social questions; there will never be serious and durable reforms without its solution." Part of this project was instruction that was "free and complete for every child of both sexes," which Education Nouvelle placed in the context of promoting the "the best training possible for private life, professional life, and political or social life." Indeed, most of the persons active in Education Nouvelle were women who had personal experience of educational inequality. Following a line of argument traced by Rousseau, some republican men also advocated female education, as explained by the Jacobin newspaper *Le Père Duchêne:* "citizens, if you only realized how much the revolution depends on women you would open you eyes to girls' education. . . . it is on the knees of *citoyennes* that we learn to bray our first words." V. Manière was particularly active in promoting professional education for young women in her capacity as director of a women's vocational school. A member of Education Nouvelle, she sought "a progressive education, entirely freed from prejudices," organized by elected groups of workers and teachers. Vaillant, the Commune's Delegate for Education, supported such reforms, arguing "it is vital that the Communal Revolution affirm its essentially socialist character" through "a reform of education assuring to each the true foundation of social equality, a complete education to which all have a right." As part of this vision of equality, Vaillant decreed that male and female teachers should receive equal pay.[54]

Another area in which association was employed as the basis for reorganizing social institutions was the arts. The Fédération des Artistes was founded under the leadership of Courbet to be the "government of the world of art by artists," for the conservation of artistic treasures of the past and "the regeneration of the future through education."[55] Courbet placed this initiative firmly within his well-articulated vision of association as the foundation of the new world. "The heroic people of Paris will vanquish the mystigogues and tormentors of Versailles," he proclaimed when calling artists to meet." "Man will govern himself," he said, "Federation

53. *Le Mot d'Ordre,* April 29; Edwards, *The Paris Commune,* 269.
54. *Le Père Duchêne,* April 9; *Le Vengeur,* April 3; *Le Cri du Peuple,* May 20 and 21. Thomas discusses women in education during the Commune, in *Women Incendiaries,* 153.
55. *Le Journal Officiel,* April 15.

will be complete, and Paris will have the greatest measure of glory that history has ever recorded." Three hundred artists took part in the elections to the Commission on April 17.[56] Under the supervision of the Delegation of Education the forty-six-member Commission Fédérale des Artistes established itself in the place of the ex-Ministry of Fine Arts. It then set about administering the museums of Paris, supervising Parisian participation in the London Exhibition, and reorganizing artistic education in the city.[57]

That the Fédération des Artistes identified itself completely with the cause of the Commune led to criticism, at the time and since, that it was an attempt to bring art under the control of the state.[58] The Commission was indeed formed by "artists of Paris who adhere to the Communal Republic," and its work was carried out under the supervision of the Communal Council's Delegation of Education. The intent of Courbet and the other artists of the Commission, however, was to free artists from "government tutelage" and replace state institutions with federations run by artists. A report by the Commission published in mid-May repeatedly stressed that it was not instituted to continue the regime of artistic supervision imposed by monarchies and empires. "Any official guidance given to a student's judgment is fatal and therefore condemned; this power does not even belong to an artistic majority," it announced. It further stated that "the Commission Fédérale des Artistes does not direct architecture along one path or another, and will never be a judge from an artistic point of view."[59] The Commission proposed ending state subsidies to artistic education institutions such as the École des Beaux Arts, which would instead be funded by artists. Associations of artists would also be responsible for funding exhibitions, again without the customary state subsidies. Prizes would be awarded only by committees of artists, and commissions would be granted only by competition. For the artists of the Commission Fédérale des Artistes the replacement of government interference with the

---

56. *Le Journal Officiel,* April 6. Of the well-known painters elected, such as Millet, Corot, Daumier, and Manet, only Courbet participated in the group; the others either were out of the city or abstained.

57. Depending on their duties the members were paid five or ten francs a day by the Commune; BHVP: Ms. 1131; *Le Journal Officiel,* May 14.

58. Jules Andrieux, a member of the Communal Council, wrote that Courbet tried to prevent the exhibition of some paintings because of the political views of the artists; Serman, *La Commune de Paris,* 383. The critic Muntz feared that the Commission Fédérale des Artistes would impose official views on artists; *La Verité,* May 9. Rials has suggested that the Commission's monopoly in artistic matters "makes one shiver, and presages certain artistic totalitarianisms of the twentieth century"; *Nouvelle histoire de Paris,* 431.

59. *Le Journal Officiel,* May 10.

liberties inherent in association was a revolutionary act. Courbet's hope of founding a new era was echoed in more political terms by an artist in a Commission meeting who said, "we seek to make the democratic revolution operative. The Louvre, once conquered by us, will be our Hôtel de ville; we will raise the red flag of painting." The comments of a conservative observer at another meeting provide more evidence of the association's radicalism: "the least observation raised murmurs, the smallest motion provoked tempests, the simplest contradiction attracted the epithet *reactionary.*" The same observer sardonically reported that when the Commission decided women could be members Courbet noted "there was no difference between *citoyens* and *citoyennes.*"[60] Although male and female artists were allowed to participate in the Fédération des Artistes, there is no record of any women actually doing so.

The same is not true of the final example of social association, the Fédération Artistique, an organization of actors, actresses, singers, and musicians. Formed in a series of meetings beginning on April 10, the Fédération Artistique began as an initiative to group all actors and musicians in one National Guard battalion, "in the name of democracy and fraternity," thereby minimizing disruptions that military service presented to mounting plays, operas, and concerts. By May 6 the battalion's organization was far enough along for it be incorporated in the Third Legion.[61] The Fédération Artistique also developed "artistic" and "social" functions, organizing concerts to benefit widows and orphans of Communards killed in combat, as well as aspiring to provide mutual aid and social security for members. Perhaps because of the military origins of the Fédération Artistique none of the organizers were women, but several woman were associated with the federation's charity benefits, notably the actress Clotilde Agar, celebrated for her renditions of the "Marseillaise."[62] Six hundred people were reportedly in attendance at the meeting of April 21 that named the committee to write the statutes. "The Fédération Artistique will rally all the members of the theatrical and musical family, and will thus accomplish the fraternal artistic fusion so long dreamed of," a newspaper reported. "This federation," the report continued, "starting

---

60. Pressensé, *Les Leçons du 18 mars,* 122; *Le Bien Publique,* April 18.

61. *Le Journal Officiel,* April 12 and May 7. Gustave Labarthe, *Le Théâtre pendant les jours du siège et de la Commune* (Paris: Fischbacher, 1910), 126, argued that the battalion's real intent was to provide a safe haven for actors. *La Commune,* May 11, complained that some actors claimed to be exempt from service.

62. *Le Journal Officiel,* May 20.

with such a republican principle, should carry out rapid and salutary reforms."[63] One such reform was the creation of societies of entertainers who would share the proceeds of their labor. Societies had already been formed for the presentation of specific plays at the salle Valentino, the Théâtre Lyrique, and the Gaité. J. Pacra, sometime president of the Fédération Artistique, organized the actors and actresses at the Eldorado into a similar society, with considerable financial success.[64]

The Fédération Artistique was less developed than the Commission Fédérale des Artistes and had no official functions besides sponsoring charity concerts. Still, the Fédération Artistique and other initiatives in the world of the theater incited an important debate about the role of the Communal Council in encouraging socialism through association. On May 19 Vaillant asked the Communal Council to confirm that theaters were under his authority as the Delegate for Education, and not under that of the Delegation of General Security. "General Security should only maintain order in the theaters; but it must not be forgotten that, just as the Revolution of '89 gave the land to the peasants, our Revolution of March 18 should assure the instruments of work and production to the worker," he said, adding, "theaters should belong to federations of artists, and that is why the Delegation of Education has thought it well that all artists should be convoked to that end."[65] Vaillant's assertion that the Commune would give the tools of production to workers just as the Great Revolution had given land to the peasants was a widespread ideal and directly paraphrased the revolutionary socialist electoral poster of February, on which Vaillant had figured as a candidate.

Félix Pyat, a sometime playwright, objected that Vaillant's proposal threatened artistic freedom. He argued that the state should not intervene in the theater, as "there should no more be a literature or science of State than there should be a religion of State." Both Frankel and Vaillant responded that the Commune, as the government of all citizens, had the right to work for justice and equality. Vaillant then directly posed the question of the Communal Council's role in transforming society: "Theaters are not only throats [for speaking and singing]; they are stomachs.

---

63. *Le Journal Officiel,* April 30. The statutes committee included actors, musicians, composers, and authors.

64. *Le Bien Publique,* March 8; *Le Rappel,* April 1; *Le Mot d'Ordre,* April 22; Labarthe, *Le Théâtre,* 133.

65. *Les Procès-Verbaux de la Commune,* 2:413. Vaillant's request was also part of the continuing battle between the majority and the minority. The Delegation of Education was dominated by the minority, while General Security was majoritarian.

There are people in them who earn an enormous amount, while others do not earn enough. Thus there are certain moral and material conditions that the Commune should regulate." Vaillant continued, "obviously we do not want *State Art.* . . . We must end all exploitation. To whom should this task belong? To the Delegation that it specifically concerns, until you have created a general Delegation that will liquidate the old society."[66] His last sentence echoes the revolutionary socialist Declaration of Principles of February 19, which envisioned a "political and social liquidation" after an intermediate period of government by the revolutionary Commune.

Vaillant clearly wanted freedom of speech and thought to be protected, but as economic enterprises theaters should be subject to the Communal Council's control in the interest of ending "all exploitation." The Communal Council agreed. Its decree incorporated the intent to protect artistic freedom by ending all state "subsidies and monopolies" for theaters, just as the Commission Fédérale des Artistes had proposed ending state subsidies to artists. The Communal Council decided that "the Delegation [of Education] is charged with ending, for theaters, the regime of exploitation by a director or a company, to replace it as quickly as possible with the regime of association."[67] The importance of this decree, and the debate that preceded it, has not been recognized among historians, who have cited it only in relation to the Commune's cultural policies. Yet it ought to be placed in the same category as the decree of April 19 allotting abandoned workshops to worker associations and as that of May 12 giving preference in awarding contracts to worker associations—as one of the strongest statements of socialist intent by the Communal Council. Association was reaffirmed as the foundation of the Communal Council's economic program, and the role of the council in promoting a restructuring of society was confirmed as well. At both the base in popular organizations and the apex in the Communal Council the Commune was founded on a similar conception of social change through popular initiative and organization.

The political facet of the program of association was most extensively

---

66. *Les Procès-Verbaux de la Commune,* 2:429.

67. A convocation of May 20 called on "citoyens et citoyennes artistes" of the Opera, Comic Opera, and Théâtre-Lyrique to meet with a representative of the Delegation of Education in order to "replace the regime of exploitation, by a director or a company, with the regime of association." The representative was Daniel Salvator, director of the Conservatory, who, like Vaillant, was part of the vigilance committee movement and had signed the Red Poster of January 6. *Le Journal Officiel,* May 20; *Les Procès-Verbaux de la Commune,* 2:438.

developed during the Commune. Popular and revolutionary political thought held that those elected to office were not representatives, free to vote as their conscience dictated, but rather bound servants or mandatories who were to carry out the specific wishes—the imperative mandate—of the people.[68] As in the draft constitution proposed by Lefrançais, there was a general understanding that the members of the Communal Council and other public officials should attend public meetings and clubs to justify their conduct. A number of meetings were held so that elected officials could give an accounting to their electors. "When Robespierre or Saint-Just came before the Convention, they were strong because they had come from the Jacobin club, or the Club des Cordeliers," Charles Amouroux, a member of the Commune, stated in one such meeting. "In the same fashion," he continued, "Marat was strong because he wrote what he had heard while in the midst of the working population."[69] Just as during the first Revolution, so too during the Commune the revolutionary leadership was considered strong only to the extent that it expressed the people's will and enthusiasm. In early May the members of the Commune for the 18th arrondissement announced daily public meetings, arguing that "those elected by the people have the duty of keeping in constant touch with their electors to give account of the mandate they have received and to submit themselves to questions."[70] One principle that prompted the founding of the Club des Prolétaires was that "the elected must always be ready to give account of his acts to his electors, in order to be constantly in touch with them."[71]

Clubs and assemblies functioned in part as intermediaries between the revolutionary leadership and the mass of Communards. Members of the Communal Council, high officials in the Communal administration, National Guard officers, and officials who administered the arrondissements often organized and attended meetings to speak and listen. Of 733 people who have been identified as clubistes, 198 had some official position of authority under the Commune, a proportion of 27 percent (see table 2; because 9 people held two positions the number in authority is

68. See Serman, *La Commune de Paris,* 314, for a fine discussion of this aspect of popular political theory.

69. *Les Procès-Verbaux de la Commune,* 2:458. According to Amouroux, two thousand people attended this meeting.

70. From a poster of May 5, cited in Edwards, *The Paris Commune,* 278. A Versailles report on the first such meeting observed that Vermorel spoke of the Committee of Public Safety, and that the assembly demanded the *leveé en masse; APP:* 364-6.

71. *Le Prolétaire,* May 10.

given there as 207). Only two of these people were women: Adélaïde Valentin, chief of the Légion des Fédérées, and a Madame Benoit who was employed at the mairie of the 5th arrondissement. The vast majority of the eighty-nine arrondissement officials listed in table 2 were members of vigilance committees that also functioned as municipal councils for their arrondissement. Seventeen of Paris's twenty arrondissements had local officials who were known to attend a club or committee. The category of National Guard officers includes only those of substantial rank, such as legion commanders, battalion chiefs, and members of arrondissement military councils. Most of the police officials listed were *commissaires,* that is, police officers, but some also held posts in the Prefecture; twelve arrondissements are known to have had police officials who were also clubistes. The "diverse" category includes persons such as Achille Revillon, director of Customs, who was noted at the Club Saint Sulpice, and Zephrin Camelinat, director of the Mint, who was a member of the Delegation of the Twenty Arrondissements. Clubs and committees linked these revolutionary leaders and militants to each other and to the mass of Communards.

The most important of these clubistes who also held official positions of authority were the members of the Communal Council. The forty-seven council members that are known to have attended popular organizations represent 60 percent of the seventy-eight members of the Communal Council. It was not uncommon for clubistes to complain that members of the council did not attend their meetings, and based on these complaints some historians have criticized the Communal Council for not maintaining close contact with popular organizations.[72] It is undeniable, however,

TABLE 2.   Clubistes in Positions of Authority

	Number	% of 207
Arrondissement officials	89	43
Members of the Commune	47	22.8
National Guard officers	29	14
Police officials	26	12.5
Diverse	16	7.7
Total	207	100

72. Edwards, *The Paris Commune,* 281. Rougerie observed that "few" members appeared in meetings; *Paris Libre,* 222. Rihs argued the Communal Council lacked "direct contact" with the mass of Communards; *La Commune de Paris,* 52.

that despite extensive duties at the Hôtel de ville and in the arrondissements, the majority of Communal Council members did indeed attend
clubs and committees, though one can well imagine that they did not do so
to the extent desired by other clubistes. Since two-thirds of the Communal
Council had been active in the revolutionary socialist movement or in vigilance committees before the Commune, it is not surprising that most
members of the Commune were active in vigilance committees and other
special purpose committees. Only nineteen are known to have attended the
large popular clubs and public assemblies, but even this number represented 24 percent of the Communal Council. Given the fragmentary evidence available these figures surely underrepresent the number of council
members that attended such meetings.

When clubs passed resolutions members of the Communal Council
often responded to the people's will. Members of the Commune who
attended clubs sometimes made club decisions known to the Communal
Council. Vésinier brought to the Communal Council's attention a set of
propositions passed at the Club Communal held in Saint Nicolas des
Champs. On another occasion Champy told the Commune that the "committee of the 20th arrondissement" proposed that the Commune declare
the Versailles Assembly dissolved.[73] The most important instance of the
Communal Council taking note of the propositions and requests of popular clubs and committees has been oddly neglected by historians, however.
On April 24 the vigilance committee of the 19th arrondissement proposed,
and the public meeting of the salle Marseillaise adopted, a statement asking that "the Commune proceed without delay to form in its midst a Committee of Public Safety, supplied with the full power to decree victory and
with the force necessary to have its decisions executed."[74] Four days later
Jules Miot, a member of the Communal Council from the 19th arrondissement, proposed the creation of such a committee, a measure that eventually split the Commune into rival factions.

As these examples show, association was also considered the avenue by
which the people could directly participate in forming policy and shaping
the revolution. This idea was a prominent feature of the Program of the
Commune, which declared one of the rights inherent in the Commune to
be "the permanent intervention by citizens in communal affairs, through

---

73. *Les Procès-Verbaux de la Commune,* 2:89, 436.

74. *Le Mot d'Ordre,* April 26. As I mentioned in chapter 2, the vigilance committee of the
19th had itself formed a Committee of Public Safety to counter the threat of Prussians occupying the city in late February.

the free expression of their ideas, and the free defense of their interests."
These rights were accompanied by a radical limitation on the function of
government, for the Commune was "only responsible for assuring the free
and just exercise of the rights of association and the press."[75] To promote
this "permanent intervention" by citizens, the municipal council of the 1st
arrondissement, composed of vigilance committee members, outlined a
project for "consultative councils," to be formed by six delegates from
public meetings in each of the four *quartiers* of the arrondissement. These
consultative councils would "second the members of the Commune, by
aiding them with their understanding and their counsels, and by directly
representing the wishes of the population, with whom they will be in constant contact."[76]

The leaders of the Club des Prolétaires also envisioned an elaborate system of popular assemblies organized alongside representative bodies such
as the Communal Council.[77] This system would establish a permanent
mechanism for holding referenda so that the people could be consulted on
both specific issues and general policy. The club leaders were suspicious of
representative systems that put private interests above the common good,
and they sought a return to popular, direct democracy based on assemblies
of citizens. The questions to be put to the people would always be phrased
to elicit a yes or no answer, as in, for example, "Should one be forbidden
from working for wages that are less than those thought the absolute minimum to live?" The other example given also dealt with an issue of economic justice: "Should some be allowed to possess more than needed if the
basic necessities are guaranteed to everyone?" An article in the May 17
issue of *La Rouge* asked all the clubs and meetings of the capital to debate
whether the Communal Council should declare itself the government of
France, so that when the Communal Council took up the issue it would
know the will of the people. Many popular organizations presented resolutions to the Communal Council. In going to meetings Communards
were not merely expressing their opinions; they were also directing their
revolution.

The most important component of political association was the belief
that popular assemblies were sovereign entities in and of themselves. This
was of course the fundamental principle behind the vigilance committee
movement and the revolutionary Commune of January 1, and it was also

75. Reprinted in Rougerie, *Paris Libre,* 154.
76. *Le Cri du Peuple,* April 16.
77. *Le Prolétaire,* May 10.

the theoretical basis for the action of the Federation of the National Guard.[78] Because Paris was under the control of a revolutionary government during the Commune this aspect of association was generally not put into practice then, but it remained an accepted assumption. Under the Commune Parisians "had finally found the exact formula for popular sovereignty," according to Arthur Arnould, a member of the Communal Council for the 4th arrondissement. The Central Committee of the Artillery of the National Guard described itself as "emanating from universal suffrage, a democratic institution in its largest sense." Several assemblies solemnly voted to rescind the mandate given the National Assembly, thereby revoking its legitimacy, and indicating that Communards intended to maintain their status as sovereign citizens through the structures of association.[79] Another way of underscoring the illegitimacy of the National Assembly—and the ability of clubs to act as sovereign entities—was found by Guillaume, known as Mouton, a member of the Club de la Révolution of the rue Cujas (5th arrondissement), who had the assembly vote to put a price on the head of Adolphe Thiers and Jules Favre and contributed the first 11.5 francs himself.[80]

Evolutions within the club movement and outside circumstances such as the course of the civil war combined to create three phases in associationism during the Commune. The first period, from March 18 to mid-April, witnessed the consolidation of the revolution at the three levels of power in the city, the Communal Council, arrondissement mairies, and public spaces such as squares and meeting halls. In addition, moderates launched conciliatory groups in hopes of bringing about a pacific settlement between Paris and Versailles. The club movement of the early Commune was a continuation of that of the siege and armistice and was built on the foundation of vigilance committees. Even, or perhaps especially, in the ten arrondissements where vigilance committees formed the core of the local municipal councils they remained at the center of local club and committee activity. In fifteen arrondissements vigilance committees can be conclusively associated with at least one club or public meeting during the Commune, and there is good reason to believe that vigilance committees

78. Michel Dominique Alner has argued to the contrary that clubs were politically marginal and did not present a "functional alternative to challenge centralized power"; "The Jacobins in the Paris Commune of 1871" (Ph.D. diss., Columbia University, 1978), 295.
79. Arnould, *Histoire Populaire,* 1:44; Maillard, *Affiches,* 193; *Le Cri du Peuple,* April 25; *Le Journal Officiel,* May 9.
80. AHG: Ly 22.

initiated clubs or public meetings in two others (the 10th and 20th); only the 9th, 15th, and 16th arrondissements appear not to have had a club or public meeting associated with a vigilance committee. Clubs and committees, based mainly on the vigilance committee movement of the siege and armistice, were still fairly closely coordinated through the Delegation of the Twenty Arrondissements, and the main thrust of club and committee action was to preserve and protect the young insurrection.

With the outbreak of civil war and the realization that possibilities actually existed for the reformation of society a second phase of the political evolution of clubs and committees began, in which the insurrection was transformed into a revolution. New organizations and groups were created to implement a thoroughgoing restructuring of society based on association. For example, the Union des Femmes pour la Défense de Paris et les Soins aux Blessés was founded on April 11 to mobilize women for a variety of tasks, including building barricades and reorganizing production of National Guard uniforms by association. The Alliance Républicaine des Départements was established to enlighten the provinces and enlist their aid against the Versailles government. In this period assemblies of doctors, artists, and others were formed. As is shown by the elections of March 26, the revolutionary left in the clubs and committees, centered in the Delegation of the Twenty Arrondissements, was the strongest organized political element in the city. Yet the same centrifugal forces of disintegration that had made the construction of a citywide revolutionary socialist movement so difficult in the siege were also at work during the Commune. After the first weeks the impetus toward localism grew even stronger, partially demolishing the coordinated club and committee movement. Not only were many militants absorbed with administrative and military duties at either the arrondissement mairies, the Hôtel de ville, or the front lines, but the new configuration of political and social power in the capital appears to have caught the former revolutionary socialist leadership off balance. Club and committee activists had always been in opposition, first to the Empire, then to the Government of National Defense, and finally to the National Assembly. From the inception of the strategy for a "revolutionary Commune" in the late siege the whole movement had been structured with the understanding that revolutionaries were a minority who required unified effort to overcome numerical inferiority and attain power. These assumptions no longer held once a revolutionary government was in control of the city, and a large part of the original rationale for the revolutionary socialist movement disappeared. Clubistes did not arrive at a new conception of the place of clubs and committees under a revolutionary regime until late April and May, by which time the central Delegation had fallen into impotence and the local vigilance committees had traveled down divergent paths. While the Delegation of the Twenty Arrondissements momentarily declined in influence, new club networks were formed to link and multiply club initiatives. At the same time, Communards either intimidated or overwhelmed moderate and conciliatory groups, so that all public discourse was in the hands of revolutionaries. Also in this second period, from late April to early May, club rhetoric grew increasingly radical, with demands for war to the finish and threats of violence against opponents. Implementing the revolution hardened positions and heightened tensions between the minority of Communards and the rest of the population in the city, leading to ever more arrests and ever more incitements to further revolutionary measures.

Finally, in early and mid-May the beginning of a third phase in the political evolution of clubs may be discerned. The first fall of the strategic Issy Fortress on April 30 and its definitive loss on May 9 made the prospect of defeat increasingly real. In this third phase invocations of popular sovereignty by clubistes took on a new tone, especially in the massive club meetings held in requisitioned churches. Church and state were declared separate by a law of April 2, and church buildings were declared national property. Arrondissement administrators and police agents then inventoried church property, in some cases closing churches to worship. Some local officials charged the faithful rent for the use of the churches, the origin of some allegations of extortion by Communards, as at Notre-Dame des Victoires, where back rent amounting to twelve thousand francs was reportedly demanded. Lefrançais proposed in the Communal Council that churches be rented to their congregations, though there was no formal decision on the matter. His proposal was echoed, though, at the Club des Prolétaires on May 12, when someone suggested that churches be rented for the benefit of widows and orphans.[81] Some churches were emptied of their contents, but mostly through administrative seizure rather than theft. For example, the contents of Notre-Dame de Lorette were found at the Mint after the Commune.[82]

Churches were in great demand by clubistes: they were free, centrally

81. *La Commune à Notre-Dame des Victoires* (Paris: Simon Raçon, 1871), 6; *Les Procès-Verbaux de la Commune,* 2:98; AHG: 16e conseil 820, dossier Lesueur.

82. AHG: 13e conseil, 189, dossier Lemoussou. Only eight people were convicted of stealing from churches after the Commune; General Appert, *Rapport d'ensemble . . . sur les opérations de la justice militaire relatives à l'insurrection de 1871,* Annales de l'Assemblée Nationale, vol. 43 (Paris: Imprimerie Nationale, 1875), 43.

located, and spacious, but most importantly, they were churches. Communards did not lack for other free meeting places in schools, museums, theaters, and other civic buildings, but churches held a special attraction. A witness testified that Pierre Burdaille tried repeatedly to open a club in Saint Eloi despite being offered other locales by clerics, "but Burdaille didn't care, it was the church that he wanted."[83] One observer listed several reasons why he thought meetings in churches were more inconvenient than in other locales, concluding that clubistes wanted to use churches not for their convenience or spaciousness but for the meanings their possession conveyed. Clubistes especially appreciated the opportunity to bring enlightenment and truth into dark sanctuaries of superstition. Joseph Chaussade told a neighbor, "It has been long enough that you have used the churches, it's our turn to preach the truth." Jean Allemane told a cleric who complained of clubs in his church, "Well, what evil do you see in that? If discussion unveils light, and you possess the truth, then you cannot but gain from the debate."[84] At the installation of the Club de la Révolution Sociale in the Saint Michel des Batignolles Church, a speaker struck a common theme. "It's been long enough that our oppressors have cast darkness around the people, without whom they would be nothing," he said, adding, "I demand light; each one of us should know our rights and make them respected. Our turn has come. The keystone of the modern world is the proletarian; I thus propose that the Club de la Révolution Sociale meet daily."[85] Here again club action was placed in the context of creating a new, "modern world," in contrast to a discredited world of clerics and superstition.

The ideal of self-enlightenment was echoed in the poster announcing meetings at Saint Nicolas des Champs, and again it was envisioned as part of the larger revolutionary purpose. "A grand revolutionary act has just been achieved: the population of the 3d arrondissement has, in order to politically educate the people, finally taken possession of a public monument that to this day only served a caste that was a born enemy of all progress," club organizers proclaimed, urging, "follow our example, open communal clubs in all the churches; the priests can officiate during the

---

83. AHG: 5e conseil 545. Budaille organized many public meetings during the late Empire but was compromised by revelations that he had contacts with the government.

84. *Sous la Commune: Récits et souvenirs d'un Parisien* (Paris: Dentu, 1873), 69; AHG: 5e conseil 919, dossier Chaussade; Allemane, *Mémoires d'un Communard*, 113.

85. Quoted by the conservative literary critic Maxime Du Camp in *Les Convulsions de Paris*, 5th ed., 3 vols. (Paris: Dentu, 1881), 2:251.

day, and you will educate the people in the evening."[86] The transformation of a church from a place of mystification to one of enlightenment was thus a "revolutionary act." On May 12 the Club des Terres-Fortes, directed by the vigilance committee of the 12th arrondissement, was installed in the Saint Eloi Church. One hostile observer described Philippe, mayor of the arrondissement and an avid clubiste, as saying, "we are going to found a new society, a truly democratic and social society, where there will never be neither rich nor poor, since the rich—should there be any—will be obliged to abandon their goods to the poor." The account then observed that someone replied, "begin by abolishing Rothschild," which received an explosion of applause from the assembly.[87] In making this particular speech at the inauguration of the new location Philippe clearly meant to show that the club was an important component of the new society, in this case as a place in which to form consensus around revolutionary goals.

As the continuing failure of the struggle against Versailles cast doubt on the Communal Council's leadership, criticism of the political and military administration grew in direct proportion to the likelihood of defeat. While an article in the May 13 issue of *La Justice* still professed that the revolution would "renovate the European old world," it stated as well that "the impotence of the Commune as a government is evident. The specific importance of its work will have been to break the governmental old world." More denunciations of the political and military administration of the city were heard in the National Guard as well. Most contemporaries observed an increasing hostility toward those in authority as Versailles forces moved ever closer to breaching the fortifications around the city. During the last week desperation and exasperation led to many threats of physical violence. Allemane described guardsmen as mutinous and vengeful; he had to lock up Legion Commander Piazza to save him from his troops. As a radical revolutionary Allemane himself contributed to this tendency to criticize the leadership of the Commune. "He always wore a large red belt, his rifle over his shoulder, and a revolver in the belt," said a

---

86. *Les Murailles Politiques,* 2:145.

87. Fontoulieu, *Les Églises,* 62. Since Fontoulieu is such a vital source of evidence about the clubs held in churches it is important to stress that his account of this speech echoes similar statements and is therefore unlikely to have been a pure invention or falsification. At a club during the late siege Israel Schneider allegedly said, "the government of the Commune will confiscate the goods of the rich to distribute them to the poor"; Cresson, *Cent jours,* 129. During the Commune Charles Lesueur reportedly said at the Club des Prolétaires that the inventory of the merchants who left Paris should be sold for the benefit of the local arrondissement; AHG: 16e conseil 820.

witness at his trial, who claimed that "in the clubs, there was no more violent or vulgar orator. He even accused the members of the Commune of
not being energetic enough."[88] A Versailles agent reported hearing complaints about inequality of guard service, and one guardsman complained
that "the Commune has sold out to Versailles."[89]

In the May 19 issue of *Le Prolétaire,* the newspaper of the Club des Prolétaires, C. G. Jacqueline called the members of the Communal Council
"exploiters of the revolution," who in general were not worthy of their
post. "The Commune is the people themselves, demonstrating their will
through legal deliberation on the acts of their agents," he declared,
demanding, "let us do everything ourselves, and not wait for the pressure
of the bridle or the stimulant of the spur to show the path to follow." The
May 6 issue of *Le Bulletin Communal,* the newspaper of the Club Communal held in Saint Nicolas des Champs, expressed much the same impatience with the members of the Communal Council. "People, govern yourself by yourself through your public meetings, through your press," it
counseled, saying, "pressure those who represent you; they will never go
far enough along the revolutionary road." Communards in clubs began to
assert their sovereign rights more forcefully during this final phase of the
revolution. On May 17 the Club Communal even held extralegal elections
to fill a vacant seat on the Communal Council for the 3d arrondissement.[90]

There were a number of reports that in the last few days of the Commune several clubs voted to dissolve the Communal Council or revoke its
mandate. The salle Marseillaise voted on May 11 to support the Central
Committee of the National Guard in its disputes with the Communal
Council.[91] On May 21, the day Versailles forces first entered the city, the
Club Saint Pierre de Montrouge voted in favor of the "déchéance" (revo-
cation in disgrace) of the Commune because it was "not revolutionary
enough."[92] During the Commune, then, the political trajectory of clubs
and committees in some ways replicated the experience of the siege. As the
governments in question appeared increasingly incompetent or insuffi-
ciently revolutionary, clubs and committees became the vehicles for the

88. AHG: 5e conseil 338; Allemane, *Mémoires d'un Communard,* 140. As a member of the
Communal Council Vallès was repeatedly insulted by guardsmen: "your place isn't here,"
one told him at a barricade, ordering him to "go and decide something!"; Vallès, *Oeuvres
complets,* vol. 2, *L'Insurgé* (Paris: Livre Club Diderot, 1969), 558.
89. APP: Ba 364-4, report of May 11.
90. AHG: 17e conseil 252, dossier Paysant; 17e conseil, 742, dossier Landeck.
91. APP: Ba 364-6.
92. Quoted in Fontoulieu, *Les Églises,* 208.

assertion of direct sovereignty by means of association. This process was not fully developed by the time the Commune was defeated, but the increasingly harsh criticisms of the Communal Council in the press and clubs is unmistakable. Had the Commune managed to last longer it is certain that leftist factions of the clubs and committees and National Guard would have posed serious, organized opposition to the Communal Council. While loyalty to the Commune was the dominant theme of club discourse to the end, the perception of imminent defeat and the hardships caused by bombardment, siege, and pitiless civil war were pushing many Communards far to the left of the Communal Council.[93] In these circumstances association once again was employed, and it continued to be employed, to express and implement the revolutionary will of the sovereign people.

---

93. At the Club des Prolétaires on May 14 an orator accused the Commune of incompetence and cowardice, and there was so much uproar that the organ had to be played to reestablish order; AHG: Ly 22.

CHAPTER 5

The Structures of Club Society

Prosecution: What were his political convictions?
Witness: He was what one called a clubiste.

—Joseph Borrel

Popular organizations during the Commune were characterized by several frameworks that conditioned the political culture that arose within them. The organizational structures of clubs and committees provided an institutional context, comprising relations between clubs, such as the creation of affiliated club networks and coordination among distinct popular assemblies. The social context reflected a unique social geography, from the implantation of clubs in certain districts of the capital, to the social composition of club participants. Social identity and institutional frameworks shaped the evolution of popular organizations, creating a revolutionary community out of public assemblies.

It is unclear how many clubs and committees functioned at any one time during the Commune; some were ephemeral, and others changed name or location. Some groups, like the Union des Femmes and the Alliance Républicaine des Départements, held many small committee meetings as well as large assemblies, adding to the difficulties of an exact enumeration. For example, on May 7 the Alliance Républicaine des Départements sponsored nine department committee meetings, and its executive committee also met in a general assembly with the Défenseurs de la République, the Union Centrale Républicain, the Delegation of the Twenty Arrondissements, and the Alliance Républicain, to form the Fédération des Sociétés Républicaines. To count all ten meetings on this day inflates the number of clubs and committees, and to count all these committees as only one group underrepresents the amplitude of the activ-

---

Epigraph from Joseph Borrel, testifying at the trial of Armand Avrillon, a member of the vigilance committee of the 4th arrondissement and the Club Bourdon; AHG: 15e conseil 177. During the Commune Avrillon had denounced Borrel as a draft dodger.

ity. Finally, many notices in the press said that assemblies were held "every day," though some of these groups met only three times a week. Perhaps thirty to thirty-five large popular clubs were in operation by early May, in addition to a somewhat larger number of special purpose committees and associations. In the first week of May, for example, sixty-five separate meetings were advertised, the large majority of which were department meetings under the auspices of the Alliance Républicaine des Départements. In contrast, in the early weeks of the Commune sometimes only ten or so meetings were advertised. Both of these numbers underrepresent the actual extent of the club and committee movement, however, because many popular organizations met regularly and did not issue a notice for every meeting. Also, for the early period a certain amount of activity went unnoticed because of the chaos of revolution. Still, it is clear that measured by both number of meetings and number of groups the club and committee movement grew rapidly in April and early May. The movement was still growing, though less rapidly, in the middle of May, which indicates that the defeat of the Commune ended a movement that was still in its infancy.

The same problems that make enumerating the size of club and committee activity difficult also hinder mapping its geographic contours. In every arrondissement groups were founded and then lost to sight, other groups changed meeting place, and still others were fully active without any mention in the press. Although most historians who pay attention to this issue have noted that some arrondissements had no clubs, in fact the club and committee movement was felt in every arrondissement of the capital.[1] In addition, there were many groups that were not centered on a particular arrondissement or that had local branches in several arrondissements, such as the Federation of Elders, the Union des Femmes, the Défenseurs de la République, and especially the Alliance Républicaine des Départements. Several arrondissements had particularly active club movements; others have left far less evidence, as a rapid review demonstrates. In the 1st arrondissement, for example, the Club of the Republican Electoral Committee of Federated National Guardsmen met at the salle de la Rédoute beginning on April 1. It is very likely that this was the continuation of meetings held there by the arrondissement vigilance committee and the Delegation of the Twenty Arrondissements under the name Club Central during the late siege and armistice. This supposition is reinforced by the

---

1. Serman, who has written the most recent important history of the Commune, noted that the 8th, 10th, and 16th arrondissements were without clubs; *La Commune de Paris,* 292.

formation of a Club Central under the auspices of the Delegation of the Twenty Arrondissements in the Saint Eustache Church, which probably was just a new home for the meetings formerly held at the salle de la Rédoute. Beginning on April 6 the salle Valentino, continuing the moderate republican meetings of the siege held there, welcomed meetings for conciliation, though by the end of April Communard elements had forced this assembly to pass resolutions favoring the Commune. The executive committee of the Ligue d'Union des Droits de Paris, which was created at these meetings, remained officially neutral until the end of the Commune, however. The Ligue apparently stopped holding public meetings at the salle Valentino in late April, no doubt because of their increasingly radical nature. The Louvre (pavilion Colbert) was the temporary home of the Delegation of the Twenty Arrondissements until it moved in mid-April to Victoria Avenue in the 4th arrondissement. Similarly, one meeting, apparently of the Union des Femmes, was held in the Saint Germain l'Auxerrois Church on April 29. Some clubistes tried to open a club at Saint Roch, but they raised so much opposition that the attempt was called off. Finally, a Club Communal was opened in Saint Leu on May 12 by the founders of the original Club Communal at Saint Nicolas des Champs.

In the 2d arrondissement the salle cour des Miracles on the place du Caire witnessed "everyday" meetings, probably associated with the vigilance committee that had met there during the siege. The agenda for one meeting, for example, was "on the revolution; study of social problems."[2] The school on the place du Caire also hosted department committee meetings. The 2d was a "bourgeois" arrondissement, home of the Stock Exchange and Bank of France, and was noted for its hostility to the Commune. The mairie was only in the hands of Communards after April 13. The 3d arrondissement was one of the most active meeting places for clubs and committees. Meetings of the club sponsored by the vigilance committee were hosted by the salle Molière from March 23 until April 24, when it moved to Saint Nicolas des Champs and became the Club Communal. Another branch of the club was opened at Sainte Elisabeth du Temple on May 1 by Laurent of the vigilance committee, "because of the great abundance of people" crowding into Saint Nicolas.[3] The Corderie, original home of the Central Committee of the Twenty Arrondissements, also hosted the International and the Federation of Worker's Societies. The

---

2. *La Commune,* April 29. This vigilance committee was composed mainly of members of the International.

3. *Le Bulletin Communal,* May 6; Fontoulieu, *Les Églises,* 213.

École Turgot was the main meeting place of the Alliance Républicaine des Départements in late April and May. A variety of other groups met in the 3d arrondissement, from the Union des Femmes (April 11 at the salle Larched and April 13 at the mairie), to Education Nouvelle (École Turgot), to the Club for the Revindication of the Rights of Man and of the Citizen, which was formed during the siege but apparently only met once during the Commune. In addition, the Cirque National and Arts et Métiers hosted a number of different groups and assemblies, among them the Federation of Republican Societies. Even the Stock Exchange hosted meetings, ironically for the Society of Former Political Prisoners.

The 4th arrondissement was the scene of meetings at the salle Bourdon, under the auspices of the vigilance committee. These meetings were then moved to the Théâtre Lyrique (on the place du Châtelet) on May 4. The vigilance committee moved its meetings again on May 17 to the Saint Paul-Saint Louis Church, but meetings were also held after that date at the Théâtre Lyrique. The Public Assistance building, with entrances on the Avenue Victoria and the Quai des Gesvres, hosted the Delegation of the Twenty Arrondissements as well as some department meetings it sponsored. The Society of Former Political Prisoners met at the mairie. The club movements in the 5th and 6th arrondissements were also dominated by the activity of vigilance committees. That of the 5th called itself the "democratic and social committee of the 5th arrondissement," as it had during the later siege. It sponsored public meetings and clubs in at least five locations during both the siege and Commune: at the rue Arras, rue Cujas (École de Droit), École de Pharmacie, Collège de France, and salle Vieux-Chêne (on the rue Mouffetard). The Club Arras, known as the Club de la Révolution Sociale and the Club de la Révolution, moved to the Pantheon on April 25. In May the Saint Severin, Saint Jacques du Haut Pas, and Saint Etienne du Mont Churches also served as meeting places, probably for the vigilance committee clubs. In the 6th arrondissement the Association Républicaine, which was the vigilance committee of the arrondissement and a section of the AIT, continued sponsoring meetings at the École de Médecine. A women's club under the auspices of the Union des Femmes met at the girls school of the rue Saint Benoit. Saint Sulpice was the scene of violent disputes between clubistes and the faithful, though the club was definitively installed by mid-May.[4]

---

4. Fontoulieu, *Les Églises,* 248; Du Camp, *Les Convulsions de Paris,* 253. Fontoulieu wrote that church services were still held during the day, but a Versailles police report noted the church was closed to all except clubistes; APP: Ba 365-1.

The club movement was relatively less well represented in the more prosperous and bourgeois 7th, 8th, 9th, and 10th arrondissements. The salle Pré-aux-Clercs in the 7th arrondissement held meetings every day, and meetings were also held on the rue Vannueau. That of the Pré-aux-Clercs, at least, was associated with the vigilance committee. In the 8th arrondissement the Triat Gymnasium held meetings every day under the auspices of the vigilance committee, which administered the mairie in partnership with, and then in replacement of, Allix. The mairie was also home to the Women's Committee of the Social Commune Society, which held a joint meeting with Education Nouvelle on "Social Measures and Education."[5] In the 9th arrondissement a meeting at the Théâtre Seraphin in the passage Jouffroy was held under several names, first Club National, a continuation from the siege, then simply Club Jouffroy or Club Seraphin. While known as the Club National it was linked to the Union National de Commerce et de l'Industrie, a business group. At first this club favored conciliation and was the meeting place of the "federation of groups for conciliation," but in late April the balance tipped in favor of the Commune.[6] The Casino de la rue Cadet was the scene of a "republican club" every day in late April and May. The Notre-Dame de Loirette and Trinity Churches also housed clubs, sponsored by the Union des Femmes in particular. In the 10th arrondissement the only meeting hall known to have been active during the Commune was the salle du Dix-Neuvième siècle, which beginning on March 26 held meetings every day.

The 11th through 14th arrondissements all had important club movements. In the 11th the vigilance committee sponsored the Club des Prolétaires held in early May at Saint Ambroise, and it later opened a branch at Sainte-Marguerite (11th arrondissement). The Club Ambroise was one of the largest in the capital and is the only one for which detailed minutes have survived. The vigilance committee of the 12th arrondissement sponsored meetings in the salle des Terres-Fortes throughout March and April and moved to Saint Eloi in May. A battalion of women was formed there under the command of Adélaïde Valentin to seek out refractories and build and fight on barricades. A club also met in the rue Citeaux. In the 13th arrondissement the local sections of the AIT, those of the Légion Garibaldienne, and the Club Démocratique et Socialiste du 13e Arrondissement combined on March 6 as the Gobelins section of the AIT. This reorganization was probably brought about to implement the Revo-

5. *La Commune,* April 22.
6. *Sous la Commune,* 50; *Le Mot d'Ordre,* April 22.

lutionary Socialist Declaration of Principles, as noted in chapter 2. Each group apparently kept its independence, however, as in April and May the group was known as the Federated Associations of the Thirteenth Arrondissement. A Club de la Fraternité also functioned in mid-May on the avenue d'Italy.[7] The vigilance committee of the 14th arrondissement ran the mairie and also sponsored clubs at the salle Maison-Dieu, the École des Soeurs (on the place de la mairie), and the École Communale (on the rue de la Tombe-Issoire). Other clubs were held on the rue de Maine and in the Saint Pierre de Montrouge and Notre Dame de Plaisance Churches.

In contrast, the sparsely populated 15th and 16th arrondissements saw little club activity. The 15th was home to the Cercle des Jacobins, which met in the basement of Saint Lambert. The Union des Femmes met in the same building. In early March meetings were held at the salle Ragache, though it is unclear whether they continued during the Commune. The only club activity known in the 16th arrondissement was a meeting of the Club des Citoyennes de Passy, held in the mairie on April 23. The arrondissement was administered by a committee drawn mainly from vigilance committee members from other arrondissements.

Finally, the last four arrondissements, all of them mainly working-class in composition, again gave life to large and active clubs. In the 17th arrondissement the salle Levis was the home of the Club de la Révolution Sociale, which moved to Saint Michel des Batignolles in early May. A women's club and vigilance committee met in the rue des Acacias. Saint Ferdinand also housed a club. The Club de la Révolution of the 18th arrondissement not only ran the mairie and National Guard of the arrondissement but sponsored meetings in the salle Robert, salle Perrot, salle de la Réine-Blanche, and Saint Bernard. According to the curé the club in Saint Bernard was begun around April 20, making it perhaps the first permanent church club in Paris.[8] The vigilance committee of women of the 18th arrondissement met and sponsored a club at the Boule Noir, at the boulevard Rochechoart, and occasionally at other locations. In the 19th arrondissement the vigilance committee sponsored clubs at the salle Marseillaise, the rue de Meaux, and Saint Christophe. A club was also held in the Café de la Grand Villette. Finally, in the 20th arrondissement the Union des Femmes sponsored a club in the Menilmontant Church.

---

7. *Le Cri du Peuple,* March 6 and May 8; *La Sociale,* April 3 and May 13.
8. Individual meetings had occurred at other churches. AHG: 16e conseil 96, dossier Cordier-Joly.

This listing of clubs and committees prompts several conclusions. First, some clubs in the same arrondissement were linked by networks centered on the vigilance committee. In the 11th arrondissement Clubs des Prolétaires were instituted in Saint Ambroise and Sainte Marguerite. Clubs Communal were founded in Saint Nicolas des Champs and Sainte Elizabeth in the 3d, as well as at Saint Leu in the 1st. As shown, the Club de la Révolution of the 18th arrondissement sponsored several clubs, as did the vigilance committees in the 5th and 14th arrondissements. The vigilance committee in the 19th arrondissement divided the arrondissement into "districts," each of which would have a club; one of these was the "district de la Marseillaise." This was the same terminology used by the Club de la Révolution in the 18th and recalls the districts and sections of the Great Revolution. This process of forming networks was organized in various ways. Sometimes it was merely a matter of one leader's initiative; other times formal motions were carried by the original club. The Club Communal appears to have had the most formal structure, as it had a Society of Clubs presided by Landeck. As secretary of this society, Joseph Paysant was paid one hundred francs a month; this money may have come from admission fees and donations at the clubs.[9] This Society of Clubs was formed by participants of the salle Molière, which was the meeting associated with the vigilance committee of the 3d. Both Landeck and Michau were members of the salle Molière, and Laurent, delegated to open the Club Communal at Saint Leu, had been president once. In forming club networks members of vigilance committees were carrying out the strategy codified in the Resolutions concerning Committees of Vigilance, a founding document of the Revolutionary Socialist Party. The Resolutions and the Declaration of Principles that accompanied them stated that all members of vigilance committees belonged to the Revolutionary Socialist Party, and that each vigilance committee was to form "groups of adherents" in an attempt to unite the revolutionary socialist forces in each arrondissement. That the vigilance committees acted relatively uniformly in forming networks of clubs during the Commune suggests that the vision of February was still intact.

A second conclusion relates to the division in both function and participants between the large, popular clubs and the smaller, special purpose committees. Committees that are not explicitly devoted only to the affairs of one arrondissement tended to draw participants from across the city,

---

9. AHG: 17e conseil 252, dossier Paysant; *Les Murailles Politiques,* 2:145.

while the large assemblies seem to have attracted persons mainly from the arrondissement where the club met. For example, of the persons known to attend clubs located in the 5th arrondissement and whose home address is also known, eight of nine lived in the 5th. Among members of the Club des Prolétaires seven of eight whose address is known lived in the 11th, where the club was located. For the Club de la Révolution at Saint Bernard (18th arrondissement) the proportion was thirteen of fourteen. The Club de la Révolution Sociale at Saint Michel des Batignolles (17th arrondissement) was somewhat more mixed: of sixteen members whose address is known, nine lived in the 17th, three in the 18th (which borders the 17th), and one each in the 10th, 11th, 15th, and 19th. Because the sample is somewhat weighted in favor of leaders and activists and is so small in relation to the size of the clubs, club membership was probably not quite so highly concentrated as these figures suggest, but the tendency for the large, popular clubs to attract participants primarily from the immediate vicinity is clear.

Special purpose committees, in contrast, naturally attracted persons from all over the city who were interested in the activity in question. As these special purpose committees were generally small, often there are only one or two participants whose address is also known, but the results for the few groups that have sufficient information for analysis are at least indicative. Of the six members of Education Nouvelle whose address is known, two each were from the 4th and the 10th arrondissement, and one each lived in the 11th and 17th; the group itself generally met in the 3d. The members of the Alliance Républicaine des Départements came from all over the city, though the left bank was poorly represented. Analysis of those who attended the Club Central of the Central Committee of the Twenty Arrondissements at Saint Eustache suggests that it was indeed a central club that drew participants from across the city: all seven participants whose address is known came from different arrondissements, a striking contrast to the other church clubs.

Finally, the connection between clubs and vigilance committees, on the one hand, and between vigilance committees and the administration of Paris, on the other, suggests that throughout the city the revolutionary leadership and the mass of Communards were in direct contact on a daily basis. In these circumstances the distance between the leadership and the rank and file was virtually nonexistent. One of the central paradoxes of mass movements is that they require leaders, who by their very function become differentiated from the mass. Under the Commune this problem, which has caused so many revolutions born of hope to end in tyranny, was perhaps reduced to its minimum by the application of association. Clubistes were among the most ardent Communards, and they constituted the mass base of the movement. While service in the National Guard was often coerced or was necessary because of lack of other employment, club participation was wholly voluntary. Nonpolitical motivations were no doubt present, such as a desire to cut an important figure, but these cannot account for the magnitude of the movement during the Commune. Clubs then are a window into the ideals, hatreds, and aspirations of dedicated Communards.

The social composition of popular organizations provides important evidence supporting the contention that clubistes represented a key segment of the population devoted to the Commune. The set of related events and ideas that is called the Commune was shaped by rank-and-file militants as much as—and perhaps more than—the leadership in the Communal Council and the National Guard Central Committee. Altogether 733 individual clubistes have been identified, the largest group of Communards that has yet been subject to social analysis.[10] Of these, the gender of 729 may be identified; 85 percent were male, while 113 were female. From anecdotal and other evidence it is clear that women accounted for a far higher percentage of the clubiste population than this sample would indicate. Women are probably underrepresented because they were less likely to be club leaders and orators. Yet the 15 percent known to be women in the sample is relatively large, given that of the 35,771 adults arrested as Communards 819 (2.2 percent) were women, and only 115 of these were actually convicted. Women were a significant segment, and by some accounts even a majority, of the clubiste population. This is the first indication among several to be encountered that clubistes offer a more accu-

---

10. I used a variety of sources to identify clubistes, from posters, newspapers, and memoirs, to trial records and club minutes. I also systematically mined Maitron's *DBMOF* for references to Communards noted for attending clubs, and it was the single most important source for identifying clubistes. It relies on dossiers in the National Archives, which are themselves summaries of dossiers in the army's archive at Vincennes. The army dossiers were consulted for approximately 175 people. Alner, "The Jacobins in the Paris Commune of 1871," analyzed fewer than three hundred individuals. Jean Maitron, "Étude critique du Rapport Appert: Essai de 'contre-rapport'" *Le Mouvement Social* 79 (April–June, 1972): 95–122, rests on about four hundred members of the AIT. The only previously available information about the social composition of Parisian clubs is a petition of about one hundred names that dates from the siege, in Bruhat, Dautry, and Tersen, *La Commune de 1871,* 161.

rate image of Communard militants and activists than the portrait painted by official statistics for all those arrested as Communards.[11]

The age of these clubistes breaks down as indicated in table 3, where the percentages given relate to the total for each column. The similar proportion of persons in each age category regardless of gender is remarkable and indicates that these 415 clubistes are distributed fairly evenly. Comparing the age of clubistes to the general population of Paris and to those convicted for Communard activity is enlightening. Table 4 includes only men so that the data will be comparable. The number in parentheses is the ratio by which the figure given differs from a perfect correspondence with the general population. The proportion of both clubistes and convicted Communards over sixty is far less than the proportion of those over sixty in the general male population. The most notable distinction between clubistes and Communards is that clubistes were very unlikely to be young and somewhat more likely to be fully mature (age forty-one to sixty). Though examples of youthful clubistes are known, in general it required a certain weight of years to be accepted as a club leader and orator, and these older people are most likely to be found in the sample.

TABLE 3.   Ages of Clubistes

	All Clubistes		Men		Women	
Age 16 to 20	8	(2%)	6	(1.5%)	2	(0.5%)
Age 21 to 40	243	(58.5)	218	(59)	25	(55)
Age 41 to 60	153	(37)	136	(37)	17	(38)
Over 61	11	(2.5)	10	(2.7)	1	(2.2)
All ages	415	(100)	370	(100)	45	(100)

Note: Percentages are in parentheses.

11. In general, two sets of comparisons can be made: clubistes in relation to the total Parisian population, and clubistes in relation to those arrested as Communards after the Commune. The national census of 1866 provides data about the Parisian population. For Communards, General Appert prepared for the National Assembly a statistical report detailing many characteristics of those arrested for Communard activity, and while his evidence and findings are subject to some suspicion, they still provide the most complete statistical portrait of those identified by military authorities as Communards; Appert, *Rapport d'ensemble.* Maitron, in "Étude critique du Rapport Appert," and Schulkind, in "Socialist Women," 129, have argued that the selection of those arrested and Appert's prejudices render his report nearly useless. Rougerie mined the Appert report for his "Composition d'un population insurgée: L'Example de la Commune," *Le Mouvement Social* 48 (July–September, 1964): 31–47, and the figures given below for Communards are taken from his article unless otherwise noted. See also Roger V. Gould, *Insurgent Identities.*

TABLE 4.   Age Comparison of Male Communards and Clubistes

	Male Population in 1866	Communards ($N = 9,949$)	Clubistes ($N = 370$)
Age 16 to 20	8.6%	9.6% (1.1)	1.5% (0.17)
Age 21 to 40	52	64.2 (1.23)	59 (1.13)
Age 41 to 60	30.6	25.6 (0.83)	37 (1.23)
Over 61	8.8	0.6 (0.07)	2.7 (0.3)

Note: Ratios are in parentheses.

The marital status of clubistes, reported in tables 5 and 6, offers confirmation of the relative maturity of these militants. Again, the percentages relate to the total for each column. One remarkable difference between men and women is the high rate of "concubinage" among women. The term *concubinage* was used to describe free unions and common-law marriages that helped to paint a picture of Communard men and women as immoral enemies of the most revered social conventions. The reasons for the higher observed rate for women are uncertain; it may be that "immoral" women were more likely to be reported as clubistes, and their illegitimate living arrangements duly indicated, by the eyewitnesses and military authorities that are the primary sources of the sample. Given the double standard of morality it would not be surprising if men's irregular living arrangements were deemed less noteworthy. It may be, as well, that a certain indifference to bourgeois marital customs among women accorded with a willingness to embrace radical politics—it is clear from club discourse on the family that much was found wanting in the established order in this regard. Another area of difference is the relatively lower proportion of married women than men in the sample, and the same types of considerations perhaps explain this result as well. The relatively high percentage of widowed women in the sample of clubistes (18 percent) suggests that the maturity and freedom associated with widowhood, and perhaps a difficult economic situation, encouraged participation in radical clubs. Among the women arrested for Communard activity only 6 percent were reported to be widows, and this proportion should be reduced by an unknown number who were widowed but living in concubinage.[12] Clubistes were apparently much more likely to be married than those arrested

---

12. Unfortunately this information on marital status is only approximately comparable to the figures given by General Appert, because his figures combine information from different categories. In particular, the number of persons "in concubinage" in his report included persons listed here as married, single, and widowed, making detailed comparisons difficult.

as Communards, 60 percent versus 45 percent. Conversely, only 20 percent of clubistes were single, while 47 percent of Communards were. This
may be an indication that clubistes were not at all a marginal or alienated
group but instead were drawn primarily from the established, mature population of the capital.[13]

The geographic origin of clubistes holds some surprises. There are no
sure figures for the place of birth of the general population. Following
Rougerie, the 34,952 men arrested after the Commune may perhaps be
taken as a proxy for the working population of the capital.[14] Of these, 24.3
percent were born in the department of the Seine, which is essentially con-
tiguous with Paris, while 18.8 percent of the clubistes were born there.
Within the city, the clubistes in the sample lived in every one of Paris's
twenty arrondissements. Yet they were clearly concentrated in the work-

TABLE 5.   Marital Status of Clubistes

	All Clubistes		Men		Women	
Single	68	(20%)	58	(20.7%)	10	(16%)
Married	203	(60)	178	(64)	25	(41)
Widowed	33	(9.7)	22	(7.8)	11	(18)
Concubinage	30	(8.8)	17	(6)	13	(21)
Separated	6	(1.7)	4	(1.4)	2	(3)
Total	340	(100)	279	(100)	61	(100)

Note: Percentages are in parentheses.

TABLE 6.   Women's Marital Status

	Convicted Communards ($N = 102$)	Union des Femmes ($N = 139$)	Clubistes ($N = 61$)
Single	25.5%	30.2%	16%
Married	56.8	58.2	41
Widowed	17.6	11.5	18
Concubinage	—	—	21
Separated	—	—	3.2

13. There is rather better evidence available about the marital status of women, thanks to
Maitron's study of women convicted as Communards and Eugene Schulkind's analysis of
women in the Union des Femmes; Maitron, "Étude critique du Rapport Appert," 104;
Schulkind, "Socialist Women," 156. Again, however, these studies do not indicate how many
in each category were in fact living in concubinage.

14. Rougerie, "Composition d'un population insurgée," 45.

ing-class areas, which were also the arrondissements with the largest populations. Table 7 ranks the arrondissements by the number of known clubistes who lived in each. The top six arrondissements account for over half the clubistes, and the top ten account for nearly 80 percent. The only surprise in the top arrondissements is the appearance of the bourgeois 8th arrondissement; its vigilance committee left an unusually rich record. The scarcity of clubistes in the 3d arrondissement is less easily explained. It was the scene of several important clubs, especially Saint Nicolas des Champs, though it is generally considered a "bourgeois" area. Again, the scarcity of clubistes in the 20th arrondissement is also difficult to explain; it had several thriving clubs and was one of the most populous areas of the capital. One factor may be its distance from the center of the city, where information was collected and disseminated through posters and newspapers. Otherwise the level of clubiste residence in the arrondissements of the capital is fairly commensurate with the social composition and population of the area in question. This conclusion is confirmed by an analysis of the occupation of clubistes (male and female) broken down by arrondissement (see table 8). Journalists were the largest occupational category of clubistes living in the 9th arrondissement, where most newspapers and publishers were based. *Négociants,* that is, businesspeople, were the largest group in the bourgeois 6th, 7th, and 8th arrondissements. This category also included the liberal professions. Metalworkers and industrial workers were well represented in the 11th, 13th, 15th, 19th, and 20th, regions that were close to the large complexes of heavy industry on the eastern and southern outskirts of the city. Small trades and merchants were found especially in the older core of the city. This evidence suggests that club participation reflected in broad outlines the social geography of the capital.

Three final areas of analysis will allow a more rigorous social and political definition of clubistes. The severity of the penalties inflicted on clubistes may be taken as a measure of the extent of their activity and devotion to the Commune; the past criminal history of clubistes can help illuminate the contentious issue of the connection between crime and revolution; and their occupational categories will show them to exhibit interesting ambiguities, especially in relation to other Communards. The sentences imposed on clubistes were far harsher than those convicted of being Communards (see table 9). The figures in table 9 include only those sentenced in person, in order to correct for the tendency of the military courts to impose harsher penalties on the absent, who made up two-thirds of those sentenced. Very clearly clubistes were considered more guilty than ordinary Communards, and rightly so. The list of clubistes condemned to death, for example, displays in miniature the full range of clubiste activity. It included Theophile Ferré, Jean Dupont, and Jean Fenouillas (called Phillippe) of the Communal Council, as well as François David, known as "the Proletarian," founder of the Club des Prolétaires and administrator in the 11th arrondissement. Louis Dalivous of the Club Saint Germain L'Auxerrois was executed for having participated in killing hostages at the rue Haxo, and Marie Guyard of the Club Saint Jacques du Haut Pas was sentenced to death, but not executed, for having built barricades and inciting others to murder. As administrators in the mairies and members of the Communal Council, as officers in the guard and as radicals who arrested and denounced enemies, clubistes paid the price for their devotion to revolution. They were far more likely (by a factor of three) to be given the three highest sentences and far less likely to be dealt with leniently.

The relationship between crime and revolution has been debated by historians, but for most contemporaries the connection was self-evident.[15] Appert's figures show that 21 percent of those arrested as Communards

TABLE 7   Clubistes by Arrondissement

Rank	Arrondissement	No. of Clubistes	% of 288
1	18	39	13.5
2	14	37	12.8
3	11	29	10
4	5	25	8.6
5	17	24	8.3
6	4	23	8
7	2	19	6.6
8	10	18	6.2
9	8 and 12	17	6
10	6 and 13	15	5.2
11	1 and 19	12	4
12	9	9	3
13	3	8	2.7
14	15 and 20	5	1.7
15	7	4	1.3
16	outside the city	3	1
17	16	1	0.3

15. Some historians of the Commune have minimized this connection, perhaps to purify the motives or morality of Communards. Using data from 1869 Rougerie argued that crime and poverty were not associated with the same professions; adding in the profession of those arrested as Communards, he draws the conclusion that crime, poverty, and revolt may have

TABLE 8. Residence and Occupation of Clubistes

Arrondissement	No. with Known Occupation	No. in Largest Occupation	
1	6	2	*négociants*
2	13	3	clothing/textiles
3	6	2	luxury trades
4	11	3	building
5	23	4	*employés*
6	14	6	*négociants*
7	4	2	*négociants*
8	14	3	*négociants* and
		3	merchants
9	7	2	journalists
10	11	4	*employés*
11	25	7	metal/industry
12	15	6	clothing/textiles
13	14	4	metal/industry
14	22	4	building
15	5	2	metal/building
16	0	0	
17	23	5	merchants
18	37	9	clothing/textiles
19	10	2	shoes and
		2	metal/industry
20	5	2	*employés* and
		2	metal/industry

TABLE 9. Sentences of Communards and Clubistes

	Communards		Clubistes		
	No.	%	No.	%	Ratio
Death	95	0.9	11	5.4	6
Hard labor	251	2.5	25	12.2	4.9
Deportation and imprisonment	1,169	11.6	55	27	2.3
Deportation without imprisonment	3,417	33.9	56	27.5	0.8
Imprisonment, more than 1 year	1,305	13	31	15.2	1.2
Imprisonment, less than 1 year	2,054	20.4	10	5	0.24
Detention, public works	1,333	13.2	16	7.8	0.6
Exile, probation	458	4.5	0		
Total	10,082	100	204	100	

had prior records for crimes ranging from the very minor to the most heinous. Although there is no comparable data for the population as a whole, this proportion appears quite high. Yet of the 369 clubistes who were sentenced after the Commune (which entailed an investigation of their judicial history), 38 percent had some prior conviction. Clubistes had thus felt the weight of the Second Empire more fully than others, and their revolutionary action should be seen as part of a long struggle against established authorities. This point becomes more compelling when the types of crimes committed by clubistes are compared to those arrested as Communards. Table 10 includes only those clubistes and Communards known to have a prior record. Comparing data sets of such differing size is hazardous, but once again the clear pattern that emerges suggests certain conclusions are possible. Clubistes were far more likely to have been sentenced for crimes against "public order," a category that includes rebellion, defamation of religion, crimes of press and speech, and inciting strikes. They were less likely to have been sentenced for the categories of crime that included injuring others, offending public morality, or theft. These figures demonstrate that many clubistes had waged an unequal political fight against the Second Empire. A large number of the sentences for political crimes were indeed the result of speaking out in the public meetings of 1868–70. As for the relatively high proportion of clubistes who had been convicted of property crimes, it seems reasonable that those who had been punished for breaking the rules of the old order should seek to make a new one.

Even more than the issues of criminality and revolt, the occupational characteristics of Communards have been the subject of much attention. Whole interpretative schools depend on whether Communards are defined as workers or artisans, *le peuple* or proletarians. The social composition of Communards has become one of the battlefields where the political and social interpretations clash, focusing on the question of whether Commu-

---

had an inverse relationship. For example, bronze workers were not very prone to be poor or have records, but they were quite likely to be Communards; "Composition d'un population insurgée," 45. Maitron, refining Appert's numbers, argues that of the 115 women convicted after the Commune only 13 percent, rather than 28.7 percent, had prior convictions; "Étude critique du Rapport Appert," 106. Yet Maitron has eliminated as a "crime" exactly those behaviors that conservative contemporaries thought most immoral and hence most dangerous: adultery, offending public morality, and incitement to debauchery. It is more fruitful to use the contemporary definition of crime, rather than to impose a later standard, because only then can the cultural and ideological context within which Communards acted be fully understood.

nards represent the future or the past, whether the Commune was the dawn of proletarian revolution or the sunset of nineteenth-century artisanal revolts. The profession of 482 of the 733 clubistes is known, a proportion of 66 percent. Of these, 416 were men and 66 were women, although only men are included in table 11 so that the figures may be compared to those provided in the Appert report. Except for artists and journalists the professional categories used were dictated by the Appert report. Within the categories no distinction is possible between employees, masters, workers, or patrons. The category *employés* includes salaried workers, store clerks, and some lower-level government employees. *Négociants* includes the liberal professions (lawyers, doctors, professors) as well as businesspeople, again to conform to Appert's categories. Clubistes were approximately proportionally represented in the categories of shoes, leather, luxury goods *(travail d'art)*, metal/industry, and *employés.* These occupations appear to have little in common, and no firm conclusions are possible for these categories. Clubistes were underrepresented in agriculture, woodworking, construction, day labor, domestic service, and the diverse small trades (hairdresser, student, cork maker, etc.); all of these except woodworking and some of the diverse small trades appear to be unskilled or semiskilled occupations, though the construction category includes some skilled crafts. Clubistes were overrepresented in the categories of clothing/textiles, book trades, small merchants (including grocers, bakers, etc.), and *négociant*/liberal professions. Except for clothing/textiles these occupations are associated with higher-than-average literacy. The two categories with the highest overrepresentation—small merchants and *négociant*/liberal professions—may be considered petit bourgeois or bourgeois categories. If journalists were included in the *négociant*/liberal profession category, where Appert probably placed them, this group would account for nearly 17 percent of the 416 male

TABLE 10. Comparative Criminality of Communards and Clubistes

	Communards		Clubistes		
	No.	%	No.	%	Ratio
Public order	1,584	21.2	71	50.7	2.4
Persons	1,481	19.9	19	13.6	0.7
Morality	879	11.8	4	2.8	0.25
Property	3,516	47	46	32.8	0.7
Total	7,460	100	140	100	

clubistes whose occupation is known, just over five times the proportion of this category among Communards in general. The presence of so many artists—painters, sculptors, musicians, actors—in the sample of clubistes is explained by the richness of documentation left by Courbet's Fédération des Artistes and by the theatrical Fédération Artistique. Even excluding these artists and actors, the club leaders and orators who tended to be noted by the sources were clearly drawn disproportionately from occupations that involved speaking, writing, and thinking.

Comparing the occupations of men and women clubistes reveals some interesting traits (see table 12, where the percentages relate to the total for each column). The concentration of women in clothing and textile trades, including laundry, makes that the largest single category for all clubistes. Second and third in overall size are the categories of merchants and *négociants,* though it was the number of men that gave these categories their high ranking. Unfortunately the Appert report does not provide comparable information, but one study of the 115 women convicted for Communard activity suggests that if anything the clothing and textile trades are underrepresented in the sample of clubistes, since 49 percent of the 88

TABLE 11. Occupational Analysis

	Communards No.	Communards %	Clubistes No.	Clubistes %	Ratio
Agriculture	398	1.1	0	0	—
Wood	2,791	8	22	5.3	0.6
Clothing	1,348	3.9	38	9.1	2.3
Shoes	1,496	4.3	16	3.8	0.9
Leather	381	1.1	5	1.2	1.1
Luxury goods	2,413	6.9	24	5.7	0.8
Book trades	925	2.7	18	4.3	1.6
Metal/Industry	4,135	11.9	41	9.8	0.8
Construction	5,458	15.7	22	5.3	0.3
Day laborers	5,198	14.9	13	3.1	0.2
Domestics	1,699	4.9	4	1	0.2
Merchants	1,516	4.3	46	11	2.6
Employés	2,790	8	41	9.8	1.2
Négociants	1,169	3.3	47	11.2	3.4
Artists	—	—	44	10.6	—
Journalists	—	—	23	5.5	—
Diverse	3,005	9	12	2.8	0.3
Total	34,722	100	416	100	

convicted women whose occupation was known were in the clothing and textile trades, compared to 38 percent of clubiste women.[16] This conclusion is reinforced by a study of 111 women in the Union des Femmes, over 62 percent of whom were in the clothing and textile trades.[17] This high proportion reflects the work of the Union des Femmes in organizing women to provide uniforms for the National Guard.

The occupational categories of Communards and clubistes may be further refined to get at two related questions: To what extent were Communards *ouvriers*? And to what extent were they "proletarians of the modern sort"? In his study of 402 men in the International, Maitron has suggested that the categories of metalworking/industry, construction, leather, shoes, clothing/textiles, and diverse small trades as used by Appert may be taken as including almost exclusively workers, so that 55 percent of the members of the International may be defined as workers.[18] Using these same

TABLE 12.   Occupations of Clubistes by Gender

	Male		Female		Total	
	No.	%	No.	%	No.	%
Agriculture	0	0	0	0	0	0
Wood	22	5.3	1	1.5	23	4.7
Clothing	38	9.1	25	38	63	13
Shoes	16	3.8	1	1.5	17	3.5
Leather	5	1.2	0	0	5	1
Luxury goods	24	5.7	0	0	24	5
Printing	18	4.3	3	4.5	21	4.3
Metal	41	9.8	3	4.5	44	9.1
Construction	22	5.3	2	3	24	5
Day laborers	13	3.1	2	3	15	3.1
Domestics	4	1	4	6	8	1.6
Merchants	46	11	7	10.5	53	11
Employés	41	9.8	5	7.5	46	9.5
Négociants	47	11.2	2	3	49	10.1
Artists	44	10.6	2	3	46	9.5
Journalists	23	5.5	3	4.5	26	5.4
Diverse	12	2.8	6	9	18	3.7
Total	416		66		482	

16. Maitron, "Étude critique du Rapport Appert," 104.

17. Schulkind, "Socialist Women," 156.

18. Following Jean Maitron's analysis of the Appert report, "Étude critique du Rapport Appert," 115.

categories, only 29 percent of the clubistes were workers, a ratio of .53. Communards as a whole, based on Appert's figures for those arrested, were drawn from the working classes in a proportion of 44 percent, meaning that members of the International were more likely to be workers than were Communards (by a factor of 1.25), while clubistes were less likely (by a factor of .65). While Maitron's method of defining workers necessarily relies on several assumptions, these findings correspond well with the nature of the samples: clubistes were drawn from a wide range of occupations, with emphasis on higher status and higher literacy professions, while members of the International were drawn mainly from the working classes to which the group addressed itself.

Maitron also joins in the dawn or sunset debate over the nature of the Commune by defining some workers as "proletarians of a modern type." Without elaborating on what was meant by this term, he defined these modern proletarians as *mechaniciens, ferblantiers, plombier-zingueurs,* and others in the general metalworking/industry category. Table 13, which includes only men, uses Maitron's definitions and methods to compare Communards, members of the International, and clubistes. Just as members of the AIT were more likely to be workers, so they were more likely to be proletarians. Similarly, clubistes were less likely to fall into either category.[19] Clubistes, then, were more likely to be mature and married than were members of the general population. The people included in this study lived in all the arrondissements of the capital, though certain areas, such as the 3d and 20th arrondissements, were underrepresented. Similarly, clubistes came from a variety of social backgrounds and occupations, including a large cohort of "bourgeois" and learned professions. Clubistes were much more likely than most Communards to have been convicted of a political crime before the Commune, indicating prior commitment to political action. Reflecting the fact that about one-third of the sample held positions of authority in the Communal administration, clubistes were far more likely to be sentenced to harsher penalties than most of those convicted as Communards. Clubs were not the preserve of a single class but that of a revolutionary political culture.

The influence of the vigilance committee movement on this political culture was so great that the Delegation of the Twenty Arrondissements may be considered an institutional structure in its own right. After having dom-

---

19. Yet one historian's "proletarian" may be another's artisan. For example, Rougerie classifies the building trades as "new," distinguishing them from "traditional" trades such as clothing/textiles and woodworking; "Composition d'un population insurgée," 39.

inated the elections of March 26, however, the Delegation, with most of its
leaders now in the Communal Council, entered a period of decline. In the
first three weeks of April there were almost no press notices calling meetings, and judging from what little evidence remains Delegation meetings
were sparsely attended. It is exactly during this period that the group
exhibited the most confusion over what name to give itself; the inter-
changing usage of the titles Delegation of the Twenty Arrondissements
and Central Committee of the Twenty Arrondissements in this context
appears to be a sign that the group had lost confidence in its identity and
purpose. By late April, however, the Delegation exhibited clear signs of a
renaissance. It began once again to play a leading role in directing popular
organizations, making it an important part of the institutional framework
shaping the Parisian club movement.

In early April that rebirth was still distant, and the Delegation moved at
crosscurrent to the larger Communal movement. Already the moderation
of the Delegation has been observed in relation to the elections of March
26, both in the Delegation's choice to support elections and in its electoral
statements. Even afterward, while most Communards were increasingly
radicalized by the experience of civil war and revolution, the Delegation
remained committed to noncoercive means to secure the success of the
Commune. In three instances, for example, the Delegation opposed
extreme or "revolutionary" measures. In the first, the Delegation several
times called on the Communal Council to double the number of its members in order to have enough members to adequately administer the city
and to give its deliberations greater force. It argued that "if the Commune
of Paris had been composed of 180 to 200 members, and had they all been
revolutionaries and socialists, the Assembly of Versailles, composed of
traitors and royalists, would have refrained from attacking Paris." The
Communal Council, however, moved in the opposite direction, concentrating power in fewer and fewer hands over the course of the Commune,

TABLE 13.   Proletarians and Politics (males only)

	Communards %	AIT %	AIT Ratio	Clubistes %	Clubistes Ratio
Workers as a percentage of all occupations	44	55	1.25	29.3	0.65
Proletarians as a percentage of all occupations	12	16.6	1.4	9.8	0.8

centralizing authority rather than broadening it.[20] In the second example, the Delegation advocated reorganizing the National Guard in ways contradictory to prevailing notions. The Communal Council imposed a *levée en masse* of all Parisian men aged eighteen to forty, and Communards constantly called for stricter measures against those who refused to serve in the guard. In contrast, the Delegation advocated ending the *levée en masse* and relying instead on volunteers who would be paid 5 francs a day (versus the customary 1.5 francs) and would live in barracks rather than at home, so as to be constantly available for action.[21] These measures would have in effect created a professional Communal army, while most Communards and the Communal Council distrusted standing armies as instruments of oppression and dictatorship. Finally, the Delegation remained committed to the strategy begun during the electoral campaign of March 26 of organizing and uniting a broad, diverse republican coalition. Meanwhile, the evolution of most Communards was toward intolerance of differences, violent rhetoric, and revolutionary purity. While intimidation, arrests, and terror became ever more frequent, the Delegation participated in several initiatives to unite a large coalition of organizations around the Commune. In all three instances the Delegation sought broad, noncoercive methods for supporting the Commune and was at odds with the larger, exclusionist tendencies. In any one of these cases the differences may not seem significant, but taken together they form a pattern of moderate, measured action that was out of step with the larger Communal movement. This strategy began in the first days of the Commune and was continued until the end.[22] Previously it had shaken governments and helped make an insurrection; now it was reduced to sending unsolicited advice to the Communal Council.[23]

In part the decline of the Delegation was a consequence of the dissolu-

---

20. Choury, *La Commune au coeur de Paris*, 273; *L'Affranchi*, April 8. On April 20 the Communal Council disbanded previous commissions that had collective responsibility, replacing them with individual delegates. The creation of the Committee of Public Safety on May 1 was the culmination of this trend.

21. APP: Ba 364-6.

22. The Delegation did remain active, issuing statements that were both laudatory and critical of the Communal Council. See *Le Journal Officiel*, March 31; Dautry and Scheler, *Le Comité Central*, 243–5; *Le Cri du Peuple*, April 2; AHG: Ly 22; Rougerie, "Quelques documents nouveaux," 29.

23. Choury gives the Delegation credit for inciting the Communal Council to call the by-elections for April 16, but the Delegation had previously made several such requests with no result; *La Commune au coeur de Paris*, 273. Dautry and Scheler, *Le Comité Central*, 247, first pointed out the "decadence" of the Delegation, although they dated this decline too early.

tion of ties between the center and the local vigilance committees. A notice calling a meeting of "delegates to the old Central Committee and the Delegation of the Twenty Arrondissements" listed the agenda as "reconstruction of the arrondissement committees and elections," indicating that the Delegation had lost touch with some of the vigilance committees.[24] The lack of coordination between the central Delegation and the arrondissement committees is clearly evident in the by-elections of April 16. Initially called for April 5 the elections had twice been postponed because of combat and were only decided on definitively on April 12. Thirty-two seats were vacant, but the rate of abstention was so high that the Communal Council only validated twenty-one elections, which because of resignations and multiple elections added only seventeen new members. Even taking into account the battalions at the front lines and the dislocations of civil war, the low turnout must be interpreted as a sign of either hostility or indifference by the majority of Parisians. Yet those who did vote were by and large the most radical elements, meaning that in most cases those elected were dedicated revolutionaries who generally received 70 to 90 percent of the votes cast. Although Communards were a minority in the city, the elections provide evidence of fairly great unanimity within the Communal movement.[25]

While the February and March elections had revealed differences between the center and the arrondissements, the elections of April exhibit an almost complete disconnection between the two. The Delegation issued a list of candidates on April 4, when the elections were to be held on April 5, but does not appear to have updated the list for the elections of April 16. Of the twenty-two candidates on the Delegation list, only seven are also known to have been on local vigilance committee lists. Only in the 2d arrondissement did this list fully agree with that supported by a local vigilance committee. Only in the 1st and 9th arrondissements did the list partially agree with that of the local vigilance committee. In the other four cases in which the list of the Delegation and that of the local vigilance committee can be compared (in the 8th, 12th, 18th, and 19th arrondisse-

24. *La Sociale,* April 14. Dautry and Scheler, *Le Comité Central,* 273, take this as an indication that the local vigilance committees had stopped meeting, but to the contrary they were often absorbed with administrative duties, and most were indeed sponsoring public meetings.
25. The high rate of abstentions has been explained away by historians sympathetic to the Commune, who generally argue that Communards by this time preferred the bullet to the ballot; Bruhat, Dautry, and Tersen, *La Commune de 1871,* 132. But see also Rials, *Nouvelle histoire de Paris,* 306; Serman, *La Commune de Paris,* 276.

ments) there were no candidates in common.[26] Indeed, the vigilance committees of the 9th and 12th arrondissements protested against the candidates recommended for their arrondissements by the Delegation.[27] The results of the elections were mixed for Delegation and vigilance committee candidates. Ten of the Delegation's twenty-two candidates were elected, and taking into account resignations and multiple elections Delegation candidates made up nine of the seventeen new members of the Communal Council. Local vigilance committee candidates won at least half the seats in five arrondissements (the 1st, 2d, 7th, 9th, and 19th) but failed in five others (the 3d, 6th, 8th, 12th, and 18th). No vigilance committee list was found for the 13th, 16th, 17th, and 20th arrondissements, which in all these cases except the 16th is most likely due to loss of evidence rather than to inactivity. Overall the results suggest that the central Delegation was out of touch with the arrondissements; the local committees were still influential, but a decline in their authority as well is apparent.

The relative failure of vigilance committee and Delegation candidates in April in comparison with the elections of March 26 was most likely related to lack of cooperation with both local guard committees and the Central Committee of the National Guard. By mid-April the Central Committee and the Communal Council were well down the path of mutual hostility and suspicion that would lead in May to threats of arrests and coups d'état on both sides. These divisions were also reflected in the arrondissements. In those districts for which evidence is available the guard structures tended to support different candidates than those of the Delegation and vigilance committees, and in these cases they tended to defeat the Delegation and vigilance committee candidates.[28] In these conditions new members of the Delegation of the Twenty Arrondissements came into prominence, whose attitudes and actions help explain the evolu-

---

26. In the seven other arrondissements that had elections either no vigilance committee list has been found or the Delegation did not provide a recommendation. The Delegation list, presented as being from the Comité Central des Vingt Arrondissements, was published in *La Commune,* April 4. Choury, *La Commune au coeur de Paris,* 275, provides the list of the 2d arrondissement. For lack of a later list some of the lists used for comparison were intended for the elections when they were scheduled for April 5 or April 10.

27. Meeting in common with the local AIT section the committee in the 12th issued a statement strongly protesting the Delegation's choices, emphasizing that they were decided on without the participation of the committee and did not express its will. The vigilance committee of the 9th seconded the protest and declared its support for its own list over that of the Delegation. Maillard, *Affiches,* 198, 204.

28. Wolfe, "The Parisian *Club de la Révolution,*" 118, observed this trend in the 18th arrondissement, and it is also evident in the 1st and 12th arrondissements.

tion of the group during the last half of the Commune. Two such members were Charles Trohel and Auguste Briosne, and the contrast between them illustrates as well the role the Delegation still played in uniting disparate elements of the revolutionary socialist coalition. Charles Trohel was fifty-one years old in 1871, an ex-sailor who joined the vigilance committee of the 8th arrondissement during the siege. "Trohel was a *grand gaillard,*" a contemporary wrote, "a strapping man of five and a half feet; wild hair, a large black beard, sunburnt, eyes grey as the sea, which, when calm, had a certain softness. At the least contradiction he became stormy; his eyes resembled those of a ferocious beast."[29] He had participated in all the insurrections of the last nine months, beginning with the revolution of September 4 overthrowing the Empire. He occupied the mairie of the 8th arrondissement on March 20 and evidently was an administrator there until the end of the Commune.[30]

Trohel admired the young, well-known Blanquist Raoul Rigault, whom he nominated for election to the Communal Council.[31] In two let-ters to Rigault, the Commune's prefect of police, Trohel wrote that he wished to see him "surpass St. Just. . . . you know the adage that he adopted: those who make half a revolution only serve to dig a grave." He argued that the Commune "greatly needs someone to give it an infusion of a little virile blood in its veins, for it is fairly foundering. If I had the honor to belong to it, I would do my best to eliminate at least two-thirds of it, and I would finish with the bourgeoisie in a single blow." He counseled, "take over the Bank of France, imitate the woodcutter Lincoln and pay a five thousand franc bonus to volunteers, take care of the families of the dead and injured, shoot whoever did not want to march, send two hundred mil-lion francs to serve as capital for the International." But he added, "I fear the Commune will not rise to this level." Trohel was also the sometime

29. Fontoulieu, *Les Églises,* 284, reported that Trohel carried Pyat on his shoulders to the Hôtel de ville on October 31, and that on January 22 he had his coat pierced by several bul-lets fired by the defenders of the Hôtel de ville. See also Maitron, *DBMOF,* 9:238.

30. He explained to his prosecutors after the Commune that he hoped to use seventy-four thousand francs found at the mairie to aid more needy arrondissements; he also proposed on March 25 that guardsmen of the 8th arrondissement loyal to the Commune be called out to support the insurrection; AHG: 9e conseil 687, dossier Trohel; AHG: Ly 16. During the Commune he signed a number of statements from the Delegation of the Twenty Arrondisse-ment, at one point as the Delegation's president; *L'Enquête Parlementaire sur l'Insurrection du 18 mars,* 535; Dautry and Scheler, *Le Comité Central,* 246.

31. Trohel helped oversee the elections, and all the candidates on the list were elected. Fontoulieu, *Les Églises,* 285; AHG: 9e conseil 687; AHG: 3e conseil 901, dossier Piquet (another member of the vigilance committee).

president of the club in the Saint Severin Church, formed in May. The abbé of the church later testified that Trohel was responsible for preserving the sanctuary and choir from sacrilege, and that he had willingly tried to free an imprisoned curé through his contacts at the Ex-Prefecture of Police, all of which earned Trohel the epithets "Versaillais" and "priest-lover" at the club. Trohel's concierge said she relied on his influence for protection during the Commune, and that he had given her a pass to leave the city and return so she could visit her nephew, a soldier in the army of Versailles.[32] Yet he also presided over a meeting at Saint Severin on May 13 in which two thousand people unanimously passed several violent resolutions: draft dodgers and the wives of police agents should be arrested and sent into battle ahead of the Communard forces, and the archbishop—already taken hostage to try to prevent Versailles forces from executing Communard prisoners—should be shot if Blanqui were not released.[33]

Trohel may be taken as broadly representative of many of the new participants in the Delegation during the Commune, who were important at a local level for their role in clubs and at the mairie, but who had not previously been a significant force in the central Delegation during either the siege or the armistice. For political or personal reasons relations between these men and others in the Delegation may not always have been easy, as they did not have the long history of common action in the Republican Central Committee and the Delegation. Trohel, for example, was highly critical of Auguste Briosne, lumping him with "decorated dunces, Tartuffes from every club, Briosne, Gaillard, and their consorts."[34] Briosne was, however, probably the most important figure consistently active in the Delegation during the Commune.

A forty-six-year-old printer, Briosne was well-known from the public meetings of the late Empire, having been subject to several political condemnations dating to the 1850s. Although he suffered from tuberculosis, by common agreement he was one of the finest orators of the day. "As

32. She reported he was evasive whenever she asked him what he did: "for the mairie, he said he distributed goods to the poor," and "for what he did at the church, he said he prevented people from smoking"; AHG: 9e conseil 687. The Communal Council had abolished the Prefecture of Police, but because it remained in operation under Rigault, it was called the Ex-Prefecture.

33. AN: BB24 783; Fontoulieu, *Les Églises*, 284, citing a newspaper report.

34. Napoleon Gaillard, an active clubiste noted for his originality of expression, was in charge of building barricades for the Commune but was often criticized for doing nothing more than wearing a highly decorated uniform; Maitron, *DBMOF*, 6:115; Fontoulieu, *Les Églises*, 286.

soon as this tormented figure appeared at the tribune—framed by his black hair and beard, his forehead cut by thick eyebrows, his eyes bright with fever—silence immediately fell. You felt there was *someone* in this thin body, consumed by sickness," recalled Lefrançais, describing Briosne during the Second Empire. "Almost a communist when he refuted the Proudhonians," continued Lefrançais, "he again became an individualist against the defenders of Babeuf and Cabet. Thus he had everyone against him. Yet all loved him and acclaimed him, for they knew him to be sincere and disinterested." Vallès was also an admirer: "Every night for three hours he lived more fully than others did in a year: enlarging the present moment with his eloquence, encroaching, through his vision, upon the future." Vallès described Briosne as "this sickly man casting the welfare of his words to a legion of workers with shoulders like athletes and chests like iron, all of them moved by seeing this laborer without lungs kill himself in defending their rights."[35] Both Lefrançais and Vallès stressed the emotional impact of Briosne's speeches, linking the effect to the contrast between his weak health and strong voice.

Briosne did not play a significant role in the Delegation until after the insurrection of March 18. On his proposition the Delegation publicly stated its support for the Central Committee of the National Guard when it appeared that the elected mayors and deputies of Paris were not going to cooperate in holding elections; his name was on all the signed statements of the Delegation in the first crucial weeks of the insurrection. Candidate of the Delegation for the 9th arrondissement in the elections of both March and April, he was elected in the latter but resigned "despite my strong desire to take my place on the benches of the Commune," because he did not receive the vote of one-eighth of the registered voters.[36] Briosne's participation in the Delegation during the Commune gave it greater visibility and perhaps a certain respectability: he was listed as president when the Delegation met with other radical republican groups to form the Fédération des Sociétés Républicaines, putting him on equal footing with such republican notables as Ledru-Rollin, Dupont du Bussac, and Bayeaux-Dumesnil.[37] Like Trohel, Briosne was also active at a

---

35. Both quoted in Maitron, *DBMOF,* 4:420–21.

36. He received 77 percent of the vote, but only 3,177 citizens out of 26,608 registered went to the polls; *Les Procès-Verbaux de la Commune,* 1:339.

37. *La Verité,* May 4.

local club, in his case the Club du passage Jouffroy in the 9th arrondissement.[38] A knowledgeable anonymous observer hostile to the Commune
has left a brief description of Briosne at the club, urging the bourgeoisie to
make concessions to "the people."[39] Briosne allegedly had a plan for conciliation but would not divulge it, saying, "search for yourselves, gentlemen of the bourgeoisie, you are intelligent, you will find it, since I, a simple worker, I, the people, have found it." When another speaker
threatened to reveal the plan, Briosne interrupted him with "the cry of a
wild beast," saying, "do you want my head, citizen G   ? Haven't you
read the decree, and don't you know that when there is a law of suspects,
it is always friends that are arrested first."[40] This incident forms an enlightening contrast with the revolutionary exhortations of Trohel. While one
leader was calling for mass arrests and executions, the other sought conciliation and was fearful of arrest himself. Trohel was mainly interested in
practical measures to defend the Commune, Briosne in social reform. One
was primarily revolutionary, the other primarily socialist; the Delegation's
continued role as an umbrella group linking elements of the revolutionary
socialist coalition could hardly be more clearly demonstrated.

The decline of the Delegation of the Twenty Arrondissements as the
center of the revolutionary socialist movement was most clearly reflected
in the Communal Council. Under the pressures of civil war and revolution
the revolutionary socialist coalition that formed the core of the Communal
Council split into rival factions. The division in the Communal Council
has been the subject of much controversy and requires discussion here
only for the insight it provides into the revolutionary coalition that created
and administered the Commune. Even in the early days of the Commune
the council divided into factions, which have been given various labels by
contemporaries and historians. Nearly all agree, however, that in general

---

38. A Club National had met in the passage Jouffroy (a covered narrow street that thus
became a kind of pedestrian mall) during the armistice, and for a time during the Commune
it was linked to projects for conciliation. It was also known as Club Seraphin because it met
in the Théâtre Seraphin, which formerly presented shadow-puppet shows.

39. *Sous la Commune,* 66–67. The author had spent much time in the clubs of the siege and
Commune. Briosne was not mentioned by name but designated as "citizen X," who was
described as having been elected to the Commune on April 16 and as having resigned for lack
of sufficient votes, a description that can apply to Briosne only. The author used such codes
to denote orators who had not been arrested after the Commune, such as Briosne. Similarly,
the club was called only an unspecified "club of the faubourg Montmartre," but internal evidence reveals it to be that of the passage Jouffroy, in the faubourg Montmartre.

40. The law in question was evidently that specifying the categories of persons subject to
being held hostage, an attempt to stop the execution of guardsmen taken prisoner.

the Communal Council was divided between a majority who tended to favor radical and violent measures in the political tradition of 1793, and a minority who tended to favor more measured policies of social reform. A minority and majority could be discerned as early as the first meeting of the Communal Council, originally dividing over whether the minutes of its meetings should be published; a compromise was worked out that entailed publishing edited accounts of meetings. The lack of coordination through the Delegation, the new demands and circumstances of maintaining power, and the radicalizing dynamic of defending a cause under attack from within and without produced centripetal forces that pulled the coalition apart, as I have already noted occurred in several arrondissements.

The decisive schism in the Communal Council occurred in May, when the majority voted to form a Committee of Public Safety of five members, which was intended to have the authority to take energetic measures to defend the cause. The CPS, composed wholly of members of the majority, purged members of the minority from several commissions, most importantly that of war. On May 15 twenty-two members of the minority declared they were retiring from the Communal Council but would continue to administer their arrondissement mairies. While most of the minority later returned to the Communal Council it remained deeply split. Maxime Vuillaume later reported that Raoul Rigault, who had been given the title "Prosecutor of the Commune," which Fouquier-Tinville bore in 1793, had prepared arrest warrants for the minority. Jules Andrieux noted that he and other members of the minority lived under constant threat of imprisonment in the middle of May.[41]

While individual motives differed and a variety of factors were at work, the schism in the Communal Council reflected at its most fundamental level the fact that the Commune was born largely from a coalition of revolutionaries and socialists created during the siege and armistice. Lefrançais, a member of the minority, noted the Communal Council was divided primarily between "revolutionaries" and "socialists," in other words, between the two wings of the revolutionary socialist coalition.[42] These appellations should not be construed as exclusive, however, for over twenty members of the revolutionary majority were members of the International, and the minority also included the Blanquist Tridon and oth-

---

41. Vuillaume cited in Rihs, *La Commune de Paris,* 105; Andrieux, *Notes pour servir à l'histoire de la Commune de Paris de 1871* (Paris: Spartacus, 1971), 112.

42. Lefrançais also included a category of "conservatives," who resigned after the first week; *Étude,* 79.

ers—such as Varlin—who had devoted their lives to revolution. Revolutionary and socialist sentiment were present to some degree in nearly all the members of the Communal Council. In late April and May, the question key to each member became, On which side of the balance do I fall? With Versailles troops literally within yards of the walls of Paris many came to accept that radical and extreme means were needed to safeguard the Commune, including mass arrests of draft dodgers and political enemies. By early May both the majority and minority met separately from the other, and the majority had its own letterhead, used to invite members to its meetings: it called itself the Fraction Révolutionnaire Radicale de la Commune de Paris.[43] As the name indicated, the majority considered itself more radical, more revolutionary, than the minority, meaning it was more willing to resort to violence and coercion. Grousset, a leader of the Radical Revolutionary Faction, derisively likened the minority to the "Girondins," referring to moderates in the Great Revolution who were purged from the Convention in 1793 and later executed by Robespierre's supporters. Pyat's newspaper called the majority "the left," indicating that the minority's alleged hesitation to take forceful action against the enemies of the Commune was a sign of insufficient revolutionary zeal.[44]

The schism in the Communal Council broke apart the revolutionary socialist coalition that had been patched together during the later siege and armistice. This break can be demonstrated in two ways. Twenty-eight of the seventy-eight definitive members of the Commune (35.6 percent) had previously signed the Red Poster of January 6, which announced the creation of the Delegation of the Twenty Arrondissements, that is, the revolutionary Commune of January 1.[45] Of these twenty-eight, sixteen were later part of the majority (57 percent), while eight signed the declaration of the minority (28.6 percent). In addition, three of the twenty-eight (10.7 percent) voted not to call the Committee of Public Safety by that name but rather to give it the less frightening name Executive Committee, indicating that they occupied a middle position between the two sides.[46] Another way

43. Grousset was the *questeur,* or administrator, of the radical revolutionary faction. Its usual meeting place was the mairie of the 1st arrondissement. Bibliothique Nationale: Lb57 2085.

44. *Les Procès-Verbaux de la Commune,* 2:389; *Le Vengeur,* May 12.

45. Thirty people had been elected to the Commune, but Duval was killed in battle and Fruneau resigned.

46. The majority as defined here includes those who voted for the name Committee of Public Safety or for the entire decree instituting the committee. The minority is defined as the twenty-two who signed the declaration of the minority. The position of one of the twenty-eight members, Puget, is unclear.

of confirming that the majority/minority dispute involved a split in the revolutionary socialist coalition relates to the fifty members of the Communal Council who were previously or currently active in vigilance committees. Of these fifty, thirty were members of the majority (60 percent), while fourteen were of the minority (28 percent). Another five voted against the decree creating the CPS but did not sign the declaration of the minority (10 percent), again indicating a middle or uncommitted position. Thus no matter whether members of the revolutionary socialist coalition in the Communal Council are defined as those who signed the Red Poster or as members of vigilance committees the result is the same: just under one-third were of the minority, just under two-thirds were of the majority, and about one-tenth were not fully committed.

The difficulties raised for revolutionary socialists by the debate on the Jacobin-inspired Committee of Public Safety are apparent in considering the hesitations of Leo Frankel. A dedicated socialist and even Marxist, he nonetheless voted for the Committee of Public Safety, "not wanting to allow insinuations against my revolutionary socialist opinions." Yet Frankel later signed the declaration of the minority and defended himself against Grousset's accusation that the minority were Girondins, by underscoring the difference between "the bourgeoisie and we revolutionary socialists."[47] Although Frankel implied that the minority alone was composed of revolutionary socialists, in fact the schism divided the old revolutionary socialist coalition, generally along the central fault line between revolutionary and socialist, but with some nuances. Many who had a long history of socialist militancy voted with the majority; some who might seem from past rhetoric and action to have been more purely politically revolutionary joined the minority. During the Commune, as in all revolutions, the pace of political and ideological transformation quickened under new and rapidly evolving circumstances; the factional affiliations that had developed under the late Empire and siege no longer adequately described the reality of ideological positions as they developed during the Commune. There was no previous equivalent, for example, of the title Radical Revolutionary Faction of the Commune of Paris, which the majority gave itself.[48]

---

47. *Les Procès-Verbaux de la Commune,* 2:35, 408.

48. The minority did not have a recognized title beyond "minority," nor were they as well organized as the majority. After the Commune both Malon and Lefrançais referred to their group as the "socialist minority," but that term was not used at the time and does not reflect the fact that over twenty of those who voted for the CPS were members of the International; Malon, *La Troisième défaite,* 318; Lefrançais, *Étude,* 303.

In creating the Committee of Public Safety the Radical Revolutionary majority hoped to better defend the Commune. The minority argued instead that the CPS was a dictatorship that contradicted the principles of the Commune. In fact the CPS was always subject to the Communal Council, which could make and unmake it at will. It was not a dictatorship, because its powers derived from and depended on the elected Communal Council. Given the balance of forces in the Communal Council, however, it represented and implemented the desires of the Radical Revolutionary Faction, and this is what the schism was really about. Minority and majority were contending for control of the revolution, as the chronology of the schism proves. The minority did not issue their declaration until two weeks after the actual creation of the Committee of Public Safety, after members of the minority in key positions had been replaced by members of the majority. Neither was the CPS a dictatorship in the sense that it was imposed against the will of the mass of Communards. The very impetus for creating a Committee of Public Safety originated with the vigilance committee of the salle Marseillaise (19th arrondissement), that is, from a popular assembly.[49] On April 24 the committee passed a resolution calling for instituting a CPS; four days later, Jules Miot, a Commune member representing the district, proposed to the Commune that it create the Committee of Public Safety.[50] There are no known club or committee declarations opposed to the CPS, and several were favorable. A special meeting of the International did not blame the minority for their declaration but asked them to return to the Communal Council. The Comité démocratique de la Somme made the same request, calling their action "two-faced" and "impetuous." A meeting at the Théâtre Lyrique called on the minority to return to the Commune.[51] The nearest an orator came to criticizing the CPS was when Pinparait at the Club de la Révolution, salle

---

49. Recall that this committee and that of the 6th arrondissement had formed committees of public safety in late February to counter the threat of Prussian occupation.

50. While Miot's proposal was not explicitly linked to that of the vigilance committee, the similar timing, the fact that Miot represented the same arrondissement, and the similarities of language reveal a clear connection. The committee noted, "la situation de Paris devient de plus en plus grave"; and Miot's proposal argued from "la gravité des circonstances." The committee suggested, "il est nécessaire de montrer d'autant plus d'énergie"; and Miot proposed, "la nécessité de prendre promptment les measures les plus radicales, les plus énergiques." This version of Miot's proposal dates from May 3 and might not be the original. *Le Mot d'Ordre,* April 28; *Les Procès-Verbaux de la Commune,* 1:556.

51. *Le Journal Officiel,* May 20; AHG: 16e conseil 96, dossier Cordier-Joly; *Les Procès-Verbaux de la Commune,* 2:469.

Cujas (5th arrondissement), asked that a delegation be named to oversee the CPS—apparently more an assertion of popular sovereignty than a statement of opposition to the committee.[52] An editorial in *Le Prolétaire* of May 19, the newspaper of the Club des Prolétaires, also asserted a vision of direct democracy—and increased impatience with the Communal Council—stating, "majority or minority, what does it matter to us? Your persons are of little weight in the balance of the Commune. The People are tired of saviors, from now on they intend to discuss your acts." Another article in the same issue by Parthenay, treasurer of the Club des Prolétaires, dismissed the minority, but also the Commune in general, saying, "oh, yes, go back to your respective mairies; we've been groaning too long already under your hours of useless chatter." Malon, an important member of the minority, later conceded that in the clubs, "those ardent hearths of popular passion," the Commune was considered moderate, and the minority reactionary, meaning unwilling to take the forceful and violent measures needed to assure the survival of the revolution.[53]

While the relatively unified revolutionary socialist movement disintegrated during the Commune, the Delegation evolved a new strategy for dealing with the changed circumstances in Paris. In late April and early May the Delegation began or joined a series of initiatives designed to more effectively unite popular organizations. It started a Federation of Clubs, was a key participant in the Fédération des Sociétés Républicaines, directed the Club Central that met in the Saint Eustache Church, and created groups to elicit the aid of the provinces in the struggle with Versailles. Although the Delegation never succeeded in fully regaining its lost influence these efforts show it to be responding in new ways to the crisis in the capital and are a sign of the Delegation's continued vitality. Had the Commune survived it is almost certain that these projects would have once again made the Delegation the center of the revolutionary club and committee movement, as it had been during the siege and armistice.[54]

The Fédération des Clubs was begun on the initiative of the club of the salle Molière, an assembly organized and directed by the vigilance com-

---

52. AHG: Ly 22, meeting of May 9.

53. Malon, *La Troisième défaite,* 271.

54. Thus Dautry and Scheler, *Le Comité Central,* 249, were misguided in stating that the Fédération des Sociétés Républicaines was simply "gathering the ruins of the past," because in fact the Delegation, through the Fédération des Clubs, was attempting to assure the future of the Commune.

mittee of the 3d arrondissement.[55] A poster of May 1 announcing the creation of the federation stated that the salle Molière "believes that it is urgent that all the clubs and public meetings of Paris be united by the bond of federation," and it asked that three delegates from each club meet at the mairie of the 3d arrondissement. After May 5 the Comité de la Fédération des Clubs met at the Public Assistance building, the new home of the Delegation.[56] By May 7 the group had matured to the point that it was able to issue a statement of mission. It sought to defend the Republic, uphold the "principle of the Commune," and allow all popular organizations in the city to discuss propositions put forth by individual meetings. The committee of the Fédération des Clubs, formed by delegates from each meeting, would then send to the Commune any propositions deemed worthy. Finally, it would remain in daily communication with the Communal Council to transmit its decisions and any important military news directly to the clubs and committees of the city, thereby avoiding the "lies" often found in the press. The Fédération des Clubs would then become "a guarantee against the incompetence of some and the ambition of others."[57] One orator at the Club Communal in the Saint Nicolas des Champs Church echoed these goals, expressing a typical desire to actively participate in governing the city through association when he said that the Fédération des Clubs should collect propositions by clubs and committees and then submit them to the Communal Council for action.[58] By May 7 eleven clubs and committees had joined the Fédération des Clubs, and it had sponsored propositions in a number of meetings.[59] According to one

---

55. *Le Vengeur,* May 1. Choury, *La Commune au coeur de Paris,* 292, states that the group was begun by the AIT. The evidence he presents is dated after the salle Molière's announcement, and in any case it does not appear related to the federation. Many members of the vigilance committee of the 3d were also members of the AIT.

56. APP: 364-6; *Le Vengeur,* May 1. Dautry and Scheler, *Le Comité Central,* 248, were the first to point out the links between the Fédération des Clubs and the Delegation. For a short while the Delegation was housed in the Louvre, before moving to the Public Assistance building. Both locations had an entrance on Victoria Avenue, the usual address given for Delegation meetings. Camille Treillard, a member of the AIT and of the Delegation, was director of public assistance during the Commune.

57. *Le Vengeur,* May 7.

58. The report citing the meeting observed, "this club federation would bring about more rapid communications among the various meetings, and would establish a link that would give an even more imposing force to these demonstrations of the people's sentiments." The orator was an unnamed "citizen delegate at the 11th arrondissement," meaning a member of the municipal council. *Le Journal Officiel,* May 16.

59. In his pioneer study of the popular movement under the Commune the Soviet historian Molok stated that the Fédération des Clubs was never effectively organized; "Les Ouvri-

anonymous account, motions for creating women's battalions, for destroying Napoleon's tomb at the Invalides, and for prosecuting for treason leaders in the Government of National Defense and the Versailles government were all put forth simultaneously in several clubs on the initiative of the Fédération des Clubs. The same source asserted that the federation was intended to be a vehicle to power for those shut out of the Communal Council and the Central Committee. With the will of the people behind their propositions, they could then little by little substitute themselves for the more regularly constituted authorities. While exaggerated, this assertion again demonstrates that political association, imbued with the theory of the general will, was commonly taken as one basis for power.[60]

The Delegation of the Twenty Arrondissements was also involved in another effort to coordinate club and committee action. It is unclear whether any one group initiated this effort, but its four main members were the radical republican groups Alliance Républicaine, Union Républicaine, and Défenseurs de la République, as well as the Delegation (sometimes under the name Central Committee of the Twenty Arrondissements). The goal was originally "the *fusion* of all these *truly* republican societies into one vast association called the Association for Communal Defense." The compromises this fusion would have required were apparently too great, however, for after several meetings in mid-May the less militant title Fédération des Sociétés Républicaines was decided on, along with the more limited ambition that "while still conserving their autonomy, these diverse societies can combine their efforts to assure the victory of the Commune."[61] The Fédération des Sociétés Républicaines united exactly those groups that had attempted to agree on a common list for the elections of February. This attempted coalition's breakup over whether to support Blanquist candidates constituted a crucial step in the development of the Revolutionary Socialist Party. Because, since the elections of March, the Delegation had adopted a strategy of inclusion and unity on

---

ers de Paris pendant la Commune," 618. Eight of the eleven organizations that had adhered to the group were associated with vigilance committees; *Le Vengeur,* May 7; BHVP: Ms. 1125, fol. 284. For example, the Club du passage Jouffroy, also known as the Club National, voted on May 2 to send three delegates to the meetings of the Fédération des Clubs; *Sous la Commune,* 73. On May 9 the Club des Prolétaires elected three delegates to represent it in the Fédération des Clubs; AHG: Ly 22.

60. The Fédération des Clubs met regularly until the end of the Commune; *La Commune,* May 16 and 19; *Sous la Commune,* 73–74.

61. *La Verité,* May 4; *Le Cri du Peuple,* May 18. A Versailles police report took note of the project; APP: Ba 364-6.

the left, the four groups were now able to form a working partnership. Again the Delegation was moving to the right in an effort to broaden the base of the Commune. It must be recalled, too, that since February the three radical republican groups had moved to the left under the radicalizing dynamic of civil war and the threat from the monarchist Versailles Assembly, pushed by general assemblies of their rank-and-file members.

For some people the Fédération des Sociétés Républicaines was a key stage along the path toward full acceptance of the Communal revolution. At its meeting of May 7 at the Alcazar there was much discussion about whether to revoke the mandate of the deputies elected to the Assembly from Paris.[62] Although the meeting voted in the affirmative, to even discuss such an issue after five weeks of combat was an indication of considerable moderation and perhaps even of hesitation about taking sides in the conflict. Seen from this perspective the Delegation's participation in the Fédération des Sociétés Républicaines was no doubt influential in bringing the radical republican leadership to embrace the Commune, vindicating the Delegation's policy of inclusion and compromise. By late May the Masons had joined the group, and there were hopes that the Alliance Républicaine des Départements, the International, the Federal Chamber of Worker Societies and the Central Committee of the National Guard would join as well. The possible inclusion of the worker's groups was a sign that the Fédération des Sociétés Républicaines was indeed fulfilling its intent to include all republican associations, "from the most moderate to the most advanced."[63]

At the same time that the Delegation was initiating the Fédération des Clubs and participating in the Fédération des Sociétés Républicaines it created a Club Central, again to coordinate and centralize the Communard club movement. During the siege the Club Central had met at the salle de la Rédoute in the 1st arrondissement, but nothing was heard of it after the armistice. In early May the Delegation returned to the idea of directing a central club in which delegates from all clubs and committees could meet. This club would differ from the concurrent Fédération des Clubs in that it would be open to the public and would unite delegates from popular clubs, rather than being a directing committee that gathered

---

62. The meeting was presided by Bayeaux-Dumesnil of the Défenseurs de la République, and its assessors were Dupont du Bussac and Dujardinier of the Union Républicaine Centrale. The only other person mentioned was Armand Levy, active in the Delegation, the Association Républicaine du 6e Arrondissement, and the AIT. *Le Cri du Peuple,* May 10.

63. *Le Cri du Peuple,* May 18.

club leaders behind closed doors. Beginning on May 5 the Central Club of
Paris, held by the Central Committee of the Twenty Arrondissements, met
every day in the Saint Eustache Church in the 1st arrondissement. An English clergyman attended a meeting, afterward noting in his diary that it was
"regarded as a central meeting, delegates attending from all the clubs, and
two or three members of the Central Committee always being present."
The entire church was filled, leading the minister to exclaim, "Oh, for such
an audience to preach the Gospel to!"[64] Another observer reported that
the number attending the club was "always very considerable," adding
that it was "the most orderly and best policed" of all the clubs held in
churches.[65]

The Club Central did indeed centralize club initiatives. One newspaper
article described a set of propositions voted at the Club Eustache, that is,
the Club Central, which were later voted at the Club Communal in the
Saint Nicolas des Champs Church.[66] Indeed, the Club Central was probably the most successful of the unifying ventures of the Central Committee
of the Twenty Arrondissements, as in late May it was one foundation of an
announcement for a newspaper called "*The Revolutionary,* organ of the
Committee of the Twenty Arrondissements, the Club Central, and of public meetings."[67] Eugène Chatelain, the longtime pillar of the vigilance committee movement, was to be the editor, although the paper never
appeared, because Versailles forces entered the city the day after this
announcement. That by late May the Republican Central Committee had
the ambition of founding a newspaper was a sign of renewed strength and
vigor after the decline and dissolution of mid-April. Through the Republican Central Committee that sponsored it, the Club Central may have been
linked to the "minority" of the Commune, as the "majority" of the Com-

64. *Les Murailles Politiques,* 3:409; William Gibson, *Paris during the Commune* (New
York: Haskell House, 1874), 239. Gibson was probably referring to the Republican Central
Committee rather than the Central Committee of the National Guard.

65. He described the clubistes as "the most bizarre mob, where there were more women
than men"; Fontoulieu, *Les Églises,* 13.

66. These resolutions called for creating a line of barricades to be built by guardsmen and
"young citizens aged twelve to eighteen," expelling from Paris the wives of Versailles police
agents and administrators, demanding from the Versaillais a list of prisoners, and forcing
landlords to give a receipt to their tenants for the next two quarters of rent; renters who normally pay less than five hundred francs a year would not have to pay, and rents above that
would be reduced by one-third; *Le Journal Officiel,* May 16. The Communal Council had
already decreed that rents due during the siege and armistice would not have to be paid, and
any amounts already paid would be applied to future terms. Rents were generally paid three
months at a time.

67. *Paris Libre,* May 20.

mune that had voted to create the Committee of Public Safety on May 1 had a project to imitate it. "The majority of the Commune has resolved to form a central club analogous to that of the Jacobins, composed of delegates from all the clubs of Paris," a newspaper well connected with the majority announced. "This club," the newspaper reported, "will be in continuous contact with the majority of the Commune, which will gauge public opinion there."[68] Although like many initiatives for political association this statement was linked to the Great Revolution, the Club Central at Saint Eustache may have been the trigger, as is shown by the use of the phrase *central club* in the statement.

While the Delegation's and the Republican Central Committee's efforts to unite popular organizations appear to have been only moderately successful, the strategy does show that a framework for the future was constructed in a relatively brief period. No longer in opposition, but not in actual possession of the levers of power either, the Delegation had not yet found a new role in early and mid-April. While it did revitalize itself through new goals and missions by mid-May, the relatively unified and unrelentingly radical direction implicit in the Revolutionary Socialist Party of February and March was lost. Instead, the more moderate strategy of inclusion and unity against Versailles, begun in the campaign for the elections of March 26, was carried forward in May by the foundation of umbrella groups. Within the social and institutional structures of club society there evolved a coherent and viable movement in pursuit of revolutionary transformation.

---

68. *Le Vengeur*, May 17.

CHAPTER 6

The Components of Club Culture

Chaussade was told, you don't have the right to threaten people, and
he replied, "I have that right in order to defend our cause."

—Witness

Clubistes were revolutionary militants who helped shape the Commune,
but they were not derived from any single class or occupational category.
Just as the Commune was the result of conscious preparation—it was created—so the nature of the Commune cannot be adequately understood
unless it is placed in the context of a revolutionary club culture. A Versailles police report of May 14 reported with horror, for example, that "a
person who attended the club held the day before yesterday in the Sainte
Marie of Batignolles Church told me that the confessionals serve as uri-
nals. What more can I say?"[1] One history of Paris during the Commune
uses the term *revolutionary vandalism* for the destruction of property and
symbols associated with the old order, which suggests that such behavior
was criminal or without meaning. Although most historians of both interpretative schools have emphasized the Commune's lack of ideological
clarity, clubiste discourse and action reveals a remarkably uniform conception of the social and ideological struggles underway.[2] Individual formulations varied in detail, but in general Communards believed themselves to be taking part in a vital conflict between two worlds, and they

---

Epigraph from an apology for revolutionary violence, reported by a witness testifying
against Joseph Chaussade, a clubiste of the 17th arrondissement; AHG: 5e conseil 919.

1. APP: Ba 364-6.

2. Rials used the term *revolutionary vandalism; Nouvelle histoire de Paris.* Rougerie
argued that the social antagonisms of the average Communard were "vagues et mal fixés";
Procès des Communards, 203. R. D. Price similarly noted the "vague ideals" of Communards;
"Ideology and Motivation in the Paris Commune of 1871," *Historical Journal* 15 (1972): 75.
Marxist and most socialist analyses generally ascribe the failure of the Commune to the lack
of a disciplined worker's party. See, for example, Bruhat, Dautry, and Tersen, *La Commune
de 1871.*

constructed their revolution on this dichotomy.[3] If some clubistes urinated in confessionals it was not simply from urgent need; it was as much a statement as was a speech or pamphlet. This realization is all the more essential when such acts took place in churches in which the statue of Jesus "is dressed as a republican and coiffed with a red bonnet, [and] the Virgin is dressed in a women's canteen uniform, a pipe in her mouth."[4] The symbolics and practices of clubiste political culture were not merely discursive, however, as they were instrumental in reshaping social and political relations. An anthropology of clubs is needed, then, to understand the meanings within such incidents in these workshops of the new world.

Four patterns of action and analysis characterized clubiste action during the Commune: they rejected some sets of ideas and enemies; they identified themselves with other groups, ideas, and actions; they inverted "normal" social relations; and they positioned themselves in the larger historical evolution of the revolutionary struggle. Through rejection, identification, inversion, and positioning, clubistes destroyed certain aspects of the old order and constructed their vision of the new. At their most profound level revolutions are transformations in the way the world is interpreted and understood; the changes associated with them, whether in political institutions, social structures, or other areas, derive from the recognition and acceptance that a different order of things is possible.[5]

Clubiste political culture unfolded within the contexts of meeting halls, which were at the same time social, discursive, and physical spaces. Meetings were publicized through newspapers and posters, and through word of mouth by proselytizing clubistes. "The club is mortally boring, unless some renowned Communard orator was expected, and the organizers knew it well," according to one account of the Club Jouffroy, which

3. For example, the official Program of the Commune stated that "the Communal revolution, begun by popular initiative on March 18, inaugurates a new era of experimental, positivist, scientific politics," and it explicitly rejected the "governmental and clerical old world"; reprinted in Rougerie, *Paris Libre,* 155. In another of the many examples, *Le Cri du Peuple,* April 6, characterized the civil war as "the white flag against the red, the old world against the new."

4. Rials is particularly indignant about the Communal Council's decrees to destroy the Vendôme column, Adolphe Thiers house, and the chapel raised in memory of Louis XVI; *Nouvelle histoire de Paris,* 471. An eyewitness described the Virgin at the church at Notre-Dame de Lorette to a Versailles agent; APP: Ba 365-1.

5. Revolutions are also, in the words of Aristide Zolberg, "moments of madness" when all seems possible, including vengeance or justice; "Moments of Madness," *Politics and Society* 2 (winter 1972): 183–207. See also Sidney Tarrow, "Cycles of Collective Action: Between Moments of Madness and the Repertoire of Contention," in *Repertoirs and Cycles of Collective Action,* ed. Mark Traugott (Durham, N.C.: Duke University Press, 1995): 89–116.

explains that "as they had to cover their costs (the hall was rented and one paid, on entry, a minor sum of twenty-five or fifty centimes), they placed at the doors a panel announcing that such and such a citizen would speak."[6] Individuals also did their part. Marie Rualt "made a lot of propaganda, and encouraged people to go to the meeting," one person testified, saying, "she dragged me along once."[7] Similarly, a neighbor testified of another clubiste, "everyday I saw the Louis woman pass before my house going to the club of the Church of La Villette, and as she went she cried, 'Who is going to the raven's barn?'"[8] Often entire families went together to clubs. Hippolyte Cordier-Joly gave a fiery speech at the club held in the Saint Bernard Church, then sat down next to his wife and two daughters. Jean-Baptist Elouis was said to go to clubs every night with his wife and daughter. The widow Neckbecker went to the Clubs Saint Eloi and Saint Bernard with her seven-year-old daughter. The Masson, Rabany, Barrabino, and Magot families were also said to be avid clubistes.[9]

People said they went to clubs for a variety of reasons, but often they were speaking before a military court and so had reason to dissimulate. Joseph Chaussade said he went to "sejourner" or hang out at the club because it was across the street from his house, and that his wife did the same. Many said they went out of curiosity. "I went two times to the club," Sidonie Letteron testified, explaining, "they said the organ was going to play, and I was curious to hear it. Another time they said a woman was going to speak, and I wanted to see what she might say." Even Letteron's attempt to excuse her attendance reveals that she wanted to hear what would be said. The same applies to Marie Rogissart, who said she went to the Club Saint Eloi "two or three times out of curiosity, and to hear the speeches"—a damning explanation when before prosecutors.[10] The excuse of curiosity in fact only underscores one's interest in what went on in clubs. Some said they went to clubs for diversion. The anonymous, well-

---

6. *Sous la Commune,* 58. The Club Jouffroy was in the bourgeois 9th arrondissement; in the "popular" quartiers either clubs were free or attendees gave five centimes.

7. AHG: 4e conseil 514, dossier Rault. The meeting in question was the Club de la Révolution at Saint Michel des Batignolles.

8. Another neighbor also confirmed this account; AHG: 26e conseil 212, dossier Sidonie Letteron. Jacques Gache, who frequented the Club of the École de Médecine, invited a neighbor to go with him; Gache had also participated in the October 31 insurrection and was known to read revolutionary newspapers; AHG: 4e conseil 400.

9. AHG: 16e conseil 96, dossier Cordier-Joly; 5e conseil 694, dossier Elouis; 26e conseil 94, dossier Neckbecker; 5e conseil 59, dossier Masson; 11e conseil 576, dossier Rabany; 16e conseil 68, dossier Barrabino; 4e conseil 100, dossier Magot.

10. AHG: 26e conseil 212, dossier Letteron; 20e conseil 528, dossier Rogissart.

informed author of *Sous la Commune,* for example, noted that he went to clubs for lack of things to do, but his explanation highlights the other possibilities for amusement: he had already walked about near the bombarded areas, watched the artillery fire, eaten at restaurants, and gone to the theaters—one wonders if anything could have kept the author out of the clubs.[11] The Communard journalist Vuillaume gave another account of going to a club for entertainment. He recounted a chance meeting with the caricaturist Gill, who was depressed over his realization that the Commune would be defeated. In an effort to cheer himself up Gill suggested they go to a club because, he said, "it ought to be funny."[12]

There were strong reasons for not going to revolutionary clubs during a period of civil war, and that so many did go indicates some degree of interest. This interest can easily be shown in cases where individuals can be identified and their club activity can be correlated to other Communard activity. Even for the generally anonymous masses of clubistes, though, the fact that one went to clubs was often known in the *quartier.* The concierge, the neighbors, the shopkeepers—all the elements of community surveillance in a city that still maintained ties of local solidarity and sociability based on the *quartier* were in play, as many found to their regret when put on trial for their activities. After the Commune, police employed this network of informal oversight to identify large numbers of Parisians as Communards, as clubistes, or as guardsmen. Simply going to clubs was a public political statement that entailed the risk of retribution. The stakes were even higher for those who were notable for their oratory, devotion, or violence. Most of the clubistes who can be identified fall into these categories.[13] Spread throughout the arrondissements of the capital, club activists and casual participants formed the largest base of militants who elaborated and implemented the Communal revolution.

Song and symbol demarcated a space for the elaboration of revolutionary discourse. Most club meetings began and ended with the *Marseillaise,* but sometimes other revolutionary songs were heard. By May, when most

11. *Sous la Commune,* 56.
12. Vuillaume, *Mes Cahiers rouges,* 275.
13. After the Commune Gustave Calvinhac was recognized on the street and denounced by someone who had seen him speak at the Club Jouffroy; Joseph Paysant was similarly denounced; Edmond de Pressensé recognized many "distinguished clubistes" among the audience at a court martial during the Commune, showing the notoriety of clubistes. AHG: 4e conseil 84, dossier Calvinhac; AHG: 17e conseil 252, dossier Paysant; Pressensé quoted in Guy La Batut, *Les Pavés de Paris,* 2 vols. (Paris: Éditions Sociales Internationales, 1937), 2:34.

large clubs had established themselves in churches, the opening of meetings was also generally accompanied by the display of red symbols such as flags and banners, which were removed at the end of the night. At Saint Ambroise the Club des Prolétaires began with the raising of the red flag in the choir. The Club Communal at Saint Nicolas des Champs was inaugurated by placing a red sash around the statue of Christ, while a *café-concert* singer treated the assembly to the *Marseillaise;* the club even had a paid organist. At Saint Severin meetings ended with a guard officer waving the red flag as the club members sang the *Marseillaise.* Songs and organ music during meetings helped fill in time between speakers and raised spirits when news from the battlefield was grim. While the words of the songs certainly inspired some, perhaps even more important was the collective experience of singing. Marie-Anne Rault, for example, was seen "standing on her chair, singing with everyone and shouting, 'Long Live the Commune!'"[14] Rituals of song and gesture, such as installing a red flag in the choir of a church, built a common foundation and encouraged shared action. In song, the people were one and indivisible, at least until the last echoes faded from the vaults.

Most clubs appear to have had a core group that organized meetings, were the principle officers and orators, and drew up manifestos or newspaper articles. Paul Fontoulieu, an acute observer of the Commune's clubs, noted that each club had its star, its favored speaker. "The bigwigs, the orators favored by the public, arrived at the Club Saint Christophe at about 8 P.M.," he wrote, "always followed by a cortege of *brothers.*"[15] There were also lesser lights in the club firmament, from assessors to secretaries to ushers. Mathurin Rault was a *commissaire,* or usher, at the Club Batignolles in the Saint Michel Church (17th arrondissement) until, as he testified, "one day someone brought a horse into the church, I had it removed, [and] I was set upon and my armband torn off; from that day I stopped going to meetings." His duties were to seat people, prevent disorder, and make sure nothing was broken. Joseph Chaussade was also an usher at the same club. A neighbor testified that his duties included "going all over, seating people and telling them to be quiet; when someone cried, 'Long live the Commune!' he said it was better to cry, 'Long live the Com-

---

14. Fontoulieu, *Les Églises,* 126, 154; Vuillaume, *Mes Cahiers rouges,* 278; AHG: 4e conseil 514. On singing see Serman, *La Commune de Paris,* 45. Perrot found that workers on strike used song to maintain solidarity; *Les Ouvriers en grève,* 275.

15. Fontoulieu, *Les Églises,* 176.

mune!' than 'Long live the good Lord!' "[16] Other club duties might include collecting donations or opening the church for meetings. Moise Pillioud, an important figure in the vigilance committee in the 19th arrondissement, said that "every night I went to the meetings [of the salle Marseillaise], and when I saw people who strayed, and who were in the wrong, who wanted to do arbitrary things, I tried to return them to reason."[17] Despite his attempt to put the best face on things, it is clear that Pillioud supervised meetings as a member of the vigilance committee.

Because popular organizations provided so many officials in the Communal administration, both at the Hôtel de ville and in the arrondissement mairies, in practice the local club leadership often administered guard and civil affairs in the arrondissement. Pillioud, as legion commander, was the head of the guard in the 19th arrondissement, a powerful post; Claude Serment, who sometimes attended the clubs of the 14th arrondissement, was president of the vigilance committee that administered that arrondissement's mairie.[18] Such examples could be greatly multiplied. Even less exalted officials must have had a powerful effect when presiding over or simply attending club meetings: many agents in the Commune's police apparatus were known to attend clubs, with obvious possibilities for intimidation. The implicit or *de facto* supervision of clubs by persons in positions of power made clubs more than discussion groups. They were vital centers of communication within the revolutionary movement, places where leadership and mass interacted. Club discourse took place in an atmosphere charged with significance, where words were weapons and one's revolutionary credentials had to be constantly on display.

One became a notable clubiste in a variety of ways. Jean Trohel claimed he was elected president of the Club Severin because he was known to be a member of the Republican Central Committee of the Twenty Arrondissements, and perhaps because of his "maturity"—he was fifty-one.[19] Revolutionary ardor was generally a prerequisite, combined with some engaging oratorical or personal trait. Voice and gestures were the most remarked on features distinguishing club notables. Gustave Flourens, killed in the first days of the civil war, conquered his large following with

---

16. AHG: 5e conseil 919, dossier Chaussade; 4e conseil 514, dossier Rault (the husband of Marie, cited in chap. 6 n. 7). Chaussade was a member of the AIT and held a minor post at the mairie of the 17th arrondissement during the Commune.

17. AHG: 3e conseil 923, dossier Vésinier; AHG: 4e conseil 1432, dossier Pillioud; Maitron, *DBMOF,* 5:96.

18. AHG: 19e conseil 134, dossier Sermet.

19. AHG: 9e conseil 687, dossier Trohel.

"his nervous, cutting gestures, his strident voice, sometimes soft and caressing, sometimes torn and grating," according to one account, which claims that "everything in him was made to win over heated spirits, to seduce listeners who applauded in this patrician both the professor and the combatant."[20] The oratory of Tony Révillon inspired a journalist thirty years later to write, "I have kept an enthusiastic memory of his warm and vibrant voice, of his passionate eloquence. Never at any epoch has an orator made such a profound impression."[21] A host of clubistes made names for themselves by their eloquence and fervor. A neighbor of Jacques Gache said, "he is a southerner and a good talker; he consequently often had around him a little group who listened to him with a sort of admiration, and to whom he did a lot of harm with his revolutionary speeches."[22] Amédée Combault, a founder of the International, "spoke without rushing, choosing well his expressions and well rounding-out his sentences."[23]

Some club orators prepared written notes or outlines for their speeches. Hector Peru, a member of a committee uniting natives of the Gironde, wrote out a draft outline justifying the actions of Paris, which presents one Communard's view of the events of the last year, emphasizing patriotic anger.

War declared on Prussia—why, how, and by who?
Surrender of our fortresses—what are the principal causes
The retreat of our armies to the walls of Paris
Siege of Paris, and exposé of suffering during the siege
Paris is sold-out and handed over
Entry of Prussians and their thievery
Paris saves for the nation a part of its arms and munitions
Seizure of these cannons and munitions, what do the gendarmes and
    police agents want?
Civil war—why, and the motives?
Present state of Paris
Conclusion[24]

20. Described by Jules Clartie, *Histoire de la Révolution de 1870–71* (Paris: L'Eclipse, 1872), 40. Flourens had been revoked from the Collège de France for his radical lectures, then he had joined the war for the independence of Crete; Guiraudon and Rebondy, *Gustave Flourens.*

21. Alexandre Zévaès, *Tony Révillon, 1831–1898* (Paris: Arthème Fayard, 1950), 26.

22. AHG: 4e conseil 400, dossier Gache.

23. Fontoulieu, *Les Églises,* 221.

24. AHG: 4e conseil 1587. Peru left Paris in mid-May after having told a neighbor that he was going to the Gironde; these notes were probably for speeches he hoped to give in his native department.

A "draft of a harangue" was found in Marie Orlowska's apartment. Allegedly known to the Club Batignolles as "la mére Duchêne" because of her revolutionary devotion, according to police she had also composed "a list of proscription that she admitted having had the idea of sending to the members of the Commune, an idea that she later gave up."[25] A "compromising" notebook was found in Nicolas Montelle's dwelling.[26] These examples convey the importance attached to voice, rhetoric, and gesture in club culture during what was still an age of public speaking.

In contrast, Théophile Ferré did not apparently owe his influence to his voice or manner. He was once derisively described as a funny-looking man, "but what is funnier is when he speaks: he raises up on the points of his feet like an angry rooster and emits sharp sounds, which constitute what one can improperly call his voice." Another, perhaps more discerning observer recalled, "he had determination and one could easily see that he was capable of anything."[27] Here one's resolution was the test, and Ferré certainly passed; it was he who ordered the execution of the Archbishop of Paris.

Ferré's order was only the most extreme example of a prominent feature of club culture, its thoroughgoing anticlericalism. Clubiste rhetoric almost invariably omitted ecclesiastical designations such as *Saint* from titles and place names. The Club Communal in the Saint Nicolas des Champs Church was described by its leadership as meeting at "Nicolas des Champs . . . a monument that up to this day has only served a caste that was the born enemy of all progress."[28] In this cleansing of their language of clerical references clubistes were following an established practice of the left. The Blanquist Raoul Rigault made a fetish of never pronouncing the word *Saint,* and his friend Pilotell, the caricaturist, followed suit, giving his address as "rue André des arts," rather than Saint André des arts. When the Club de la Revindication announced meetings during the siege they took place not in the faubourg Saint Antoine but in the "faubourg

25. AN: BB24 760 6427.

26. A member of the Communal Council and vigilance committee and an enthusiastic clubiste of the 4th arrondissement, Montelle argued that they were notes of speeches he heard, rather than gave. AHG: 3e conseil 176.

27. Maitron, *DBMOF,* 6:38; Sutter-Lauman, *Histoire d'un Trente Sous (1870–1871)* (Paris: Albert Savine, 1891), 221.

28. *Les Murailles Politiques,* 3:145. Fontoulieu, an abbot, self-consciously referred to the club in the Saint Eloi Church as simply "Club Eloi—as it was put at the time," his explanation indicating that dropping the word *Saint* was general among Communards; *Les Églises,* 61.

Antoine." This verbal secularism was reflected in the official decrees of the Commune as well. On May 10 the Committee of Public Safety referred to "George Square," rather than Saint George Square.[29] This rejection of ecclesiastical titles signaled that religion in general and the Catholic Church in particular had been demystified. Clubistes called priests "merchants of religion"; churches were called "shops" or "the raven's barn."[30] A note by Benjamin Lemoussou, a member of the vigilance committee of the 18th arrondissement and an active clubiste, presented a thorough indictment of the church, in part by redefining vocabulary. Acting in his capacity as policeman of the Carrières *quartier,* Lemoussou justified closing a church and arresting its clergy, "given that priests are bandits and that churches are the lairs where they have morally assassinated the masses by bending France under the talons of the infamous Bonaparte, Favre, and Trochu."[31]

Revolutions generally contain a puritanical element, and the purifying function of clubiste language—eradicating offending terms and ideas—constitutes a mirrorlike inversion of the Catholic Church's role in the purification of sins. Yet the clubiste process of inverting the church's place in society and culture involved far more than dropping *Saint* from place names. The pervasiveness of anticlerical attitudes in clubs helps explain why clubistes were in the forefront of the movement for secularization during the Commune, often providing the personnel that expelled religion from schools and hospitals. Communards in general and clubistes in particular took clerics hostage, desecrated sanctuaries, and put secular teachers and nurses in the place of nuns in schools and hospitals. All of this was accompanied by violence and threats of violence. In the destruction of church influence and the creation of new mechanisms clubistes again were the shock troops of the new world, revealing more passionate hatred and loftier ambition in this domain than in any other. Examples of bloodcurdling rhetoric and threats could be cited indefinitely and are well represented in most histories of the Commune. According to a neighbor, Hippolyte Cordier-Joly declared at the Club (Saint) Bernard "that priests and

---

29. *Le Combat,* January 4 and 8; *Le Journal Officiel,* May 11.

30. AHG: 26e conseil 212, dossier Letteron. The use of vocabulary derived from the realm of consumer and economic issues has prompted Edith Thomas to suggest that "In the eyes of the people of Paris, the Church was closely linked to bourgeois interests: they were rejecting both at the same time," a social analysis of anticlericalism that is fully compatible with, but only part of, the culturally centered view presented here; *Women Incendiaries,* 128.

31. The church was probably Saint Pierre de Montmartre; Lemoussou quoted in André Zeller, *Les Hommes de la Commune* (Paris: Perrin, 1969), 291.

religious instruction were not necessary and it was imperative to suppress that sect."[32] Violence and threats against hostages served to channel anger, and there were what might be termed "constructive" aspects of such rhetoric, including the way it created the foundation for specific policies to be put into effect. It is not sufficient to cite brutal language and massacres without showing that these practices were part of a revolutionary culture that also fulfilled "legitimate," if contentious, objectives.

The record of clubiste action to implement the Commune's anticlerical policies is long. As in the example of Lemoussou, who ordered a church closed and the priests arrested, these clubistes were acting in official capacities as administrators and police agents. Yet they often owed those positions to the notoriety they gained in the clubs or to the contacts they had made there in the revolutionary movement, and they formed and expressed there the projects that they then carried out. Jules Endres, a member of the vigilance committee of the 7th arrondissement and a leader of the Club Pré-aux-Clercs, was the administrator of the mairie of the 7th arrondissement during the Commune, for example, and as such purged schools and hospitals of nuns. Edouard Bourdeille, a member of the vigilance committee of the 18th arrondissement and the Club Elysée-Montmartre, as Civil Delegate took possession of the Ministry of Cultes.[33] Jean Fenouillas, a member of the Communal Council for the 12th arrondissement and an avid clubiste, was particularly assiduous in expelling nuns from schools and charitable institutions in his arrondissement.[34] Leon Jacob, of the AIT and vigilance committee of the 3d arrondissement, was on the board of the communal orphanage, replacing clerical supervision. Eugene Froissart, a vigilance committee member in the 10th arrondissement and a Civil Delegate, searched and inventoried several churches.[35] The citations could be multiplied, but in general all over Paris, particularly in the eighteen of twenty arrondissements represented or run predominantly by revolutionary socialists, many of the Communards who carried out secularization were also clubistes. Their actions in this regard fulfilled the programs set forth in the clubs of the siege and Commune, in the same

---

32. AHG: 16e conseil 96, dossier Cordier-Joly.

33. Maitron, *DBMOF,* 5:460; APP: Ba 364-5.

34. François Gérardin also helped carry out the secularization of his arrondissement. He was a member of the vigilance committee of the 4th arrondissement and the Club Saint Paul-Saint Louis, and he was also part of the group Act as you Think, an influential society of freethinkers; Maitron, *DBMOF,* 6:34, 170.

35. *Le Journal Officiel,* May 18; Maitron, *DBMOF,* 6:103.

manner that the seizure of power was prepared in revolutionary socialist clubs and committees.[36]

In all these aspects of its relations with religion and the church the Commune differed markedly from 1848. The revolution of 1848 had seen the blessing of Trees of Liberty and masses said for victims of February; it was colored by the powerful romanticism of the day, when many argued that revolution was compatible with religion. Clubs were not held in churches, which generally remained untouched by revolutionary militants.[37] The Commune of 1871 took place in a more positivist age, when "iron and blood" decided the great issues of the day. On the left science was associated with progress and liberty, the church with obscurantism and oppression, a sentiment that the *Syllabus of Errors* of 1864 and the Declaration of Infallibility of 1870 served only to strengthen. During the Second Empire French troops protected the Pope from the people of Rome and later from the government of Italy, connecting opposition to the Empire in France with opposition to the church. Anticlericalism in later nineteenth-century France was not a mere ritual without substance. Nor does the scope of anticlericalism in Communard discourse reveal a backward or traditional outlook.[38] Communards, and in particular clubistes, acted from an analysis of the old order that they had come to despise and sought to destroy. In its place they would build, through violence if need be, the new world.

The powerful discourse of violence that pervaded clubiste political culture was founded on a conception of revolutionary justice. The leaders of the Club Communal at Saint Nicolas des Champs defined justice as a

---

36. However, the effect of replacing nuns in charitable institutions was not wholly to the liking of some of those served. A Versailles police agent noted that those on relief in the 11th and 20th arrondissements were complaining about the meals distributed by the guardsmen; APP: 364-5.

37. Gossez, *Les Ouvriers de Paris,* 183. Peter H. Amann cites two instances of clubs in churches in 1848: one was no longer used for services, and the other was the basement of Saint Sulpice; *Revolution and Mass Democracy: The Paris Club Movement in 1848* (Princeton: Princeton University Press, 1975), 58. Edward Berenson has argued that 1871 was atheist while 1848 was not; *Populist Religion and Left-Wing Politics in France, 1830–52* (Princeton: Princeton University Press, 1984). Magraw echoes this conclusion; *A History of the French Working Class,* 1:253.

38. As Hutton suggests in relation to the Blanquists, in *The Cult of the Revolutionary Tradition.* For Rougerie, anticlericalism links Communards to the sansculottes of the First Republic, prompting him to conclude, "what is a Communard but a belated sansculotte?"; *Procès des Communards,* 208. He added that some Communards went beyond the sansculotte mentality, especially by their socialism. These conclusions were repeated later in *Paris Libre,* 224.

higher law than the formal codes created by politicians. In a poster of late April they distinguished between *légalité* and *droit,* between mere legality and fundamental law, or rights. Legality worked to the profit of reactionaries and had been one of the props of Napoleon III, but law worked for the benefit of justice. The Club leaders then urged the Communal Council to more revolutionary measures: "Step outside of legality, to enter into justice."[39] Under this doctrine of a higher law above the self-serving rules created by previous holders of power, Communards could sincerely deny acting illegally. When prosecutors asked Louise Michel why she supported a regime that ordered "illegal arrests, theft, pillage, assassination, and arson," she responded, "we never ordered illegal arrests, theft, pillage, arson; all that they did, to my knowledge, was perfectly legal."[40] Michel did not deny that the actions occurred, only that they were illegal. Operating within their two conceptions of legality both sides were correct, and both imposed their definition of legality when able. The Versaillais did so by interpreting Communard action as criminal; Communards also persecuted, jailed, and threatened their enemies when they had the means to do so. The Communard police agent Bertin provides an example as he searched, inventoried, and carried away some of the contents of Notre-Dame de la Plaisance. "Silence!" he commanded a cleric who protested, "or I'll have you put under wraps by my men." Then he looked at the work accomplished, saying, "that's fine, if I had done that under the Empire I'd get ten years of hard labor for it." The inversion of social relations and power was so clearly demonstrated that Bertin had to smile as he remarked on it.[41]

The assumptions informing the language of clubistes, their violent anticlericalism, and even their speaking and attending the workshops of the new world that clubs had become express this Communard conception that they were fighting for a higher order, a set of principles that gave purpose and legitimacy to their rhetoric and actions. Whether in contradistinction to the hierarchical and aristocratic social relations inherent in traditional forms of address or set against superstition and clerical influence, the higher law of revolution and the new world provided another aspect of the underlying unity of the Communal revolution. Certainly the specific features of this underlying vision differed among different individuals, but

39. *Les Murailles Politiques,* 3:145.
40. AHG: 6e conseil 135.
41. Fontoulieu, *Les Églises,* 241. This account was from an eyewitness, probably the cleric.

the same could be said for any large movement. The elements of commonality among clubiste visions are instead far more remarkable than the differences, and a cult of violence—its creation, characteristics, and functions—was one of the most striking unifying elements in the Communal
revolution. Because of the sharpness of the political struggle with Versailles, the depth of the social divisions within French society, and the
model for revolutionary action implicit in the historical memory of Communards, verbal and real violence was an organic part of the Commune.

Clubs and clubistes played a vital role in generating a culture of revolutionary violence in Paris; they created the framework within which opposition could be silenced, and they opened up space for the elaboration and
implementation of Communard visions. In this, as in most other traits,
clubistes expressed in sometimes exaggerated form characteristics general
among the revolutionary left. Guns and other weapons were a notable feature of the cult of violence. About fifty thousand revolvers were distributed during the Commune, prompting a journalist to decry the "mania for
fire arms, above all revolvers. . . . soon, you won't see a single person who
isn't wearing these arms in their belt." Orators, club officers, and members
in general often brought their weapons to meetings; Fonséques, for example, "always had his revolver in his hand," at the Club (Saint) Eustache.[42]
Alexandre Barrabino "frequented clubs, as did his wife, and often prof-
fered words against the army and the regular government. He always carried a sharpened, serrated knife, and said he would well know how to use
it when needed." Non-Communards, too, carried weapons. One man
described successfully resisting some guardsmen trying to arrest him as a
draft dodger: "I seized a revolver that I always carried on me, and threatened to shoot them if they moved."[43] Weapons in the hands of clubistes
were far more than symbols, although they were that. They were also
instruments of power used to implement the policies of the revolution.
Clubistes denounced draft dodgers, and many then carried out arrests.
Pierre Marechal, a member of the vigilance committee in the 5th
arrondissement, was accused of attempting to arrest a draft dodger.
Clotilde Legros and Mairie Rogissart, both clubistes, were accused of
denouncing réfractaires.[44]

---

42. Serman, *La Commune de Paris,* 475; *La Verité,* May 8; Fontoulieu, *Les Églises,* 14.
43. AN: BB24 746 3967, dossier Barrabino; AHG: 3e conseil 1742, dossier Marechal.
44. A Versailles report described women of the *quartiers populeux:* "deprived of their husbands, showing great irritation against the men that they meet, they call them 'cowards' and
have them arrested as refractories"; APP: 364-4; AHG: 3e conseil 742, dossier Marechal;
AHG: 20e conseil 528, dossier Rogissart; Maitron, *DBMOF,* 7:101.

In most instances of arrests, as for secularization, clubistes were acting as administrators or police agents when they arrested *réfractaires.* Nevertheless, threats and violence were possible in any social situation, and while physical harm was rare, the potential for violence created an environment of fear—even terror—among some non-Communards. Chaussade, a sometime officer of the Club Batignolles and an employee at the mairie of the 17th arrondissement, is illuminating in this regard. "I know him to be an eccentric, very fanatical man," his neighbor Marie Guerin testified, saying, "I saw him frequently parading about and gesturing with his revolver." Another witness testified that "during the Commune Chaussade was very fanatical. He was a militant, always shouting, and even threatening me. He told me one day, striking me on the shoulder, 'If we win we will chop your head off' (because I didn't want to march)." Chaussade admitted at his trial, "often, under my jacket, I wore a revolver in my belt, but sometimes I didn't wear it; my belt was indeed red, but I didn't wear it in a demonstrative manner." One day Guerin and Louis Laloire were looking at the fighting through a telescope from a fourth-floor balcony when Chaussade saw them from his fourth-floor apartment directly across the street. He pointed his revolver at them, shouting to Laloire, "Go get a rifle and get over there, coward, and take a good look." Frightened, Guerin cried out, "He's going to kill me!" and ran into the apartment. The next day Laloire complained at the mairie. When the guard captain on duty told Chaussade he did not have the right to threaten people, he replied, "I have that right in order to defend our cause; besides, this citizen could signal to the Versailles troops with his telescope."[45] For Chaussade, as for clubistes and Communards in general, serving the higher law of "our cause" implied the authority to threaten violence, a right he did not fail to exercise. His revolver, carried in clubs and in the street, was both the symbol and the actual guarantor of the right to commit violence.

Violence and the threat of violence in pursuit of a higher vision was integral to the revolution, as it had been to that of 1789. Weapons and the culture of violence, far from being a tangential or excessive aspect of the Commune, are packages of linked meanings that go to the center of the Communal revolution. Often weapons and violence were found in con-

---

45. AHG: 5e conseil 519, dossier Chaussade. Laloire's wife provided the testimony about the telescope incident; Laloire described his complaint and Chaussade's response. According to Chaussade the threats were not all on one side, as he testified at his trial that Laloire on another occasion told him, "soon they would have us all [Communards] shot." But Chaussade surely did himself no good by adding, "I didn't threaten him and I didn't have him arrested, which would have been easy for me; I didn't even denounce him."

junction with red symbols. Red symbols conferred legitimacy, joining specific actions that may have been contentious—such as arrests, denunciations, and threats—to larger authorities that can provide psychic reassurance. Chaussade's red belt, worn beneath his outer garments, comes to mind. The usage of red scarfs, belts, sashes, and other items also was a sign of office, which covered one's actions with the authority of the cause. Finally, red dress and accessories expressed the crossing of the threshold into the new world, part of the constellation of transformations that signaled that a revolution was under construction. The revolutionary cycle that culminated in the insurrection of March 18 may be said to have begun, for example, on February 24, when the Red Flag was hoisted to the top of the Bastille column by guardsmen who were both celebrating the anniversary of 1848 and defying the monarchist National Assembly.[46] Revolutions bring with them changes in dress, style, or grooming—as do counterrevolutions—and the Commune was no different. Just as the Empire's police agents had to cut off their "Imperial" mustaches after the founding of the Republic, so too red clothing became a potent symbol for the revolutionary left before the Commune. Michel admitted to her prosecutors, "I haven't gone without my red belt since September 4," the day the Republic was proclaimed.[47] Leo Meilliet's club dress and manner incited the following description from the prefect of police: "as an actor he was a terror; when he went to the clubs, he pulled off his suit coat and appeared in a red shirt and vest; he drew from his clothes a red flag; these gestures, this action, had a powerful effect on the masses."[48] Meilliet continued his promotion of red symbolism under the Commune. A member of the Communal Council, he gave the Pantheon section of the AIT one hundred francs "for fabricating red sashes."[49]

Delegates, orators, police agents, and other officials wore red as a sign of office. The clerk of a clothing store testified that Civil Delegate Lemoussou's common-law wife asked him for "a scarf in red silk ('whatever you have that is the most red,' she said) for my husband who is going to arrest an important person this very night." Etienne Canal said he wore a red rosette as his boutonnier, "as a member of the [vigilance] committee of the 19th arrondissement." Michau, leader of a delegation from the salle

46. See Maurice Dommanget, *Le Drapeau rouge* (Paris: Éditions Sociales, 1965).

47. Henri Guillemin, *L'Héroïque défense de Paris (1870–1871)* (Paris: Gallimard, 1959), 54; AHG: 6e conseil 135, dossier Michel.

48. "What phantasmogory!" remarked the prefect's interlocutor. "It was a real melodrama," replied Cresson. *L'Enquête Parlementaire su l'Insurrection du Dix-Huit mars,* 2:132.

49. The receipt was signed Octavia Tardif, April 12, 1871; APP: Ba 364-4.

Molière, wore a red belt.[50] Club meetings were surrounded with red symbols, banners, and flags. The *Journal Officiel* of May 5 reported the pulpit of the Saint Michel des Batignolles Church was "transformed henceforth into a people's tribune" by the addition of a red banner. Dress differentiated two worlds in uneasy juxtaposition, and some Communards associated black with reactionaries or clericals. J. B. Clement, a clubiste and a member of the Commune, wrote an article entitled "The Mischievous Women in Black," criticizing the women who constantly complained about high prices, republicanism, and the persecution of the church: "they are almost always in black, from the dress, shawl, hat, corsage, to their fan, and even to their dog." Jean-Baptiste Larocque described the bourgeois reactionaries who hounded him as "black suits."[51] Distinctions in dress between social classes and political groups were striking in this age when workers wore caps and the middle-class wore top hats. Newspaper vendors, for example, knew very well whom to offer prohibited conservative newspapers; "they hardly ever were mistaken."[52] The two worlds could be easily differentiated by those with discernment.

Wearing red belts, gesturing with revolvers, and proclaiming the new world, clubistes also threatened destruction and vengeance. Clubs were not simply debating societies; they played a crucial role in elaborating and then implementing the revolution. The clubiste culture of revolutionary violence considered execution, arson, and terror to be necessary for the transformation of society. The efforts of 1792 and 1848 were interpreted as proving this necessity; the first effort was successful through violence, the second failed without it. An orator at Notre-Dame de la Croix was notorious for repeating, "We must cleanse society with the blood of priests and aristocrats."[53] This rhetoric reflected both the revolutionary vision and the physical reality of Communards in a city surrounded and bombarded. Incitements to burn, execute, and arrest were typical in club discourse. In addition to priests, Communards targeted for retribution former police agents, the wives of Versailles sympathizers who had fled, and landlords.[54]

---

50. AHG: 13e conseil 185, dossier Canal; Fontoulieu, *Les Églises,* 154.

51. *Le Cri du Peuple,* April 21; Larocque, *1871,* 345.

52. Dabot, *Griffonnages quotidiens,* 198. Another observer also remarked on the keen eyes of newspaper vendors; Bergerand, *Paris sous la Commune,* 141.

53. Fontoulieu, *Les Églises,* 115.

54. Rougerie, in *Paris Libre* and *Procès des Communards,* has convincingly argued that the hatred shown these groups by Communards translated underlying social and political conflicts, and here it only needs noting that many clubistes carried out these projects, moving from words to action.

At their trials after the Commune many clubistes were described as "the terror of the *quartier*" for having threatened, attacked, and arrested their enemies. This label is found both in police reports of clubiste activity and in the depositions of neighbors and other witnesses. In the stairwells of apartment buildings, in the streets, in casual conversation, and in the public squares, clubistes spoke and acted for their cause and against their enemies. To be a "terror," then, was the mark of revolutionary militants who brought their convictions into every aspect of life under the Commune. Constant Demeulle, a member of the vigilance committee and the municipal commission of the 4th arrondissement, allegedly terrorized his neighbors. A married couple fled the city as a result of his threats to make the husband march for the Commune, and he was said to have threatened everyone in his building.[55] Jacques Gache "went daily to the clubs," according to his postman, "and openly criticized those who didn't go, as well as those who didn't march [for the Commune]." A neighbor confirmed that Gache "did everything he could to make the inhabitants of the building take up arms; many times he even threatened to make them march and to shoot them."[56] Both Ajax Faure, known to attend the Club École de Droit, and his wife were, according to a neighbor, "very feared; in the *quartier* you heard only of them, and everyone fled them." Each time Isadore Lecharpentier, a clubiste of the 13th arrondissement, encountered the wife of a former police agent who lived in his building he called her "the mother assassin." Jean Brousse of the Club Arras, 5th arrondissement, threatened that "the Republic would not be soft" and tried several times to have a neighbor arrested.[57] These citations, which could be multiplied, create a picture of clubiste action that did indeed make clubistes the "terrors" of their neighborhoods.

These and other actions created a climate of fear among many non-Communards in the city. The wife and daughter of a gendarme, for example, fled their home in Montrouge because they feared a crowd that had demanded they be sent to the front—placing the wives of gendarmes in the line of fire was a common threat in clubs. This incident may be related to a Versailles police report of April 1 based on information from train travelers arriving from Paris. It reported a rumor that "the wife of a police agent of Montrouge was killed last night. Many wives of police agents

55. AHG: 5e conseil 565, dossier Demeulle.
56. AHG: 4e conseil 400, dossier Gache.
57. AHG: 13e conseil 212, dossier Faure; AHG: 6e conseil 670, dossier Brousse; AN: BB24 737 1178, dossier Lecharpentier.

arrived by this train."[58] Fear intimidated potential opposition. Charles Bergerand's memoir recounts, "the honest people whom poverty or necessity retains in Paris hide, and are in any case silent. No one leaves his house without first checking his pockets to be sure they don't contain compromising papers. It's vain to search for another work for it; there is none: it's the Terror."[59] The sense of fear among some nonrevolutionaries, perhaps excessive given the actual incidence of physical harm, was an inherent part of constructing the new world—which entailed the destruction of the old.

In the heat of the struggle clubistes did not hesitate to proclaim their desire to see Paris burn rather than submit to Versailles, just as under the siege many said Paris should be destroyed rather than handed over to the Prussians. In this, however, the Communards were more faithful to their word, for in the last days of fighting parts of Paris were torched. Most fires had a defensive purpose, some were accidental, and some were purely destructive, but all were welcomed by those like Charles Bas, of the Club Sainte Marguerite, who was heard to say, "Paris is burning, we are the masters, let Paris burn." Another person heard him hope that "all those [hostages] at Mazas Prison will be burned like pigs."[60] Isidore Cochu, of the Clubs Bernard and Robert, and his wife were seen to "dance for joy" when they heard that demolition crews had begun destroying Thiers' house, as ordered by the Communal Council.[61] In looking out at the destruction in the midst of Bloody Week, Bergerand thought, "there is no doubt about it, they have burned the Tuileries! Everything that they said in the clubs was true, then. This infernal project to burn Paris, they conceived it, and they are going to try to execute it!"[62] He was right. The fires that consumed parts of the city, no matter their cause, were—like arrests, threats, attacks, and executions—an expression of the cult of violence fostered within clubiste political culture.[63] The fires were the translation of

---

58. Dabot, *Griffonnages quotidiennes,* 181; APP: 364-4.

59. Bergerand, *Paris sous la Commune,* 132.

60. AHG: 5e conseil 681, dossier Bas. The burning of parts of Paris during Bloody Week and allegations of willful destruction by "women incendiaries" have been extensively debated. For three well-informed and contrasting perspectives see Thomas, *Women Incendiaries;* Rials, *Nouvelle histoire de Paris;* Gay L. Gullickson, *"La Pétroleuse:* Representing Revolution," *Feminist Studies* 17 (summer 1991): 241–65.

61. AHG: 17e conseil 166, dossier Cochu.

62. Bergerand, *Paris sous la Commune,* 94.

63. Dalotel, Faure, and Freiermuth noted that the execution of hostages was the "logical fulfillment of an indictment made for two years of public meetings" during the Empire, but they are on less solid ground when they agree the executions were justified by the occupation and social class of the victims (police agents, clerics, and a banker); *Aux Origines,* 208.

words to deeds in the context of a pitiless civil war, in the same way that the Commune was founded in the rhetoric, symbols, and practices of the revolutionary movement centered in clubs. As the most fervent militants in the revolutionary struggle, clubistes outlined and acted on their visions, a process many believed intrinsically required violence.

Communard violence and terror was not gratuitous, not a glorification of violence for its own sake. Within every threat or act lay a vision of how conditions must be changed to construct the new world. Clubs and committees were one framework within which that world took shape; as expressions of the three faces of association they in effect constituted the girders and pillars of the future society, and it was in clubs and committees that the new world received its fullest elaboration and implementation. The culture of revolutionary violence generated in them was inspired by and preparatory to a larger vision, the fundamental basis of which was the virtually sacrosanct revolutionary trinity: Liberty, Equality, Fraternity. The descriptive labels in the names of the groups founded to promote the revolution and the Commune were *association, federation, solidarity, union, alliance*—that is, variations on the theme of fraternity. In the topics raised and actions taken by clubistes within the context of association, that is, fraternity, one sees as well dedication to liberty and equality. Arguing that clubistes in particular and Communards in general were dedicated to liberty may seem paradoxical, given the real and threatened violence directed toward enemies and the abrogation of public discourse by Communards. Yet when instances of violent rhetoric and action are examined closely, they show that many clubistes well understood that liberty can be defined and implemented in several ways. Persons suspected of opposing the Commune or tainted because of their past were often shouted down before even beginning a speech, although when Abbé Delmas debated the Communes decrees on religion at the Club des Prolétaires he supposedly won many sympathizers.[64] Pierre Burdaille was not so lucky. At a meeting in the auditorium of Arts et Métiers the assembly did not allow him to speak, probably because his position had been compromised several years before by the publication of letters declaring his devotion to the Empire.[65]

---

64. Delmas added that when he was allowed to speak some clubistes left muttering, "well then, it's no longer a club!"; Abbé Guillaume Delmas, *La Terreur et l'Église en 1871* (Paris: Dentu, 1871), 83, 97.

65. *Le Cri du Peuple,* April 24. Burdaille later testified that he had been arrested after speaking in favor of the government of Versailles at the salle Sax, 9th arrondissement; AHG: 5e conseil 545.

A Versailles report citing an eyewitness's account stated that a fight had broken out in the Saint Michel des Batignolles Church, and that a woman who spoke in favor of the Versailles government was nearly hung.[66] At the Club Saint Eloi a man who told the assembly that it should have no master other than God was forced to descend from the pulpit amid shouts of "à la porte le mouchard!"[67]

Although club discourse was limited to those who accepted the principle of the Commune, there was considerable latitude for debate and criticism. Disputes and arguments were often noted in clubs. Nicolas Montelle told prosecutors that he had a "fairly sharp" argument with Viard, a member of the Commune for the 20th arrondissement, at the Club du Châtelet (Théâtre Lyrique), "and the assembly was against me."[68] At the Club des Prolétaires an orator who complained about the military administration of the arrondissement "treated the bureau in a really cavalier manner," according to the minutes, and President David replied, "to such insolence one can only respond with disdain." David and other leaders of the club were some of the highest officials in the arrondissement guard administration.[69] At the Club Saint Bernard (18th) "we are told that the orators fought each other in support of their positions," according to a Versailles report.[70] Trohel was called a "calotin" (priest-lover) at the Club Saint Severin after announcing that he hoped to secure a cleric's release from prison.[71] In the 17th arrondissement Chalain and Malon of the Communal Council reportedly had a bitter quarrel in the Club Saint Michel des Batignolles. According to one account Chalain accused Malon of treason, and another source reported that Chalain said that even though they were friends, if Malon did not change his mind Chalain would "blow his head off."[72] Some moderates and conservatives used the violence and lack of freedom in clubs as an indictment of the supposed anarchic, primitive

---

66. APP: Ba 364-4.

67. AHG: 5e conseil 545, dossier Burdaille.

68. AHG: 3e conseil 176, dossier Montelle.

69. AHG: Ly 22. The secretary, probably Paysant, added, "I have observed that every time the question of battalions are on the table, this occasions tumult, anger, and above all much lost time that one could better employ."

70. APP: Ba 364-6.

71. AHG: 9e conseil 687, dossier Trohel.

72. D'Esbeoufs, *Trahison,* 48; Fontoulieu, *Les Églises,* 222. Neither source knew what the argument was about. Fontoulieu said this was around May 18, which was just after the publication of the declaration of the minority; Malon was part of the minority, Chalain of the majority, and this incident was likely connected to the increasing polarization of the Communal Council.

ideas of clubistes.[73] For Communards, however, the intimidation exercised by popular assemblies was a positive attribute and a source of strength for the revolution. In the Communal Council, for example, Rastoul once complained that the Committee of Public Safety had suppressed some newspapers and had decreed that attacks against the Commune and the Republic could be referred to a court-martial. While he agreed that attacks on "the ideal of the Commune" should be suppressed, he noted that the decree was useless because journalists "will go to the clubs to say what they would have published and that is the same thing." An anonymous member of the council replied, "the journalists will at least find contradictors in the clubs, and, if they go once, they will not be tempted to return."[74] Thus restriction of discussion through the culture of revolutionary violence was applauded for its services to the Commune. Baillache, one of the leaders of the Club des Prolétaires, demanded quite simply that all newspapers be suppressed since journalists were not serving in the guard and were spreading false reports.[75] These instances of disputes and arguments, and the many more that could be cited, took place within proscribed limits. Individuals and even the Communal Council could be attacked, but not the principle of the Commune and the Republic; the liberty of Communards was coextensive with and defined by revolutionary politics.

Even more prevalent in the clubs of the Commune were themes of equality. Generally these themes were not debated or described in abstract terms but were part of the discussion of everyday problems and concerns. The Communard conception of equality tended to be practical and real, and it was intended to be implemented, not just discussed. Equality was applied to all aspects of life. One of the most pressing economic concerns of Parisians throughout the siege and Commune was the rent question. Though the Commune had decreed that rents due during the last nine months did not have to be paid, the issue was still of critical importance to many. Both the Club Central at Saint Eustache and the Club Communal at Saint Nicolas des Champs passed a motion on May 16 asking the Commune to decree that rent for the next six months would not have to be paid. Citoyenne Thyou proposed much the same thing at the Club des

---

73. "What else can be expected from an assembly of drunkards and thieves?"; Fontoulieu, *Les Églises*, 245.

74. *Les Procès-Verbaux de la Commune*, 2:432.

75. AHG: Ly 22. Baillache's was an ironic proposal, since the Club des Prolétaires had its own newspaper, *Le Prolétaire.*

Prolétaires.[76] Some Communards and clubistes, among them several anonymous members of an open-air club in late March, thought that not paying rent was not enough; according to a conservative newspaper they demanded as well the "suppression of property."[77]

The dynamic of inversion in Communard thought was particularly pronounced in discussion of the rent question. Martin Masson, a clubiste of the 11th arrondissement, refused to move out of his apartment and told his landlord that "the Commune would triumph, and would put renters in the place of landlords." While having a drink with the concierge of his building, Constant Demeulle, a member of the vigilance committee of the 4th arrondissement, said, "soon there will be neither concierges nor landlords." A caricature of the time twisted these sentiments to comic effect, depicting an orator shouting from a pulpit, "No more landlords! Everybody rents!"[78] Similarly, Georges Melotte, sometime president of the Club Notre-Dame des Victoires, told neighbors he encountered in the stairwell of his building, "the roles are going to change; the age of the petit bourgeoisie is over."[79] The rent question fused personal and political motives; denunciations of rapacious landlords arose from both the experience and the discourse of property relations. Sylvian Bouisson, for example, denounced his landlord, M. Pompei, at the Club de l'École de Médecine for being a former police officer, helping draft dodgers, and hiding weapons. The club then voted for Pompei's arrest; Pompei later testified that Bouisson had also asked the club to condemn him to death. Bouisson, who may have been a Communard police official, later arrested Pompei and took him to the Prefecture of Police, where Pompei was shown a complaint signed by many names, which he believed was a club petition. This was Pompei's second arrest on the same charges, and Bouisson's resorting to the club for backing may have been prompted by Pompei's earlier release. The dynamic of inversion was complete when Bouisson bragged to Pompei's maid that he had seen Pompei in prison—the landlord and the renter in an unusual reversal.[80]

---

76. *Le Journal Officiel,* May 16; AHG: Ly 22.

77. *La Gazette des Tribunaux,* March 31.

78. AN: BB24 752 5149, dossier Masson; AHG: 5e conseil 565, dossier Demeulle; Leith, *Images of the Commune,* 133.

79. "Educated and intelligent" according to the police, Melotte was also a member of the AIT; AHG: 10e conseil 584.

80. Pompei remained in prison until freed by Versailles troops during the *semaine sanglante.* Bouisson showed Communard police a red card, which the Versailles prosecutors later took to be a police identity card; it might also have been a club or vigilance committee membership card. AN: BB24 749 #4675; AHG: 3e conseil 362.

Equality in duties and in responsibility, including equality in hardship, were the central axes of citizenship for republicans and revolutionaries of the left during the siege and Commune. During the siege the liberal Government of National Defense only hesitantly rationed some necessities, prompting classic "food riots" in which goods were seized by crowds and sold at a "just price."[81] Jules Favre of the Government of National Defense wrote later in his memoirs that he found it "singularly bizarre" that during the siege Paris willingly submitted to the requisitioning of some goods but protested in the name of liberty any measures taken against political troublemakers. He still did not understand that in a time of crisis many Parisians would sacrifice economic "freedom" but not their republican liberties.[82] The Communal Council and other civil and military authorities always paid for goods that were requisitioned for the war effort and to feed the city. Even the money taken from the Bank of France was either from the account of the City of Paris or a loan. As for food, under the Commune there was no threat of starvation; prices did rise, and many complained of want for lack of work, but there was no subsistence crisis as there had been in the later siege. Hence it is all the more significant that clubistes did not stop demanding requisitioning. In the new circumstances of the city, requisitioning was demanded no longer out of necessity but on the basis of equality in sacrifice and responsibility. Pursuit of this ideal explains the great desire among Communards for requisitions of necessities and universal service in the guard.

Former officials of the Second Empire and Government of National Defense were to bear the burden of punishment and confiscation as well. Isidore Cochu, a member of the Club de la Révolution Saint Bernard and a Communard police agent reassured the wife of a police officer who was imprisoned that her husband would not be shot. "We're not so vile as that," he told her, explaining, "your husband is held because they have assaulted Blanqui, if they had given him back, the hostages would have been returned. What will be done probably is that all your goods will be seized and you will be expelled from the city."[83] The rich were generally expected to share in sacrifice in a variety of ways as well, from limits on the amount of money they could earn in interest—an attack on wealth not

---

81. On November 7, for example, a crowd forced a merchant to sell ham at a reduced price—he had attempted to return to his warehouse from a public market with ham that was unsold because the price was so high; APP: Ba 363-1.
82. Favre, *Le Gouvernement de la Défense Nationale,* 1:297.
83. AHG: 17e conseil 166, dossier Cochu.

earned by work—to confiscation of wealth to pay the costs of the war or the indemnity to the Prussians.[84] An orator at the Club de la Révolution Sociale in Saint Michel des Batignolles on May 14 proposed that all the shopkeepers who fled Paris be fined one hundred francs a day for a week, and that the goods of those who did not return be confiscated and sold for the benefit of the Commune and of widows and orphans. The minutes report that "the entire assembly applauded this decision and a delegation was immediately named to submit this just demand to the Commune." At the Club des Prolétaires there was even discussion of allocating three hundred francs and some land to men who had fought for the Commune.[85] Not all shopkeepers were to be expropriated, however, only those who had "treasonably" fled the city. Communards considered these measures to be a punishment as well as a means toward greater equality, and in general they were to be directed only against enemies. The Communal Council decreed that only defenders of the city were eligible to receive items from the municipal pawn shop for free. Similarly, families and persons with connections to Versailles were not eligible to receive pensions from the Commune.[86] Equality operated to the benefit of Communards—that is, to the victory of the revolution—and to the detriment of their opponents, who included reactionaries, aristocrats, and monarchists, no matter their economic condition. The foundations for these demands, as well as the targets selected, suggest that class antagonism was only one element at work, and that political and cultural elements conditioned Communard behavior as well.

Clubistes also demanded equality among Communards. The decree limiting salaries of Communard officials to six thousand francs, about four times a skilled worker's salary, was welcomed by guardsmen gathered in front of the Hôtel de ville, who wanted "no more huge appointments," because "everyone has to live."[87] At the Club de la Révolution Sociale an orator complained that musicians soliciting donations for widows and orphans of killed Communards were earning too much, four to eight francs a day.[88] This may seem a petty demand in a city under attack, but equality was to operate at all levels, so long as the equality in operation

84. Fontoulieu, *Les Églises,* 78, 159; Firmin Maillard, *Histoire des journaux publiés à Paris pendant le siège et la Commune, 4 septembre au 28 mai, 1871* (Paris: Dentu, 1871), 218.
85. AHG: Ly 22.
86. *Les Procès-Verbaux de la Commune,* 2:421, 245.
87. APP: Ba 364-4.
88. AHG: Ly 22.

was the Communard vision of equality. The Central Comité Électoral, Républicain, Démocrate, Socialiste du XIe Arrondissement expressed the same vision at a higher plane in a poster for the elections of March 26. "Revolution is the march of peoples toward equality of rights and duties," its statement of principles began, stating, "the Democratic and Social Republic is this equality realized. All men should be in solidarity. Law should be the progressive expression of eternal right. The People must affirm the rights and sovereignty that reside in them." This remarkable statement thus combines a fully realized conception of equality, a concept of a higher revolutionary law, and an affirmation of popular sovereignty.[89] This formal statement is more abstract than most daily club speech, but the structures of thought and purpose are the same whether in this electoral statement, in the complaint that musicians in the service of the Commune were paid too well, or in the demand that those who did not fulfill the duties of citizenship should have their goods seized.[90] All were part of the continuing struggle to attain a new society.

Examining one club in depth may further clarify clubiste political culture. The Club Communal exhibits in specific ways many of the general traits of Communard clubs. Like most, it developed from an earlier public meeting sponsored by the local vigilance committee, in this case that of the 3d arrondissement, most of whose members were also members of the International. During the siege and armistice the committee sponsored meetings at the salle Molière, where committee members conquered a significant following, and during the Commune they dominated the local municipal commission. All of those elected to the Commune from the 3d had participated in the revolutionary socialist movement, and the ties between the club and administrators at the mairie and Hôtel de ville remained strong.[91] One observer described the public at the salle Molière as "populaire; beaucoup de femmes," who were "white-hot" in their extremism.[92] By late April the crowd had grown so large that club leaders,

89. *Les Murailles Politiques,* 2:54–55.

90. Rougerie argues that the question of requisitions is part of an "old quarrel" with roots in the Great Revolution and is therefore evidence of archaism and the backward-looking nature of the Commune; *Procès de Communards,* 206. Rather, the issue was absolutely current. And not all property holders as a class were to be expropriated, as implied when terms such as *dictatorship of the proletariat* are applied to the Commune by some scholars who employ the social interpretation.

91. Antoine Arnaud, a member of the municipality and the Commune, reported that the club had been opened "by order of the municipality"; *Les Procès-Verbaux de la Commune,* 1:518.

92. *Sous la Commune,* 68.

several of whom were on the municipal commission, decided to move the meetings to the Saint Nicolas des Champs Church. They presented a municipal order to the beadle, who on April 24 was forced to open his doors to a different sort of faithful; to protect their churches clerics often helped accommodate clubistes. One abbé recalled that he "put up barriers in the transept, lit the lamps, unfolded the chairs, and had the door opened a little before eight."[93]

Marc Villiers de l'Isle-Adam wrote a remarkable newspaper article describing the Club Communal at Saint Nicolas des Champs, incorporating several important themes in the Communard mentality. "Agreed, then: from five in the morning to five at night the churches are for the clergy," he wrote, explaining that "at five, the usher rearranges the prayer benches, puts the holy vases in the armoire, clears the sanctuary, and invites the faithful to retire. At eight o'clock, the people enter."[94] Villiers' fundamental opposition of "the faithful" versus "the people" is continued in the form *fideles* versus *foule* in his description of the enormous crowd thronging the streets leading to the club and in the interior of the church itself. "Never would the services of Mary's month [May] attract so many faithful. . . . Under the astonished ancient vaults, which usually resound to austere chants, is heard the confused murmur of the crowd." Villiers wrote that the effect the scene had on him when he entered the church was "gripping," and he was not alone in sensing a change of atmosphere in the presence of so many Communards in a holy place; an English minister echoed Villiers, writing, "the effect produced on my mind on entering the church was peculiar, and almost indefinable." When revolutionaries shouted from the pulpit it was remarkable to the whole neighborhood, as when three people testified separately that they heard that a neighbor, Achille Martin, had spoken from the choir of Saint Severin.[95]

Villiers continued playing on oppositions in his description of club orators: "In the choir, instead of a priest in white surplice or a capuchin in fustian cloth, stands a man who, hand on the hilt of his saber, kepi low on his forehead, a red scarf around his waist, addresses to the multitude a sermon of a new genre." A newspaper article confirms this picture, describing the "club communaliste" where "popular orators, most of them belonging to the National Guard, express, explain, and comment on the theories whose

93. The beadle testified at Landeck's trial; AHG: 17e conseil 742. Delmas was referring to the Club Central in Saint Eustache; *La Terreur,* 83.

94. *Le Tribune du Peuple,* May 19, under the pseudonym Marius.

95. Gibson, *Paris during the Commune,* 240; AHG: 6e conseil 220, dossier Martin.

triumph is currently the object of fighting between Paris and Versailles."[96] During their new sermon, according to Villiers, "the church resounds with virile and audacious accents forgotten for centuries," the emphasis on the orator's masculinity serving to heighten the contrast with the celibate priesthood. Villiers then changed the focus of the fundamental dichotomy evident throughout his article, writing, "these men, those who speak as well as those who listen, are they apostles? Whatever they be, they are going to shed their blood for their cause. Do you hear the canon roar? The doors of the sanctuary might open before the martyrs." By referring to clubistes as apostles and to guardsmen as martyrs, Villiers raised devotion to the Commune to the spiritual level, linking revolution and salvation. "An entire people is discussing grave issues; for the first time you hear workers exchanging their evaluations of problems, which up to now only philosophers grappled with," Villiers observed. "Before," he continued, "when this same people left unsteady from the dance halls on the outskirts of town, the bourgeois turned aside, saying low, 'If these people were free, what would become of us? What would become of them?' They are free, and they no longer dance. They are free, and they work. They are free, and they fight." Villiers then returned to a theme that implicitly informed his entire description: "When a man of good faith passes near them today, he understands that a new century has just burst forth." Identifying with one-half of the paired oppositions he describes, and rejecting the other, Villiers positioned orators in church clubs within a conception of history, recognizing in them the apostles of a new era.

Such sentiments, expressed more prosaically, were shared by the leaders of the Club Communal who installed the club in the Saint Nicolas des Champs Church. Their declaration of principles asserted that the club was founded to fight the enemies of the Commune and the Republic, to educate the people and defend their rights, and to uphold popular sovereignty by supervising elected officials.[97] As in other arrondissements, however, there was opposition to the invasion of the church. Clubiste possession of Saint Sulpice, for example, caused considerable disorder, and on May 10 the faithful were able to prevent a club meeting, despite the intervention of guardsmen sent by the municipality. On the next day clubistes entered the church in the midst of services, and a war of songs ensued. According to one account, "The clubistes shouted the *Marseillaise,* and the faithful intoned the *Magnificat;* then came the singing of the *Girondins,* to which

96. *Le Mot d'Ordre,* April 29.
97. *Le Bulletin Communal,* May 6.

one responded with the *Salve Regina.*" When the clubistes yelled "Long live the Commune!" the faithful shouted "Long live Jesus Christ!" The clubistes prevailed; on May 18 a Versaillais police report stated that although the church was closed for services, it was open for a men's club in the afternoon and for a women's club in the evening.[98] Similarly, a published letter of protest by the priest of Saint Nicolas des Champs incited a ceremonial seizure of the edifice several days after the club had already been installed there. The club newspaper reported that on April 30, which not coincidentally was a Sunday, a crowd of ten thousand people filled the streets around the church. Accompanied by drumrolls and trumpet blasts the crowd enthusiastically shouted, "Vive la Commune, vive la République!" After a speech by Bernard Landeck, sometime club president, the Red Flag was hoisted onto the church, in a combination of symbolic and effective action, revolutionary ritual and practice.[99]

Like many clubistes in the revolutionary socialist movement, Landeck, a thirty-nine-year-old jewelry worker and a member of the International, had participated in the two major revolts of the siege, those on October 31 and January 22. "Landeck's goal was to raise the masses," testified the beadle of Saint Nicolas des Champs, who said, "he wanted to force everyone to march." The concierge of his building reported that "Landeck was extremely fanatical. They even said he was crazy. . . . He was an original." According to the beadle Landeck was perhaps the best-armed orator in Paris, as "he usually came armed with a rifle, a saber, and a revolver." As police commissioner of the 1st arrondissement Landeck used these weapons, or at least he used the revolutionary power they represented. Early in May he had the building he lived in surrounded, went inside with several guardsmen, and came out holding three young men in custody for not serving the Commune. One of them later testified with good reason that like so many other clubistes Landeck "was feared in the *quartier.*"[100] Also like other clubistes, Landeck united revolutionary symbolism and intimidation with effective action in the name of the Commune.

The secretary of the Club Communal, Joseph Paysant, also illuminates the clubiste culture of violence. He, too, wore a revolver, and on one

98. Fontoulieu, *Les Églises,* 248; Du Camp, *Les Convulsions de Paris,* 4:253; APP: Ba 365-1.

99. *Le Bulletin Communal,* May 6.

100. AHG: 17e conseil 742, dossier Landeck. Landeck was also a delegate to the provinces in late May, along with Amouroux, a Communal Council member for the 4th arrondissement; AHG: 3e conseil 332, dossier Amouroux.

evening at the club he demanded the arrest of his landlord for harboring draft evaders. He, too, spread fear among his neighbors according to witnesses, and in addition he lived with a woman of doubtful morals, who drank and was said to be as frightful as he; both were also "chefs de barricade" and "the terrors of the *quartier.*"[101] A thirty-year-old artisan in textile production, Paysant was known as "Iron Foot" because of the apparatus he wore to correct for legs of unequal length. "Endowed with a certain intelligence" according to his prosecutors, Paysant was well equipped to play an important role in clubs, due to his "fairly great ease of elocution." He helped Landeck and others install branches of the Club Communal at both Saint Leu and Sainte Elisabeth, so his excuse for a draft speech that called government officials "the valets of tyranny" could only fall on deaf ears: "What would you have? You must run with the wolves; to combat certain [club] propositions you have to put yourself on their level." Indeed, at his trial Paysant lied extravagantly to try to avoid punishment; at one point, he told prosecutors that he only spoke of "agricultural questions, the constant goal of my life; but soon I realized that this theory was not to the taste of my audience, and on May 15 I thought it my duty to retire [from the club]." Although somewhat craven before army prosecutors, Paysant served the Commune to the end, supervising a barricade during the *semaine sanglante.*[102]

Those who attended and spoke at the Club Communal along with Landeck and Paysant appear to have been broadly representative of club assemblies across Paris. On different occasions attendance was said to be from four thousand to six thousand, which is not inconceivable given that the two branches of the club at Saint Leu and Sainte Elisabeth were opened due to overcrowding of the large church.[103] Among the attendees were many Communard notables, including members of the Communal Council, such as Vésinier, Johannard, Amouroux, and Varlin. In any such club there were even those who were hostile, seeking intelligence about Communard projects. In addition to the ubiquitous Versailles police informants, Abbé Martin attended the Club Communal "disguised as a

---

101. AHG: 17e conseil 252, dossier Paysant.

102. Paysant had indeed written on agriculture, and he had even presented a public lecture on the topic; AHG: 17e conseil 252; *Le Mot d'Ordre,* February 26.

103. *Le Bulletin Communal,* May 6. Fontoulieu, *Les Églises,* 159, cites six thousand attendees at the meeting of May 3. A petition to the Communal Council cited five thousand in attendance on May 1; *Les Procès-Verbaux de la Commune,* 2:89.

National Guard."[104] Like most clubs, the participants appear to have lived in the immediate vicinity, which in this case meant the 2d, 3d, and 4th arrondissements almost exclusively. Most were artisans and shopkeepers, and as in other clubs, the leaders and orators included a large proportion of journalists and others in occupations that required some education. The role of women in the club was somewhat ambiguous, conforming to contradictory ideals and practices. The statutes allowed women to attend the twice-weekly meetings of club members and leaders, which were held in addition to public assemblies, but they prohibited women from taking part in the deliberations. Women's club membership cards gave them rights to "a special place in public meetings," but this suggestion of segregation was not carried out in practice, for women and men mingled freely in club meetings. Women suspected of immorality could be excluded from the club, although the statutes made no such provision for men. Still, as at most clubs, women gave speeches, and some accounts describe meetings in which women constituted the majority. Indeed, Marie-Jean Bouquet was seen on the dais with club leaders, and another woman, Paysant's companion, was said to be the club treasurer.[105]

The speeches and decisions of the Club Communal also appear to have conformed to patterns typical of most popular organizations. Denunciations of draft dodgers mixed with warnings about treason by supporters of Versailles; death sentences were passed on the hostages and the archbishop of Paris; the leaders of the National Assembly were declared outlaws, their property, and that of army officers, confiscated for the families of wounded and killed guardsmen. One proposal unanimously accepted called for a moratorium on rents below five hundred francs, with higher rents discounted 30 percent. Defense of the Commune was a constant concern, as when the club outlined a detailed plan of barricades and fortifications to be constructed by those too young to serve in the guard. On April 28 Paysant was delegated by the three thousand people in attendance to take a sample of the guard's meat ration to the Commune, in order to prove its inadequacy. Régère, a member for the 6th arrondisse-

---

104. A Versailles report of May 7 signaled a speech by Varlin at the club; APP: Ba 364-6. A curé testified about the abbé's espionage, AHG: 17e conseil 742.

105. *Le Bulletin Communal,* May 6; AN: BB24, 746, 4082. Paysant's concierge said he and the woman lived well on funds stolen from the club; AHG: 17e conseil 252.

ment who met with Paysant, agreed it was too small, and he promised remedial action.[106]

As this example shows, the Club Communal took seriously its stated goal of expressing the will of the people to their elected officials. On May 1 Vésinier presented the Communal Council with the club's congratulations for voting to form the Committee of Public Safety, but he also presented a demand that supplementary elections be held to fill vacant seats on the assembly. The petition even threatened that if the Commune did not hold the elections, "the club, representing the majority of the electors, will convoke them itself." Landeck, who had moved this proposition at the club, was particularly interested in holding elections, because, as Paysant told prosecutors, "Landeck wanted at any price to be a member of the Commune." Landeck had been a candidate in the April 16 by-election, but although he had gained the most votes in the 3d arrondissement, he was among those not allowed to sit because they had not received the votes of a high enough proportion of the registered voters. When the Communal Council did not call elections as the club requested, it carried through on its threat and on May 17 elected Landeck to represent the arrondissement by a simple raising of hands.[107]

The election of Landeck to the Communal Council by the Club Communal, even though he never tried to take his seat, is an illuminating expression of clubiste political culture. Episodes of threats and violence that can appear random or without meaning, as when Chaussade pointed his revolver at a man for looking at the fighting through a telescope, must be inserted into this larger culture to be explicable. The symbolism of red flags ceremoniously unfurled on church spires formed part of that culture, but club institutions and the social positions of club members also formed the contexts for resolute action. Landeck (arresting draft dodgers), Paysant (building barricades during the *semaine sanglante*), and clubistes (shouting in the stairwells of their buildings) partook of this nexus of practices, symbols, rhetoric, and contexts that defined the revolution Communards crafted.

---

106. *Le Journal Officiel,* May 16; *Le Bulletin Communal,* May 6; Maillard, *Histoire des journaux,* 218; AHG: 17e conseil 742.

107. AHG: 17e conseil 252; *Le Bulletin Communal,* May 6. The election was described by an eyewitness; AHG: 17e conseil, 742.

CHAPTER 7

Gender and Clubiste Political Culture

The social revolution will not be operative until women are equal to
men. Until then, you have only the appearance of revolution.
—"Citoyenne Destree"

In May 1871, as the Versailles army threatened to breach the defenses of
the Commune, many Parisians were startled by the spectacle of "armed
citoyennes" wearing red armbands and marching in the streets of the capital. About one hundred women reportedly received weapons at a ceremony at the Hôtel de ville, while in the 12th arrondissement the Légion des
Fédérées—a battalion of women federated with the National Guard—
organized demonstrations and enforced Communard control of the district.[1] When the Versailles forces finally entered the city, women in these
armed groups built barricades and died in their defense during the street
fighting of the *semaine sanglante*.[2] These armed women's groups arose
from a complex interaction of ideals of revolutionary citizenship and the
collective memory of the revolutionary tradition. Within the framework of
the popular organizations of the Commune, Communard men and women
created a political culture that combined representations of the past and
current revolutionary practice, with novel results. Contradicting traditional gender definitions, Communard women in the Légion des Fédérées

Epigraph from Citoyenne Destree at the Club de l'École de Médecine; *La Lutte à Outrance,*
19 Nivôse 79 [January 9, 1871?].

1. APP: Ba 365-1, Versailles police reports dated May 17 and 21; AHG: 4e conseil 100,
dossier Magot; AN: BB24 756 5805, dossier Neckbecker; *La Justice,* May 15.

2. While the existence of armed women's groups has long been known in a piecemeal
manner, the extent and implications of their activity merit systematic investigation. In the
best study of the Union des Femmes, the group that organized much of this activity,
Schulkind devoted two sentences to the group's military action; "Socialist Women."
Thomas, *Women Incendiaries,* only mentioned the Légion des Fédérées in passing. David A.
Shafer, "*Plus que des Ambulancières:* Women in Articulation and Defence of their Ideals during the Paris Commune (1871)," *French History* 7 (1993): 85–101, did not discuss women's
armed defense of the Commune.

and other armed groups asserted their right to organize and to arm themselves in pursuit of political ideals, significantly contributing to the Communal movement. Armed women in paramilitary formation undermined one of the central assumptions justifying the denial of civic identity to women, that only men could be warriors, and therefore citizens.[3] Communards who supported and participated in these armed units accepted the identification of citizenship with soldiery, but in the circumstances of a desperate civil war they claimed a right for women to both identities.[4]

Clubs and assemblies were the stages for the elaboration of political culture, providing the social space for the enactment of revolutionary rhetoric and practices. Association created forums for stating objectives, declaring allegiances, and taking action. Through the practice of association women attained a large degree of functional and practical equality with men. By arming themselves and participating in clubs, women often expressed themselves and acted in ways that were similar to Communard men. This was one of the key reasons why Communard women were such a shocking phenomenon to so many. Women shouted threats from pulpits, wore red symbols of revolutionary devotion, brandished revolvers, and demanded the execution of hostages. Observers often described club meetings in which women constituted the majority, as at the Club des Prolétaires at Saint Ambroise, where on May 13 there were "three thousand *citoyennes* and about one thousand *citoyens.*" Many women marched for the Commune, and some died for it. The participation of women in the Commune on these and other planes of actual, if not always admitted, equality with men shook the foundations of the old order to the core. This practical equality between genders was also one of the most widely applied, and most profound, elements of the new world under construction in the clubs and committees of the Commune. Virtually every club speech that mentioned women contained a vision of greater gender equality. "A woman perfume merchant of the rue de l'Arbre Sec demanded the

---

3. On the relationship between gendered constructions of war and women's political rights more generally, see W. B. Tyrell, *Amazons: A Study in Athenian Mythmaking* (Baltimore: Johns Hopkins University Press, 1984); J. B. Elshtain and S. Tobias, eds., *Women, Militarism, and War: Essays in History, Politics, and Social Theory* (Savage, Md.: Rowman and Littlefield, 1990); Carol Berkin and Clara Lovett, eds., *Women, War, and Revolution* (New York: Holmes and Meier, 1980).

4. The several surveys of historical memory do not discuss women or gender: Patrick Hutton, *History as an Art of Memory* (Hanover, Vt.: University of New England Press, 1994); Gildea, *The Past in French History.* Another thorough survey of studies about memory decried the lack of attention to women: James Fentress and Chris Wickham, *Social Memory* (Cambridge, Mass.: Blackwell, 1992), 137.

complete emancipation of women, and a cantinière of the Vengeurs de Paris proposed a desire in favor of divorce," Fontoulieu observed of a club in Saint Germain l'Auxerrois. "Her motion was adopted with enthusiasm," he continued, "and a deputation, composed of four women, was named that instant to go the next day to Citizen Protot with the wish formulated by the assembly."[5]

References to women as *citoyennes* reveal the importance of civic identity in revolutionary action. The armed women's groups of the Commune were founded on a unique Communard vision of citizenship. In recent years citizenship has emerged as a privileged window for investigating political, social, and gender structures and representations.[6] Historians of women and gender in particular have explored definitions of citizenship to reveal the components and assumptions informing the gendered nature of politics in the revolutionary era and the nineteenth century.[7] These studies suggest that women's claims to and exclusion from citizenship cannot be divorced from more general conceptions of citizenship for men, an understanding that is confirmed in the case of the Commune. Communard women and men developed parallel visions of revolutionary citizenship, both of which recognized gender as a significant category of difference yet also partially inverted traditional social and gender hierarchies.

Communards drew a sharp distinction between *citoyens* and *citoyennes* who supported the Commune, on the one hand, and non-Communards, described variously as Versaillais, aristocrats, or simply as "gentlemen" (*messieurs*) and "ladies" (*mesdames*), on the other. As in 1789 and 1848, revolutionaries in 1871 replaced the hierarchical, aristocratic appellation

---

5. *Le Prolétaire,* May 15; Fontoulieu, *Les Églises,* 184. Protot was the Commune's Delegate for Justice.

6. A useful introduction to the literature and theory of citizenship is J. M. Barbalet, *Citizenship: Rights, Struggle, and Class Inequality* (Minneapolis: University of Minnesota, 1988). See also Rogers Brubaker, *Citizenship and Nationhood in France and Germany* (Cambridge: Harvard University Press, 1992); Catherine Wihtol de Wenden, ed., *La Citoyenneté* (Paris: Fondation Diderot, 1988).

7. See, for example, Renée Waldinger, Philip Dawson, and Isser Woloch, eds., *The French Revolution and the Meaning of Citizenship* (London: Greenwood, 1993); Olwen Hufton, *Women and the Limits of Citizenship in the French Revolution* (Toronto: University of Toronto Press, 1992); Dominique Godineau, *Citoyennes Tricoteuses: Les Femmes du peuple à Paris pendant la Révolution française* (Aix-en-Provence: Alines, 1988); Candice E. Proctor, *Women, Equality, and the French Revolution* (New York: Greenwood, 1990); Claire Goldberg Moses, *French Feminism in the Nineteenth Century* (Albany: State University of New York Press, 1984); Christine Faure, *Democracy without Women: Feminism and the Rise of Liberal Individualism in France,* trans. Claudia Gorbman and John Berk (Bloomington: Indiana University Press, 1991).

gentleman with the egalitarian, fraternal title *citizen.* Communards no longer recognized the validity of old forms of address and the power relations they encoded in the new world of the Republic and the Commune. Revolutionaries before and during the Commune used the term *citoyen* to associate themselves with the continuing struggle begun by the Great Revolution. Lefrançais noted that until late 1868 orators in the public meetings allowed during the later Empire used the formula "Ladies and Gentlemen," but that one night someone began a speech "Citoyens et Citoyennes," inspiring thunderous applause. "In lancing his *citoyen,*" Lefrançais recalled, "[the orator] evoked, consciously or not—who knows?—an entire world of memories and hopes. Everyone shuddered, shivered. . . ."[8] A provincial journalist at the time of the Commune also expressed the organic connection between the term *citoyen* and the hopes and fears of the revolution. He wrote that "In proclamations *citizen* is brilliant as a star. In the clubs they gobble up *citizen* with full mouths." Yet he observed that for some "*citizen* has the effect of a cigar smoked on a barrel of powder. *Citizen* freezes them with fright; it gives them a foretaste of the guillotine."[9] Use of the republican title *citoyen* was more widespread—but only somewhat less contentious—during the Prussian siege. The *Revue des Deux-Mondes* reported that National Guard officers in certain bourgeois districts had difficulty not calling their soldiers "gentlemen," and that the habit of saying *citoyen* came hard to some.[10] In February 1871 a republican deputy addressed the National Assembly—composed mainly of monarchists—as "Citizens," provoking a storm of protest.[11] Both sides were well aware of the political and social distinctions embedded in the terms *citoyens* and *messieurs.*

During the Commune, with the revolution only provisionally victori-

---

8. Lefrançais, *Souvenirs d'un révolutionnaire,* 300. Among the left opposition to the Empire, *citoyen* was a badge of honor. In December 1868, an underground newspaper created by journalists in the Sainte-Pelagie Prison noted, "You enter here a *monsieur,* you leave a *citoyen*"; Roger Bellet, *Presse et journalisme sous le Second Empire* (Paris: Armand Colin, 1967), 184. Jules Allix wrote a pamphlet in which he divided the nation into the two contending factions of *citoyens* and *messieurs;* Maitron, *DBMOF,* 4:109.

9. *Le Salut Public* (Lyon), May 1.

10. Cited in Armand Lanoux, *Une Histoire de la Commune de Paris,* vol. 1, *La Polka des Canons* (Paris: Bernard Grasset, 1971), 449. Just before the insurrection of March 18 some guardians of the peace (a police corps held over from the Empire) who were clearing the streets of illegal vendors were heard to say, "circulate gentlemen (excuse me! Citizens!)"; *Le Bien Public,* March 12.

11. The young Émile Zola ironically commented, "What, do those people think that they're in a republic?" Quoted in Henri Guillemin, *L'Héroïque défense de Paris,* 53.

ous in Paris, the different worlds represented by the two forms of address coexisted uneasily, often in immediate juxtaposition. For example, *Citoyenne* Thiourt told the Club des Prolétaires that she had asked directions of a *citoyen* in the square in front of the stock market, a predominantly bourgeois area. He had replied that in that *quartier* there lived no citizens, only "ladies and gentlemen," an unmistakable repudiation of egalitarian principles and Communard politics. *Citoyenne* Thiourt's reaction shows that she understood this, for she recommended that the club place canons on the square to silence reactionaries, a declaration of war on the old order.[12] Communard awareness of such distinctions was also evident at a meeting called to promote a truce between Paris and Versailles. The newspaper account noted that when one man attempted to bridge the gap between the two worlds by beginning his speech with the inventive "Citizens and Gentlemen," "this last term as usual raised a certain murmur in the assembly, which appeared to see therein an undemocratic distinction, and the orator began again, 'Citizens, . . . ' *(Ah! Ah! That's better!)*"[13] While the speaker had hoped to reconcile *citoyens* and *messieurs,* the two terms were simply considered incompatible by the majority of the meeting's attendees. The division over identities reflected the politics of the assembly, which rejected conciliation with Versailles and voted full support for the Commune.

As part of the same process by which Communards repudiated old political and social distinctions, they also created new distinctions erected on new foundations. For rather than attempting to reconcile the two worlds, Communards consciously inverted the original relationship between "citizens" and "gentlemen." Thus an orator critical of the Commune's Delegate of War took pains to call him *monsieur* at every opportunity, but another clubiste defended the delegate, saying, "he did not merit being insulted by the term *monsieur.*"[14] One businessman even went so far as to apologize to several members of the Commune for calling them "gentlemen" during negotiations for a temporary truce.[15] With the reimposition of "order" after the defeat of the Commune, the predominance of *messieurs* over *citoyens* was restored. Maxime Vuillaume recounted how he was nearly set free after questioning by a Versaillais interrogator, but he

12. AHG: Ly 22, meeting of May 13.
13. *Le National de '69,* May 3.
14. At an April 23 meeting of the Club Casino; R. P. Edouard Prampain, *Souvenirs de Vaugirard: Mon journal pendant le siège et pendant la Commune 1870–1871* (Paris: Société Anonyme de Publications Périodiques, 1887), 119.
15. Jules Amigues, *Les Aveux d'un conspirateur Bonapartiste,* 95.

let slip the word *citoyen.* "Citizen!" cried the agent, "Citizen! In the name of God! That's too much—don't call me citizen." Vuillaume explained his arrest: "I called this man 'citizen'; I could only be a dangerous rogue."[16]

The Communard definition of citizenship legitimated coercive measures and restrictions on the rights of noncitizens, that is, those who did not support the Commune. While Communards threatened, attacked, and jailed others for a variety of reasons, a refusal to recognize non-Communards as full citizens was common to most coercion. The Communal Council made this differentiation official policy by a variety of measures, as when it decreed that only those who fought for the Commune could receive items from the municipal pawn shop without charge. Similarly, those with connections to Versailles were not eligible for pensions. Citizen Mousseron at the Club des Prolétaires expressed the same sentiment when he argued that draft dodgers were "not worthy of the title *citizen.*" The club agreed, later deciding that the property of draft dodgers should be requisitioned for the benefit of the families of Communards killed in battle.[17] Violence and coercion were facilitated when citizenship was denied to the victims, as when a Communard officer threatened to take hostages from a group of clerics: "Look here, Citizens—I'm mistaken, you are not worthy of bearing that name. Look here, Gentlemen . . ."[18] As *citoyens* Communards seized jurisdiction over clerics, landlords, former police agents, and officials of the defunct Second Empire. Since Communards were derived primarily from the working classes of the city, Communard citizenship functioned to invert the former social hierarchy and was an important component of the social revolution carried out by Communards.[19]

The Communard conception of citizenship also challenged the nineteenth-century gender hierarchy. While general declarations of full equality between genders were rare, the identity of *citoyenne* authorized Communard women to seize many of the attributes of citizenship usually reserved for men. Most often the patriotism, sacrifice, and devotion of women to the Commune was invoked to lay claim to the title *citoyenne,*

---

16. Vuillaume, *Mes Cahiers rouges,* 1:19.

17. *Les Procès-Verbaux de la Commune,* 2:421, 245; AHG: Ly 22.

18. Henri D'Alméras, *La Vie Parisienne pendant le siège et sous la Commune* (Paris: Albin Michel, [1925?]), 484.

19. A social analysis by Roger V. Gould confirms previous conclusions that the mass of Communards were from the artisanal and working classes; "Trade Cohesion, Class Unity, and Urban Insurrection: Artisanal Activism in the Paris Commune," *American Journal of Sociology* 98 (January 1993): 721–54.

legitimating actions that conflicted with traditional gender distinctions. When some Communard officers refused to allow women on the battlefield to tend the wounded, the Club de la Révolution Sociale adopted a statement saying that these "devoted *citoyennes*" and "brave daughters of the people" should be welcomed instead, that "it would be an act of *lèse-humanité* to refuse the concourse of these brave and devoted patriots." A notice published in the Communard press underscored the gender-based linkage of citizenship and military valor, praising a *citoyenne* for her "most virile conduct" in caring for the wounded even under a hail of shell fire.[20] In a similar vein, a women's club declared that "the *Citoyennes* of Montmartre, [having] met in assembly, have decided to put themselves at the disposition of the Commune to form first-aid units that will follow those corps engaged with the enemy," adding that "by acts of devotion and by the revolutionary spirit that animates them the women of Montmartre will prove their patriotism to the Commune."[21] This declaration makes a distinction between women and *citoyennes,* arguing that women can attain citizenship by supporting the Commune. This distinction—parallel to that between *citoyens* and gentlemen—was also expressed at the Club Boule Noire, which was associated with the Comité de Vigilance des Citoyennes du 18e Arrondissement. Béatrix Excoffon, known as "La Républicaine," was seen at the podium, "speaking against some women who were making fun of her in the *quartier* of La Chapelle because she wore a red sash, adding that all those women were bad *citoyennes* and it was vital that they be made to disappear." This red sash was the symbol of Excoffon's leadership in the vigilance committee, and it symbolized her adherence to the Commune; ridiculing it deprived women of the right to be considered good *citoyennes.*[22]

In addition, the analogy of society as a family was invoked to permit women a public role analogous to the importance widely accorded women as mothers. According to a hostile observer, the widow Chabert gave a speech at the club in Saint Sulpice to the effect that "in Paris, there should only be a single and same family, in which everything is in common: money, work, and women."[23] Certainly this presents an incomplete version of what was actually said, but it is just as certain that Chabert argued

20. *Le Cri du Peuple,* May 20; *La Commune,* April 13.

21. Fontoulieu, *Les Églises,* 50, citing a poster on the door of the church signed, "Anna Jaclard, André Leo, Poirier, Buissard."

22. AHG: 4e conseil 57, dossier Excoffon.

23. Fontoulieu, *Les Églises,* 137.

for some kind of integral equality based on an analogy to the family. Similarly, a witness described Nathalie Lemel's speaking at a club in the Trinity Church, noting that she discussed "the way mothers of families should behave in order to make citizens and other things of that sort, that it was important to form societies of workers."[24] There is evidence that in the last days of the Commune the struggle by *citoyennes* for the recognition of larger rights may have been altering traditional gender distinctions among men as well. In the Communal Council Eugène Gérardin noted that in regard to pensions "*citoyennes* are obviously *citoyens.*" In late May the Alliance Républicaine des Départements, an electoral association founded to win the provinces over to the Commune, began for the first time to call on *citoyennes* to attend its meetings.[25]

Communard women not only constituted themselves as *citoyennes;* like *citoyens* they acted on this identity to threaten and arrest enemies of the revolution. Indeed, the Comité de Vigilance des Citoyennes du 18e Arrondissement well earned its title by the surveillance it exercised in the district. Its "presidente," Sophie Poirier, admitted signing a note denouncing the wife of a former gendarme who had fled Paris and was said to be in contact with Versailles police. Poirier also admitted telling other women to "go find" a man who had then been arrested, but she denied telling them to go there armed, as apparently they did. She denied as well requesting a search of the cloister of "forty novice monks carrying packages a little too heavy for their size." Another note Poirier denied writing called for the arrest of one Monsieur Nourry because he "goes back and forth to Versailles and always brings back bad news." Still another, unsigned but with the committee's seal, identified a man as "good for arrest."[26]

The rights and duties claimed by *citoyennes* reached their most radical form in the creation of armed women's groups. Such aspirations were not new, for both the Great Revolution and 1848 had seen projects to form women's battalions, even though none was carried out. Armed women participated in demonstrations in 1792 and 1793, but not as members of organized units.[27] A poster of March 1848 called for creating battalions of

24. Lemel was organizing women's producer association in conjunction with the aid of the Communal Council; she was so affected by the defeat of the Commune that she attempted suicide; AHG: 4e conseil 688; Maitron, *DBMOF,* 7:114.

25. *Les Procès-Verbaux de la Commune,* 2:421; *Le Cri du Peuple,* May 19 and 23.

26. AHG: 26e conseil 101, dossier Poirier.

27. See two articles by Harriet B. Applewhite and Darline G. Levy: "Women, Radicalization, and the Fall of the French Monarchy," in *Women and Politics in the Age of Democratic Revolution,* ed. Harriet B. Applewhite and Darline G. Levy (Ann Arbor: University of

"Vésuviennes," but the women who later identified themselves under that name did not claim the right to bear arms.[28] The siege of 1870–71 renewed interest in women's battalions. The Women's Committee of the rue d'Arras hoped to form an "armed legion to gather the wounded on the battlefield, care for them in fixed or mobile hospitals, and if necessary replace men at the ramparts." Another proposal envisioned ten battalions of "Amazones de la Seine" to guard barricades and nurse the wounded. The author, Félix Belly, argued that shared hardship and sacrifice would prove that women merited "emancipation and civil equality," an argument underscoring the connection between military service and citizenship. Some women attempted to fulfill these hopes. Belly wrote that fifteen hundred signed up for the Amazones but were rebuffed by military authorities, and Louise Michel was arrested when she led a group requesting weapons from the government.[29] These projects thus remained ineffectual. Only during the Commune did women form organized, armed units that engaged in combat for the defense of the cause.

The women's units of the Commune arose from the convergence of these ideals of citizenship and the collective memory of the revolutionary tradition. On April 3, at the beginning of the civil war between Paris and Versailles, an appeal by "une véritable *citoyenne*" appeared in the Communard press, accompanied by declarations exalting women's role in October 1789, prompting some women to attempt a similar march on Versailles. Over the next several days large crowds of women were turned back at the gates of the city by the National Guard so that they would not be harmed on the battlefield. "There were between seven hundred and eight hundred women," one of the participants, Béatrix Excoffon, later recalled of a group of women on the place de la Concorde. "Some," she said, "talked about explaining to Versailles what Paris wanted; others talked about how things were a hundred years ago, when the women of

---

Michigan Press, 1990): 81–107; and "Women and Militant Citizenship in Revolutionary Paris," in *Rebel Daughters: Women and the French Revolution,* ed. Sara E. Melzer and Leslie W. Rabine (New York: Oxford University Press, 1992): 79–101. See also Proctor, *Women, Equality, and the French Revolution,* 154; Hufton, *Women and the Limits of Citizenship,* 29.

28. They sought mandatory military service for women, but only in work, supply, and charity units; see Laura S. Sturmingher, "The *Vésuviennes:* Images of Women Warriors in 1848 and Their Significance for French History," *History of European Ideas* 8 (1986): 451–88; Joan S. Moon, "Woman as Agent of Social Change: Women's Rights during the Second French Republic," in *Views of Women's Lives in Western Tradition,* ed. Frances R. Keller (Lewiston, N.Y.: Edwin Mellon, 1990), 322–59; Moses, *French Feminism,* 130; Edith Thomas, *Les Femmes de 1848* (Paris: Presses Universitaires de France, 1948).

29. *La Patrie en Danger,* 11 October 1870; Thomas, *Women Incendiaries,* 44.

Paris had once before gone to Versailles to carry off the baker and the baker's wife and the baker's little boy, as they said then."[30] This demonstration, the largest by women during the Commune, was founded on a collective memory of the October Days of 1789, when revolutionary market women and the National Guard had forced the royal family to return to Paris, an example invoked by Communard women to legitimate revolutionary action.

The precise size and number of the demonstrations that resulted from this movement are impossible to determine. One group of women went up the Champs-Élysées toward a bridge over the Seine, while another was stopped at the porte de Versailles. A third, composed of "young women of the people, quite well dressed, some even in black silk dresses and hats," marching four abreast, headed toward the bridge at Grenelle. It was accompanied by perhaps thirty gamins singing the *Chant du Départ*, "all of this done with a seriousness and gravity corresponding to the circumstances, which did not fail to make an original and touching impression."[31] As to participants, Excoffon spoke of seven hundred to eight hundred women in one group, and newspaper accounts mention groups of one hundred, five hundred, and seven hundred. The purpose of the march on Versailles was also open to some confusion. When asked what she was doing one woman responded, "we are going to Versailles to join our husbands." Perhaps she meant that they were going to encourage their husbands in combat, for another woman, after having complained that some men would rather hide than fight, said their group would be leaving "from the place de la Concorde, bearing a red flag, to provide leadership for the men." Still another account asserted that the women hoped to "set an example" for men, again suggesting that their valor was intended as a reproach to those men who did not fight for the Commune. Indeed, some women armed with the latest rifles were reported to be guarding the porte d'Auteuil. Rather than a call to arms, however, the "véritable citoyenne" whose appeal started the movement had asked that women explain the Parisian revolution to Versailles, believing that the revolt would be accepted by the government once it was properly understood.

Although the attempted marches on Versailles had no immediate effect

---

30. Béatrix Excoffon cited in Thomas, *Women Incendiaries,* 59; APP: Ba 364-4, reports of April 6 and 7.

31. *L'Affranchi,* April 5 and 7; *Le Bien Public,* April 5; APP: 364-4; AHG: 4e conseil 57, dossier Excoffon. For a somewhat different account of the marches on Versailles see Thomas, *Women Incendiaries,* 56–62.

on the course of the civil war, their appeal to the historical memory played an essential role in mobilizing women in support of the Commune. After one march Excoffon told the women gathered that "although there were not enough of us to go to Versailles, there were enough to go tend the injured in the Commune's marching companies." Within days the Communard *Journal Officiel* published an appeal by a "groupe de citoyennes" calling on the "*citoyennes* of Paris, descendants of the women of the Great Revolution, the women who, in the name of the people and justice, marched on Versailles and carried off Louis XVI as a captive," to organize a "women's movement for the defense of Paris." From this initiative resulted the Union des Femmes pour la Défense de Paris et les Soins aux Blessées (Women's Union for the Defense of Paris and Aid for the Wounded). The Union des Femmes quickly grew into one of the most important popular associations in Paris, eventually organizing political meetings, first-aid units, and even armed women's groups for fighting on barricades and forcing men to fight for the Commune.[32]

The connection between the Versailles marches and the founding of the Union des Femmes demonstrates that the historical memory of the revolutionary past was vital for legitimating women's collective action. That the memory of women's role in the Great Revolution was important for inciting action in a specifically revolutionary sense in 1871 is shown by the existence of an alternative image of women's action, that of the Sabine women of Roman legend. A statement signed by one Marie Carlon appeared in *Le Rappel* at the same moment that women were marching on Versailles and called on women to "renew the heroism of the immortal Sabines" who had prevented combat between their Roman husbands and their Sabine fathers and brothers, thereby conquering war by love: "Yes, our cries will conquer the tumult of war, for love is stronger than death; weapons will fall from their hands, and the ground will be soaked only with our tears." This apolitical vision of wives and daughters bringing reconciliation and peace reveals the tension between revolutionary and traditional roles for women and was at odds with Communard demands. The Union des Femmes, for example, always met appeals for conciliation with indignant denunciations of the Versailles government. But Excoffon, a Union des Femmes leader, played on the distinction between women's political and nonpolitical public action, arguing at her trial that she and the other marchers were simply going to Versailles "to propose the means

---

32. AHG: 4e conseil 57, dossier Excoffon; *Le Journal Officiel,* April 11, quoted in Thomas, *Women Incendiaries,* 59, 65; Schulkind, *The Paris Commune,* 171.

of conciliation to the chief of the executive power [Adolphe Thiers] and to attempt to avoid bloodshed." Despite Excoffon's understandable deception at her trial, Carlon's appeal to the memory of the Sabines did not express the sentiment of most of the women who marched on Versailles. The prominence of red flags, the participation of a committed Communard such as Excoffon, and the fact that the movement was the springboard for launching the Union des Femmes demonstrate instead that this was primarily a revolutionary, rather than a conciliatory, endeavor. Even the pursuit of conciliation raised some concerns about women's proper role, however. The liberal journalist Charles Vrignault expressed a widespread rejection of any form of women's public action, counseling women to stay at home because even pacific demonstrations were dangerous: "remain good housewives: you may begin as a Sabine, but you will end up a *tricoteuse.*" The same journal published a letter—signed significantly "a *Parisienne,*" rather than "a *citoyenne*"—that echoed these sentiments, · protesting against both the civil war and public demonstrations by women. "Comfort those who return to the hearth," the *Parisienne* urged women, pleading, "be their consolation and their refuge."[33]

True to its origins in the movement to march on Versailles, organizing women to militarily defend the Commune was the dominant motive for creating the Union des Femmes.[34] On April 11 a stirring call to arms by a group of women appeared in the *Journal Officiel,* publicizing a meeting of all patriotic *citoyennes* devoted to creating "a women's movement for the defense of Paris." The notice asked for the aid of women who were willing "to fight and die" for the revolution and made no mention of nursing or of workshops, which later grew to be important Union des Femmes activities.[35] A seven-member "comité central des citoyennes" was elected at the April 11 meeting, but the group only later took its definitive name, which indicated it would also care for the wounded. The members of the new

---

33. *Le Rappel* cited in *Le Bien Public,* April 5; AHG: 4e conseil 57, dossier Excoffon.

34. Studies of the Union des Femmes have neglected its military and police functions, concentrating instead on its role organizing women's cooperative workshops and care for the wounded, which were indeed important Union des Femmes activities. Schulkind's article on the Union des Femmes gives the impression that organizing fighting units was not a systematic endeavor on the part of the Union, and he does not note that the Union's statutes mentioned petroleum and weapons; "Socialist Women," 159, 149. Thomas cites the participation of Union des Femmes members in the fighting of Bloody Week, but she does not draw general conclusions about the role of the Union des Femmes, nor does she show the sustained nature of its preparations for combat; *Women Incendiaries,* 155–56.

35. *Le Journal Officiel,* April 11, cited in Schulkind, *The Paris Commune of 1871,* 172.

committee appealed to the Commune for help in an address that dealt only with the need to mobilize women for military service, and which connected this function to an expanded vision of citizenship for women. They argued that given the imminent danger of defeat, "it is everyone's duty and right to fight for the grand cause of the people, for the revolution," and that "all individual efforts should fuse to form a collective resistance by the entire population." This statement was a sustained argument for the rights of *citoyennes* to defend the Commune given their interest in a thorough "social renovation" based on the "just demands of the entire population, without distinctions of sex—distinctions created and maintained by the need for antagonism on which rests the privileges of the governing classes." The committee stated that many *citoyennes* had resolved, "in the event the enemy passes the gates of Paris, to fight and conquer or die for the defense of our Communal rights," but the aid of the Commune was needed to facilitate "a firm organization of this revolutionary element into a force capable of providing effective and vigorous support to the Commune." Thus the committee asked for money to print posters as well as for meeting rooms in the twenty town halls, so committees of women could "organize the defense of Paris."[36]

The military vocation of the Union des Femmes was continued in its definitive statutes published on April 20, which noted that some of its money would be used for buying petroleum and weapons for the *citoyennes* who would fight. As the Union des Femmes evolved, socialist women with a history of activism emerged as leaders of its executive commission. Among them were Elizabeth Dmitrieff, a correspondent of Karl Marx, and Nathalie Lemel, who had founded a bookbinder's mutual aid society with Eugène Varlin.[37] By May the Union des Femmes had developed an elaborate program for creating women's cooperatives that was being implemented when the Commune was defeated. Yet the group emphasized its military function in a declaration of May 6, stating, "the women of Paris will prove to France and the world that they too, like their brothers, will know how to give their blood and their lives—on the barricades, on the ramparts of Paris if the reactionaries force the gates—for the

---

36. *Le Cri du Peuple,* April 16; Thomas, *Women Incendiaries,* 77.

37. Dmitrieff was also on the committee elected April 11, but Thomas cites no evidence for her assertion that Dmitrieff founded the group; *Women Incendiaries,* 70. Schulkind leaves open the question of whether women members of the International such as Dmitrieff founded the Union des Femmes; "Socialist Women," 145.

defense of the Commune, that is, the people."[38] Women were thus comparable to men in their capacity to fight and sacrifice, one of the foundations of Communard citizenship for women.

To fulfill these aspirations the Central Committee of the Union des Femmes sponsored meetings throughout the city, and its local chapters held others, during which women were urged to sign up for barricade and ambulance duty. Lemel is known to have recruited on at least two occasions. "She called on women to take up arms to defend the Commune and fight to the last drop of their blood," according to one source describing her at a club in the Trinity Church. The source continues, "'We are coming,' she cried, 'to the supreme moment when one must know how to die for the country. No more lethargy, no more uncertainty! Everyone into combat! Everyone to their duty! We must crush the Versaillais' *(Prolonged applause)*."[39] At Lemel's trial a woman testified to seeing her at a meeting in the town hall of the 4th arrondissement: "she said that any woman that wanted to go to the barricades, to build them or defend them, should give their name and sign up, and that those who wanted to tend the wounded should do the same." One such register of barricade fighters was found at the town hall of the 10th arrondissement, where the Union des Femmes made its headquarters during the *semaine sanglante*.[40] A woman at a Union des Femmes meeting in the 3d arrondissement also asked women to take up arms to defend the Commune, and a Union des Femmes leader did the same at clubs in the 11th and 12th arrondissements.[41]

Besides these cases in which the Union des Femmes organized barricade duty, there are other instances in which Union des Femmes involvement was likely but cannot be proven. A garbled report of a "Club des Citoyennes de Passy" (16th arrondissement) described a woman orator urging the women in attendance to fight for the Commune. The meeting was held at the mairie, it was said to be convened by the "société centrale," its leaders were dressed in black and red, and a speaker stated that it was the last of similar assemblies organized in every arrondissement of the capital—all of which suggests that the meeting was in fact called by the *comité central* of the Union des Femmes. One woman spoke of the benefits the

---

38. *Le Cri du Peuple,* May 10.

39. Fontoulieu, *Les Églises,* 274.

40. AHG: 4e conseil 388, dossier Lemel. The report noting the register did not list the names; AHG: Ly 27.

41. AHG: 3e conseil 40, dossier Leroy; AHG: Ly 22. The Union des Femmes leader in the last two instances was Adélaïde Valentin.

Commune would bring, such as ending exploitation and the power of priests, then finished with a call for volunteers: "if you had seen, like me, all the dead, all the blood in the aid stations, on the battlefield, you would want, as I do, to go fight and march out in front of the men." Of the one hundred fifty women present, a dozen signed up with the organizers of the meeting.[42] Another account described a unit of "femmes fédérées" who met at the École de Droit (5th arrondissement).[43] At a club in the 13th arrondissement a woman argued that women should take up arms, and the Comité des Citoyennes du 17e Arrondissement appealed to women to join their group and help the wounded or fight on barricades. Finally, the Club Seraphin in the 9th arrondissement passed a motion agreeing to support the formation of women's battalions.[44] Ten arrondissements are known to have witnessed such efforts to organize groups of barricade fighters, a remarkable record given the extremely fragmentary nature of the evidence, and an indication of the importance the Union des Femmes and other groups attached to women's battalions.

The Légion des Fédérées in the 12th arrondissement is the best-documented armed women's group. According to a poster the Légion was officially founded on May 10 under the patronage of Jean Fenouillas (known as Phillippe), a member of the Commune for the area as well as the local mayor, and Jules Montels, the commander of the local National Guard. According to Malon an "organized and armed" company of woman volunteers marched with the Commune's Twelfth Legion on May 12.[45] Two days would hardly have sufficed to recruit and provision the Légion des Fédérées, however, and the origins of the Légion are in fact more complex than the announcement of May 10 would suggest. The headquarters of the Légion des Fédérées was the Saint Eloi Church, and according to a well-informed eyewitness, Légion members were obligated

---

42. Baron Marc de Villiers, *Histoire des clubs de femmes et des légions d'Amazones: 1793–1848–1871* (Paris: Plon, 1910), 401.

43. A.-M. Blanchecotte, *Tablettes d'une femme pendant la Commune* (Paris: Didier, 1872), 258.

44. The wording of the appeal by the committee of the 17th almost exactly replicated that of the Union des Femmes's request for aid from the Commune; *Le Cri du Peuple,* May 2; Thomas, *Women Incendiaries,* 94. A member of the committee, Josephine Delattre, reportedly said that she was a delegate of the Commune, and that she had a cache of fifty old rifles; AHG: 26e conseil 92, dossier Delattre; *Sous la Commune,* 74.

45. *Les Murailles Politiques,* 2:305; Malon, *La Troisième défaite,* 279. The vice-mayor, Louis Magot, whose wife was a Légion member, claimed at his trial to have opposed the organization of the "battalion des femmes" by Phillippe and Montels; AHG: 4e conseil 100, dossier Magot.

to attend meetings of the club held at Saint Eloi.[46] This club had been formerly located on the rue des Terres-Fortes and was sponsored by the local vigilance committee, whose members included Phillippe and Montels. Members of the Communal Council, officials in the local town hall, and National Guard officers attended the Club Eloi, and it became the key center linking the revolutionary mass and leadership in the arrondissement.

Club Eloi was one thread leading to the Légion; another was the Comité de Républicaines (Committee of Republican Women) in the 12th arrondissement, which was probably the local branch of the Union des Femmes. Local members of the Commune, including Phillippe, gave the committee a formal role in reorganizing public assistance in the district. Adélaïde Valentin, the future *colonelle* of the Légion, was probably on this committee, for after the Commune she was accused by another committee member, Julie Magot—also a Légion member—of taking part in the expulsion of nuns from a local charitable institution. Colonelle Valentin was also said to be the mistress of Phillippe.[47] The Légion des Fédérées arose from the entangled connections among the Comité des Républicaines, the Communard leadership in the arrondissement, and the Union des Femmes, and it is very probable that the May 10 poster by Phillippe and Montels forming the Légion was merely a recognition of official patronage for a group that had its real origins in the local committee of the Union des Femmes.

The best evidence for this conclusion is that Colonelle Valentin of the Légion des Fédérées was also a founding member of the Union des Femmes. An *ouvrière* who lived in the 10th arrondissement, her name was listed first among those who signed the original manifesto of the Union des Femmes, which incorporated a vision of citizenship for women based on service to the Commune, including armed combat should the Versaillais enter the city.[48] Little else is known about her. Magot, who at her own trial tried to exculpate herself by implicating others, said Valentin was "a very

---

46. The witness was Martin Bourgeois, who attended seven meetings. A "fabricant de draperies" who seemed to make a hobby of keeping track of Communard activity in the arrondissement, he testified at several trials of Communards from the 12th arrondissement; AHG: 20e conseil 528, dossier Rogissart.

47. *Les Murailles Politiques,* 3:335; AHG: 4e conseil 100, dossier Magot. Fontoulieu asserted Valentin's liaison with Phillippe; *Les Églises,* 198.

48. *Le Cri du Peuple,* April 16. Thomas was aware of Valentin's role in both groups separately but does not appeared to have connected these facts; *Women Incendiaries,* 67, 143.

violent clubiste. . . . she threatened my husband." The anti-Communard, but often reliable, Fontoulieu said that she was at the Club Eloi on May 16 shouting, "I urge all women to *denounce their husbands* and to make them take up arms. If they refuse, *shoot them!*"[49] This hysterical portrait is somewhat modified by Valentin's speech at the Club des Prolétaires in the Saint Ambroise Church on May 20. The minutes of the meeting are elliptical, but Valentin seems to have hoped to recruit women for the Légion des Fédérées. In terms reminiscent of the Union des Femmes manifesto she called on "all *citoyennes* to make themselves useful to the cause that we defend today" and "guard positions in Paris while the men go to fight" at the front. Yet her martial address ended with a request that the flowers found in front of the Virgin at the church (May was Mary's month) be removed and given to poor schoolchildren, as "this would adorn the garrets where our poor families live." After Valentin's speech a club officer thanked her for coming to the club and "strongly urged her to return," suggesting an appreciation of her position as *colonelle* of the Légion.[50]

The Légion des Fédérées also had a *capitaine* and a flag bearer. Versailles prosecutors said that Capitaine Louise Neckbecker was a prostitute, but they were sometimes free with that accusation. During the Commune Neckbecker, a lace maker, was employed by the town hall of the 12th arrondissement at a first-aid station, activity typical of Union des Femmes members. She admitted attending the Club de la Révolution in Saint Bernard as well as the Club Eloi.[51] Catherine Rogissart was said by her neighbors to have been flag bearer of the Légion and the vice president of the Club Eloi. In describing Rogissart one witness said, "although uneducated, she had an easy way with words, which she misused to talk politics." Another witness said Rogissart went to the Club Eloi every night, and a third reported that "sometimes women, in more or less considerable

---

49. AHG: 4e conseil 100; Fontoulieu, *Les Églises,* 64. An eyewitness testified to seeing a woman at the Club Eloi tell women to shoot their husbands if they refused to march, but the witness did not specify that the woman was Valentin; AHG: 5e conseil 545.

50. AHG: Ly 22; it could be, too, that the club officer was showing deference to Valentin as Phillippe's mistress—if such she was—because Phillippe was also an important figure in the Club des Prolétaires, having inaugurated a branch of the club in the Saint Marguerite Church.

51. Neckbecker spoke at every one of the seven Légion meetings one witness attended; AN: BB24 756 5805. The devotion of many prostitutes to the Commune was nicely explained by Louise Michel, who noted that no one had more right to serve the revolution than "the saddest victims of the old world"; *La Commune,* 286. Michel was complaining about the hesitation of Communard leaders to accept prostitutes as nurses.

numbers, came to get her to go to the Saint Eloi Church."[52] The only other known member of the Légion des Fédérées, Julie Magot, was an *employée* at the town hall who used her control over public assistance funds to recruit for the Légion. A laundress later testified that being without work she asked Magot for aid, but, "she told me that she would only give it if I enrolled in the women's regiment. I often saw the woman Magot walking the streets of the *quartier* with a red belt and a revolver. She threatened to arrest me because I responded to her insults."[53]

In addition to its regular meetings at the Club Eloi, the Légion des Fédérées organized several demonstrations in the 12th arrondissement, most likely to encourage recruits and demonstrate their support of the Commune. Sometime in May Neckbecker was seen "adorned with a red armband, in front of the town hall of the 12th arrondissement, receiving from the hands of the woman Valentin a red flag, which she bore to the Hôtel de ville, escorted by about a hundred other women."[54] The flag bore the inscription "The Commune or Death!" The site of this ceremony in front of the town hall again underscores the linkages between the Légion and local authorities. Another witness described what was probably a different demonstration. He saw "the women's battalion" marching to the Bastille around May 10 or 15. In this demonstration there were about twenty-five women, not one hundred, though each of them also wore a red armband. Still another witness said that at some point in May she saw fifty or so women of the battalion marching behind a red flag, going to the local town hall.[55]

These demonstrations by the Légion des Fédérées were part of a Parisian-wide movement that has left only slight traces in the historical record. The broad nature of the movement strongly suggests that the Union des Femmes was at its origin; it alone had the capacity to mobilize women in many arrondissements for a common action. The Fédération des Clubs also supported the formation of women's battalions.[56] Indeed, on May 14 a member of the Committee of Public Safety reportedly distributed rifles to about one hundred women who had marched to the Hôtel de ville to ask for weapons.[57] A Versailles police agent reported on May 17

52. AHG: 20e conseil 528, dossier Rogissart.
53. Note again that the Communard conception of citizenship implied providing aid and pensions to only those who supported the cause; AHG: 4e conseil 100, dossier Magot.
54. AN: BB24 756 5805, dossier Neckbecker.
55. AHG: 4e conseil 100, dossier Magot; 20e conseil 528, dossier Rogissart.
56. *Sous la Commune,* 74.
57. *La Justice,* May 15; Thomas, *Women Incendiaries,* 121.

that "more than five hundred women with armbands took themselves to the Hôtel de ville, after having made the rounds of several *quartiers,* to ask from the Commune the favor of judging draft dodgers." According to this report, "throughout their route they alarmed the inhabitants by their songs, shouts, and gestures; *several were drunk.*" Four days later another Versailles agent reported "bands of armed *citoyennes,* preceded by a brass band," that traversed the city before going to the Hôtel de ville.[58] The military band again connotes official endorsement, made explicit in the distribution of arms by the Committee of Public Safety.

While the Union des Femmes and Colonelle Valentin of the Légion des Fédérées organized women to fight on barricades should the Versaillais enter the city, policing the internal enemies of the Commune was a more immediate daily concern. Club discourse by both men and women recognized that women had legitimate jurisdiction and rights in many areas. Just as teachers and artists regulated their own interests in associations, so too some argued that women should regulate through association matters that particularly pertained to women. Blanche Lefebvre, a member of the Union des Femmes, proposed at the Club de la Révolution Sociale in Saint Michel des Batignolles that "a woman be placed at every gate with a secret password, so as to know if a *citoyenne* may or may not leave the city."[59] Women were thus to have a formal public role in supporting the revolution, though in this case one confined to surveillance of other women. Women such as Josephine Delattre of the Club Boule Noire and the Club de la Révolution in Saint Bernard threatened and denounced wives of gendarmes, often leading to arrests.[60] The five hundred women who demonstrated in front of the Hôtel de ville had specifically asked for jurisdiction over draft dodgers, and there are numerous examples of women—many of whom were also members of the Union des Femmes—denouncing and threatening those who refused to march for the Commune. Two members of the Légion des Fédérées also sought out draft dodgers. Rogissart, the flag bearer, had several men arrested for not serving in the National

---

58. APP: Ba 365-1. Over the course of the Commune mention of public drunkenness grew more frequent in these reports and in other sources as well. Susanna Barrows has explored the political use made of these accusations of drunkenness, in "After the Commune: Alcoholism, Temperance, and Literature in the Early Third Republic," in *Consciousness and Class Experience in Nineteenth-Century Europe,* ed. John M. Merriman (New York: Holmes and Meier, 1979): 205–18.

59. Thomas, *Women Incendiaries,* 86.

60. AHG: 26e conseil 92, dossier Delattre.

Guard.[61] One was her landlord, who later testified that she "threatened the men of the *quartier* all the time: 'I will make you all go [to fight],' she said, 'you are nothing but loafers; I, a woman, have more courage than all of you. For good or ill, you will fight against those Versailles assassins.'" Rogissart's emphasis on her own courage, a vital element in constructing the Communard identity of *citoyenne,* is also instrumental here in demeaning the masculinity of draft dodgers and justifying her power over them. Magot also initiated arrests. She "was always about, wrapped in a red belt and armed with a revolver," a witness at her trial said. "Busying herself greatly with politics," the witness continued, "she frequented the clubs and denounced to her husband those who resisted the Commune. Threatening everyone with arrest or with her revolver, she was the terror of the *quartier.*"[62] Summarizing the information collected about the Légion des Fédérées, the prosecution in Rogissart's trial asserted, "The role of this battalion was to search for draft dodgers, to bring them before the battalion, to strike them and shoot them if they refused to march." Indeed, one witness did accuse the Légion des Fédérées of having executed several people, but this accusation was not officially made against any Légion member.[63]

The movement to form armed women's groups, founded on the memory of the October Days and a vision of revolutionary citizenship for women, demonstrates the power of the collective memory of the revolutionary tradition in shaping Communard rhetoric and action. The French sociologist Maurice Halbwachs initiated the modern study of collective memory with his insight that "social frameworks" shape memory and that memory in turn shapes social behavior.[64] There has been, however, pro-

---

61. AHG: 20e conseil 528, dossier Rogissart; *La Gazette des Tribunaux,* August 7, 1872. A witness testified she heard Rogissart say of one of the men, "that Lutz deserved to have his damn head filled with lead." Rogissart claimed she had Lutz arrested because he was disturbing the peace, but her explanation contained several contradictions. Thomas was oddly unwilling to recognize that Communard women inflicted and precipitated violence, as is clearly shown in the case of Rogissart: she was in the Légion and had two men arrested, but Thomas wrote she could hardly have been held guilty of anything more than living with someone; *Women Incendiaries,* 188.

62. AHG: 4e conseil 100, dossier Magot.

63. AHG: 20e conseil 528, dossier Rogissart.

64. *The Collective Memory,* trans. Francis J. Ditter, Jr. (New York: Harper and Row, 1980; French ed., 1923). Halbwachs was referring specifically to such "social frameworks" as family, class, or generation. Nathan Wachtel provides a brief annotated bibliography of collective memory, focusing on anthropological aspects, in "Memory and History: An Introduction," *History and Anthropology* 2 (1986): 207–24; for a study combining theory and prac-

found disagreement about whether gender should be included in this analysis.[65] "The essential problem for anyone wishing to identify a distinctly female view of the past," suggest James Fentress and Chris Wickham, "is hegemony: that of a dominant ideology and a dominance over narration, as expressed through the male-female relationship." Fentress and Wickham assert that language, commemorative occasions, and the narrative process itself are so deeply dominated by male voices and actors as to make all but impossible the identification of an independent women's historical consciousness.[66] Yet folklorists and ethnologists, who have generally preceded historians in exploring these issues, have often found clear differences in the ways men and women recount the past, implying that gender is a significant category of difference in regard to collective memory and traditions.[67]

The Commune is an ideal vehicle for exploring the intersection of collective memory, gender, and political culture, because not only were women remarkably active in the Communal movement, but its origins and key features were shaped by the memory of the French revolutionary tra-

---

tice from a sociological perspective see Barry Schwartz, "Social Change and Collective Memory: The Democratization of George Washington," *American Sociological Review* 56 (April 1991): 221–37.

65. Sylvie Vandecastle-Schweitzer and Danièle Voldman have argued that memory is not related to one's gender but to the "events of the individual's life," and they warn against constructing a "feminine historical object" after having demolished a "masculinized historical object"; "The Oral Sources for Women's History," in *Writing Women's History,* ed. Michelle Perrot, trans. Felcia Pheasant (Oxford: Blackwell, 1992), 41, 49. While rejecting the possibility of gendered memory, the authors acknowledge the existence of class-based memory.

66. They cite, for example, a study by P. Dronke that demonstrates that chronicles written by medieval nuns did not substantially differ from those written by monks. Fentress and Wickham do not reject the possibility of a "women's memory," but they find it difficult to locate and analyze, given their assessment that women often do not form autonomous social groups; *Social Memory,* 138.

67. Mary P. Coote has pointed out, for example, that nineteenth-century Serbs created two types of songs, "heroic" and "women's"; "On the Composition of Women's Songs," *Oral Tradition* 7 (1992): 332–48. In Tunisia, men tell "true tales" and women tell "fantasy tales"; Susan Webber, "Women's Folk Narratives and Social Change," in *Women in the Family in the Middle East,* ed. E. W. Fernes (Austin: University of Texas Press, 1985): 310–16. See also Joan Newlon Radner, *Feminist Messages: Coding in Women's Folk Culture* (Urbana: University of Illinois Press, 1993); Rosan A. Jordan and Susan J. Kalcik, *Women's Folklore, Womens Culture* (Philadelphia: University of Pennsylvania Press, 1985). Fentress and Wickham survey some of this literature in *Social Memory,* 140. The language used here is intended to evoke Joan Wallach Scott's essay, "Gender: A Useful Category of Analysis," in *Gender and the Politics of History* (New York: Columbia University Press, 1988).

dition.[68] The extent of references to the past has meant that the contours and meaning of the popular historical memory have long been points of contention in the historiography of the Commune.[69] Karl Marx antici-pated several of the positions in the debate over the role of collective mem-ory in the Commune. In 1869 he welcomed a book on Louis-Napoléon's coup of 1851, writing, "a very interesting movement is going on in France. The Parisians are making a regular study of their recent revolutionary past to prepare themselves for the business of the impending new revolution." A year later, however, he expressed concern about relying overmuch on the revolutionary tradition for guidance, warning that the "great memo-ries" of the Revolution could become a "reactionary cult of the past." Finally, in a letter written while the Commune still ruled Paris, he appears to have overcome any doubts about its progressive nature, remarking, "whatever the immediate outcome may be, a new point of departure, of importance in world history, has been gained."[70] Rougerie, perhaps the foremost recent scholar of the Commune, agreed that it was backward-looking, more "prisoner of a grand memory" of the Revolution "than con-scious of its future."[71] Differences over the weight of the revolutionary tra-dition lie at the heart of the two interpretive approaches to the Commune, which divide in part over whether it should be considered a vestige of the past or a harbinger of future world revolution.

Foreign invasion and resurgent monarchism characterized both 1793 and 1871, creating the foundation for the cult of revolution. In the period preceding the Commune the saturation of political discourse by the lan-guage and vocabulary of the first Revolution was not, however, a natural

---

68. For a recent discussion of the revolutionary tradition see Christine Piette, "Réflexions Historiques sur les Traditions Révolutionnaires à Paris au XIXe siècle," *Historical Reflections/Réflexions Historiques* 12 (1985): 403–18. See also Albert Soboul, "Tradition et création dans le mouvement révolutionnaire français au XIXe siècle," *Le Mouvement Social* 79 (1972): 15–31; Hutton, *The Cult of the Revolutionary Tradition.*

69. Rougerie has given this issue the most sustained attention in *Procès des Communards* and *Paris Libre.* See also Robert Tombs, "Paris and the Rural Hordes: An Exploration of Myth and Reality in the French Civil War of 1871," *Historical Journal* 29 (1986): 795–808.

70. Edwards, *The Paris Commune,* 31; Jacques Le Goff, *History and Memory,* trans. Steven Rendall and Elizabeth Claman (New York: Columbia University Press, 1992), 15; Schulkind, *The Paris Commune of 1871,* 199.

71. Rougerie added that some Communards went beyond the sansculotte mentality by their socialism; *Procès des Communards,* 240, 208. These conclusions were later repeated in *Paris Libre,* 224. Tombs has suggested that Communards were so devoted to the past that they were unable to recognize or cope effectively with reality; "Paris and the Rural Hordes," 806. Stéfane Rials phrases this "classic question" as "Insurrection du passé? Insurrection por-teuse d'avenir?" in *Nouvelle histoire de Paris,* 514.

or unmediated phenomenon. Although club orators in 1848 only rarely referred to the Great Revolution, it provided the terms of political analysis in 1871 because Parisians consciously identified points of commonality between their present and the past revolutionary experience of their forebears.[72] As Halbwachs suggested, social beliefs have a double character: "they are collective traditions or recollections, but they are also ideas or conventions that result from a knowledge of the present."[73] During the Prussian siege of Paris, for example, a radical journalist asserted that the Montagnards of the first Revolution had purged the Girondins and thereby saved France. He then argued that the current government was composed of latter-day Girondins who also had to be driven from power to establish a Commune that could again save France.[74] This conscious and utilitarian approach to the past, founded on current conditions, is again evident in the commemorations organized by republicans in honor of Eugene Baudin, a deputy killed during Louis Napoleon's coup of 2 December 1851. Beginning in 1867 annual processions to Baudin's tomb were celebrated as reminders of the irregular origins of the Second Empire. The procession was again held in December 1870, after the overthrow of the Empire, but with transformed meaning and function. Having placed a wreath at Baudin's tomb, the demonstrators went to the Hôtel de ville to demand the release of prisoners arrested after the unsuccessful October 31 insurrection.[75] The memory of Baudin, resurrected as a weapon against the Empire, thus became a vehicle for mobilizing radicals against the policies of the moderate republican Government of National Defense. Revolutionaries shaped their use of the past to correspond with the changing requirements of current circumstances.

The perpetuation of the collective memory of revolution was effectuated in part by a rich oral tradition passed from generation to generation. "Children are brought up hearing revolutions glorified," one contemporary remarked when explaining the origins of the Commune, and several Communards recalled that as young men they had learned of past upris-

---

72. Amann found only three evocations of 1793 in the clubs of 1848; *Revolution and Mass Democracy,* 39. According to Jean Dubois political discussion was "inundated" by references to the revolution beginning about 1868; *Le Vocabulaire politique,* 103.

73. Halbwachs, *The Collective Memory,* 88. Amos Funkenstein has similarly noted, "memory is always derived from the *present* and from the contents of the present"; "Collective Memory and Historical Consciousness," *History and Memory* 1 (spring/summer 1989), 9.

74. "Saillard" in the Blanquist newspaper, *La Patrie en Danger,* 1 and 2 November 1870.

75. *L'Enquête Parlementaire sur les actes du Gouvernement de Défense National,* 10 vols. (Paris: Germer-Baillère, 1873–75), 5:147; Molinari, *Les Clubs rouges,* 124.

ings from older workers or peasants who told them stories of the First Republic or 1848.[76] While much of the evidence has been lost and that which remains is sketchy and episodic, women do not appear to have participated to any considerable extent in this oral culture of revolution. For example, Suzanne Voilquin, the utopian socialist and feminist, described her father as an ardent revolutionary who took his sons to festivals on the Champs de Mars, but she wrote that her own upbringing was dominated by her pious mother's religiosity.[77] During the early years of the Great Revolution women had participated in the *journées* and popular revolution clubs, but public assemblies and demonstrations by women were forbidden by the Jacobin-dominated Convention in October 1793. Already under the Directory the revolutionary habit of calling women *citoyennes,* which recognized a public identity, was undermined, *madame* being increasingly used instead. The participation of "civic women" in the Revolution was thus not incorporated into oral traditions in the nineteenth century, an absence of mention corresponding to the successful repression of women's political action after 1793. Discussion of politics and revolution was evidently an aspect of working-class male sociability, part of a construction of masculinity in café and workshop that necessarily excluded women. Communard memoirs often show the importance of cafés as sites for political discussion, but none gives prominence to women.[78] Similarly, the vast historical, literary, and iconographic harvest of the first Revolution and subsequent uprisings only tangentially included women as historical agents.[79] Women appear to have had little role in communicating the political legacy of the past.

---

76. Jean Héligon, Jules Vallès, and Maxime Vuillaume all recalled that when they were young older men had introduced them to the revolutionary tradition; cited in Edwards, *The Paris Commune,* 17. In the 1840s an old peasant regaled the young Benôit Malon with tales of the First Republic and Empire; Vincent, *Between Marxism and Anarchism,* 8. Halbwachs has linked the transmission of collective memory to generational identity; *On Collective Memory,* ed. and trans. Lewis Coser (Chicago: University of Chicago Press, 1992), 24.

77. Voilquin's memoirs are partially translated in Marc Traugott, ed. and trans., *The French Worker: Autobiographies from the Early Industrial Era* (Berkeley: University of California Press, 1993), 98. Louise Michel recalled that as a child she heard both fairy tales and revolutionary stories, and that she reenacted the Terror by staging the elaborate guillotining of a playmate; *The Red Virgin: Memoirs of Louise Michel,* ed. and trans. Bullit Lowry and Elizabeth Ellington Gunter (University, Ala.: University of Alabama Press, 1981), 36.

78. See, for example, Lefrançais, *Souvenirs d'un révolutionnaire;* Bauer, *Mémoires;* Vuillaume, *Mes Cahiers rouges.* See also Haine, "'Café-Friend'"; Courtine, *La Vie Parisienne;* Robert A. Nye, *Masculinity and Male Codes of Honor in Modern France* (London: Oxford University Press, 1993).

79. See Thérèse Moreau, *Le Sang de l'histoire: Michelet, l'histoire, et l'idée de la femme au XIXe siècle* (Paris: Flammarion, 1982); Helga Grubitzsch, "A Paradigm of Androcentric His-

This void is significant when considering the ways the collective memory of the revolutionary tradition affected political discourse in the period preceding the Commune. One important function it served was to provide categories for differentiation among the competing elements of the political spectrum. "In the nineteenth century," François Furet has observed, "France could think about politics only through history." It was in the 1860s that historians such as Edgar Quinet first recognized 1789 and 1793 as distinct phases of the Great Revolution.[80] In the public meetings and freer press of the "Liberal Empire" a further distinction was often drawn between Robespierre and sansculotte idols such as Hébert and Marat, with some revolutionaries portraying the Jacobins as bourgeois oppressors of the people. These distinctions shaped the way Parisians conceived of the political fault lines dividing them, with neo-Jacobins and Hébertists vying for the mantle of revolution, while conservatives were equally obsessed with exorcizing the spirit of the Terror.[81] Analysis of the questions and issues raised by the Revolution, which were still considered to be vital and significant, had the effect of sharpening distinctions between all segments of the French political spectrum.

References to the revolutionary tradition could also operate at a more general level to facilitate consensus. Evoking the Great Revolution for guidance or inspiration could be narrowly or broadly phrased, depending on the desired effect. Election posters, appeals for support of policies or actions, and other attempts at mass mobilization were often couched in terms reminiscent of 1789 or 1793. Although it was dedicated to a specific vision of political action, the revolutionary left nonetheless constantly referred to the revolutionary past to rally support from a larger audience. In this way the revolutionary tradition served as a point of common ground between political and revolutionary leaders and the mass of Parisians. Contentious actions could also be legitimated by reference to the common history of revolution, as when a group of revolutionaries

---

toriography: Michelet's *Les Femmes dans la Révolution,*" in *Current Issues in Women's History,* ed. Arina Angerman et al. (New York: Routledge, 1989): 271–88. Marilyn Yalom, *Blood Sisters: The French Revolution in Women's Memory* (New York: Basic Books, 1993), explores women's biographies during the Revolution, rather than memory.

80. François Furet, *La gauche et la Révolution française au milieu du XIXe siècle: Edgar Quinet et la question du jacobinisme, 1865–1870* (Paris: Hachette, 1986), 8, 112.

81. Jacques Rougerie, "Belleville," in *Les Élections de 1869,* ed. Louis Girard (Paris: Marcel Rivière, 1960), 17; Louis Girard, *Étude comparée des mouvements révolutionnaires en France en 1830, 1848, et 1870–71,* 2 vols. (Paris: Centre de Documentation Universitaire, n.d.). In his study of conservative opinion, J. M. Roberts noted, "one is struck above all by historical evocations and resonances"; *The Paris Commune Considered from the Right* (London: Longman, 1973), 89.

urged revolt during the siege of Paris: "Will the great people of '89, who destroy Bastilles and overthrow thrones, wait in passive despair as cold and famine freeze its hearts under the eyes of the enemy?" The right of revolt, a central element of the revolutionary tradition, was reiterated by a club orator who referred to the momentarily successful uprising of October 31, 1870: "we held [the government], and we had the right, because we can invoke the grand example of our first Revolution." Even the Commune's examination to establish the competence and loyalty of National Guard officer candidates tested principally their knowledge and interpretation of the Revolution and Napoleon.[82] The language and categories of political analysis and action from the late 1860s through the Commune were to a great extent derived from the revolutionary tradition.

Just as men dominated the avenues for communicating the revolutionary tradition and discussing politics, so too the collective memory was gendered in that it was generally invoked by men and was about men. One of the phrases repeatedly used to evoke the Revolution for inspiration or guidance was *nos pères,* as when an election poster of February 1871 recalled "our fathers of '89" and sought support for the regeneration of France. In another case, a Communard journalist used this formula when arguing that the revolution "proclaimed by our fathers" was still unfinished.[83] The need to fight internal enemies, combined with the circumstances of war against an enemy that shot prisoners as a matter of policy, meant that many counseled a return to the tactics of 1793, when the Jacobins had surmounted a similar crisis. A neo-Jacobin newspaper in 1871 argued, "For each head of a patriot that Versailles causes to fall, let the head of a Bonapartist, an Orleanist, a Legitimist, roll in response. So be it! Versailles wants it: The Terror!" Victory was associated with the Terror, during the siege a club orator had demanded, "what we need are new Robespierres and Marats. . . . what we need is a new '93!" When a club established a tribunal to judge whether a member had been a police spy during the Second Empire, one of the judges asserted, "it is the duty of Jacobins to be suspicious of one another; in '93, everyone was suspect." During the Commune another clubiste called for reinstating the "law of suspects" that had unleashed the Great Terror in 1793.[84] The collective

---

82. From the Red Poster of January 6, reprinted in Schulkind, *The Paris Commune,* 86; Molinari, *Les Clubs rouges,* 67; Jacques Rougerie, "Comment les Communards voyaient la Commune," *Le Mouvement Social* 37 (1961), 63.

83. *Les Murailles Politiques,* 3:117; *L'Affranchi,* April 2.

84. Molinari, *Les Clubs rouges,* 80; *L'Affranchi,* April 5; *Le Petit Journal,* November 22, 1870; *Le Bulletin Communal,* May 6.

memory of the revolutionary past functioned to legitimate violence, but
the Terror was not the only example of the achievements of "our fathers
of '92" that was used as a guide for action and analysis throughout the
siege and the Commune. In September the International stated that to
fight reactionaries "We are organizing committees of vigilance in every
quartier and are urging the formation of districts that were so useful in
'93."[85]

Relatively few names and events were retained in the collective memory
of the Revolution, but for contemporaries they powerfully evoked images
of revolutionary action. Individual Communards often identified themselves or others with figures from the Revolution, elevating their struggle
to the same historical level as that of 1793. Louis Magot, an organizer of
radical clubs in the 12th arrondissement, is reported to have regularly
asserted, "I want to be a second Marat." When the socialist journalist
Auguste Vermorel explained to his readers why he started his newspaper
he wrote, "I wanted to create a publication analogous to that of the
Courier de Provence by Mirabeau, to the letters of Robespierre to his electors, to the friend of the people Marat!" An obituary for Flourens, killed
by a Versailles officer after having surrendered, declared that "the saber
blow from a gendarme felled him to the earth, just as on 9 Thermidor, the
pistol shot of a gendarme shattered the skull of Robespierre."[86] Magot as
Marat, Vermorel as Mirabeau, Flourens as Robespierre—all reveal how
the revolutionary tradition provided identity and models for Communard
men. Repeated invocations of Marat, Robespierre, the Bastille, the Terror, Jacobins, Chouans, Girondins, and the guillotine helped to define
policies, identify enemies, rally supporters, and place the Commune in the
continuum of revolution.

The Committee of Public Safety of May 1 was the most controversial
result of the cult of revolution. Debate about the Committee of Public
Safety was largely concerned with the appropriateness of a title that so
directly evoked the Terror. A minority thought the name given the committee was too slavish an imitation of 1793, but the energy and terror associated with the first Committee of Public Safety was precisely what recommended the name to the majority of the Communal Council and to
militant rank-and-file Communards. Jules Miot, who made the proposal,
argued that there was incompetence and even treason in the Commune; he

---

85. Quoted in Rougerie, "Quelques documents nouveau," 7.
86. Fontoulieu, *Les Églises,* 62. Vermorel named his journal after Marat's newspaper;
L'Ami du Peuple, April 28, 1870; *L'Action,* April 7.

requested the committee so that "heads would roll," an illuminating reference to guillotines in an age of firing squads. Speaking in favor, Vermorel said members of the Commune should "have the courage of our convictions. Under the government of September 4, the word *Commune* was feared; let us therefore not fear words."[87] That the Committee of Public Safety had violent and revolutionary associations for the mass of Parisians is demonstrated in two examples from divergent political perspectives. On May 7 the Commune's "reporter" on public opinion wrote that people in the streets were asking, "when will the Committee of Public Safety take its first truly energetic act?" In contrast, a Versailles police spy reported that same week that "people are worried about measures the Committee of Public Safety might take, and speak of mass arrests."[88] Although the creation of the Committee of Public Safety reveals a shift toward radical measures by the Communal Council under the pressures of civil war and demonstrates the power of the revolutionary tradition, it did not institute another Terror. Instead it contented itself with such acts as attaching civil commissioners to the three armies of the National Guard in direct imitation of 1793, on the grounds that "our fathers" had understood the need to guard against military dictatorship.[89]

The use of the term *nos pères* simply made explicit the gendered assumptions underpinning the revolutionary tradition, for in general there was a remarkable imbalance in the usage of the revolutionary past between Communard women and men. In comparison to men, women only rarely appealed to the revolutionary tradition, as when a female canteen worker in a National Guard battalion told a club that "there should be four guillotines in permanent operation in Paris, to terrify the aristocrats: on the Champs de Mars, the Luxembourg, the place du Trône, and the place de la Bastille."[90] In contrast to the many references to Marat or Robespierre, the popular collective memory in 1871 did not retain the name of any revolutionary woman—neither Olympe de Gouges, nor Théroigne de Méricourt, nor Pauline Léon, nor any others. The only historical woman known to be mentioned in newspaper articles or club speeches in 1871 was Jeanne Hachette (born Laisné), the heroine of 1474 who earned her nickname and her renown defending her native town

87. *Les Procès-Verbaux de la Commune,* 1:562, 565.
88. Dauban, *Le fond de la société,* 240; APP: Ba 363-4.
89. Malon, *La Troisième défaite,* 332.
90. Each place named was associated with important events of the Great Revolution; Fontoulieu, *Les Églises,* 106.

against a Burgundian siege: a woman speaker at a club in the 13th arrondissement used Hachette as an example of courage to be emulated.[91] Perhaps the women of 1789–93, especially de Gouges or Méricourt, were not sufficiently revolutionary to appeal to Communards. Still, in 1871 individual women were not recognized as important characters in the drama of the Revolution or in the revolutionary tradition.

Rejecting alternative visions of women's role in civil war, such as that of conciliatory Sabines or that of helpmates who remain by the domestic hearth, Communard women selected the October Days from the repertoire of images of women's public action because they corresponded to their revolutionary aspirations. Thus in some ways the relatively rare evocations of the revolutionary past by women were similar to those of men. Both in part interpreted the present through the past, using images and examples derived from the revolutionary tradition, such as the guillotine and the Terror, for guidance and inspiration. Both attempted to use the legacy of the Revolution to mobilize support for the Commune. Yet the differences between them are more striking. When men referred to the revolutionary tradition the intent was not to underscore action by men as such, even if the language and examples used were inherently gendered. Gender was invisible in their analysis, while they consciously highlighted political and social distinctions. When women referred to the revolutionary tradition they usually referred explicitly to action by women, as shown in the remembrance of the October Days. This indicates a conscious attempt to legitimate public action by women, recognizing them as historical actors with a distinct identity.[92] Women invoked the collective memory of the Revolution with less frequency than men, but with perhaps even greater consequence. For Communard men, one of the key functions of the revolutionary tradition was to sharpen political definitions; for Communard women, the Revolution provided a model of group solidarity.

---

91. Thomas, *Women Incendiaries,* 95. Joan of Arc was not mentioned, perhaps because she had become the property of Catholic conservatism. On the problem of expropriating Joan for the left see Susan Dunn, "Michelet and Lamartine: Making and Unmaking the Nationalist Myth of Jeanne d'Arc," *Romanic Review* 80 (May 1989): 404–19.

92. In a study of histories written by women in the nineteenth century, Billie Melman suggested that "women as such were outside history and that, as a group, they had no place in the collective memory," but this was not the case for Communard women. From studying 782 histories written in English by sixty-six women from 1840 to 1940, Melman found that women were first constructed as a "collectivity with a historical identity" in the 1870s; "Gender, History, and Memory: The Invention of Women's Past in the Nineteenth and Early Twentieth Centuries," *History and Memory* 5 (spring/summer 1993), 17.

Collective memory then became a foundation for collective action: "We are only simple women," reads the caption of a lithograph depicting a women's club of 1870, "but we are made from a cloth no less strong than our ancestors of '93. Let us rise up and act."[93] The "our ancestors" formulation used here contrasts with that of the more usual "our fathers," underscoring the discrimination inherent in most conceptualizations of the revolutionary tradition.

Indeed, in the period up to and including the Commune some women felt alienated from the revolutionary tradition precisely because it excluded women. Already in 1843 Flora Tristan had described the Declaration of the Rights of Man as a "solemn act that proclaimed the neglect and contempt of the new men for them [women]." Jenny d'Héricourt, a feminist author of the Second Empire, argued in *La Femme Affranchi* (1860) that women did not embrace the revolutionary tradition in part because the Declaration excluded them from the benefits of the revolution. Addressing republicans in general she wrote, "all your struggles are in vain if women do not march with you." She asserted that 1789 and 1848 had used women and then abandoned them, and she concluded for the future that "woman is like the people: she no longer seeks your revolutions that decimate us for the profit of a few ambitious talkers."[94] In the same vein the journalist Léonide Béra, who wrote under the name André Léo, criticized Communards for not allowing women full participation in the revolution. In this regard she lamented that the largest chapter of an imaginary book dealing with "the inconsistencies of revolutionary movements" would deal with women, "and it would show how these movements have always found a way to drive half the troops over to the enemy."[95]

The ambivalence of the legacy that the Great Revolution left to women clarifies an important issue in the Commune, why many Communard women appear to have been more radical or class conscious than most

---

93. The lithograph adorns the statutes of the Club des femmes Patriotes de Montrouge et de Belleville; Archives Départementales de l'Isère, *La Commune et les origines de la IIIe République vues de l'Isère: Exposition Grenoble, janvière-juin 1972* (Grenoble: Allier, 1972), 39.

94. Tristan quoted in Susan Groag Bell and Karen M. Offen, eds., *Women, the Family, and Freedom: The Debate in Documents,* 2 vols. (Stanford: Stanford University Press, 1983), 1:213; Héricourt cited in Thomas, *Women Incendiaries,* 25, and in Maité Albistur and Daniel Armogathe, *Histoire du Feminisme Français,* 2 vols. (Paris: Éditions des Femmes, 1977), 1:479.

95. André Léo in *La Sociale,* May 8, translated in Kathleen Jones and François Vergès, "'Aux Citoyennes!' Women, Politics, and the Paris Commune of 1871," *History of European Ideas* 13 (1991), 722.

Communard men. Contemporaries and historians alike have remarked that women's club speeches and published declarations were particularly committed to a thoroughgoing social revolution. Eugene Schulkind has drawn attention to the "remarkable degree of programmatic and organizational cohesiveness" of the Union des Femmes, which he characterized as the first organization of French women to explain gender inequality by a class analysis. While historians' explanations for the attractiveness of socialism to Communard women are generally persuasive, the differential legacy of the Revolution must also be considered a crucial factor.[96] Using language and categories of analysis derived mainly from the revolutionary tradition, most Communard men—even socialists—advocated a primarily political view of revolution. For women, however, adopting a revolutionary approach generally required accepting a larger view of revolution than that encompassed in the revolutionary tradition, a tradition that rendered women themselves nearly invisible and also emphasized political and civil changes that often did not apply to them. This helps explain why none of the Communard women leaders was known as a Jacobin or by other political labels; all were socialists. The redefinition of the revolution was clearly stated by Citoyenne Destree at a club in January 1871, who said that although women were not strong enough for combat, they should still go to public meetings to enlighten themselves: "For the revolution to be serious, it must be social. And the social revolution will not be operative until women are equal to men. Until then, you have only the appearance of revolution." Such remarks indicate that some felt keenly the paradoxical legacy of the Great Revolution. Louise Michel, later known as the "Red Virgin," recalled, for example, that in the clubs she led "one felt free, beholding the past without overly copying '93, and at the same time viewing the future without fear of the unknown."[97] This evidence suggests that the content of the collective memory was not hegemonic—that is, allowing no room for alternative formulations—but fluid, constituting another space for the definition of both identity and politics.

The extent of Communard references to 1793 do not, however, reveal

---

96. Rougerie has suggested that women were more class conscious because they were victims of a "double exploitation" by boss and husband; *Procès des Communards*, 214. Schulkind has used the similar term *hyperexploitation;* "Socialist Women," 133, 139. Thomas presented several examples of women's devotion to the Commune, with the explanation that women "are more emotional than men"; *Women Incendiaries*, 62–63.

97. Destree at the Club de l'École de Médecine cited in *La Lutte à Outrance*, 19 Nivôse 79 [January 9, 1871?]; Louise Michel, *La Commune*, 32. On the "Red Virgin" see Marie Marmo Mullany, "Sexual Politics in the Career of Louise Michel," *Signs* 15 (1990): 300–322.

an inability to recognize reality. Nor does evoking the revolutionary tradition in itself indicate a backward-looking perspective, as Rougerie argued when he claimed that Communard anticlericalism was similar to that of the First Republic, concluding, "what is a Communard but a belated sans-culotte?"[98] Violence against clerics and other actions recalling the Great Revolution were rooted in resentments arising from experience and were not simply vestiges of the past. "Priests and nuns are rotten to the core; we must get rid of these vermin in black without overlooking a single one," Marie Lucas proclaimed at the Club Communal, but her concluding remark is particularly enlightening: "in this century that we live in, everyone should work." Along with evidence of supposed anticlerical archaism Lucas expressed a desire common among Communards that the new social order would be founded on labor. Charles Beslay, a moderate socialist member of the Communal Council, echoed this sentiment, "Work?" he asked, asserting, "that is the grand word of the new world that is rising up."[99] These analyses inserted the Commune in the revolutionary continuum and affirm that a new stage in the evolution of society was at hand.

For many Communard women, as the Légion des Fédérées demonstrates, the novelty inherent in the identity of *citoyenne* was bound up with armed defense of the revolution. Weapons in the hands of women both symbolized and actualized the power of *citoyennes* over noncitizens, and they were often used to intimidate opposition or underscore a point. One witness testified that at the Club Eloi, headquarters of the Légion des Fédérées, "I saw a woman step up to the pulpit with a revolver in her hand. She said that she would blow her husband's head off if he refused to march [for the Commune], and that all women should do the same." Most likely this woman was a member of the Légion, and she may have been Colonelle Valentin.[100] Louise Michel described how useful a gun could be during the siege when presiding or speaking at a club: "I ordinarily kept close to me on the desk a small ancient pistol without a hammer, which artfully placed, and grasped at the right moment, often checked the men of 'order.'"[101]

---

98. Tombs, "Paris and the Rural Hordes," 806; Rougerie, *Procès des Communards,* 208.

99. Lucas was arrested after the Commune for having defended a barricade; AN: BB24 746 4082, dossier Lucas; *Le Journal Officiel,* April 28.

100. AHG: 5e conseil 545, dossier Budaille. As seen earlier in this chapter, Fontoulieu attributed nearly the same words to Valentin; *Les Églises,* 64.

101. Louise Michel, *La Commune,* 34. Paule Mink wore a revolver in clubs; Maitron, *DBMOF,* 7:370.

Citoyennes used these weapons in combat after Versailles troops entered Paris. After the walls of Paris had been breached, organized and armed units of women fulfilled the program of the Union des Femmes by building and fighting on barricades. While this combat can be directly linked to the Union des Femmes in only a few instances, given its role in advocating and forming armed women's groups there can be little doubt that the Union des Femmes was an important foundation for women's armed defense of the Commune, whether individually or in groups. The leadership of the Union des Femmes mustered women at the town halls of the 4th and 10th arrondissements, who then defended the barricades at the place Pigalle, the place Blanche, the place de Clichy, and the boulevard Magenta. Nathalie Lemel was apparently their commander, and an eyewitness recalled, "her appearance impressed me, for she was the only older woman amid a group of young girls, all armed with rifles and wearing ambulance nurses' armbands as well as red scarfs."[102] Blanche Lefebvre, one of the founding members of the Union des Femmes, was killed in the fighting. Lemel herself denied firing, but she did admit that when she built the Pigalle barricade she wore "a red sash at the waist and a red *cocarde* on the stomach." This description closely matches an account of the women who fought on the barricade at the place du Pantheon (5th arrondissement): "the women *fédérées* who meet at the Law School have also turned out in field dress. Those who seem to be the leaders wear large red sashes over a black dress; in addition they have a *cocarde* on the breast."[103] Red armbands, sashes, and *cocardes*—all symbolic of specific functions as well as of the new world of the Commune—constituted a kind of uniform for women's armed groups. Indeed, the women of the Comité de Vigilance des Citoyennes du 18e Arrondissement that met at the Boule Noire seem to have had a uniform common to their group, as Presidente Poirier stated that "the Lemarchand woman in fact made us all skirts bordered in red." While Poirier herself is not known to have fought on the barricades, two members of the vigilance committee did so, and at the same barricade, indicating coordinated action.

Descriptions of women fighting during Bloody Week are not wanting. "On the rue l'Abbaye, at the corner by the Café Sergent, I saw a group of

---

102. AHG: 4e conseil 688, dossier Lemel, quoted in Thomas, *Women Incendiaries,* 156. Thomas emphasizes the actions of individual women and argues that most women fought because their husband or lover was in the guard.

103. Blanchecotte, *Tablettes,* 258. The president of this group also supervised the secularization of the arrondissement's orphanages, activity typical of Union des Femmes members; Allemane, *Mémoires d'un Communard,* 105.

women pass by, rifles on their shoulders, cartridges at their sides, skirts hiked up," recalled one male Communard, who continues, "They shouted 'Long live the Commune.' One of them had a red flag that she fervently waved." At a barricade on the rue Lepic this Communard fought next to about twenty of these women, commanded by a woman in a Tyrolean cap who was probably Dmitrieff; three or four guards and five or six women were killed or injured. When the battle was clearly lost and only a few "enragés" remained, the "grande belle jeune femme" who commanded the "troup féminine" stood on the barricade in defiance, "the red flag in one hand, a revolver in the other."[104] The symbolic brandishing of weapons in popular assemblies had become the physical assertion of Communal power in combat, revealing the way clubiste and Communard political culture seamlessly joined discursive and instrumental practices. Another barricade held by women was on the place du Château-d'Eau. "Just at the moment when the National Guards began to retreat, a women's battalion turned up," an eyewitness reported, adding that "they came forward on the double and began to fire, crying 'Long live the Commune.' They were armed with Snider carbines and shot admirably. They fought like devils."[105]

The number of women who participated in armed groups or fought for the Commune will never be known. The Communard journalist Prosper-Oliver Lissagaray wrote of one hundred twenty women at the place Blanche barricade. Prosecutors said that fifty women left a Union des Femmes meeting on May 21 to go fight. The Versailles report of five hundred women demanding weapons at the Hôtel de ville was based on hearsay, but demonstrations of fifty to one hundred are better documented. After the Commune only a handful of women were accused or convicted of armed resistance,[106] although contemporaries reported seeing many dead women in the streets, victims of the barricade fighting or the massacres that followed. Certainly for contemporaries the horror inspired

---

104. Sutter-Laumann, *Histoire d'un Trente Sous,* 304.

105. AHG: 26e conseil 101, dossier Poirier; AHG: 26e conseil 92, dossier Delattre; Thomas, *Women Incendiaries,* 154. At her trial Louise Michel denied that women fought for the Commune, saying, "there never was a troop of women armed for combat; they met as a troop only for a demonstration." But Edith Thomas has demonstrated that Michel sought to shield others at her trial, and this assertion should be seen in that light. Michel later admitted that women fought on the barricade at the place Blanche; *The Red Virgin,* 67; AHG: 6e conseil 135, dossier Michel; *Women Incendiaries,* 197.

106. Maitron, in "Étude critique du Rapport Appert," examines the official statistics relating to the 115 women convicted of supporting the Commune; officially, 1,054 women were arrested, but many were released without being counted.

by armed women was based less on numbers than on their transgression of gender boundaries. In large part the disfigurement of Communard women into wild-eyed *pétroleuses* by partisans of "the moral order" functioned to defuse the explosive reality of women bearing weapons and using them for political purposes.[107] By defending the Commune with arms, speaking in clubs, arresting draft dodgers, marching in demonstrations, and eventually fighting on barricades, *citoyennes* such as those in the Union des Femmes and the Légion des Fédérées approached full equality with *citoyens* in the exercise of rights and duties. Yet the limits of this equality are also striking, and in them one sees another aspect of the permanent dynamic of continuity and change in gender definitions, even in times of revolutionary ferment.

While women's devotion to the Commune and service in its behalf could make them *citoyennes,* it could not make them fully *citoyens.* The clearest limit on full gender equality during the Commune was the exclusion of women from formal political processes. Though in many domains Communard women exercised public roles, with very few exceptions they did not demand, nor did they ever attain, equality in making political and policy decisions. While women often spoke in the public meetings of the late Empire, they were excluded during electoral periods when candidates were selected or programs defined. During the Parisian insurrection of October 31, 1870, women were asked to leave the room when a revolutionary club elected a committee to seize the local town hall.[108] Women attended one electoral assembly in February 1871 but were not allowed to speak "until they gain their political rights."[109] Women did not vote in the elections for the Commune, nor were there any women in its official governing bodies, which included the Communal Council, the local municipal councils, and the major bureaucracies.[110]

---

107. This argument is somewhat at odds with that of G. Gullickson, who in "*La Pétroleuse*" has argued that the image of the *pétroleuse* reflected men's sexual anxieties.

108. Vésinier, future member of the Communal Council, noted this fact at his trial in order to underscore the regularity of the proceedings; *La Gazette des Tribunaux,* February 24.

109. This was at the salle de la Redoute, meeting place of the Club Central; Molinari, *Les Clubs rouges,* 282. The statutes of the Club Communal stipulated that women could not speak and were to sit in reserved areas, although these provisions were not observed in practice; *Le Bulletin Communal,* May 6.

110. Schulkind states that the Commune was the first French government to employ women in positions of responsibility, but his evidence refers only to examples of women administering specific charity or educational institutions; "Socialist Women," 136. Shafer argues that Communard men and women were "distinct but equal"; "*Plus que des Ambulancières,*" 100–101.

Indeed, women who defined themselves as *citoyennes* and sought to bear arms acted in contradiction to attitudes about traditional separate-sphere distinctions shared by both opponents and proponents of the Commune. One anti-Communard noted "the noise, the agitation of the *forum* do not agree with the delicate nature of woman," and he lamented efforts by women to "obtain what nature refused her, the ability to exercise the rights and fulfill the duties of man." Another wished for the days when Roman matrons were honored with the epitaph "She stayed home and spun wool." For conservative critics the attempt by Communard women to expand their rights by identifying themselves as *citoyennes*—and inflicting violence in that capacity—deprived them of femininity: the prosecutor at one trial of women declaimed, "I blush to give them the name woman." He then went on to raise the specter of women lawyers, judges, or deputies, ending with the nearly unthinkable: ". . . and—for all we know—commandants? Generals of the army?"[111] Yet armed women's units were also controversial among Communards of both genders. At the Club Seraphin a motion to raise women's battalions was attacked by several orators and excited murmurs in the assembly, though in the end it was approved. A Communard woman at a club in the 13th arrondissement spoke against women actually fighting on barricades and asked that they help in hospitals instead. At her trial Marie Leroy claimed that she gave a club speech against arming women, arguing that such arming "completely displaced women and took from them their mission of aid and consolation."[112] While the rights of *citoyens* were universally acknowledged among Communards, those of *citoyennes* were still problematic.

Despite the continuity of such attitudes, the seizure of the title *citoyenne* by Communard women represented a considerable enlargement of women's rights, even—or, better said, especially—relative to the experience of women in the Great Revolution and the Second Republic. The Jacobins excluded women from organized political life, and the decree of August 1793 instituting the *levée en masse* asked only that women sew tents and uniforms and serve in hospitals. The Club des Femmes of 1848 was closed even before the June Days. The Communal Council, however, actively promoted organized political action by women by providing assembly

---

111. *Journal de l'Insurrection du 18 mars et des événements qui l'ont précédée par un spectateur philosophe* (Paris: Jules Taride, 1871), 88; Thomas, *Women Incendiaries,* 152, 179.

112. *Sous la Commune,* 74; Thomas, *Women Incendiaries,* 94; AHG: 3e conseil 40, dossier Leroy. Leroy had led the Union des Femmes in the 7th arrondissement and may have been playing to the prejudices of the court.

halls and resources for printing posters. The Union des Femmes was a full partner of the Commune's Commission on Work and Exchange in the organization of women's cooperatives. Some Communal and local officials encouraged and armed women's battalions, even providing military bands for their demonstrations.

If Communards of both genders accepted and encouraged expanded rights for women it was because the Communard conception of citizenship was informed and circumscribed by political affiliation as well as gender category: as *citoyens* Communard men were elevated above gentlemen; as *citoyennes* Communard women exercised wide powers over women and over men who were not deemed citizens. *Citoyens* could vote, hold high office, and fight at the front; *citoyennes* could influence decisions through clubs and demonstrations, exercise authority over non-Communard men, and build and fight on barricades. Rather than eliminate social and gender distinctions, the unique Communard hierarchy of citizenship partially inverted them. Although most Communards and non-Communards did not actively endorse armed women's units, in the context of a brutal civil war some women sought to expand their rights through what was traditionally a defining characteristic of citizenship, the bearing of arms. Based on their political identity as *citoyennes,* founded in a unique vision of the revolutionary tradition, women wielded physical, coercive power over some men, rather than being subservient as their gender should have dictated. The right to inflict violence, so crucial for constructing citizenship, was no longer only a man's domain.

Although the gendered legacy of the revolutionary tradition and ideals of citizenship shaped the behavior and ideals of Communard men and women differently, the shared elements of that legacy allowed mobilization of broad segments of Parisian society in support of the Commune. Analysis of the past provided the language and categories for delineating contemporary politics, such that men and women endowed the revolutionary tradition with meanings that conformed to their experience and visions. Communards of both genders evoked the most wrenching revolution known to them not because they were prisoners of grand memories but because they hoped to force an analogous transformation. These varied elements fused in an incident on April 7 in the 19th arrondissement, a working-class district of Paris. A crowd had gathered in anger and grief over the death of a neighborhood man, one of the first casualties in the civil war. A gendarme who had served the Second Empire was known to live in the building, and from the midst of the crowd Sidonie Letteron, a widowed day laborer who lived near by, shouted that they should search everywhere for the servant of the former regime. She then led a large group in forcing open the door and searching the building "from basement to attic." Although the gendarme had fled they found his old uniform, and they placed his hat on the end of a pole for triumphant display.[113] Letteron and the crowd certainly acted in conformity to a collective memory of violence rooted in the Revolution when they placed the hat on the pole, in imitation of severed heads on pikes. Yet at the same moment that Letteron and the crowd triumphantly paraded behind the gendarme's hat, an image redolent of de Launay's fate at the Bastille in the revolutionary past, Letteron also carried a red flag, the symbol of the new world. In what was only an apparent paradox, Communards celebrated the cult of revolution precisely because they sought a radical break with the past, identifying themselves with the revolutionary alternative of social renewal.

With the crisis of Bloody Week the Communal Council acted in conformity with these sentiments: "let even the women join their brothers, their fathers, their husbands! Those who have no weapons can tend the wounded and can haul pavement stones up into their rooms to crush the invader."[114] This appeal accepting an auxiliary role for women in combat echoed the founding statement of the Union des Femmes, reflecting the way armed women's groups sponsored by the Union des Femmes partially attained demands made by women since 1793 and 1848 for the military rights and duties of citizenship. Women's associations, and popular organizations more generally, had become a means of stating and enforcing an inversion of power relations. A Communard police agent expressed this gender revolution when he defended a *citoyenne* against a national guardsman who had told her to stay out of affairs that did not concern her. "When will you understand that woman, too, has a role to play? Does she not have, like us, her future and that of her children to defend?" he asked, "and why then do you send her to her needle when she asks for a rifle?"[115] Instead of going to their sewing, the *citoyennes* of the Commune took up rifles. Emphasizing elements of shared identity with the "population

---

113. Testimony by Letteron's concierge, who added that "each time this woman went downstairs, I hid in my apartment." A neighbor declared, "everyone was afraid of her, women hid their husbands fearing that they would be denounced, she was always with the most fanatical Guardsmen, in a word, she was the terror of the entire *quartier*." Letteron frequented the club in the Église de la Vilette; AHG: 26e conseil 212, dossier Letteron.

114. Thomas, *Women Incendiaries,* 151, 66.

115. Report dated May 15, quoted in Dauban, *Le fond de la société,* 311.

entière," they sought to prove that they also shared the rights of citizenship. By fulfilling military duties they partially overcame one crucial gender distinction used to justify depriving women of civic identity since the creation of Western conceptions of citizenship. Their own analysis and actions demonstrate that the *citoyennes* of 1871 were not mistaken in their conviction that the Commune "bears within it the seeds of social revolution."[116]

---

116. "Manifeste du comité central" of the Union des Femmes, dated 6 May; *Le Cri du Peuple,* May 10.

Conclusion: The Legacies
of the Commune

It is a lesson of history: when a people arrive at a moral low point—
even decadence—because of despotism, an enormous crisis, an
important revolution, is needed to save the people.
                    —Manifesto by Parisian natives of the Oise

Versailles forces entered Paris on Sunday, May 21, through a gate rendered nearly indefensible by artillery fire and left entirely undefended by
Communard ineptitude. The army quickly overwhelmed the National
Guard in the western, more prosperous sections of Paris, but by midweek
it met more determined opposition in the central and eastern arrondissements, where support for the Commune was greater.[1] In addition, the
large-scale executions of guards taken prisoner, mainly carried out with
calculated efficiency behind the lines of combat, gave National Guards no
apparent choice except death in battle or by firing squad. Even those who
had taken no part in the fighting but had conspicuously supported the
Commune were dragged into the street and shot, so complete was the
"expiation" Thiers promised the National Assembly. Rigault and Ferré
proposed that the Commune retire to the Ile-de-la-Cité to make a last
stand amid the ashes of Notre-Dame and the bodies of the hostages.
Instead, on May 22 the council decided each member should return to
defend his arrondissement, a suitable end for an insurrection that had
begun in neighborhood clubs and guard units.

Epigraph from a manifesto by Parisian natives of the Oise to their brothers in the department, justifying the Commune and urging support; *Les Murailles Politiques,* 3:390. Copies of
this poster reached the department and were posted in several towns; AN: C2882, report by
the First President of the Cour de Clermont.

1. Bloody Week is the most intensively studied aspect of the Commune; see Horne, *The
Fall of Paris;* Bruhat, Dautry, and Terson, *La Commune de 1871;* Robert Tombs, *The War
Against Paris, 1871* (Cambridge: Cambridge University Press, 1981).

The *semaine sanglante* witnessed moments of horrifying cruelty and inspiring selflessness: Delescluze, wearing the black frock coat and top hat that distinguished him as a man of 1848, girt by his red sash denoting membership in the Communal Council, climbing to the top of a barricade and majestically seeking—and finding—death; Varlin, the leading figure among the younger socialists, enduring a veritable calvary when forced to run a gauntlet of soldiers and enraged Parisians; the execution of the archbishop of Paris and perhaps a hundred other clerics and police officers, who were taken hostage in hopes of ransoming Blanqui but became targets of popular wrath; the last desperate, almost Wagnerian battle amid the gravestones of the Père-Lachaise Cemetery, whose *mur des fédérés,* where many Communards were shot, became a place of pilgrimage for generations of socialists, radicals, and revolutionaries. The determination of the last Communards may be measured by the words of one who participated in the execution of the archbishop of Paris: "the traitors stretched out on the ground, we felt our revolutionary strength, we felt that we were already lost, we wanted to die too, but to revenge ourselves first, and we looked at our dead foes and breathed deep."[2] In the days during and after these apocalyptic scenes perhaps twenty thousand Parisians were massacred—many were not Communards but were taken for such—while some forty-seven thousand others were arrested, some as late as 1875. One hundred thousand Parisians were killed, arrested, or in exile; such was the immediate legacy of the destruction of the Commune.

Even before the repression was complete the National Assembly ordered an inquiry into the "insurrection" of March 18, and since then contemporaries and scholars alike have debated its meaning. Each political current and group had a response; none could remain silent in the face of such a brutal civil war that followed so closely on a traumatic national humiliation. The Commune as an event became quickly obscured in the Commune as legend—black or red. Scholarly inquiry into the Commune began only on the eve of the First World War, with Georges Bourgin's pioneering work,[3] so for the most part the Commune has been viewed through the polarizing lens of 1917. Instead, the binary choices implicit in the political and social interpretations might usefully be transcended

---

2. Recollection of Mégy, who first distinguished himself in February 1870 by shooting dead a police officer sent to arrest him for rioting in the aftermath of Rochefort's arrest; cited in Frank Jellinek, *The Paris Commune of 1871* (London: Victor Gollantz, 1937; reprint, New York: Grosset and Dunlap, 1965), 349.

3. Bourgin, *Histoire de la Commune.*

through the concept of political culture, as the Commune was both created and shaped by the political culture of popular organizations.

Why, then, has this record of revolutionary action not been more fully recognized? In general, both historians and participants were misled by accepted ideas about revolutions. Conditioned by a powerful revolutionary tradition, even the leaders of the revolutionary socialist movement framed their experience as a spontaneous mass uprising. Ironically, among contemporaries of the Commune only its conservative critics would have agreed that it arose from anything like revolutionary action. Their depiction of the Commune as a conspiracy perpetrated by members of the International and other outcasts reflects well-known themes in nineteenth-century political discourse.[4] In part as a reaction to this conservative image, even those who participated in the revolutionary socialist movement did not recognize the role of popular organizations in preparing the seizure of power.[5] According to the romantic vision of revolution dominant on the left, revolts were legitimate to the extent that they were democratic, popular, and spontaneous. Except for the Blanquists, whose strategy of insurrectionary conspiracy was widely rejected, planned seizures of power were associated with military and conservative coups, such as those by Napoleon Bonaparte on 9 Brumaire 1799, and by his nephew Louis-Napoleon Bonaparte on December 2, 1851. Even Vaillant, much influenced by Blanquism, favorably contrasted the Delegation of the Twenty Arrondissements with the elected Communal Council, which "could not have the unity of action and the energy of a committee arising spontaneously, revolutionarily, from a people in revolt."[6] During the siege Vaillant had helped piece together the coalition of popular organizations that created the Delegation as a "revolutionary Commune" and had even been on the insurrectionary committee that sought to install it at the Hôtel

---

4. See Louis Chevalier, *Laboring Classes and Dangerous Classes in Paris during the First Half of the Nineteenth Century* (Princeton: Princeton University Press, 1973); Barrie M. Ratcliffe, "Classes labourieuses et classes dangereuses à Paris pendant la première moitié du XIXe siècle? The Chevalier Thesis Reexamined," *French Historical Studies* 17 (1991): 542–74; Jaap van Ginneken, *Crowds, Psychology, and Politics, 1871–1899* (New York: Cambridge University Press, 1992); J. U. Laborde, *Fragments medico-psychologiques: Les Hommes et les actes de l'insurrection du Paris devant la psychologie morbide* (Paris: Germer-Baillière, 1872).

5. Vallès once observed in passing that the Commune sprang from the Republican Central Committee; *Le Cri du Peuple,* January 7, 1884.

6. *Ni Dieu, Ni Maître,* March 20, 1881, cited in Edwards, *The Paris Commune,* 294. Vaillant expressed the same sentiments twenty years later; see Dautry and Scheler, *Le Comité Central,* 251. Similarly, after describing in some detail the preparations for the insurrection of October 31 Lefrançais concluded that "events alone produced the explosion"; *Étude,* 96.

de ville in January 1871. Similarly, Leo Meilliet, an important organizer of the popular movement in the 13th arrondissement, who invaded and administered the mairie with Duval on March 18, described the Commune as "a purely spontaneous demonstration of popular instinct."[7] That these militants were blind to their own history of assiduous organizational work reveals the powerful effect that the obsession with revolutionary spontaneity had on the way Communards constructed their experience.

Another reason some revolutionary socialist Communards were incapable of recognizing that the revolution they created was the result of preparation was because of their involvement in the dispute between Marx and Bakunin within the International. Marx accused Bakunin of seeking revolution by an elite, rather than by the working class. Viewing the Commune as the fruit of conscious agitation would have appeared to validate Bakunin's alleged strategy. In addition, after the Commune Marx completed his evolution toward advocating mainly parliamentary, rather than revolutionary, means to socialism, so for political and ideological reasons he was not disposed to recognize the revolutionary preparation behind the Commune, even if he had been aware of it.[8] For his part, Bakunin accused Marx of authoritarianism, meaning both that Marx sought to control the international socialist movement and that Marx's conception of revolution was hierarchical and rigid, with state ownership of production rather than producer associations. While Bakunin, too, claimed the Commune, he was neither more knowledgeable about the origins of the insurrection than Marx nor more willing to see it as an example of "authoritarian" preparation by an organized group. Just after the defeat of the Commune in 1871 Bakunin wrote that the authoritarians believed a dictatorship would carry out the social revolution, but "our friends the socialists in Paris thought that the revolution could only be accomplished and fully developed by means of the spontaneous, continuous action of the masses—of the popular groups and associations." Like Vaillant and Meilliet, Bakunin characterized a movement organized by popular associations as spontaneous because that was the model inherited from the French rev-

---

7. *La Revue Blanche, 1871: Enquête sur la Commune de Paris* (Paris: n.p., 1897), 89.

8. See Henryk Katz, *The Emancipation of Labor: A History of the First International* (New York: Greenwood, 1992); Eric J. Hobsbawm, ed., *The History of Marxism*, vol. 1, *Marxism in Marx's Day* (Bloomington: Indiana University Press, 1982); George Lichtheim, *Marxism in Modern France* (New York: Columbia University Press, 1966); Hal Draper, *The "Dictatorship of the Proletariat" from Marx to Lenin* (New York: Monthly Review Press, 1987); John Ehrenberg, *The Dictatorship of the Proletariat: Marxism's Theory of Socialist Democracy* (New York: Routledge, 1992).

olutionary tradition.[9] Most survivors of the Commune who remained active in the exile revolutionary movement, such as Malon, Lefrançais, Vaillant, Serrailler, and Frankel, became deeply entangled in the growing conflict between Marx and Bakunin. For some, preparation smacked of Bakunin's heresies; for others, it was redolent of authoritarianism. Marx and Engels also kept up a vigorous rearguard action against Blanquist solutions, which they held could lead only to a dictatorship of a revolutionary clique rather than to leadership by the working class as a whole.[10] Trapped in these constraints, the role of revolutionary action by popular organizations, which fit no existing model, was ignored even by those who had participated in the movement.

The importance that the dispute within the International had in coloring interpretations of the Commune and in shaping revolutionary political ideology was magnified by the rise of Leninism. Building on the legacy of Marx and Engels, Lenin considered the Commune to be an example of class struggle, as well as a counterexample of inadequate party organization.[11] Both schools of Communal historiography tend to argue that the lack of effective central direction was a principle cause of the Commune's defeat, implicitly suggesting that one aspect of the Commune's significance lay in its function as a lesson for the future in this regard. Those of the political school generally argue that the lack of unity in the Commune derived from incoherence and confusion about ideals and goals.[12] As for the social interpretation, emphasizing the ideological deficiencies of Communards often serves a double purpose: it helps explain the failure of a theoretically inevitable social revolution, and in some cases it is used to confirm Lenin's insights about the need for disci-

9. Cited in Schulkind, *The Paris Commune of 1871: The View from the Left,* 220. See also Mikhail Bakounine, *Sur la guerre franco-allemande et la révolution sociale en France, 1870–1871* (Leiden: Brill, 1977).

10. Lefrançais and Malon, both of whom were closely associated with Bakunin for a time, echoed the condemnation of Marx as authoritarian; Vaillant evolved toward Blanquism and was duly excoriated by Engels. Lefrançais, *Souvenirs d'un révolutionnaire;* Malon, *La Troisième défaite;* Vincent, *Between Marxism and Anarchism;* Katz, *The Emancipation of Labor,* 93; G. D. H. Cole, *A History of Socialist Thought,* vol. 2, *Socialist Thought: Marxism and Anarchism, 1850–1890* (London: Macmillan, 1961).

11. Lenin, *Lessons of the Commune.*

12. Wolfe wrote that popular organizations expressed "vague and contradictory aspirations"; "The Parisian *Club de la Révolution,*" 119. Schulkind noted that clubistes lacked a clear conception of the path to the Social Republic and were without a unifying vision; "The Activity of Popular Organizations," 414.

pline and unity in a vanguard party.[13] Both interpretations suggest the Commune failed because there was no charismatic leader or disciplined group that could unify diversity and inspire sacrifice.

Certainly no grand personage or single group emerged to lead a disciplined Communal movement to victory. In hindsight the full implementation of the revolutionary socialist Declaration of Principles of February 19, 1871, could have allowed the Delegation of the Twenty Arrondissements to play this role. The Declaration envisioned linked networks of revolutionary socialist groups in a pyramidal structure, culminating in the central Delegation. The Commune would still have been defeated militarily, but its failure would not have been ascribed to lack of discipline or unity. It is perhaps more fruitful to suggest that the very nature of the revolution precluded such an occurrence. Communards and, more specifically, clubistes had a conception of their revolution that blocked the development of a disciplined group analogous to the Bolshevik party or other directing force. In all three of its faces—social, political, and economic—association was voluntarist and localist. It left the initiative for progress and the creation of a new world to assemblies of *citoyens* and *citoyennes* who would regulate their common interests (as members of a civil polity, as workers, as parents, as artists). This mode of organization had clear weaknesses, especially in regard to planning and implementing revolutionary action, which clubistes in the revolutionary socialist movement since the siege had tried to rectify through the Delegation of the Twenty Arrondissements and the Revolutionary Socialist Party. Even with these deficiencies, the agitation of 1870–71 revealed clubs and committees to be a powerful form of popular organization.

Historians, too, have misunderstood the role of the popular movement in preparing and shaping the Commune, in large part because they, like contemporaries, have been influenced by prevailing notions of how revolutionary movements ought to occur. A diverse coalition of assemblies gathering many social groups, a movement founded in the neighborhood and not the workshop, clubs and committees did not correspond to most later models of revolutionary action.[14] Scholars seeking revolutionary

---

13. Bruhat, Dautry, and Tersen, echoing a dominant theme among Marxist adherents of the social interpretation, concluded that in large part the failure of the Commune was due to the lack of a worker's party; *La Commune de 1871,* 360. Choury, who also represents the Marxist wing of the social interpretation, argued that the Commune did indeed represent a "new and original program" of federation; *La Commune au coeur de Paris,* 315.

14. Gould overemphasizes this element, however, when he argues that during the Commune, "the collective actors in question were neighborhoods, and their adversary was the

roots for the Commune turned first to the International but found organizational entropy rather than dynamism.[15] Furthermore, Jean Dautry and Lucien Scheler's well-respected history of the Republican Central Committee and the Delegation of the Twenty Arrondissements found that this movement had little or no role during the Commune. Finally, the way the Central Committee of the National Guard seemingly rose from oblivion to seize Paris suggested to most historians that the Commune was either a creation of circumstance or an inevitability whose specific roots were less important than its triumphal example.[16]

Scholarly inquiry into the Commune has been dominated by the looming shadows of the Bolshevik Revolution and the Cold War. With the fall of the Berlin Wall and the dissolution of the Soviet Union, previously central questions such as whether the Commune was a "dictatorship of the Proletariat" seem somehow quaint.[17] What needs explaining is the way people interpreted and acted within the historical moment. That is why this study has evoked the language of clubistes, their modes of thought, and the symbolism of revolvers and red consigns, as well as presenting a social analysis of club militants: this approach, exploiting the analytical potential of political culture, circumvents a century of interpretive debate. The memory of past struggles shaped the beliefs and actions of clubistes, yet the pervasiveness of references to the Great Revolution in no way confirms the Commune to have been backward-looking, as many in the political interpretation suggest. Judging from their rhetoric most clubistes and Communards interpreted their struggle as part of a larger process, a battle of two worlds, begun by the revolution of 1789 and continuing in new guises throughout the intervening eighty years. Some defined this primarily as a struggle of democracy against monarchy, others as labor against capital, but there was a consensus among Communards that they were fulfilling the promise of history. Similarly, the prevalence of anticlericalism in Communard and clubiste action and oratory does not denote

---

state"; *Insurgent Identities,* 135. Club and guard militants, not neighborhoods, created the Commune, and their battle was not against abstract state power but against the old world represented by monarchism and the National Assembly.

15. Rougerie, "L'AIT et le mouvement ouvrier"; Maitron, "Étude critique du Rapport Appert."

16. It is significant, however, that both monographs focusing on the popular movement before the Commune conclude that the insurrection was indeed the result of revolutionary action: Wolfe, "The Origins of the Paris Commune"; Dalotel, Faure, and Freiermuth, *Aux Origines.*

17. See Ehernberg, *The Dictatorship of the Proletariat,* 186, for a recent well-articulated argument that the Commune was such a dictatorship.

archaism; rather, both the appeal to previous revolutionary action and the attack on the authority of the church arose from an interpretation of current conditions. They were reasoned responses to events and constellations of power as they existed in 1870 and 1871, not the vestiges of outmoded struggles. The political interpretation, in stressing the links of the Commune to the past, ignores the progressive, transformative nature of clubiste and Communard political culture.

Neither do the two strands of the social interpretation adequately describe the nature of the Commune. The Commune was not a criminal attempt to destroy civilization, as contemporary conservatives argued, but a revolutionary attempt to change existing conditions, which given the assumptions of conservatives was much the same thing. Nor was it primarily rooted in class struggle, as more recent adherents of the social interpretation have contended. For twenty-five years after the inception of the "new social history" in the early 1960s, the interaction of social and economic evolutions was the dominant paradigm for understanding revolutions like the Commune. In the last decade, however, social historians have found culture virtually everywhere they look.[18] The vexing problem is to discover the linkages between subjective and objective reality, between culture and society. Just when the classic questions of class and social structure were being answered—or a range of possible answers were being identified—whole new fields opened up involving such concerns as "the language of labor," "visions of the people," and "the construction of tradition." Social antagonism and hostility as expressed in the clubiste culture of violence revolved around political allegiance and perceived appurtenance to either of the two worlds in conflict, rather than around relationship to the means of production. While the rich and privileged were targeted for violence, payment, or punishment, so too were common people who did not share the Communard vision. This was a struggle based on cultural conceptions in which class played an important, but not predominant, role. For most clubistes or Communards the primary battle was not workers versus owners but the people versus those who did not accept the rights and duties of revolutionary action. Citizenship defined in this way was in large part constructed and expressed through the culture of

18. Eric J. Hobsbawm and Terrence Ranger, eds., *The Invention of Tradition* (New York: Cambridge University Press, 1983). Joan Wallach Scott began with the glassworkers of Carmaux and now explores gender as a cultural construct; *The Glassworkers of Carmaux: French Craftsmen and Political Action in a Nineteenth-Century City* (Cambridge: Harvard University Press, 1974) and *Gender and the Politics of History*. Patrick Joyce has argued that class is also cultural construction; *Visions of the People*.

violence expressed in the clubs of the Commune, within the framework of association. That the popular clubs and committees that were the primary vehicles of revolutionary mobilization could not develop a program of class struggle was in large part because they were not composed of one class. Since these popular organizations were generally based on the neighborhood and included a wide spectrum of social groups and classes, the ideas they expressed and implemented were primarily founded on the wider conceptions of *citoyen* and *citoyenne,* rather than on the concepts of worker or proletarian narrowly defined.

The consequences of the Commune have been subject to almost as much debate as its origins and nature. The year of defeat, civil war, and massacre Hugo named the *année terrible* marks a crucial moment in French political history. After eighty years of revolution and reaction signified by the familiar milestones of 1789, 1793, 1814, 1830, 1848, 1851, and 1871, France was about to begin the longest of republics. And although the Third Republic would end in German defeat in 1940—as the Second Empire had ended in 1870—the hesitant, contested establishment of the Republic in the 1870s was definitive. Some have argued that the Commune was disastrous for republicanism and France because it polarized opinions, divided republicans, and united conservatives; according to Roger L. Williams, "the high price of human folly has rarely been better measured."[19] Most sympathizers and historians have held, to the contrary, that the Commune saved the Republic by revealing the impossibility of a monarchist restoration. During the civil war, for example, Thiers felt compelled to give delegations from France's largest cities and towns categorical assurances that he would protect the Republic; his only fight was against the assassins who ruled Paris.[20]

Repression of the Commune also demonstrated to skeptics that moderate and conservative republicans could resist radical demands for precipitous social or political transformations. In this regard François Furet has argued that the Third Republic finally resolved the century-old central problem of French politics: "the restoration of monarchy brings back the *ancien régime,* but the Republic is indivisible from dictatorship in French history and French memories."[21] The Second Empire had been one solu-

---

19. *The French Revolution of 1870–71* (New York: Norton, 1969); Edwards, *The Paris Commune,* 351; Pierre Miquel, *La Troisième République* (Paris: Fayard, 1989), 109.

20. J. P. T. Bury, *Gambetta and the Making of the Third Republic* (London: Longman, 1973), 22.

21. Furet, *Revolutionary France,* 171.

tion to this problem; the Opportunist Republic would be another. Defeat and massacre of urban revolutionaries certainly assuaged fear of popular dictatorship after both 1848 and 1871. The military victory of Thiers over the Commune in 1871 and Gambetta's repudiation of the Commune in the electoral struggles of the 1870s broke the linkage between revolution and the Republic that frightened so many.[22] One must distinguish between the Commune and its repression; it was not the Commune that made the Third Republic but rather its defeat and rejection by influential republicans. This conclusion is all the more compelling when it is remembered that former Communards were among the fiercest opponents of the Opportunist Republic. The Republic envisioned by Communard and clubiste militants was very different from the Republic that was born so hesitantly in the 1870s. Although the Commune itself did little to create the Third Republic, it engendered high ideals and bitter divisions that deeply affected the way political issues were framed and decided for the rest of the century. From the *ordre moral* government of the mid-1870s to the Dreyfus affair and beyond, many of the problems of 1871 continued to disturb French political life: redefining relations of church and state; reconciling state authority and republican liberties; navigating the transition from the politics of notables to mass politics; and integrating discontented and marginalized groups into a democratic order. There is much truth in Gordon Wright's observation that the divisions of the Commune were healed only by the blazing patriotism of the *union sacré* of 1914.[23]

The Commune also marks a crucial moment in the development of socialism in France. While the question of whether the Commune was a dictatorship of the proletariat has lost much of its resonance, the Commune must still be recognized as a seminal event in the French socialist movement. Assessing the Commune's legacies for French socialism reveals, however, a paradoxical mixture of disjunctures and continuities. Worker societies in Paris recovered rather rapidly from massacre and defeat; by October 1872 there were some forty-five in existence, and there were about one hundred by 1876. They showed little interest in strikes and

---

22. Gambetta sometimes spoke sympathetically of the republican aspirations of Communards, but he refused to endorse their amnesty; Bury, *Gambetta;* Jean Joughin, *The Paris Commune in French Politics, 1871–1880: The History of the Amnesty of 1880,* 2 vols. (Baltimore: Johns Hopkins University Press, 1955).

23. "On the floor of the Chamber of Deputies [in 1914], Edouard Vaillant, a Communard in 1871, and Albert de Mun, an officer in Thiers's army that repressed the Commune, shook hands for the first time in their political careers"; Wright, *France in Modern Times,* 302.

were primarily concerned with forming and supporting cooperative associations of production. This relatively weak and tentative labor movement was the Parisian foundation for the socialist resurrection of the late 1870s, culminating in the 1879 Congress of Marseilles, which marked the rebirth of French socialism.[24] Such a revival is all the more remarkable given the severe legal limitations on the movement: martial law was lifted in Paris only in 1879, limited public meetings were finally allowed in 1881, and unions were legalized only in 1884. In some ways the trajectory of the labor movement in the 1870s mirrors that of the authoritarian Second Empire of the 1850s and early 1860s, underscoring the importance of state and legal structures for shaping the nineteenth-century French labor movement. In both periods of repression militant workers returned to minimal political programs while strengthening their commitment to ending exploitation through producer associations. Responding to political conditions workers developed economic solutions in repressive periods and focused on political solutions in more tolerant times, as in the late Empire and late 1870s. One effect of the destruction of the Commune was that the lessons of the later Second Empire had to be relearned, and many of the decisions at Marseilles simply reiterated those of the 1868 and 1869 congresses of the International. There was one crucial difference, however. The Congress of Marseilles openly proclaimed its allegiances to the cause of the Commune and embraced political revolution as a necessary prerequisite for real social change.[25] Revolutionary socialism, forged in the spring of 1871 in Paris to merge the social and political aspirations of a dedicated minority, became after 1879 the announced goal of the majority of French socialists.

Yet in some ways the Commune was the last of the nineteenth-century revolutions, for in fact there was no other. The aspirations of the Revolutionary Socialist Party, many of which were attained in unforeseen ways during the Commune, suggest that this was not because the movement was mired in the past but because of fundamental changes in Paris and France. Lenard Berlanstein has observed that the Commune was "the formative political experience for Parisian workers of the late nineteenth century," but he also shows that they reacted to the monarchist threat by rallying

---

24. Aimée Moutet, "Le Mouvement ouvrier à Paris du lendemain de la Commune au premier congrès syndicaliste en 1876," *Le Mouvement Social* 58 (1967): 3–39.

25. Alexandre Zévaès, *Histoire du socialisme et du communisme en France de 1871 à 1947* (Paris: France-Empire, 1947), 85; Magraw, *A History of the French Working Class,* 2:83.

not to the young working-class parties in the late 1870s and early 1880s but to radicalism.[26] The socialists of the 1880s and 1890s shared a revolutionary socialist rhetoric with militant Communards but differed in their organizational forms. Rooted in neighborhoods and exquisitely responsive to the will and passions of participants, popular organizations during the prolonged crises of 1870–71 fostered a political culture that made them cells for revolutionary combat as well as militant electoral associations. In contrast, later labor and socialist movements never seriously attempted an armed seizure of power. Thus if the Commune was the last of the nineteenth-century revolutions this was because it was defeated, and because of the choices of later militants when facing new social and political conditions; the real revolutionaries of the Third Republic were the integral nationalists and anti-Semites. Had the Commune survived it would indeed have been the harbinger of a new world, for the transformations implicit in clubiste and Communard political culture constituted a fundamental reshaping of social, gender, and political relations.

Even in defeat the associationist foundations of the Commune represent an element of continuity with past and future republican practices. While Jean-Marie Mayeur has asserted that "the individualism of the age distrusted groups and associations," one finds from the 1880s onward an explosion of associations, committees, unions, federations, and syndicates. Daniel Halévy was perhaps more correct when he described this era as "the Republic of committees."[27] The most important political and social movements of the Third Republic were carried out in large part through voluntary associations and public meetings, from Boulangism to the Popular Front, from anti-Semitism to solidarism, from the Dreyfusard Ligue des Droits de l'Homme to Action Française. In this perspective the popular organizations of the siege and Commune, renewing and adapting the legacy of 1848, inaugurated an era of mass politics.[28] The Revolution-

26. Leonard R. Berlanstein, *The Working People of Paris, 1871–1914* (Baltimore: Johns Hopkins University Press, 1984), 153.

27. Jean-Marie Mayeur and Madeleine Reberioux, *The Third Republic from its Origins to the Great War, 1871–1914,* trans. Robert Foster (Cambridge: Cambridge University Press, 1984), 82; Daniel Halévy, *La République des comités: Essai d'histoire contemporaine (1895–1934)* (Paris: Bernard Grasset, 1934).

28. Amann has argued, to the contrary, that the popular organizations of 1793, 1848, and 1871 belonged to a distinct phase in political organization, when "traditional hierarchies had lost legitimacy, but before modern mass organizations had taken root"; "The Paris Club Movement in 1848," in *Revolution and Reaction: 1848 and the Second French Republic,* ed. Roger Price (London: Croom Helm, 1973), 125. Wolfe made much the same argument in the conclusion of "The Origins of the Commune."

ary Socialist Party and popular organizations in general were strategies for mobilizing opinion and action in the new context of republican civic rights. The same is true of the public assemblies of the Third Republic, as well as the clubs of 1848. Later associations differed from the practices of both 1848 and 1871, however, in not implementing that tenet of the revolutionary tradition that held that popular organizations embodied popular sovereignty. Here again the Third Republic divorced revolution and the Republic, as was the wish of its two most important founders, Gambetta and Thiers. Yet the ideal of direct popular sovereignty evident in 1848 and 1871 was also present in the soviets of 1905 and 1917, an element of continuity rather than disjuncture. Also present in the Leninist program was the consciousness of being a revolutionary minority, which was so clearly felt by revolutionary socialists in the spring of 1871. In this regard the genealogy linking 1793 to 1848 to 1871 to 1917 is valid not on the foundation of class dictatorship but in elaborating strategies for combining direction and spontaneity, leadership and mass.

The entry of the Versailles army into Paris on May 21 ended hopes for realizing the revolutionary new world elaborated by clubistes and Communards. The popular organizations of the Commune, successors to the public meetings of the late Empire and the assemblies of the siege, were definitively silenced. One of the last meetings for which a record survives was that of the Club Central at Saint-Eustache, sponsored by the Republican Central Committee of the Twenty Arrondissements—a fitting honor for the group that had done the most to nurture the Communal movement. On Monday, May 22, with the army already on the Champs de Mars, there was no bureau of club officers to organize the meeting. After the few orators spoke, the assembly sang the Marseillaise and then melted away, some to hide, others to fight and die. In describing the meeting an anonymous observer wrote an epitaph for the entire revolution: with the defeat of the Commune, "the reign of the orators vanished."[29]

---

29. *Saint-Eustache pendant la Commune* (Paris: Paul Dupont, 1871), 45.

Sources

The most important source for the history of popular organizations is the Archives de la Ministère de la Guerre (AHG), the army archive located in the Vincennes fortress outside Paris. Under martial law the army investigated and prosecuted suspected Communards, collecting tens of thousands of dossiers on individuals and hundreds of cartons of evidence. Individual dossiers generally include a report by the investigating official and testimony by witnesses and the suspect, unless the accused was being tried *in absentia.* These dossiers are subject to the usual reservations about trial documents, such as self-serving testimony, distortions to hide or magnify one's activities, malicious or dishonest prosecutors, and vengeful or naive motivations. Investigators of Charles Bas, for example, were unable to learn anything about him from several potential witnesses who reportedly feared that Bas might exact revenge (5e conseil 681). A witness in the case of Sidonie Letteron testified that Letteron said she expressed Communard sympathies only to anger her neighbors (26e conseil 212). Twenty-six *conseils de guerre* processed over thirty-six thousand suspects, though only about fifteen thousand dossiers remain. The Ly series of cartons comprises evidence collected by army prosecutors and arranged by institution or event, with materials devoted to such topics as the functioning of the National Guard, the mairies, the uprising of 31 October, and a very important carton of materials on popular organizations. These latter documents are a varied collection of manuscript club minutes seized after the Commune, notes sent between clubs, declarations, posters, and quotations from speeches.

Another important collection of archival materials on the Commune may be found in the Archives de la Préfecture de Police (APP). Ba 362 to 365, comprised of a total of twenty-three cartons, contain thousands of documents on all aspects of the Commune, providing a remarkable picture of the Commune from day to day. The Bibliothèque Historique de la Ville de Paris (BHVP) has a large collection of useful materials, notably Manuscript 1083, a previously unused collection of police reports on clubs and committees from November 1870 to January 1871. Manuscript 1131, part of Gustave Courbet's papers, has much of interest on the Fédération des Artistes.

The Archives Nationales (AN) BB24 series contains Communards' petitions for pardons. The petitions in this series generally summarize the *conseil de guerre* material at Vincennes. Yet most studies of the Commune that use archival materials rely on this much less informative source because the BB24 cartons contain dozens of cases each, while the AHG dossiers must be requested one by one (with a daily limit, seemingly dependent on the archivist, of four to six dossiers). Fortunately a most impressive and fundamental work, the incomparable *Dictionnaire biographique du mouvement ouvrier français, deuxième partie, 1864–71,* edited by Jean Maitron, has collected and published the material on Communards that is found in the BB24 series. When combined with the *conseil de guerre* dossiers the *DBMOF* allows both extensive coverage of the mass of Communards and intensive exploration of individual cases.

Finally, Paul Fontoulieu's *Les Églises de Paris sous la Commune* requires attention as a source for the history of clubs and *comités.* Abbé Fontoulieu, a sometime journalist for *Figaro,* was outraged at the Communards' treatment of churches, clerics, and believers. He personally attended some of the club meetings he described, and he also gathered information from newspapers and interviews with clerics and other witnesses. Fontoulieu's account proves highly reliable wherever the possibility to verify it exists. He reported that Etienne Canal spoke at the club held at St. Christophe, for example, and Canal was in fact a member of the vigilance committee of the 19th arrondissement that sponsored that club. Fontoulieu has also been accepted as a primary source by historians of various persuasions, from William Serman to Jean Maitron, and from Claude Perrot to Jacques Rougerie.

Archives

Archives de la Préfecture de Police (APP)

Ba 24: Surveillance des écoles, 1869–72.
Ba 86: Daily report by the Prefect of Police, November to December 1870.

Ba 362 to 365: Commune de Paris (twenty-three cartons).
Ba 366–3: Commune de Paris.
Ba 1013: Diary of Adolphe Clémence.
Ba 1615: Comité Central Républicain.

Archives du Département de la Seine (ADS)

VD⁶1239 5: Elections of March 26, 4th arrondissement.
VD⁶1336 8: Posters of the Comité de Vigilance, 5th arrondissement.
VD⁶1542 10: Republican Socialist Club, 7th arrondissement, November 1870.
VD⁶2347 5: Elections of March 26 and April 16, 17th arrondissement.
VD⁶2452 3: Elections of March 26, 18th arrondissement.

Archives Historiques de la Ministère de la Guerre (AHG)

Dossiers des Communards.
Ly 12: Events of October 31.
Ly 16: Mairies of the 2d, 4th, 5th, and 6th arrondissement.
Ly 20: Central Committee of the National Guard.
Ly 22: Clubs and *comités* during the Commune.
Ly 26: Hôtel de ville.
Ly 27: Mairies de Paris.

Archives Nationales (AN)

C 2882 to 2885: Reports on province during the Commune.
BB18 1795 9803 (1) and (2): Public meetings, 1868–69.
BB24: Dossiers de grâce des Communards.
BB30: Political reports by *procureurs généraux,* 1864–68.
F¹ᶜIII: Prefects' reports on public opinion.
F⁷ 12665: Reports on the war and seige.

Bibliothèque Historique de la Ville de Paris (BHVP)

Ms. 1083: Public meetings, November 1870 to January 1871.
Ms. 1118: Vie civile pendant le siège.
Ms. 1123: Commune de Paris, Fédération des Arts.
Ms. 1124: Commune de Paris, Comité Central Républicain.
Ms. 1125: Commune de Paris, clubs and réunions.
Ms. 1131: Commune de Paris, papiers Courbet.
Ms. 1135: Commune de Paris, avis de réunions, comités.
Ms. 1137: Commune de Paris, Comité de Vigilance.
Ms. 1142: Commune de Paris, cercle des Jacobins.
Ms. 1148: Commune de Paris, Ligue d'Union Républicaine.
Ms. 1398: Papiers Chassin, Comité Central Républicain.
Ms. 1399: Papiers Chassin, October 31.

Ms. 1400: Papiers Chassin, public meetings.
Ms. 1762: Papiers Fiaux.

Principal Newspapers

Le Bulletin Communal: Organ des Clubs, May 6, 1871. One issue, published by the Club St. Nicolas des Champs.
La Commune, March 20 to May 19, 1871. Edited by J. B. Millière after April 9.
Le Cri du Peuple, February 22 to May 23, 1871. Edited by Jules Vallès.
Le Journal Officiel de la République Français, March 20 to May 24, 1871. The official newspaper of the Commune.
Le Mot d'Ordre, February 3 to March 12, 1871, and April 1 to May 20, 1871. Henri Rochefort's newspaper.
Paris Libre, April 12 to May 24, 1871. Pierre Vésinier's newspaper.
Le Prolétaire, May 10 to May 24, 1871. Four issues, published by the Club des Prolétaires and the vigilance committee of the 11th arrondissement.
La Rouge, Journal des Jeunes, May 17 and 19, 1871.
La Sociale, March 31 to May 17, 1871.
Le Vengeur, February 3 to March 11, 1871, and March 30 to May 24, 1871. Felix Pyat's newspaper.

Published and Manuscript Sources

Agulhon, Maurice. *Le Cercle dans la France Bourgeoise.* Paris: Armand Colin, 1977.

———. *Marianne into Battle: Republican Imagery and Symbolism in France, 1789–1880.* Trans. Janet Lloyd. London: Cambridge University Press, 1981.

Agulhon, Maurice, and Maryvonne Bodiguel. *Les Associations au village.* Le Paradou: Actes Sud, 1981.

Albistur, Maité, and Daniel Armogathe. *Histoire du Feminisme Français.* 2 vols. Paris: Éditions des Femmes, 1977.

Alexander, Jeffrey C., and Steven Seidman, eds. *Culture and Society: Contemporary Debates.* New York: Cambridge University Press, 1990.

Allemane, Jean. *Mémoires d'un Communard: Des barricades au bagne.* Paris: Librairie Socialist, n.d.

Alner, Michel Dominique. "The Jacobins in the Paris Commune of 1871." Ph.D. diss., Columbia University, 1978.

Amann, Peter H. "The Paris Club Movement in 1848." In *Revolution and Reaction: 1848 and the Second French Republic,* ed. Roger Price, 115–32. London: Croom Helm, 1973.

———. *Revolution and Mass Democracy: The Paris Club Movement in 1848.* Princeton: Princeton University Press, 1975.

Amigues, Jules. *Les Aveux d'un conspirateur Bonapartiste.* Paris: Lachaud, 1874.

Aminzade, Roland. *Ballots and Barricades: Class Formation and Republican Politics in France, 1830–1871.* Princeton: Princeton University Press, 1993.

————. *Class, Politics, and Early Industrial Capitalism: A Study of Mid-Nineteenth Century Toulouse, France.* Albany: State University of New York Press, 1981.

Andrieux, Jules. *Notes pour servir à l'histoire de la Commune de Paris de 1871.* Paris: Spartacus, 1971.

Appert, General. *Rapport d'ensemble . . . sur les opérations de la justice militaire relatives à l'insurrection de 1871.* Annales de l'Assemblée Nationale, vol. 43. Paris: Imprimerie Nationale, 1875.

Applewhite, Harriet B., and Darline G. Levy. "Women and Militant Citizenship in Revolutionary Paris." In *Rebel Daughters: Women and the French Revolution,* ed. Sara E. Melzer and Leslie W. Rabine, 79–101. New York: Oxford University Press, 1992.

————. "Women, Radicalization, and the Fall of the French Monarchy." In *Women and Politics in the Age of Democratic Revolution,* ed. Harriet B. Applewhite and Darline G. Levy, 81–107. Ann Arbor: University of Michigan Press, 1990.

Aprile, S. "La République au salon: Vie et mort d'une form de sociabilité politique (1865–1885)." *Revue d'Histoire Moderne et Contemporaine* 38 (1991): 473–87.

Arago, Etienne. *L'Hôtel-de-ville de Paris au 4 septembre et pendant le siège.* Paris: Hetzel, n.d.

Archer, Julian. "La Commune de Lyon." *Le Mouvement Social* 77 (1971): 5–47.

Archives Départementales de l'Isère. *La Commune et les origines de la IIIe République vues de l'Isère: Exposition Grenoble, janvier–juin 1972.* Grenoble: Allier, 1972.

Arnould, Arthur. *Histoire populaire et parlementaire de la Commune de Paris.* 3 vols. Brussels: Librairie Socialiste de Henri Kistemaeckers, 1878.

Audebrand, Philibert. *Histoire intime de la Révolution du Dix-Huit mars.* Paris: Dentu, 1871.

Audoin-Rouzeau, Stéphane. *1870: La France dans la guerre.* Paris: Armand Colin, 1989.

Azéma, Jean-Pierre, and Michel Winock. *Les Communards.* Paris: Seuil, 1964.

B., Raoul. *Journal du siège.* Paris: Corps 9, 1984.

Baal, Gérard. *Histoire du radicalisme.* Paris: La Découverte, 1994.

Baczko, Bronislaw. *Les Imaginaires sociaux: Mémoires et espoirs collectifs.* Paris: Payot, 1984.

Baker, Keith M. Introduction to *The French Revolution and the Creation of Modern Political Culture.* Vol. 1, *The Political Culture of the Old Regime,* ed. Keith M. Baker, xi–xxiv. New York: Pergamon, 1987.

————. *Inventing the French Revolution: Essays on French Political Culture in the Eighteenth Century.* Cambridge: Cambridge University Press, 1990.

Bakounine, M. *Sur la guerre franco-allemande et la révolution sociale en France, 1870–1871.* Leiden: Brill, 1977.

Baldick, Robert. *The Siege of Paris.* New York: MacMillan, 1964.

Barbalet, J. M. *Citizenship: Rights, Struggle, and Class Inequality.* Minneapolis: University of Minnesota, 1988.

Barrows, Susanna. "After the Commune: Alcoholism, Temperance, and Literature in the Early Third Republic." In *Consciousness and Class Experience in*

Nineteenth-Century Europe, ed. John M. Merriman, 205–18. New York: Holmes and Meier, 1979.

Bauer, Henri. *Mémoires d'un jeune homme.* Paris: Charpentier, 1895.

Bell, Susan Groag, and Karen M. Offen, eds. *Women, the Family, and Freedom: The Debate in Documents.* 2 vols. Stanford: Stanford University Press, 1983.

Bellet, Roger. *Jules Vallès.* Paris: Fayard, 1995.

———. *Presse et journalisme sous le Second Empire.* Paris: Armand Colin, 1967.

Bénézit, E. *Dictionnaire critique et documentaire des peintres, sculpteurs, dessinateurs et graveurs.* Rev. ed. 10 vols. Paris: Grun, 1976.

Bennett, Tony, et al., eds. *Culture, Ideology, and Social Process: A Reader.* London: Open University Press, 1981.

Berenson, Edward. *Populist Religion and Left-Wing Politics in France, 1830–52.* Princeton: Princeton University Press, 1984.

Bergerand, Charles. *Paris sous la Commune en 1871.* Paris: Lainé, 1871.

Berkin, Carol, and Clara Lovett, eds. *Women, War, and Revolution.* New York: Holmes and Meier, 1980.

Berlanstein, Leonard R., *The Working People of Paris, 1871–1914.* Baltimore: Johns Hopkins University Press, 1984.

———. ed. *Rethinking Labor History: Essays on Discourse and Class Analysis.* Urbana: University of Illinois Press, 1993.

Bertocci, Philip A. *Jules Simon: Republican Anticlericalism and Cultural Politics in France 1848–1886.* Columbia: University of Missouri Press, 1978.

Bidouze, René. *Lissagaray: La Plume et l'épée.* Paris: Éditions Ouvrières, 1991.

Blanchecotte, A.-M. *Tablettes d'une femme pendant la Commune.* Paris: Didier, 1872.

Blanqui, Auguste. *Textes choisis.* Ed. V. P. Volguine. Paris: Éditions Sociales, 1971.

Bougeart, Alfred, et al. *Des Districts!* Paris: Association générale Typographique, [1870].

Bourgin, Georges. *Histoire de la Commune.* Paris: Cornély, 1907.

———, ed. *La Guerre de 1870–1871 et la Commune.* Paris: Flammarion, 1938.

Bourillon, Florence. *Les Villes en France au XIXe siècle.* Gap: Orphys, 1992.

Brécy, Robert. *La Chanson de la Commune: Chansons et poèmes inspirés par la Commune de 1871.* Paris: Éditions Ouvrières, 1991.

Brint, Michael. *A Genealogy of Political Culture.* Boulder: Westview, 1991.

Broue, Pierre. "Les Communeux de Grenoble: Le Club de l'école Reboul." In *Grenoble à l'époque de la Commune,* ed. P. Guillen, 71–82. Grenoble: Université des Sciences Sociales de Grenoble, 1972.

Brubaker, Rogers. *Citizenship and Nationhood in France and Germany.* Cambridge: Harvard University Press, 1992.

Bruhat, Jean. *Eugène Varlin, militant ouvrier, révolutionnaire et Communard.* Paris: Éditions Français Réunis, 1975.

———. "Pouvoir, pouvoirs, état en 1871?" *Le Mouvement Social* 79 (1972): 157–71.

Bruhat, Jean, Jean Dautry, and Emile Tersen. *La Commune de 1871.* 2d ed. Paris: Éditions Sociales, 1971.

Bury, J. P. T. *Gambetta and the Making of the Third Republic.* London: Longman, 1973.

Bury, J. P. T., and R. P. Tombs. *Thiers 1797–1877: A Political Life.* London: Allen and Unwin, 1986.

Cahiers d'Histoire de l'Institute de Recherches Marxistes 44 (1991). Special issue on the Paris Commune.

Cattelain, P. *Mémoires inédits du Chef de la Sûreté sous la Commune.* Paris: F. Juven, 1900.

Cerf, Marcel. *Edouard Moreau, l'âme du Comité Central de la Commune, centenaire de la Commune 1871–1971.* Paris: Lettres Nouvelles, 1971.

Chastenet, Jacques. "La Commune, aube des révolutions modernes on flamboyant créspuscule?" Preface to *La Commune de Paris,* by Pierre Dominique. 1948. Reprint, Paris: Hachette, 1962.

———. *Histoire de la Troisième République.* Vol. 1, *L'Enfance de la Troisième (1870–1879).* Paris: Hachette, 1952.

Chevalet, Emile. *Mon journal pendant le siège et la Commune par un bourgeois de Paris.* Paris: Librairie des Contemporains, 1871.

Chevalier, Louis. *La Formation de la population parisienne au XIXe siècle.* Paris: Presses Universitaires de France, 1950.

———. *Laboring Classes and Dangerous Classes in Paris during the First Half of the Nineteenth Century.* Princeton: Princeton University Press, 1973.

Choury, Maurice. *Bonjour, Monsieur Courbet!* Paris: Éditions Sociales, 1969.

———. *La Commune au coeur de Paris.* Paris: Éditions Sociales, 1967.

———. "Les Liasons de la Commune de Paris avec la Province d'après les Archives de la Préfecture de Police." *Pensée* 132 (1967): 83–94.

———. *Les Origines de la Commune: Paris livré.* Paris: Éditions Sociales, 1960.

———. *Le Paris Communard.* Paris: Perrin, 1970.

Christiansen, Rupert. *Paris Babylon: The Story of the Paris Commune.* New York: Viking, 1995.

Clartie, Jules. *Histoire de la Révolution de 1870–1871.* Paris: L'Éclipse, 1872.

Clère, Jules. *Les Hommes de la Commune.* Paris: Dentu, 1871.

Clifford, Dale. "Aux Armes, Citoyens! The National Guard in the Paris Commune of 1871." Ph.D. diss., University of Tennessee, 1975.

———. "Direct Democracy in the Paris Commune of 1871." *Proceedings of the Western Society for French History* 5 (1977): 397–405.

Club Républicain Démocratique et Socialiste de XIIIe Arrondissement: Règlements et statuts. Paris: Berthelemy et Cie, [Adopted November 18, 1970].

Cole, G. D. H. *A History of Socialist Thought.* Vol. 2, *Socialist Thought: Marxism and Anarchism, 1850–1890.* London: Macmillan, 1961.

Collingwood, R. G. *The Idea of History.* Oxford: Clarendon, 1948.

La Commune à Notre-Dame des Victoires. Paris: Simon Raçon, 1871.

"La Commune de 1871: Acts du colloque universitaire pour la commémoration du centenaire, Paris les 21–22–23 mai 1971." *Le Mouvement Social* 79 (1972). Special issue.

La Commune de Paris, 1871. Paris: Éditions H.I.S., 1988.

Connerton, Peter. *How Societies Remember*. Cambridge: Cambridge University Press, 1989.

Conte, Gérard. *Éléments pour une histoire de la Commune dans le XIIIe arrondissement, 5 mars–25 mai 1871*. Paris: Éditions de la Butte aux Cailles, 1981.

Coote, Mary P. "On the Composition of Women's Songs." *Oral Tradition* 7 (1992): 332–48.

Cordillot, Michel. *Eugène Varlin: Chronique d'un espoir assassiné*. Paris: Éditions Ouvrières, 1991.

Courbet raconté par lui-même et par ses amis. Geneva: Pierre Cailler, 1950.

Courtine, Robert. *La Vie Parisienne: Cafés et restaurants des boulevards, 1814–1914*. Paris: Perrin, 1984.

Cresson, E. *Cents jours du siège à la Préfecture de Police, 2 novembre 1870–11 février 1871*. Paris: Plon, 1901.

Dabot, Henri. *Griffonnages quotidiens d'un bourgeois du Quartier Latin du 14 mai 1869 au 2 décembre 1871*. Paris: Peronne, 1895.

Da Costa, Charles. *Les Blanquistes*. Paris: Marcel Rivière, 1912.

Da Costa, Gaston. *La Commune vécue*. 3 vols. Paris: Ancienne Maison Quantin, 1903–5.

D'Alméras, Henri. *La Vie Parisienne pendant le siège et sous la Commune*. Paris: Albin Michel, [1925?].

Dalotel, Alain, Alain Faure, and Jean-Claude Freiermuth. *Aux Origines de la Commune: Le Mouvement des réunions publiques à Paris 1868–1870*. Paris: Maspero, 1980.

Dalsème, A.-J. *Histoire des conspirations sous la Commune*. Paris: Dentu, 1872.

D'Andrade, Roy G., and Claudia Strauss, eds. *Human Motives and Cultural Models*. Cambridge: Cambridge University Press, 1992.

Dauban, Charles-Aimé. *Le fond de la société sous la Commune*. 1873. Reprint, Geneva: Slatkine-Megariotis Reprints, 1977.

Daubié, Marie-Victoire. *La Femme pauvre au XIXe siècle*. Paris: Côté-Femmes, 1992.

Dautry, Jean, and Lucien Scheler. *Le Comité Central Républicain des Vingt Arrondissements de Paris (septembre 1870–mai 1871)*. Paris: Éditions Sociales, 1960.

Deaucourt, Jean-Louis. *Premières loges: Paris et ses concierges au XIXe siècle*. Paris: Aubier, 1992.

Decouflé, André. *La Commune de Paris (1871): Révolution populaire et pouvoir révolutionnaire*. Paris: Cujas, 1969.

Delmas, Abbé Guillaume. *La Terreur et L'Église en 1871*. Paris: Dentu, 1871.

Deloge, Albert. *Causes de révolutions periodiques*. Paris: A. Lacroix, 1871.

Delpit, Martial. *Le Dix-Huit mars: Récit des faits et recherche des causes de l'insurrection. Rapport fait à l'Assemblée Nationale au nom de la Commission d'Enquête sur le 18 mars 1871*. Paris: L. Techener, 1872.

Derfler, Leslie. *Paul Lafargue and the Founding of French Marxism, 1842–1882*. Cambridge: Cambridge University Press, 1991.

———. *Socialism Since Marx: A Century of the European Left*. New York: St. Martin's, 1973.

D'Esboeufs, V. *Trahison et défection au sein de la Commune: Le Coin du voile.* Geneva: Blanchard, 1872.

Despats, U. *Lettres d'un homme à la femme qu'il aime pendant le siège de Paris et la Commune.* Ed. Pierre Lary. Paris: J. C. Lattes, 1980.

Dessal, Marcel. *Un révolutionnaire jacobin: Charles Delescluze 1809–1871.* Paris: Marcel Rivière, 1952.

Dirks, Nicolas B., Geoff Eley, and Sherry B. Ortner, eds. *Culture/Power/History: A Reader in Contemporary Social Theory.* Princeton: Princeton University Press, 1994.

Dominique, Pierre. *La Commune de Paris.* 1948. Reprint, Paris: Hachette, 1962.

Dommanget, Maurice. *Blanqui et l'opposition révolutionnaire à la fin du Second Empire.* Paris: Armand Colin, 1960.

———. *Blanqui, la guerre de 1870–71 et la Commune.* Paris: Domat, 1947.

———. *La Commune.* Paris: La Taupe, 1971.

———. *Le Drapeau rouge.* Paris: Éditions Sociales, 1965.

———. *L'Enseignement, l'enfance, et la culture sous la Commune.* Paris: Éditions Sociales, 1964.

———. *Eugène Pottier, membre de la Commune et chantre de'Internationale.* Paris: E.D.I., 1971.

———. *Les Idées politiques et sociales d'Auguste Blanqui.* Paris: Marcel Rivière, 1957.

Le Dossier de la Commune devante les conseils de guerre. Paris: Librairie des Bibliophiles, 1871.

Draper, Hal. *The "Dictatorship of the Proletariat" from Marx to Lenin.* New York: Monthly Review Press, 1987.

Dreyfus, Michel. *L'Europe des socialistes.* Brussels: Complexe, 1991.

Dromel, Justin. *La Loi des révolutions: Les génerations, les nationalités, les dynasties, les religions.* Paris: Didier, 1862.

Dubois, Jean. *Le Vocabulaire politique et social en France de 1869 à 1872.* Paris: Librairie Larousse, 1962.

Dubois, Raoul. *A l'assaut du ciel: La Commune raconté.* Paris: Éditions Ouvrières, 1991.

Dubreuilh, Louis, and Jules Jouff. *La Commune.* Paris: n.p., n.d.

Du Camp, Maxime. *Les Convulsions de Paris.* 5th ed. 3 vols. Paris: Dentu, 1881.

Ducatel, Paul. *Histoire de la Commune de du siège de Paris vue à travers l'imagerie populaire.* Paris: Jean Grassin, 1973.

Duclos, Jacques. *La Commune de Paris à l'assaut du ciel.* Paris: Éditions Sociales, 1970.

———. *La Prémière Internationale.* Paris: Éditions Sociales, 1964.

Dumay, Jean-Baptiste. *Mémoires d'un militant ouvrier du Creusot (1841–1905).* Grenoble: Maspero, 1976.

———. "La Proclamation de la Commune au Creusot." *La Revue Socialist* 189–90 (January–February 1966): 96–109; 191 (March 1966): 218–34; 192 (April 1966): 343–61.

Dunn, Susan. "Michelet and Lamartine: Making and Unmaking the Nationalist Myth of Jeanne D'Arc." *Romanic Review* 80 (May 1989): 404–19.

Dupâquier, Jacques, and Denis Kessler, eds. *La Société française au XIXe siècle: Tradition, transition, transformation.* Paris: Fayard, 1992.

Dupuy, Aimé. *1870–1871: La Guerre, la Commune et la presse.* Paris: Armand Colin, 1959.

Durand, Pierre. *Louise Michel: La Passion.* Paris: Messidor, 1987.

Duveau, Georges. *Le Siège de Paris, septembre 1870–janvier 1871.* Paris: Hachette, 1939.

Edwards, Stewart. *The Paris Commune, 1871.* London: Eyre and Spottiswoode, 1971.

———, ed. *The Communards of Paris, 1871.* Ithaca: Cornell University Press, 1973.

Ehrenberg, John. *The Dictatorship of the Proletariat: Marxism's Theory of Socialist Democracy.* New York: Routledge, 1992.

Ellenstein, Jean. *Réflexions sur la Commune de 1871.* Paris: Julliard, 1971.

Elshtain, J. B., and S. Tobias, eds. *Women, Militarism, and War: Essays in History, Politics, and Social Theory.* Savage, Md.: Rowman and Littlefield, 1990.

Elton, Lord. *The Revolutionary Idea in France, 1789–1871.* 2d ed. London: Edward Arnold, 1931.

Elwitt, Sanford. "Solidarity and Social Reaction: The Republic against the Commune." In *Images of the Commune,* ed. James A. Leith, 187–200. Montreal: McGill-Queens University Press, 1978.

L'Enquête Parlementaire sur les actes du Gouvernement de Défense Nationale. 10 vols. Paris: Germer Baillière, 1873–75.

L'Enquête Parlementaire sur l'Insurrection du Dix-Huit mars 1871. Paris: A. Wittersheim, 1872.

Evrard, Ferdinand. *Souvenirs d'un ôtage de la Commune.* Paris: Paul Dupont, 1871.

Faure, Christine. *Democracy without Women: Feminism and the Rise of Liberal Individualism in France.* Trans. Claudia Gorbman and John Berk. Bloomington: Indiana University Press, 1991.

Favre, Jules. *Le Gouvernement de la Défense Nationale.* 2 vols. Paris: Plon, 1871–72.

Feld, Charles, and François Hincker. *Paris au front d'insurgé: La Commune en images.* Paris: Livre Club Diderot, 1971.

Fentress, James, and Chris Wickham. *Social Memory.* Cambridge, Mass.: Blackwell, 1992.

Feu Seraphin: Histoire de ce spectacle. Lyon: N. Scheuring, 1875.

Fiaux, Louis. *Histoire de la guerre civile de 1871.* Paris: Charpentier, 1879.

Fitzpatrick, Maria. "Proudhon and the French Labour Movement: The Problem of Proudhon's Prominence." *European History Quarterly* 15 (1985): 407–30.

Flourens, Gustave. *Paris Livré.* Paris: Librairie Internationale, 1871.

Fontoulieu, Paul. *Les Églises de Paris sous la Commune.* Paris: Dentu, 1873.

Fonvielle, W. de. *La Terreur ou la Commune de Paris.* Brussels: Petit Journal, 1871.

Foucault, Michel. *Language, Counter-Memory, Practice.* Ed. Donald F. Bouchard. Ithaca: Cornell University Press, 1977.

Foulon, Maurice. *Eugène Varlin, relieur et membre de la Commune.* Clermont-Ferrand: Éditions Mont-Louis, 1934.

Funkenstein, Amos. "Collective Memory and Historical Consciousness." *History and Memory* 1 (spring/summer 1989): 1–15.

Furet, François. *La gauche et la Révolution française au milieu du XIXe siècle: Edgar Quinet et la question du jacobinisme, 1865–70.* Paris: Hachette, 1986.

———. *Penser la Révolution française.* Paris: Gallimard, 1978.

———. *Revolutionary France, 1770–1880.* Trans. Antonia Neville. Oxford: Blackwell, 1992.

Gaffney, John, and Eva Kolinsky, eds. *Political Culture in France and Germany.* London: Routledge, 1991.

Gagnière, A. *Histoire de la presse sous la Commune.* Paris: Lachaud, 1872.

Gaillard, Jeanne. "Les Associations de production et la pensée politique en France, 1852–1870." *Le Mouvement Social* 51 (1965): 59–85.

———. "La Commune: Le Mythe et le fait." *Annales: Économies, Sociétés, Civilizations* 28 (1973): 838–52.

———. "La Commune: Une Révolution ou un mythe." In *Comprendre les faits du vingtième siècle,* ed. Marc Ferro. Paris: Marabout Université, 1977.

———. *Communes de Province, Commune de Paris.* Paris: Flammarion, 1971.

———. "Les papiers de la Ligue Républicaine des Droits de Paris." *Le Mouvement Social* 56 (1966): 65–87.

Gaumont, Jean. *Histoire générale de la coopération en France.* 2 vols. Paris: Fédération Nationale des Coopératives de Consommation, 1924.

———. *Un Républicain révolutionnaire romantique, Armand Lévy (1827–1891).* Paris: Flammarion, 1932.

Geary, Dick, ed. *Labour and Socialist Movements in Europe before 1914.* New York: Berg, 1989.

Geertz, Clifford. *The Interpretation of Cultures.* New York: Basic Books, 1973.

Gibaud, Bernard. *Au conflit de deux libertés: Révolution et droit d'association.* Paris: Mutualité Française, 1989.

Gibson, William. *Paris during the Commune.* New York: Haskell House, 1874.

Gildea, Robert. *The Past in French History.* New Haven: Yale University Press, 1994.

Gille, Gaston. *Jules Vallès (1832–1885).* Paris: Jouve, 1941.

Ginneken, Jaap van. *Crowds, Psychology, and Politics, 1871–1899.* New York: Cambridge University Press, 1992.

Girard, Louis. *Étude comparée des mouvements révolutionnaires en France en 1830, 1848, et 1870–71.* 2 vols. Paris: Centre de Documentation Universitaire, n.d.

———. *La Garde Nationale, 1814–1871.* Paris: Plon, 1964.

———. *Napoléon III.* Paris: Hachette-Pluriel, 1993.

———. *Nouvelle histoire de Paris: La Deuxième République et le Second Empire, 1848–1870.* Paris: Hachette, 1981.

———, ed. *Les Élections de 1869.* Paris: Marcel Rivière, 1960.

Girardet, Raoul. *Mythes et mythologies politiques.* Paris: Seuil, 1986.

———. "Les Trois couleurs: Ni blanc, ni rouge." In *Les Lieux de mémoire,* vol. 1, *La République,* ed. Pierre Nora, 5–35. Paris: Gallimard, 1984.

Girault, Jacques. *La Commune et Bordeaux (1870–71)*. Paris: Éditions Sociales, 1971.

———. "Les Étudiants et la Commune." In *Experiences et langage de la Commune de Paris*, 95–106. Paris: 1970.

Godineau, Domique. *Citoyennes Tricoteuses: Les Femmes du peuple à Paris pendant la Révolution française.* Aix-en-Provence: Alines, 1988.

Goncourt, Edmond. *Paris under Siege, 1870–1871: From the Goncourt "Journal."* Ed. and Trans. George J. Becker. Ithaca: Cornell University Press, 1969.

Gosselin, Ronald. *Les Almanchs républicains: Traditions révolutionnaires et culture politique des masses populaires de Paris (1840–1851)*. Paris: L'Harmattan, 1993.

Gossez, Rémi. *Les Ouvriers de Paris.* La Roche-sur-Yon: Bibliothèque de la Révolution, 1967.

Gould, Roger V. *Insurgent Identities: Class, Community, and Protest in Paris from 1848 to the Commune.* Chicago: University of Chicago Press, 1995.

———. "Multiple Networks and Mobilization in the Paris Commune, 1871." *American Sociological Review* 56 (December 1991): 719–29.

———. "Social Structure and Insurgency in the Paris Commune, 1871." Ph.D. diss., Harvard University, 1990.

———. "Trade Cohesion, Class Unity, and Urban Insurrection: Artisanal Activism in the Paris Commune." *American Journal of Sociology* 98 (January 1993): 721–54.

Gourden, Jean-Michel. *Le Peuple des ateliers: Les Artisans du XIXe siècle.* Paris: Créaphis/Distique, 1992.

Greenberg, Louis M. "The Commune of 1871 as a Decentralist Reaction." *Journal of Modern History* 41 (1969): 304–318.

———. *Sisters of Liberty: Marseilles, Lyon, Paris, and the Reaction to a Centralized State, 1868–1871.* Cambridge: Harvard University Press, 1971.

Griffin, David E. "The Other Republicans: The Mayors of Paris and the Failure of Moderation, 1871." *Proceedings of the Western Society for French History* 2 (1974): 267–74.

Gromier, Marc. *Journal d'un vaincu.* Paris: Victor-Havard, 1892.

———. *Lettres d'un bon rouge à la Commune de Paris.* Paris: André Sagnier, 1873.

Grubitzsch, Helga. "A Paradigm of Androcentric Historiography: Michelet's *Les Femmes dans la Révolution.*" In *Current Issues in Women's History,* ed. Arina Angerman et al., 271–88. New York: Routledge, 1989.

Guillemin, Henri. *L'Avènement de M. Thiers et réflexions sur la Commune.* Paris: Gallimard, 1971.

———. *La Capitulation (1871).* Paris: Gallimard, 1960.

———. *Cette Curiouse guerre de '70.* Paris: Gallimard, 1956.

———. *L'Héroïque défense de Paris (1870–1871).* Paris: Gallimard, 1959.

Guillen, P., ed. *Grenoble à l'époque de la Commune.* Grenoble: Université des Sciences Sociales de Grenoble, 1972.

Guin, Yannick. *Le Mouvement ouvrier Nantais.* Paris: Maspero, 1976.

Guiraudon, Richard-Pierre, and Michel Rebondy, *Gustave Flourens: Le Chevalier rouge.* Paris: Pré au Clercs, 1987.

Gullickson, Gay L. "*La Pétroleuse:* Representing Revolution." *Feminist Studies* 17 (summer 1991): 241–65.

Haine, W. Scott. "'Café-Friend': Friendship and Fraternity in Parisian Working-Class Cafés, 1850–1914." *Journal of Contemporary History* 27 (October 1992): 607–27.

Halbwachs, Maurice. *The Collective Memory.* Trans. Francis J. Ditter, Jr. New York: Harper and Row, 1980. French ed., 1923.

———. *On Collective Memory.* Ed. and trans. Lewis Coser. Chicago: University of Chicago Press, 1992.

Halévy, Daniel. *La République des comités: Essai d'histoire contemporaine (1895–1934).* Paris: Bernard Grasset, 1934.

Halévy, Ludovic. *Notes et souvenirs, 1871–1872.* Paris: Calman Lévy, 1889.

Hamon, Léo. *Les Républicains sous le Second Empire.* Paris: Maison des Sciences de l'Homme, 1994.

Hanagan, Michael. *Nascent Proletarians: Class Formation in Post-Revolutionary France.* Oxford: Blackwell, 1989.

Hanotaux, Gabriel. *Contemporary France.* Trans. Charles Tarver. 3 vols. New York: Putnam, 1912.

Harrington, Michael. "The Misfortune of 'Great Memories': Historical Remarks on the Paris Commune." *Dissent* (October 1971): 472–77.

Haupt, Heinz-Gerhard, and Karin Hausin. "Comment adapter les moyens révolutionnaires aux buts de la Revolution? Reflexions à partir de l'éxperience de la Commune de Paris (1871)." *Le Mouvement Social* 111 (1980): 119–26.

Hazareesingh, Sudhir. *Political Traditions in Modern France.* New York: Oxford University Press, 1994.

Hemmings, F. W. J. *Theater and State in France, 1760–1905.* New York: Cambridge University Press, 1994.

Hicks, John, and Robert Tucker, eds. *Revolution and Reaction: The Paris Commune of 1871.* Boston: University of Massachusetts Press, 1973.

Hippeau, Paul. *Les Fédérations artistiques sous la Commune: Souvenirs de 1871.* Paris: Comptoir d'Édition, 1890.

Hobsbawm, Eric J., ed. *The History of Marxism.* Vol. 1, *Marxism in Marx's Day.* Bloomington: Indiana University Press, 1982.

Hobsbawm, Eric J., and Terrence Ranger, eds. *The Invention of Tradition.* New York: Cambridge University Press, 1983.

Horne, Alistair. *The Fall of Paris: The Siege and the Commune, 1870–1871.* New York: Penguin, 1965. Reprint, 1981.

Howard, Michael. *The Franco-Prussian War.* New York: Methuen, 1961.

Howorth, Jolyon. *Edouard Vaillant.* Paris: Syros, 1982.

Huard, Raymond. "Le mouvement républicain gardois devant la Commune de Paris." In *Actes du 96e Congrès des Sociétés Savantes, Toulouse, 1971,* 1:155–75. Paris: 1976.

———. *La Préhistoire des partis: Le Mouvement républicain en Bas-Languedoc 1848–1881.* Paris: Fondation Nationale des Sciences Politiques, 1982.

Hufton, Olwen. *Women and the Limits of Citizenship in the French Revolution.* Toronto: University of Toronto Press, 1992.

Hunt, Lynn. *Politics, Culture, and Class in the French Revolution.* Berkeley: University of California Press, 1984.

——, ed. *The New Cultural History.* Berkeley: University of California Press, 1989.

Hunt, Lynn, and George Sheridan. "Corporatism, Association, and the Language of Labor in France, 1750–1850." *Journal of Modern History* 58 (1986): 813–44.

Hutton, Patrick. *The Cult of the Revolutionary Tradition: The Blanquists in French Politics, 1864–1893.* Berkeley: University of California Press, 1981.

——. *History as an Art of Memory.* Hanover, Vt.: University of New England Press, 1994.

Izzo, Jean-Claude. "Esquisse pour une histoire de la Commune à Marseille." *Pensée* 161 (1972): 81–96.

Jacquemet, Gérard. *Belleville au XIXe siècle: Du Faubourg à la ville.* Paris: Éditions de l'École des Hautes Études en Sciences Sociales, 1984.

Jeanneret, Georges. *Paris Pendant la Commune révolutionnaire de '71.* Neuchâtel: n.p., 1872.

Jellinek, Frank. *The Paris Commune of 1871.* London: Victor Gollantz, 1937. Reprint, New York: Grosset and Dunlap, 1965.

Jeloubovskaïa, E. *La Chute du Second Empire et la naissance de la Troisième République en France.* Moscow: Éditions en Langues Étrangères, 1959.

Jennings, Jeremy. *Syndicalism in France: A Study of Ideas.* New York: St. Martin's, 1990.

Jones, Kathleen, and François Vergès. "'Aux Citoyennes!' Women, Politics, and the Paris Commune of 1871." *History of European Ideas* 13 (1991): 711–32.

——. "Women in the Paris Commune." *Women's Studies International Forum* 14 (1991): 491–503.

Jordan, David P. *Transforming Paris: The Life and Labors of Baron Hausmann.* New York: Free Press, 1995.

Jordan, Rossan A., and Susan J. Kalcik. *Women's Folklore, Women's Culture.* Philadelphia: University of Pennsylvania Press, 1985.

Joughin, Jean. *The Paris Commune in French Politics, 1870–1880: The History of the Amnesty of 1880.* 2 vols. Baltimore: Johns Hopkins University Press, 1955.

Journal de l'Insurrection du 18 mars et des événements qui l'ont precédée par un spectateur philosophe. Paris: Jules Taride, 1871.

Joyce, Patrick. *Visions of the People: Industrial England and the Question of Class, 1848–1914.* Cambridge: Cambridge University Press, 1991.

Judt, Tony. *Marxism and the French Left: Studies in Labour and Politics in France, 1830–1981.* New York: Oxford University Press, 1986.

Kale, Steven D. *Legitimism and the Reconstruction of French Society, 1852–1883.* Baton Rouge: Louisiana State University Press, 1992.

Katz, Henryk. *The Emancipation of Labor: A History of the First International.* New York: Greenwood, 1992.

Katznelson, Ira, and Aristide Zolberg. *Working-Class Formation: Nineteenth-Century Patterns in Western Europe and the United States.* Princeton: Princeton University Press, 1986.

Kennedy, Michael. *The Jacobin Clubs in the French Revolution: The First Years.* Princeton: Princeton University Press, 1982.

———. *The Jacobin Club of Marseilles, 1790–1794.* Ithaca: Cornell University Press, 1973.

Kleiman, Lawrence, and Florence Rochefort. *L'Égalité en march: Le Féminisme sous la Troisième République.* Paris: Fondation Nationale des Sciences Politiques, 1989.

Knoke, David. *Organizing for Collective Action: The Political Economies of Associations.* Hawthorne, N.Y.: A. de Gruyter, 1990.

Kranzberg, Melvin. *The Siege of Paris, 1870–1871: A Political and Social History.* Ithaca: Cornell University Press, 1950.

Kulstein, David. *Napoleon III and the Working Class.* Los Angeles: California State Colleges Press, 1969.

Labarthe, Gustave. *Le Théâtre pendant les jours du siège et de la Commune.* Paris: Fischbacher, 1910.

La Batut, Guy. *Les Pavés de Paris.* 2 vols. Paris: Éditions Sociales Internationales, 1937.

Laborde, J. U. *Fragments medico-psychologiques: Les Hommes et les actes de l'insurrection du Paris devant la psychologie morbide.* Paris: Germer Baillière, 1872.

Labouchère, Henri. *Diary of the Besieged Resident in Paris.* London: Hurst and Blackett, 1871.

Lamazou, Abbé. "La Place Vendôme et la Roquette." *La Correspondant: Recueil Périodique* 84 (July 10, 1871): 132–85.

Lambert, Susan. *The Franco-Prussian War and the Commune in Caricature, 1870–71.* London: Victoria and Albert Museum, 1971.

Landes, Joan B. *Women and the Public Sphere in the Age of the French Revolution.* Ithaca: Cornell University Press, 1988.

Lanjalley, Paul, and Michel Corriez. *Histoire de la Révolution du 18 mars.* Paris: Librairie Internationale, 1871. Reprint, New York: Ames, 1973.

Lanoux, Armand. *Une Histoire de la Commune de Paris.* Vol. 1, *La Polka des Canons.* Paris: Bernard Grasset, 1971.

Larocque, Jean-Baptiste. *1871: Souvenirs révolutionnaires.* Paris: Albert Savine, 1888.

Laronze, Georges. *Histoire de la Commune de 1871: La Justice.* Paris: Payot, 1928.

Lazare, Louis. *La France et Paris.* Paris: Bibliothèque Municipale, 1872.

Lazerges, J. R. H. *Des Associations artistiques.* Paris: Leclere, 1868.

Lefebvre, Henri. *La Proclamation de la Commune: 26 mars 1871.* Paris: Gallimard, 1965.

Lefèvre, André. *Histoire de la Ligue d'Union Républicaine des Droits de Paris.* Paris: Charpentier, 1881.

Lefranc, Georges. *Le Mouvement socialiste sous la Troisième République.* Paris: Éditions Ouvrières, 1963.

Lefrançais, Gustave. *Étude sur le mouvement Communaliste à Paris en 1871.* Neuchâtel: Guillaume, 1871.

———. *Souvenirs d'un révolutionnaire.* Brussels: Bibliothèque des Temps Nouveaux, 1902.

Le Goff, Jacques. *History and Memory.* Trans. Steven Rendall and Elizabeth Claman. New York: Columbia University Press, 1992.

Leith, James A., ed. *Images of the Commune.* Montreal: McGill-Queens University Press, 1978.

Lejeune-Resnick, Evelyn. *Femmes et associations, 1830–1880: Vrais democrates ou dames patonesses?* Paris: Publisud, 1991.

Lenin, V. I. *Lessons of the Commune: In Memory of the Commune.* Moscow: Foreign Languages Publishing House, n.d.

Lepelletier, Edmond. *Histoire de la Commune de 1871.* 3 vols. Paris: Mercure de France, 1911–13.

Lequin, Yves, ed. "Ouvriers dans la ville." *Le Mouvement Social* 118 (1982). Special issue.

———. *Les Ouvriers de la région Lyonnaise (1848–1914).* 2 vols. Lyon: Presses Universitaires de Lyon, 1977.

Lethève, Jacques. *La Vie quotidienne des Artistes français au XIXe siècle.* Paris: Hachette, 1968.

Leverdays, E. *La Résistance à outrance et la Ligue Républicaine.* Paris: Association Générale Typographique, 1870.

Levillain, Philippe, and Rainer Riemenschneider, eds. *La Guerre de 1870/71 et ses conséquences.* Bonn: Bouvier Verlag, 1990.

L'Hospice, Michel. *La Guerre de 70 et la Commune en 1000 images.* Paris: Cercle Européen du Livre, 1965.

L'Huillier, Fernand. *La Lutte ouvrière à la fin du Second Empire.* Paris: Armand Colin, 1957.

Lichtheim, George. *Marxism in Modern France.* New York: Columbia University Press, 1966.

Lindsay, Jack. *Gustave Courbet: His Life and Work.* London: Jupiter, 1977.

Lissagaray, Prosper Oliver. *Histoire de la Commune.* 1871. Reprint, Paris: Éditions de Delphes, 1964.

Loua, Toussaint. *Atlas statistique de la population de Paris.* Paris: J. Dejey, 1873.

Lucas, Alphonse. *Les Clubs et les clubistes.* Paris: Dentu, 1851.

Machu, J. "La Société Républicaine de Grenoble (4 Octobre 1870–7 Juillet 1871)." In *Grenoble à l'époque de la Commune,* ed. P. Guillen, 57–70. Grenoble: Université des Sciences Sociales de Grenoble, 1972.

Magraw, Roger. *A History of the French Working Class.* 2 vols. Cambridge, Mass.: Blackwell, 1992.

Maillard, Firmin. *Affiches, professions de foi, documents officiels, clubs et comités pendant la Commune.* Paris: Dentu, 1871.

———. *Histoire des journaux publiés à Paris pendant le siège et la Commune, 4 septembre au 28 mai, 1871.* Paris: Dentu, 1871.

———. *Les Publications de la rue pendant le siège et la Commune.* Paris: August Aubry, 1874.

Maitron, Jean. "Étude critique du Rapport Appert: Essai de 'contre-raport.'" *Le Mouvement Social* 79 (1972): 95–122.

———, ed. *Dictionnaire biographique du mouvement ouvrier français, deuxième partie, 1864–71.* 6 vols. Paris: Éditions Ouvrières, 1967–71.

Maitron, Jean, and Jacques Rougerie, eds. "Les Communards." *Le Mouvement Social* 37 (1961): 44–69.

Maitron, Jean, and G. M. Thomas. "L'International et la Commune à Brest." *Le Mouvement Social* 41 (1962): 46–73.

Malon, Benôit. *La Troisième défaite du prolétariat français.* Neuchâtel: G. Guillaume fils, 1871.

Margadant, Ted W. "The Paris Commune: A Revolution That Failed." *Journal of Interdisciplinary History* 7 (1976): 91–97.

Martine, Paul. *Souvenirs d'un insurgé, la Commune, 1871.* Paris: Perrin, 1971.

Marx, Karl. *The Paris Commune, 1871.* Ed. Christopher Hitchens. London: Sidwick and Jackson, 1971.

Mason, Edward S. *The Paris Commune: An Episode in the History of the Socialist Movement.* New York: Howard Fertig, 1967.

Mayeur, Jean-Marie, and Madeleine Reberioux. *The Third Republic from its Origins to the Great War, 1871–1914.* Trans. Robert Foster. Cambridge: Cambridge University Press, 1984.

McClellan, Woodford. *Revolutionary Exiles: The Russians in the First International and the Paris Commune.* London: Frank Cass, 1979.

Melman, Billie. "Gender, History, and Memory: The Invention of Women's Past in the Nineteenth and Early Twentieth Centuries." *History and Memory* 5 (spring/summer 1993): 5–41.

"Memory and Counter Memory." *Representations* 26 (spring 1989). Special issue.

Mendès, Catulle. *Les 73 journées de la Commune (Du 18 mars au 29 mai 1871).* Paris: Lachaud, 1871.

Merriman, John M. *The Red City: Limoges and the French Nineteenth Century.* New York: Oxford University Press, 1985.

Michel, Louise. *La Commune.* Paris: Stock, 1898.

———. *Mémoires écrits par elle-même.* 1886. Reprint, Paris: Maspero, 1976.

———. *The Red Virgin: Memoirs of Louise Michel.* Ed. and trans. Bullitt Lowry and Elizabeth Ellington Gunter. University, Ala.: University of Alabama Press, 1981.

———. *Souvenirs et aventures de ma vie.* Ed. Daniel Armogathe. Paris: Maspero, 1983.

Miquel, Pierre. *Le Second Empire.* Paris: Plon, 1992.

———. *La Troisième République.* Paris: Fayard, 1989.

Moilin, Tony. *La Liquidation sociale.* Paris: n.p., 1869.

———. *Programmes de discussion pour les sociétés populaires.* Paris: Imprimerie de la Gaittet, 1868.

Moissonnier, Maurice. *La Première Internationale et la Commune à Lyon (1865–1871).* Paris: Éditions Sociales, 1972.

———. "La Province et la Commune." In *1871: Jalons pour une histoire de la Commune,* ed. Jacques Rougerie, 151–82. Paris: Presses Universitaires de France, 1973.

Moissonnier, Maurice, and Claude Willard. *Barricades: Révoltes et révolutions au XIXe siècle.* Paris: Messidor, 1991.

Molinari, Gustave de. *Les Clubs rouges pendant la siège de Paris.* Paris: Garnier, 1871.

———. *Le Mouvement socialiste et les réunions publiques avant la Révolution du 4 Septembre 1870.* Paris: Garnier, 1872.

Molok, A. "Les Ouvriers de Paris pendant la Commune." *Cahiers du Communism* 5–6 (May–June 1951): 608–22, 728–75.

Montaud, C. Barral de. *Notes journalières sur l'état de Paris durant la Commune.* Paris: Paul Dupont, 1871.

Moon, Joan S. "Woman as Agent of Social Change: Women's Rights during the Second French Republic." In *Views of Women's Lives in Western Tradition,* ed. Francis R. Keller, 323–59. Lewiston, N.Y.: Edwin Mellon, 1990.

Moreau, Thérèse. *Le Sang de l'histoire: Michelet, l'histoire, et l'idée de la femme au XIXe siècle.* Paris: Flammarion, 1982.

Moriac, Édouard. *Paris Sous la Commune: 18 mars au 28 mai.* Paris: Dentu, 1872.

Moses, Claire Goldberg. *French Feminism in the Nineteenth Century.* Albany: State University of New York Press, 1984.

Moss, Bernard H. *The Origins of the French Labor Movement (1830–1914): The Socialism of Skilled Workers.* Berkeley: University of California Press, 1976.

Moutet, Aimée. "Le Mouvement ouvrier à Paris du lendemain de la Commune au premier congrès syndicaliste en 1876." *Le Mouvement Social* 58 (1967): 3–39.

Le Mouvement Social 118 (1982). Special issue on working-class neighborhoods.

Mullany, Marie Marmo. "Sexual Politics in the Career of Louise Michel." *Signs* 15 (1990): 300–322.

Munch, Richard, and Neil J. Smelser. *Theory of Culture.* Berkeley: University of California Press, 1992.

Les Murailles Politiques françaises. 3 vols. Paris: Le Chevalier, 1873–74.

Namer, Gerard. "L'Imprimerie Nationale sous la Commune." *Revue d'Histoire Économique et Sociale* 40 (1962): 342–62.

———. *Mémoire et société.* Paris: Méridiens et Klincksieck, 1987.

Nast, Gustave. "Les Mairies de Paris et le Comité Central." *Le Correspondant: Recueil Périodique* 84 (September 25, 1871): 1040–65.

Noël, Bernard. *Dictionnaire de la Commune.* Paris: Payot, 1971.

Noiriel, Gérard. *Workers in French Society in the Nineteenth and Twentieth Centuries.* Trans. Helen McPhail. New York: Berg, 1990.

Nora, Pierre. "Entre mémoire et histoire: La Problématique des lieux." In *Les Lieux de mémoire,* vol. 1, *La République,* ed. Pierre Nora, xvii–xlii. Paris: Gallimard, 1984.

Nord, Philip G. *Paris Shopkeepers and the Politics of Resentment.* Princeton: Princeton University Press, 1986.

———. "The Party of Conciliation and the Paris Commune." *French Historical Studies* 15 (1987): 1–36.

———. *The Republican Moment: Struggles for Democracy in Nineteenth-Century France.* Cambridge: Harvard University Press, 1995.

———. "Republicanism and Utopian Vision: French Freemasonry in the 1860s and 1870s." *Journal of Modern History* 63 (1991): 213–29.

Nye, Robert A. *Masculinity and Male Codes of Honor in Modern France.* London: Oxford University Press, 1993.

Olivesi, Antoine. *La Commune de 1871 à Marseille et ses origines.* Paris: Marcel Rivière, 1950.

Palmer, Bryan D. *Descent into Discourse: The Reification of Language and the Writing of Social History.* Philadelphia: Temple University Press, 1990.

Papayanis, Nicolas. *The Coachmen of Nineteenth-Century Paris: Service Workers and Class Consciousness.* Baton Rouge: Louisiana State University Press, 1993.

Pérennès, Roger. *Déportés et forçats de la Commune, de Belleville à Nouméa.* Nantes: Ouest Éditions, 1991.

Peridier, Jean. *La Commune et les artistes: Pottier, Courbet, Vallès, J. B. Clément.* Paris: Nouvelles Éditions Latines, 1980.

Perrot, Michelle. *Jeunesse de la Grève: France 1871–1890.* Paris: Seuil, 1984.

———. *Les Ouvriers en grève, France 1871–1890.* 2 vols. Paris: Mouton, 1974.

Pessin, Alain. *Le Mythe du peuple et la société française au XIXe siècle.* Paris: Presses Universitaires de France, 1992.

Piette, Christine. "Réflexions Historiques sur les Traditions Révolutionaires à Paris au XIXe siècle." *Historical Reflections/Réflexions Historiques* 12 (1985): 403–18.

Pinol, Jean-Luc. *Le Monde des villes au XIXe siècle.* Paris: Hachette, 1991.

Plamenatz, John. *The Revolutionary Movement in France 1815–1871.* London: Longmans Green, 1952.

Plessis, Alain. *The Rise and Fall of the Second Empire, 1852–1871.* Trans. Jonathan Mandelbaum. New York: Cambridge University Press, 1985. French ed., 1979.

Poulot, Denis. *Le Sublime.* Paris: Maspero, 1980.

Prampain, R. P. Edouard. *Souvenirs de Vaugirard: Mon journal pendant le siège et pendant la Commune 1870–1871.* Paris: Société Anonyme de Publications Périodiques, 1887.

Prendergast, Christopher. *Paris and the Nineteenth Century.* Cambridge, Mass.: Blackwell, 1992.

Pressensé, Edmond de. *Les Leçons du 18 mars.* Paris: Michel Lévy, 1871.

Price, R. D. "Ideology and Motivation in the Paris Commune of 1871." *Historical Journal* 15 (1972): 75–86.

Le Procès de la Commune: Compte-Rendu des débats du Conseil de Guerre. Paris: Librairie Internationale, 1871.

Les Procès-Verbaux de la Commune de 1871. Ed. Georges Bourgin and Gabriel Henriot. 2 vols. Paris: Ernest Leroux, 1924–45.

Proctor, Candice E. *Women, Equality, and the French Revolution.* New York: Greenwood, 1990.

Radner, Joan Newlon. *Feminist Messages: Coding in Women's Folk Culture.* Urbana: University of Illinois Press, 1993.

Ragache, Gilles. "Les clubs de la Commune." *Le Peuple Francais: Revue d'Histoire Populaire* 2 (April–June 1971): 5–8.

Rancière, Jacques. *The Nights of Labor: The Workers' Dream in Nineteenth-Century France.* Trans. John Drury. Philadelphia: Temple University Press, 1989.

———. "The Myth of the Artisan: Critical Reflections on a Category of Social

History." In *Work in France: Representations, Meanings, Organization, and Practice,* ed. Steven L. Kaplan and Cynthia J. Koepp, 317–34. Ithaca: Cornell University Press, 1986.

Rapport du Comité Républicain élu du IIIe arrondissement: Aux Habitants. Paris: n.p., 1870.

Ratcliffe, Barrie M. "Classes labourieuses et classes dangereuses à Paris pendant la première moitié du XIXe siècle? The Chevalier Thesis Reexamined." *French Historical Studies* 17 (Fall 1991): 542–74.

Reddy, William. *Money and Liberty in Modern Europe: A Critique of Historical Understanding.* New York: Cambridge University Press, 1987.

Remy, Tristan. *La Commune à Montmartre: 23 mai 1871.* Paris: Éditions Sociales, 1970.

Reynolds, Siân, ed. *Women, State, and Revolution: Essays on Power and Gender in Europe since 1789.* Brighton: Wheatsheaf Books, 1986.

La Revue Blanche, 1871: Enquête sur la Commune de Paris. Paris: n.p., 1897.

Rials, Stéphane. *Nouvelle histoire de Paris: De Trochu à Thiers (1870–1873).* Paris: Hachette, 1985.

Riesenberg, Peter. *Citizenship in the Western Tradition: Plato to Rousseau.* Chapel Hill: University of North Carolina Press, 1992.

Rifkin, Adrian, and Roger Thomas, eds., *Voices of the People: The Social Life of 'La Sociale' at the end of the Second Empire.* London: Routledge, 1988.

Rihs, Charles. *La Commune de Paris 1871: Sa Structure et ses doctrines.* 1955. Reprint, Paris: Seuil, 1973.

Riley, Denise. *"Am I that Name?" Feminism and the Category of "Woman" in History.* Minneapolis: University of Minnesota Press, 1988.

Roberts, J. M. *The Paris Commune from the Right.* London: Longman Group, 1973.

Rochefort, Henri. *The Adventures of My Life.* Trans. Ernest Smith. 2 vols. New York: Edward Arnold, 1896.

Rougerie, Jacques. "L'AIT et le mouvement ouvrier à Paris pendant les événements de 1870–1871." *International Review of Social History* 27 (1972): 3–102.

———. "Belleville." In *Les Elections de 1869,* ed. Louis Girard, 3–36. Paris: Marcel Rivière, 1960.

———. "Le Centenaire de la Commune: Moisson, problèmes, overtures." *Revue Historique* 246 (1971): 409–22.

———. "Comment les Communards voyaient la Commune." *Le Mouvement Social* 37 (1961): 55–73.

———. *La Commune.* Paris: Presses Universitaires de France, 1988.

———. "Composition d'un population insurgée: L'Example de la Commune." *Le Mouvement Social* 48 (1964): 31–47.

———. "Les Elections du 26 mars à la Commune de Paris." Diplôme d'Études Supérieures, n.d.

———. "Notes pour servir à l'histoire du 18 mars 1871." In *Mélanges en Histoire Sociale offerts à Jean Maitron,* 229–48. Paris: Éditions Ouvrières, 1976.

———. *Paris Libre: 1871.* Paris: Seuil, 1971.

———. "La Première Internationale à Lyon, 1865–1870, problèm d'histoire du mouvement ouvrier français." *Annali dell'Instituto Giangiacomo Feltrinelli* (1961): 126–93.

———. *Procès des Communards.* Paris: Juillard, 1964.

———. "Quelques documents nouveau pour l'histoire du Comité Central Républicain des Vingt Arrondissements." *Le Mouvement Social* 37 (1961): 3–29.

———. "Les Sections françaises de l'Association Internationale des Travailleurs." In *La Première Internationale: L'Institution, l'implantation, le rayonnement,* ed. Jacques Rougerie, 93–127. Paris: Centre National des Recherches Scientifiques, 1968.

———, ed. "Les Evenements de 1870–1871 en Province." *Recherches et Travaux: Bulletin de l'Institute d'Histoire Economique et Sociale de l'Université de Paris I* 3 (May 1973): 1–57; 4 (December 1973): 1–24.

Saint-Eustache pendant la Commune. Paris: Paul Dupont, 1871.

Sans, Emile. *Paris et la Commune.* Paris: Imprimerie Générale, 1870.

Sarcey, Francisque. *Le Siège de Paris.* Paris: Nelson, 1871.

Schulkind, Eugene. "The Activity of Popular Organizations during the Paris Commune of 1871." *French Historical Studies* 1 (1960): 394–415.

———. "Les Clubs et réunions populaires pendant la Commune de 1871." Diplôme d'Études Supérieures, [1951].

———. "Socialist Women during the 1871 Paris Commune." *Past and Present* 106 (February 1985): 124–63.

———, ed. *The Paris Commune of 1871: The View from the Left.* New York: Grove, 1972.

Schwartz, Barry. "Social Change and Collective Memory: The Democratization of George Washington." *American Sociological Review* 56 (April 1991): 221–37.

Scott, Joan Wallach. *Gender and the Politics of History.* New York: Columbia University Press, 1988.

———. *The Glassworkers of Carmaux: French Craftsmen and Political Action in a Nineteenth-Century City.* Cambridge: Harvard University Press, 1974.

Les Séances officielles de L'Internationale à Paris pendant le siège et pendant la Commune. Paris: Lachaud, 1872.

Serman, William. *La Commune.* Paris: Presses Universitaires de France, 1971.

———. *La Commune de Paris (1871).* Paris: Fayard, 1986.

Sewell, William H. *Work and Revolution in France: The Language of Labor from the Old Regime to 1848.* New York: Cambridge University Press, 1980.

Shafer, David A. "*Plus que des Ambulancières:* Women in Articulation and Defence of Their Ideals during the Paris Commune (1871)." *French History* 7 (1993): 85–101.

Sibalis, Michael D. "The Mutual aid societies of Paris, 1789–1848." *French History* 3 (1989): 1–30.

Simon, Jules. *The Government of M. Thiers, from 8th February 1871 to 24th May 1873.* 2 vols. New York: Scribner's, 1879. Singer-Lecocq, Yvonne. *Rouge Elisabeth.* Paris: Stock, 1977.

Skocpol, Theda. "Bringing the State Back In." In *Bringing the State Back In,* ed. Peter B. Evans, Dietrich Rueschmeyer, and Theda Skocpol, 3–43. New York: Cambridge University Press, 1990.

Soboul, Albert. "De l'An II à la Commune de 1871: La Double tradition révolutionnaire française." *Annales Historiques de la Révolution Francaise* 43 (1971): 535–53.

———. *The Parisian Sans-Culottes and the French Revolution, 1793–4.* Trans. Gwynne Lewis. Oxford: Clarendon, 1964.

———. "Tradition et création dans le mouvement révolutionnaire français au XIXe siècle." *Le Mouvement Social* 79 (1972): 15–31.

Soria, G. "Les Beaux arts." *Europe* 499–500 (November–December 1970): 227–36.

———. *Grande histoire de la Commune.* 5 vols. Paris: Livre Club Diderot, 1970.

Sous la Commune: Récits et souvenirs d'un Parisien. Paris: Dentu, 1873.

Stafford, David. *From Anarchism to Reformism: A Study of the Political Activities of Paul Brousse within the First International and the French Socialist Movement, 1870–90.* Toronto: University of Toronto Press, 1971.

Stedman Jones, Gareth. *Languages of Class: Studies in English Working Class History, 1832–1982.* New York: Cambridge University Press, 1983.

Strumingher, Laura S. "The *Vésuviennes:* Images of Women Warriors in 1848 and Their Significance for French History." *History of European Ideas* 8 (1986): 451–88.

Stuart, Robert. *Marxism at Work: Ideology, Class, and French Socialism during the Third Republic.* New York: Cambridge University Press, 1992.

Sutter-Laumann. *Histoire d'un Trente Sous (1870–1871).* Paris: Albert Savine, 1891.

Tales, C. *La Commune de 1871.* With a preface by Leon Trotsky. Paris: Librairie du Travail, 1921.

Tarrow, Sidney. "Cycles of Collective Action: Between Moments of Madness and the Repertoire of Contention." In *Repertoires and Cycles of Collective Action,* ed. Mark Traugott, 89–116. Durham, N.C.: Duke University Press, 1995.

Tassy, Abbé. *Menilmontant sous La Commune.* Paris: F. Wattelier, [1872].

Tchernoff, J. *Associations et Sociétés Secrétes sous la Deuxième République 1848–1851.* Paris: Felix Alean, 1905.

———. *Le Parti Républicain au coup d'état et sous le Second Empire.* Paris: A. Pedone, 1906.

Terdiman, Richard. *Present Past: Modernity and the Memory Crisis.* Ithaca: Cornell University Press, 1993.

Thomas, Edith. *Les Femmes de 1848.* Paris: Presses Universitaires de France, 1948.

———. *Louise Michel.* Trans. Penelope Williams. Montreal: Black Rose Books, 1980.

———. *Rossel, 1844–1871.* Paris: Gallimard, 1967.

———. *The Women Incendiaries.* Trans. James Atkinson and Starr Atkinson. New York: George Braziller, 1966.

Tilly, Charles. *From Mobilization to Revolution.* Breading, Mass.: Addison-Wesley, 1978.

Tombs, Robert. "L'année terrible, 1870–1871." *Historical Journal* 35 (1992): 713–24.

———. "Harbingers or Entrepreneurs? A Worker's Cooperative during the Paris Commune." *Historical Journal* 27 (1984): 969–77.

―――. "Paris and the Rural Hordes: An Exploration of Myth and Reality in the French Civil War of 1871." *Historical Journal* 29 (1986): 795–808.

―――. "Prudent Rebels: The 2nd Arrondissement during the Paris Commune of 1871." *French History* 5 (1991): 393–413.

―――. "The Thiers Government and the Outbreak of Civil War in France, February–April 1871." *Historical Journal* 23 (1980): 813–31.

―――. *The War against Paris, 1871.* Cambridge: Cambridge University Press, 1981.

Traugott, Marc. *Armies of the Poor: Determinants of Working-Class Participation in the Parisian Insurrection of June 1848.* Princeton: Princeton University Press, 1985.

――― , ed. and trans. *The French Worker: Autobiographies from the Early Industrial Era.* Berkeley: University of California Press, 1993.

Trochu, Louis Jules. *La Politique et le siège de Paris.* Paris: Hetzel, n.d.

Tyrell, W. B. *Amazons: A Study in Athenian Mythmaking.* Baltimore: Johns Hopkins University Press, 1984.

Vallès, Jules. *Oeuvres complets.* Vol. 2, *L'Insurgé.* Paris: Livre Club Diderot, 1969.

Vandecastle-Schweitzer, Sylvie, and Danièle Voldman. "The Oral Sources for Women's History." In *Writing Women's History,* ed. Michelle Perrot, trans. Felicia Pheasant, 35–52. Oxford: Blackwell, 1992.

Varlin, Eugène. *Pratique militante, écrits d'un ouvrier communard.* Presented by Paule Lejeune. Paris: Maspero, 1977.

Vésinier, Pierre. *Comment a péri la Commune.* Paris: Albert Savine, 1892.

Villiers, Baron Marc de. *Histoire des clubs de femmes et des légions d'Amazones: 1793–1848–1871.* Paris: Plon, 1910.

Vincent, Steven K. *Between Marxism and Anarchism: Benôit Malon and French Reformist Socialism.* Berkeley: University of California Press, 1992.

―――. *Pierre-Joseph Proudhon and the Rise of French Republican Socialism.* Oxford: Oxford University Press, 1984.

Voici l'aube, l'immortelle Commune de Paris, compte rendu analytique du colloque scientifique international organisé par l'Institut Maurice Thorez, Paris, 6–9 mai, 1971. Paris: Éditions Sociales, 1972.

Vuillaume, Maxime. *Mes Cahiers rouges au temps de la Commune.* Paris: Société d'Éditions Littéraires et Artistiques, 1909. Reprint, Paris: Albin Michel, 1971.

Wachtel, Nathan. "Memory and History: An Introduction." *History and Anthropology* 2 (1986): 207–24.

Waldinger, Renée, Philip Dawson, and Isser Woloch, eds. *The French Revolution and the Meaning of Citizenship.* London: Greenwood, 1993.

Waldman, Martin. "The Repression of the Communards." *Canadian Journal of History* 8 (1973): 225–45.

―――. "The Revolutionary as Criminal in Nineteenth Century France: A Study of Communards and Déportés." *Science and Society* 37 (1973): 31–55.

Webber, Susan. "Women's Folk Narratives and Social Change." In *Women in the Family in the Middle East,* ed. E. W. Fernes, 310–16. Austin: University of Texas Press, 1985.

Weill, Georges. *Histoire du mouvement social en France 1852–1924.* 3d edition. Paris: Felix Mann Alcan, 1924.

Welch, Stephen. *The Concept of Political Culture.* New York: St. Martin's, 1993.

Wihtol de Wenden, Catherine, ed. *La Citoyenneté.* Paris: Fondation Diderot, 1988.

Willbach, D. "Work and Its Satisfactions: Origins of the French Labor Movement 1864–1870." Ph.D. diss., University of Michigan, 1977.

Willette, Luc. *Raoul Rigault, 25 ans, Communard, Chef de Police.* Paris: Syros, 1984.

Williams, Roger L. *The French Revolution of 1870–71.* New York: Norton, 1969.

———, ed. *The Commune of Paris, 1871.* New York: John Wiley and Sons, 1969.

Winock, Michel. "La Commune (1871–1971)." *Esprit* 39 (1971): 965–1014.

Wolfe, R. D. "The Origins of the Paris Commune: The Popular Organizations of 1868–71." Ph.D. diss., Harvard University, 1965.

———. "The Parisian *Club de la Révolution* of the 18th Arrondissement 1870–1871." *Past and Present* 39 (April 1968): 81–119.

"Women and Memory." *Michigan Quarterly Review* 26 (winter 1987). Special issue.

Wright, Gordon. "The Anti-Commune: Paris, 1871." *French Historical Studies* 10 (spring 1977): 149–72.

———. *France in Modern Times: From the Enlightenment to the Present.* 5th ed. New York: Norton, 1995.

Yalom, Marilyn. *Blood Sisters: The French Revolution in Women's Memory.* New York: Basic Books, 1993.

Yriarte, Charles. *Les Prussiens à Paris et le 18 mars.* Paris: Plon, 1871.

Zeldin, Theodore. *Emile Ollivier and the Liberal Empire of Napoleon III.* Oxford: Clarendon, 1963.

Zeller, André. *Les Hommes de la Commune.* Paris: Perrin, 1969.

Zévaès, Alexandre. *Histoire du socialisme et du communisme en France de 1871 à 1947.* Paris: France-Empire, 1947.

———. *Tony Révillon, 1831–1898.* Paris: Fayard, 1950.

Zolberg, Aristide. "Moments of Madness." *Politics and Society* 2 (winter 1972): 183–207.

Index